Art Music

Art Music

Love, Listening, and Soulfulness

Matthew Del Nevo

Transaction Publishers
New Brunswick (U.S.A.) and London (U.K.)

Library of Congress Catalog Number: 2012042366
ISBN: 978-1-4128-5161-9
Printed in the United States of America

Library of Congress Cataloging-in-Publication Data

Del Nevo, Matthew.
Art music : love, listening, and soulfulness / by Matthew Del Nevo.
    pages cm
  Includes bibliographical references and index.
  ISBN 978-1-4128-5161-9
    1. Music--Philosophy and aesthetics.   2. Music appreciation--Psychological aspects.   3. Music--History and criticism. I. Title.
ML3800.D32 2013
781.1'7--dc23

                                                            2012042366

In grateful memory of *Jurgis Janavicius,*
for his encouragement.
To *Duncan Bridgeman* and *Jamie Catto,*
for the inspiration from your work—
1 Giant Leap's *What About Me?*
at a crucial juncture.
To *Jürgen Lawrenz,*
for your oral transmission,
central to this book.
I have been a privileged recipient of your
teaching about music, which bears the
living traces of pre-War Germany, a time
continuous with the nineteenth century, and
I carry this memory into the third
millennium. I hope this work is a fitting
tribute to your demonstrations.
To *Suzhen,*
for your love and support and wisdom.
To our daughter *Genevieve*—
especially for you.
To *Max Marco, Gabriel Monteiro, Laurence Karacsony,*
to your generation.
To *Daniel Barenboim,*
thank you.

Men's faces glitter, and their hearts are blacke,
But thou (great Mistresse of heauens gloomie racke)
Art blacke in face, and glitterst in thy heart.
There is thy glorie, riches, force, and Art.

—G. Chapman, *Hymnus in Noctern*

Contents

Introduction ix

1. Baudelaire's Aesthetic 1

2. The Metaphysics of Nostalgia 17

3. The Ladder of *Eros* 39

4. Shades of Melancholy 59

5. Gardens of Delight 81

6. Listening across Time 97

7. Beethoven and Absolute Music 125

8. Wagner and World Music 151

9. The Work of Mourning 175

10. When Time Stands Still 193

11. Beauty and Sadness 205

12. Blue in Green 231

13. Attunement 245

Play List 261

Notes 263

Index 287

Introduction

One of the features of life today is that, in the words of William Wordsworth:

The world is too much with us; late and soon
Getting and spending, we lay waste our powers:

Wordsworth wrote the sonnet that starts with these lines in 1802. The situation he refers to has not lessened. The world bears in on us and whether we like it or not we are forced to be consumers as if our life depended on it, which it probably does; certainly the economy depends on it and today the economy is virtually synonymous with society—or at least synonymous with the way we view society and understand it. The pressure to fit in with this we call stress, which we speak of with an economic inflection as something to manage, the way we ostensibly manage our lives and our businesses and the way the "business" of politics is carried out.

Later in the sonnet Wordsworth seems to talk about Nature and all the commentators say Wordsworth was a romantic. But nature in the sonnet is a mere cipher for the question which worries Wordsworth—not because he is romantic but because he is human—of how we can escape the encompassing of this world which lays waste our powers. Nature represents what is other than this world, what stands outside or beyond it and represents *another whole way of being*. Wordsworth's nature is a powerful cipher, because it connotes the *freedom* of another whole way of being which is at the same time lawful, balanced, harmonious, differentiated and continually reborn. I suggest the way into another whole way of being is by *listening*.

Listening as not merely as something you do, but as something central to a way of life. Listening has the power to put us into another way of being, without having to go anywhere, or join anything. Listening is a form of sensibility and, more importantly, it forms sensibility. What matters today is to cultivate sensibility, for it is sorely lacking, even more now than in Wordsworth's day—and there is certainly a continuity in this regard between then and now, and it is mostly downhill.

This book on art music is written from the point of view of a philosophy of sensibility. This is a kind of philosophy that has completely gone out of fashion. The French poet and academician Paul Valéry (1871–1945), who I pay tribute to in what follows, was the last great thinker on the subject of sensibility. Writing on sensibility is just as missing from psychology, ostensibly the discourse on soul. The philosophy of sensibility went out of fashion because of the Wars in Europe (1914–18, 1939–45). The period after World War One was a time of terrible social depression and disorientation before the build-up to the next conflagration; after World War Two and the emergence of the details of the Holocaust, "sensibility," associated with "culture," seemed like a weak word. Big ideology reigned—principally various forms of Marxism and Communism. Big ideology did not go in for sensibility, but propaganda, the enforcement of ideas despite sensibility and culture. Today, by contrast, democracies have been overtaken by predatory monopolizing capitalism, which is another form of "soft" totalitarianism; soft because instead of arms against its people, it utilizes the greatest industry on earth, public relations, which includes all advertising. Big capitalism is about consumerism and the globalization of the species "consumer." Consumerism is the culture of vulgarity if not worse and a consumer is always less than a real person, because they are always a target. In these circumstances sensibility is under even greater assault than under Communism, where at least it could hide and there could be resistance. Commodity capitalism appropriates resistance and sells it back to the resisters, e.g. rap music and so-called streetwear would be examples; as well, commodity capitalism is constantly making new inroads into human perversity, when it comes to making "a fast buck" nothing is sacred, as we see in the spread and diversification of pornography. It is wrong to think a philosophy of sensibility is not political, weak though the word "sensibility" may seem compared with the word ideology (a word that includes religion, often, in our time, when lacking sensibility, religion easily reduces to forms of ideology).

What is under assault from the encompassment of consumerist and militaristic teletechnoscience and bad religion is precisely *sensibility*, or what I otherwise call *soul* and all of what Julia Kristeva calls "new maladies of the soul" are related to this I believe.[1] What we seek to escape from, what afflicts us on all sides, is soullessness—and we experience soullessness in our world in myriad forms, from the mall to the car lot, even to the home. What we seek to escape *to* is not a place, not a desert, foreign land, or commune. There is nowhere to escape *to*. We must transform where we *are*. A philosophy of sensibility is about such transformation, which begins with soul and soulfulness. Music is the most powerful art. Nothing acts more immediately and transformatively on our sensibility than music. But under the conditions of hard globalizing consumerism we have lost the sound of music with which the hills were alive once upon a time; that is, music as art. Recognizing and being able to listen to art music, whether classical or contemporary (I shall discuss both), works on the sensibility—the soul—and infuses us with soulfulness. Then the world is no longer too much with us. We can only transform the world and build a better future one soul at a time.

In writing about listening to art music, I am acutely conscious of what the composer Charles Villiers Stanford once said—that "books on music are dry bones unless their readers can clothe them with a fair knowledge and sufficiently vivid memory of the sounds which they describe."[2] This is true. And I assume my reader does *not* know the music I am talking about. I assume my reader is pretty much of an outsider as far as art music is concerned, and so he or she will not have a vivid memory of the music to which I can appeal. This is where technology that was not around in Stanford's day can come into its own and serve a good purpose. The pieces I refer to are track length and easy to locate online and download. The Play List at the back of this book gives the titles of the works I refer to in one place for easy reference.

With Stanford's warning in mind I have been careful to limit the number of musical works I refer to. It is very easy for a book on music to lose readers in a maze of titles of works that they might not know and for it to comprise more works than they could realistically get to know. I avoid this. For each of my music chapters I have limited my references to only a few works, and then I refer to only *parts* of each of those works. In this way, I believe my reader will easily be able to follow me and that my words will not be dry bones.

Readers who are familiar with art music, on the other hand, will be able to think of many *other* works that I have not mentioned but that

illustrate what I am saying; however, I leave that to them. The importance of this book for the music teacher or the musically literate reader
is with understanding the *metaphysics of nostalgia*. This is missing
from nearly all musical and compositional instruction because it is
something that, over time, even teachers have lost sight of. One of the
purposes of this book is to bring it back before our culture. And so in
being a book about listening to art music, this is a book no less about
sensibility and its cultivation, which in its object form we call "culture."

I am also conscious of the view that says one enjoys a sport more if
one understands the rules; therefore one enjoys the music more if one
understands the music. This is true. But it is also true that one does not
go to the game to watch the rules being played. It is love of sport that
sends you to the game. The rules do not make the game happen; the
players do. The game is not about the rules or even about winning, but
about sporting prowess that pays tribute to a great game. The rules are
enabling factors in all this, but they are governed by the sporting spirit.

Equally in music, the rules are governed by a musical spirit, by a
love of music that constitutes the rules in the first place. Love and
desire precede the rules. And in music the rules are more malleable
than those in sport; in fact they are continually being overturned.
Unlike sport, which has to stick to the rules, music can be jazzed up or
rocked or intellectualized or minimized, and so on; the rules follow the
music, the music does not follow the rules. Music is free. If a sense of
music is lost, if the love is lost, the rules become unknown. If the spirit
of sport is lost, the game looks like a futile and foolish exercise: big
meaty men in tight-fitting shorts chasing a little ball around a big field.
With art music what is lost is both a sense of art and a sense of music
as well. In music (but not in sport), things that are not art are called
art, and things that lack music altogether are everywhere referred
to as music without a second thought. This marks a lack of sensibility
and the reign of soullessness, as well as the triumph of consumerism,
which is interested only in selling us something, even if it is rubbish.
This is a fairly recent turn of events, dating back to the late twentieth
century, and can more easily change than those who are conscious of
what I am saying might imagine. The loss of sensibility, loss of art, and
the loss of a sense of music, all of which are social and cultural losses
essentially, are the central problems that the present work addresses
and attempts to redress.

This is a book about truth as much as one about music, for to my
mind the two go together. Divorced from truth, music becomes more

easily prey to reductions, such as that to technique and technicality, or more broadly in our culture, to music's total commodification. The unabated commodification of culture is difficult to criticize because we are always already *inside* it. We are inside the commodification of culture in our day more than Theodor Adorno was in Germany and America in the middle of the last century, when he complained so vociferously about it. Henry Miller's "air-conditioned nightmare" is more frightening now than in 1945, when it was already bad enough. It is impossible to criticize the commodification of culture with any objectivity and with any "outsider" perspective at all, however, we can, within reason, describe its shadowing *presence*. This I think we need to do, for the sake of truth. For truth matters in philosophy and in art. Divorced from truth, the art *in* music (but not necessarily the art *of* music) is lost. This may seem like a hairsplitting distinction, but as we shall see, it reveals a huge gulf of difference. For the truth in music is not some abstract or extraneous truth applied from the outside: it is truth intrinsic to sound and to our attunement to what we hear and what we love, for the two go together: love and truth. A disorder in our love is a disorder in our nature, and loss of art in music is a denaturing; this book addresses this problem, but with the positive accent upon attunement. The truth in music is the truth of our selves, in the sense of our *soulfulness*. It is not a didactic truth, but a truth to experience for oneself and prove to oneself, or not, as experience testifies. But this book is written because, in our time, such experience of soulful sensibility is becoming more and more impossible as monopolistic and irresponsible pecuniary interests (big capitalism, in other words) bring commercialization into every aspect of culture, and prostitute it. While we shall not be able to criticize this commercialization from "outside" it, we shall note its shadow from time to time in passing. For I try to provide something of what I consider to be a lost teaching in this book. Part of the teaching says that no real wellbeing is possible without soulfulness or without music—that is, art music, and our future as a civilization depends much more than we commonly imagine upon such music and such soulfulness.

1

Baudelaire's Aesthetic

Beauty is sovereign appearance.
—Paul Valéry, "Mallarmé"

I begin not with hypotheses and theories of art and music, but by invoking an authority on the subject. The authority is that of the French poet Charles Baudelaire.[1] We shall take our cue in this book from Baudelaire's sensibility as an artist with a sense of beauty and an ability to articulate it. Baudelaire will give us a definition of art that will hold us in good stead for understanding art music. His authority will enable us to cut through the prolixity of theory that embroils the subject of art and the aesthetic and, in fact, has completely bogged it down so that any sense of truth in art today is buried beneath words.

Charles Baudelaire (1821–1867) is commonly regarded as the father of modern poetry and this is partly because he is the first truly *urban* poet. Baudelaire's aesthetic (by which I mean his view of art and beauty, which go together for him) will frame everything we have to say in this book. Some have called Baudelaire's aesthetic an "interarts theory";[2] which is to say that Baudelaire's aesthetic goes for any art. This is true. But it is not just a theory. Baudelaire's major work, *Les Fleurs du mal* (*The Flowers of Evil*), which was published in 1857, when he was thirty-six, is an actual living example in art *of* his aesthetic. Also, Baudelaire's modernity is important to us, as art is not what it was, and neither is sensibility—we are sensible of much that is new and insensible to much that is old and passé. Lastly, Baudelaire's authority is important. He is authoritative and, as an authority on art, what I have to say *stands with* him. The nineteenth-century French poet Paul Verlaine said of Baudelaire that he was profoundly original and powerfully represented the modern times and modern art, and I think he is right.

While Baudelaire's authority as a poet and critic is widely recognized in aesthetics and cultural studies, as well as in literature and philosophy, the clamor of theory today has drowned out Baudelaire's aesthetic, and therefore I am *reminding us* of it. If we lose this sense of art, we will lose *any* sense of art. This is already happening and has been happening for quite some time. All the more reason to adopt Baudelaire's aesthetic!

"Baudelaire's aesthetic" answers the question, "What is art?" It provides us with a genuine sense of art because, as I have just indicated, in our time it is not at all clear what art is, and all sorts of things parade themselves as art, or are advertised as art, or are assumed to be art, but do not match the criteria set by Baudelaire's aesthetic, and so at least, as art, they are questionable—if not (sometimes) laughable. It is with a genuine sense of art that is a discerning sense (able at least to see what fails as art) that we can talk in a strong truth-bearing way about listening, music and soul.

When Baudelaire published *Les Fleurs du mal* in 1857 there was a public outcry and he was prosecuted by the civic authorities for outraging public decency. He found, as he might have predicted, that his work was offensive to public taste—but for us, precisely in that transgressive quality he is modern, as so much modern art, or at least so much *avant garde* modern art tries to set new standards for taste, quite often by offending established taste. Of course I realize that this situation is both complicated and normalized once it gets caught up with the politics of disestablishment, as it did in the late 1960s. But in Baudelaire's day transgression was real, not a fashion, a pose, or a publicity stunt.

Les Fleurs du mal is a Faustian work for a Faustian age, such as ours. To write it Baudelaire had to make a pact with the Devil—not the literal Devil of course, which is a personification. Baudelaire had to make a pact with his inner demons, his addictions: drugs and his women. He may have had addictions but it would be wide of the mark therefore to see in Baudelaire a "victim" and a "case study" who, had he not had these addictions, would have been much better off. Rather, my view is that his demons were necessary ways that he instinctively took to discover his art and achieve it. Had he lost his demons he would have lost his angels, as the later poet, Rainer Maria Rilke said of himself to Lou Andreas-Salomé. Baudelaire courted his demons because he had to in order to become the "Baudelaire" that we know and love and regard as authoritative. But it killed him. His death was the real price of his art—as it was for Rilke and is for all great artists. Baudelaire's life was a sacrifice once and for all and he knew it.

Freeing Beauty

The idea that art is a matter of taste is modern. For in Sections 8 and 9 of the *Critique of Judgment*, Kant said that, while *the good* is represented "only by means of a concept," *the beautiful* is what universally pleases without being dependent on concepts, but rather on what he calls the "free play of the cognitive faculties, particularly of imagination and understanding"[3] (and his whole book backs up the thesis). Formal beauty for Kant is free beauty, to which no formal canons of something called "beauty" apply. It is free because it presents itself to judgment as obviously and inescapably beautiful, or beautiful in and *for itself,* rather than as in what we would regard as a "purely subjective" judgment of something beautiful *for me,* which for Kant is merely something agreeable and pleasant, not something really beautiful at all. As always, Kant avoids objectivism on one hand, and subjectivism on the other. Yet, beauty, as a judgment of taste, is objective in the sense that it is universal and necessary (or obvious and inescapable, to avoid scholastic jargon), and beauty as an *aesthetic experience* has to be subjective.

In short, the rules of beauty that philosophers of aesthetic theory had sought for ages and at times seemed even to have discovered, and the properties of beauty that they enshrined as a result, were shown by Kant to be a chimera to begin with and to never have existed. Beauty is free after Kant.[4]

Kant distinguished *free beauty*, which is altogether independent of interests or ends, and *dependent beauty*, in which interests and ends are introduced. Kant ranked the human figure, classically the most beautiful of representations, under dependent beauty because, he said, we respond to it in terms of our gendered identities, as man, woman or child. Kant was aware of how dependent beauty was culturally relative. Nowadays many people tend to see *all* beauty in "dependent" terms (that is, it is all culturally relative, or gender relative); but Kant would regard such absolutism as a simulacrum of true universalism—in other words, as a failure of taste due to the cultural collapse of sensibilities that makes us blind to beauty.

Hence, Baudelaire is thoroughly modern in looking for beauty not merely in ugliness, where, in any case, previous artists had dug it up; for instance, in realistic depictions such as those of Grünewald, of Christ's suffering, or of Bosch, of hell, but Baudelaire sought beauty in perversity—or he sought beauty perversely. Either way, Baudelaire's poems are incomparable flowers of evil.

Freeing beauty from the concept, that is to say, beauty *without* a concept, in pure appearance as such, means that Kant considered art overtly nonconceptual.[5] Kant came to this realization out of his critical philosophy rather than from looking at artworks, of which, critics say, he was largely ignorant. However, Kant's notion of free beauty lays the precondition for abstract art, even for conceptual art ironically enough. It also lays a precondition for the replacement of beauty by all sorts of other concerns from which beauty would soon be marginalized. Meantime, painters such as Turner already had an instinctual sense of free beauty and would be immensely influential. Whistler was working in Paris in the mid-1850s and the conversations he had there at that time with Baudelaire influenced his idea of art. This was the same idea of art that Baudelaire was working out in poetry.

If we do not understand beauty we do not understand sovereignty— that something reigns in its own right over us, and comes from beyond us, not of our making. If we do not understand beauty, we do not understand that transcendence *has being*. And this "understanding" is not something logical that one can be persuaded to understand or be talked into, but it is sheerly a matter of imagination, or of its lack.

Baudelaire says what he means by beauty in his *Journaux intimes*:

> I have discovered the definition of Beauty—of *my* Beauty.
>
> It is something ardent and sad, something slightly vague, giving rein to conjecture.
>
> I shall, if you wish, apply my ideas to a perceptible object; to the most interesting object to be found in society, namely, a woman's face, I mean—it is something that makes you dream simultaneously but confusedly of sensual pleasure and of sorrow. It conveys the idea of melancholy, of weariness, even of satiety—and at the same time a contrary idea: an ardor, a desire to live, coupled with a recurrent bitterness, such as might come of privation or despair. Mystery and regret, too, are characteristics of Beauty.[6]

With beauty, Baudelaire loved a dark enchantment. In his poem, "Obsession," he says:

> What pleasure you would give me, Night! without these stars
>
> which by their light speak a language I know.[7]

He already knows the language of light. His pleasure is the language of Night. Of course there is a harking back here, in Baudelaire's case, to the Renaissance, to Bruno or Paracelsus, or, more directly, to the mystic Emanuel Swedenborg (1688–1772), whose writings Baudelaire knew, as did Kant.[8]

Baudelaire would sometimes read his poems to friends in a café on the Rue Dauphine. One critic remembers: "He would recite to us in a voice at once mincing, soft, fluty, oily, and yet mordant, some enormity or other—The contrast between the violence of the images and the perfect placidity, the suave and emphatic accentuation of the delivery was truly striking."[9]

The city of Paris was going through a tumultuous period during Baudelaire's lifetime: the run-down little medieval streets were being torn down to make way for the new boulevards which were being built for the heavy traffic of horses and coaches which, today, of course, has turned into "motor cars" or "automobiles." As a poet of the city, what strikes us in Baudelaire's poetry is that there are no poems about the city as such.[10] The city is an absent presence, and yet very much a presence even more so than if the city were everywhere actually referenced.

Le Printemps adorable a perdu son odeur!

(The adorable springtime has lost its scentedness!)[11]

Paris is transmuted through a ground-mood, spleen, through which the city is *felt*, and a resultant artistic sensibility. The splenetic temperament is the poetic temperament *par excellence*. According to tradition there were four temperaments. If one of them has the dominance it enslaves our being with its mood. According to Jacob Boehme, the melancholy temperament is that of the exile, the outsider, who feels trapped and who stalks the earth—or tramps the city streets at night, in Baudelaire's case—subconsciously seeking his place in the world, but always to no avail.[12]

When low and heavy sky weighs like a lid

Upon the spirit moaning in ennui,

And when, spanning a circle of the world,

It pours a black day sadder than our nights.[13]

It is Paris, this great city of culture and history, that commands Baudelaire's spleen. Spleen is the only fitting and true reaction to this postmodern condition at the end of history and culture, as it feels to him—and as it would feel to many others in the century to come, and especially toward the end of the millennium. But the city is always indicative of social conditions: on the one hand, capitalist self-interest, accumulation in the hands of a few, and the invisible power of the "hand of capitalism" which could have streets and buildings torn down and raised up again; and on the other hand, the very visible lack of power in the poverty, the indigence and the slums. At dawn Baudelaire pictures for us the whores still in make-up in a stupor of sleep, open-mouthed; it is a depressing thought.

His Paris is still the Paris of revolution—no longer the revolution of the Enlightenment, but potentially, perhaps, of the proletariat. Marx had been in Paris in the 1840s; it was there that he met Friedrich Engels at the Café de la Régence on the Place du Palais. Engels showed Marx his new book, *The Condition of the Working Class in England in 1844*, and they became convinced that the working class would be the source of the next emancipatory revolutions. Marx was back in Paris during the 1848 uprising, which temporarily deposed King Louis-Philippe. In 1857, when Baudelaire had finished *Les Fleurs du mal*, Marx was in exile from continental Europe, in London, 800 pages into the notes that would lie behind *Das Kapital*, the first volume of which would appear in 1867, the year of Baudelaire's death from syphilis.

We must imagine Paris as a hotbed of revolution, as a hiding place and breeding ground. Baudelaire draws from Edgar Allan Poe's alcoholic imagination to help him express his melancholy attempt—perhaps "macabre" would be a better word, a word we associate with Poe—to recover from being a lost soul in this city.[14]

In *Rêve parisien* ("Parisian Dream"), a poem dedicated to Constantin Guys, Baudelaire refers directly to the city as a "Babel of stairs and arcades/it is an infinite palace/full of falling fountains and waterfalls, in mat or burnished gold."[15] The description is like a dreamscape, like a modernist painting, expressivist, surrealist, and cubist—all of these. It is Guys, rather, who points toward the greater celebration of Paris in the Impressionists of the next generation and the one after that brings on this "magic show" in the mind of Baudelaire. But when, he says, he opens his burning eyes, behold: "I see the horror of my wretched lodgings,"[16] and, he says, the barb of everything accursed comes back through my (his) soul.

Baudelaire's Aesthetic

Spleen et idéal is the name of the first eighty-five poems comprising the main, front section of *Les Fleurs du mal*. The *idéal* is the dynamic with which spleen is caught up in the flux of life. The trapped albatross is an image of the coalescence of the two: the great bird of the sea, trapped by man, its "great white wings, dragging like useless oars."[17] This is an image of the state of poetry, an image of the impossibility of poetry in the new, capitalist city. We are trapped, and especially are the have-nots—what is trapped is the poetic spirit, which is the making of all art. Spleen is the mood felt *qua* the ideal. Between the ideal and the flux of life is a fundamental *correspondence* that is the core of Baudelaire's modern aesthetic, which we will examine more closely now.

The poem entitled in French *Correspondances* is usually pointed to as indicative of Baudelaire's aesthetic. From one point of view—looking at the matter directly—Baudelaire got the idea of correspondences from Swedenborg. He pictures man in this poem as moving within a forest of symbols of which humanity is itself a symbol too. And everything is a symbol of something else, of an ideal elsewhere, with which it corresponds. Correspondence is not just an idea. Correspondences *name a kind of inner sensibility and sensitivity.* Correspondences refer to—and refer us to—the *state of an inner ecology.*[18] Correspondences are familiar in Catholic culture as equivalent to a notion of sacramentality—a notion echoing the saying of St. Paul that "invisible things are understood by things that are made,"[19] one of St. Augustine's favorite lines of Scripture. Baudelaire's aesthetic is culturally Catholic but it is also generatively modern, and we will see how it is very shortly.

Baudelaire's aesthetic is also romantic, although we have to be careful with this word applied in art, as it is often a quite meaningless judgment. For Baudelaire, "Romanticism is neither in the choice of subjects nor in adherence to truth. It is in the manner of feeling a subject."[20] Feeling a subject means for the most part the feeling for *beauty.* Romanticism is (if it is anything) a *sense for beauty.* And for Baudelaire as a modern artist, "there are as many forms of beauty as there are traditional ways of seeking happiness."[21] Beauty is free. Baudelaire seeks her in the underbelly of the city.

Baudelaire's clearest statement of his aesthetic comes from his posthumously published work, *L'Art romantique* (published in 1868). We have said that for Baudelaire *romantique* chiefly means a feeling for beauty. Baudelaire writes:

> Beauty is made of an eternal, unchanging element which makes
> it excessively difficult to determine and an element that is relative

and circumstantial, which will be what we see, completely made up from its time, fashion, morality, feeling. Without the second element, which is the amusing, titillating, appetizing, icing on the divine cake, the first element would be indigestible, impossible to appreciate, unadapted to us and unappropriable by human nature. I defy anyone to discover a sample of whatever is beautiful that does not contain both elements.[22]

The error of the academics that Baudelaire goes on to refer to on the next page of the essay is to try to understand beauty in terms of some concept like happiness, and thereby to rob beauty of what he calls its *aristocratic character*, in other words, its dimension of *height*.[23]

"Beauty is *sovereign appearance*."[24]

Beauty is the essence of correspondence—always remembering that the correspondence a valid artwork makes is in the relationship between two "terms" or aspects, one absolute and the other relative. Alternatively, in an analytical way of saying the same thing, the correspondence the artwork makes is always two-pronged.

To recap this important point: on the one side of the aesthetic of correspondences is the ideal, the eternal, unchanging element; on the other side of the aesthetic is the amusing, the titillating, and sensual, and clearly the sensual in the most trivial sense of the concept. Between the two is a correspondence and *dimension of height*.

Inner-Height

Height is spoken of with reference to our inner sensibility and sensitivity, which is synonymous with what we once called our *soul*. We can think about it this way: everywhere indoors, in every interior setting of our lives, we have a ceiling, which limits our upward look. Some rooms have low ceilings. In most modern functionalist buildings a tall person like myself can reach up and touch the ceiling. But if I walk into a gothic cathedral the ceiling rears up to dizzying heights. The space is different and I am different in it. The acoustics are different, song is possible, and beauty is possible. And I think this is comparable with our inner lives. Each of us has a sensitivity and sensibility that is constitutive of who and what we are. I define sensibility as our *feeling* for things, or our wise intuition (*nous*, in Greek) or discernment (*diakrisis*). Sensibility is our *attunement to being*—our own being and that of the world of beings—and to the being of the world. And so, we can metaphorically ask ourselves: what height is my inner ceiling? How high is my inner-world ceiling, which I carry around with me, *as* me? Can I touch it, or can I even see it? Height with regard to soul is the *sine qua non* of all good art—art worthy of being so called. If a work has no height in this soul sense, then aesthetic experience is impossible, and if a work does not give aesthetic experience, it is not an artwork—no matter what people *say*.

Adorno, in his book *Aesthetic Theory* (1970), one of the most important texts in modernist aesthetics in print, calls this eternal unchanging element of beauty the dimension of "spiritualization."[25] Spiritualization as Adorno envisages it, "works toward the identity of the artwork with itself."[26] This does not mean art for art's sake, but rather the artwork as *end in itself*, saying what cannot be said any other way, but like *this*. At the same time, therefore, (to add to Adorno) "spiritualization" means that the artwork *heightens* our inner sensibility and sensitivity. In old-fashioned language, the art works on our soul. Adorno's "spiritualization" I shall call "soul making," because the artwork (this kind of artwork at least) elevates our inner sensibility and sensibility, perhaps by breaking our prejudgmental threshold, our inner ceiling as I have pictured it.

In speaking of the eternal, timeless or "unchanging" element, Baudelaire is not referring to a positive attribute as such. Timeless and unchanging, like infinite and absolute, are negative words or negations. This is why Baudelaire adds that this quality is something *difficult to determine* or *indeterminate*. The eternal, timeless or unchanging element is something indeterminate, or *a lack* that gives the work its greatness, and that brings people back to it time after time. What is it about *Hamlet* or Baudelaire's own poetry that enables us to say it has this quality, where something else does not? Poor art does not have that "X" factor, as it has been popularly called. In another idiom altogether, this is Martin Heidegger's "enigma" signature of Being;[27] or, in another idiom, what psychoanalyst Jacques Lacan's called "*objét a*"; the indeterminate quality, and in that sense, the "something missing."

Paul Valéry puts it in a nutshell when he writes, "The quality of *indetermination* is the key to music's magic."[28] This indetermination *underlies* the several other criteria of a work's "lastingness."

The Timeless Element

Here I shall identify seven criteria of this timeless element Baudelaire speaks of and by which we may say whether or not it is there. First is the *critical acclaim* of an artwork among art lovers. Critical acclaim is different from mere publicity, and it is different from the hysterical accolades from various so-called critics that accompany commercial simulations of art. Critical acclaim in Baudelaire's case was extremely censorious, although since his time this has gradually changed. We can think of other examples, of Dostoyevsky's novels for example, or Dickens'. What critical acclaim *acclaims* is the *aesthetic experience* to be had from the work. Other people hearing about it then want to see or hear for themselves. "Is it true that this aesthetic experience is possible?" they ask themselves. The great work with the "eternal" quality is work that sustains the critical acclaim. "Yes it is true," we come away thinking, and pass the message on to our friends. And so an oral tradition arises to surround the work; this is its "aura," which is so necessary to its life. Writing by itself cannot sustain the artwork's greatness—writing in a sense is at a remove—but what writing does is, at some time or another, give landmarks that anchor the oral tradition.

The second criterion is *longevity.* An artwork needs to abide over time. Critical acclaim is not enough. A work needs to appeal to a more popular imagination over time. Longevity is a real test. Longevity culturally validates critical acclaim by taking it up and keeping it alive and present, or else time discards it to oblivion. Dostoyevsky and Dickens have obviously passed the test of longevity, as has Baudelaire.[29] This means that death is a criterion of the timeless element: the death of the artist. Longevity does not really begin until after the death of an artist. Therefore an artist who has not sacrificed themselves for their art can hardly be said to have lived for it. Baudelaire was such an artist. In music one might think of almost any well-known nineteenth-century composer.

The third criterion is *influence.* A great work will be influential and inspire other artists, either to follow or revolt. A great work will influence artists using other media and influence the lives of non-artists, both in a private sense and in the public sphere.

A fourth criterion is a work's *translatability,* or transmittance or portability. What this means is that the work may be said to "translate" into other languages, cultures and milieus. For example, Dostoyevsky loved the novels of Dickens, which he read in Russian—or we might love Dostoyevsky or Baudelaire in English and not be able to read them in the original. This is not to say that they are not better in the original, but *they are not reducible to the original*—precisely because of the timeless element. To pick an example from painting: Monet's paintings, although controversial when he made them, are loved far and wide; this is a tribute to them. On the contrary, many other modernist painters and musicians require a particular intellectual and specialized, professional academic milieu and associated publicity machine to justify them and support their credibility, and their artworks cannot stand by themselves; as soon as the cultural buttressing and publicity vanishes, the artworks will disappear because no one really likes them, because quite simply they provide no possibility for aesthetic experience: art devoid of art.

Fifth among the criteria is an artwork's *indomitability*. This is where the artwork stands out or sticks up in time. We look back at such a work of art—or such a philosophy or other "great work" for that matter—as a sign of that time, when so much else (or almost everything) is forgotten, or, if most things are not forgotten, at least the transmission from that time is broken, such as between the ancient Egyptians and today. Indomitability in psychoanalysis is the erotic or *phallic* nature of art. Indomitability is the seed-sowing power of the artwork, the *logos spermatikos*, as the ancients called it, likening all things to a word (*logos*) and its generative power (*spermatikos*).[30]

A sixth criterion arises from Paul Valéry: a work's *productiveness*. According to Valéry, a work of art produces an impression that completes it. A work needs to be productive in order to last, and it is productive when it continues to produce an impression. For example, Shakespeare was popular in his day and continues to make an impression. Some work makes an unpopular impression in its day, which turns around after a while to produce a good impression; either way a work is productive. Baudelaire's poetry is an example of such a work.

A seventh and final criterion in the current list—from Valéry, too—is a work's *memorability*. The work must be abiding, abide *with us*, in our soul. Its "hauntingness" is linked to the work's indeterminacy, as the following quotation from Valéry makes clear:

> For it to last, to achieve a certain intensity and a certain aesthetic effect, it must haunt the memory, must be hard to define, impossible to summarize, and of such a nature that nothing I do can exhaust its efficacy. What, in a work of art, is known as *magic, beauty* and so forth results from the discovery and realization of the conditions needed to this end.[31]

And he adds: "Music is the typical example—the acme of 'obsession.'"[32]

The Voluptuous Element

Turning now to the other dimension of Baudelaire's aesthetic of correspondence, which *corresponds with* the spiritualization or dimension of height, is the *sensual*—or, to use a better, more Baudelairean word, the *voluptuous*.

Now the voluptuous (as the word suggests) is not vulgar. It may *become* vulgar because of social conditions that allow artwork to sink to that level subsequently, as Adorno suggests.[33] I would agree with Adorno on kitsch (cheap imitation) and industrialized art that produces it that there is no genuine aesthetic experience to be had but only the simulacra of it. But voluptuousness signifies correspondence in Baudelaire; it is a synonym for correspondence—the fundamental correspondence between spleen and the ideal. This is a correspondence between spiritualization and voluptuousness, a correspondence that is held in place *inwardly*, in the artist's ground-mood (spleen, in Baudelaire's case), and *outwardly*, in the artwork. Voluptuosity therefore *characterizes* Baudelaire's correspondence without constituting it.

It is *Beauty* in art that *synchronizes* the spiritualization with the voluptuousness and forms the correspondence. A correspondence between the primacy of spirit in art and what was previously taboo comes together in Baudelaire's *Le Fleurs du mal*. The dimension of height in Baudelaire's aesthetic is grounded in modernity, in his time and place, in the contingencies of urban Paris. The ideal is, for Baudelaire, "an eternal, unchanging element,"[34] but it is the *second* element that gives rise to that famous saying of the young poet Rimbaud, who was influenced by Baudelaire, and who said: "*il faut être absolument moderne*" ("we must be absolutely modern").[35] Rimbaud perfectly iterates the Baudelairean aesthetic in his art, for instance in his *Illuminations*, both in the *height* they achieve and in their absolute *novelty*, which makes them modern, free and independent in so many respects.

Baudelaire affirms the aesthetic we find in him and in Rimbaud: "Modernity is that which is ephemeral, fugitive, contingent upon the occasion; it is half of art, whose other half is the unchangeable."[36] And: "We have no right to ignore this transitory and fugitive element, whose metamorphoses are so frequent. For by doing so we forcibly fall into a void of abstract and indefinable beauty, like the unique woman before the first sin."[37] His reference here to Eve means to say that purity is not a condition of beauty. Purity and timelessness are empty and abstract. Beauty is tied to time and time passing.[38] "This modernity is the imprint of our *time* upon our perceptions."[39]

The beauty of modernity then is in all the *things* of modernity: the dress, the city, its new arcades and streets, and, above all, modern people, modern faces, modern gestures. Above all else, Baudelaire reserves his praises for women. The voluptuous and the philosophical come together in art glorifying women, Baudelaire thinks.[40] The female is not essentially a gender. This "gender" notion of woman is a conceptualization which if taken with fundamentalist literalism automatically degrades them and forfeits all that they are in truth, as shown in art. Baudelaire's praise of women could not be more extraordinary if he was Adam in the Garden of Eden seeing Eve for the first time. But, for Baudelaire, that is precisely how a woman must be seen in each and every unique instance. The woman is the most privileged object in creation. I think we can invert this perspective and say the same about man, as Donatello and Michelangelo, for instance, have unmistakably done; or, in modernity, Egon Schiele and Francis Bacon. But, for Baudelaire, there remains that *difference* that the women is always more fashionable than the man, meaning, for Baudelaire, modernity is a woman's prerogative. In a sense the city is made for her—or at least it seems that it is. To us this may seem very "Parisian."

The Longing that Binds

Baudelaire seems upon first reflection to be making a conventional, perhaps romantic, idealization of woman, but upon closer inspection I think we find this is not the point. It is in woman's possibility for defining absolute modernity that his interest lies. Moreover, Baudelaire is not idealizing women, because, as we know from the scandal surrounding his work, in his eyes, and in his art, the depraved courtesan is as beautiful as the most famous actress; the fact that the courtesan's beauty is fake—lent to her by evil, he says—makes her more beautiful: "she has invented an elegance that is barbarous and provocative," he says.[41] The danger, the *sangfroid*, about her has its unique air in every case.[42] The whole point of Baudelaire's praise of women and the fashion associated mostly with women in society is that woman is the living embodiment of Baudelaire's correspondence between the beauty that is passing and of the moment, and the beauty that is eternal.

Man is *outside* woman, literally and symbolically. Sex can momentarily draw a man closer. But man's longing is eternally greater than woman's. This is a reason why there are more male artists historically;

it is not only because, as many modern theorists have claimed, women are oppressed and unliberated, which may also be true. Lou Andreas-Salomé pointed out at the beginning of the women's movement how women's liberation caused women to imitate male longing and by this to undermine her own (feminine) nature, which does not long as a man longs, or for what a man longs. The defeminization of women in Western rationalist patriarchal culture (not all patriarchy is necessarily rational) has seen women artists increase in number, which is what, on this account, one would expect, but this does not change the fact that the inner sensibility and sensitivity of men and women are not the same, nor is their longing. Baudelaire took this for granted.

The importance then, of Baudelaire's aesthetic is that, on the one hand, it "saves the appearances" (in Owen Barfield's phrase), including the different appearance of male and female, and also the aesthetic is true to the ephemeral, the unique and particular, but, at the same time, and on the other hand, the aesthetic opens up to the dimension of height. The aesthetic opens up from the ephemeral ground of absolute modernity, infinitely. Baudelaire's aesthetic saves us from an artistic sensibility that is merely modern, in the dreary, banal sense that we see on exhibit in so many galleries of contemporary art, and yet Baudelaire's aesthetic is progressive, not conservative; popular, not elitist. And Baudelaire is not just theorizing, but his own poetic output *exemplifies* his aesthetic and becomes the touchstone of its reality.

Of course, there has to be an *inner necessity* about all of this. An art—or a philosophy for that matter—that merely construes or contrives a correspondence without the inner necessity is false. Such art is easily seen through, in any case. This inner necessity is the original creative impulse.

Adorno says, "There is no valid artwork without longing."[43] I believe this is true. Between the part of art that is eternal and unchangeable and the part that is fugitive and ephemeral is a longing that keeps the correspondence in place, at least as a possibility, and that the artist feels to be part of the creative impulse. It is what the audience picks up on—not the *artist's* longing, but the longing that is in the heart of *the one who reads or listens or gazes*. In an artwork one discovers one's own longing—that one is a creature of longing, only that one had forgotten it in all the madness of the day, but one is restored to it as to the truth; our own lives are ephemeral and our death is absolute, but the aesthetic of beauty and the artwork which serves this shows something stronger than death: that the soul to which it speaks survives, and death shall have no dominion.

So let us ask, what is art? It is something of beauty in the sense that the work can be identified as having a polarity within it, the end-terms of which correspond. The correspondence is between, on one end, an eternal unchanging element—that is, something infinitely indeterminate—and, at the other end, the relative, circumstantial and incontestably time-bound. Our taste—which belongs to our inner sensibility and sensitivity—alone can tell us whether a work has this quality of polarity or not. If it does not it may aspire to be art, but may be what we call "bad" art. If it is merely posing with these eternal and time-bound elements, especially with the first of these elements (like propaganda art, or art which illustrates a theory or concept outside the work), we would call it art, perhaps, but "bad" art. Whether the art is expressive, impressionistic, abstract or seemingly representational (not simply representational, note) does not make it good or bad in itself. There are as many ways of going about art as there are ways of being human. Good art, we recognize, coheres with Baudelaire's aesthetic. This is a view that is almost lost in a wilderness of art theory, and in a time with no time for art.

2

The Metaphysics of Nostalgia

There is no valid artwork without longing.
—Theodor Adorno, *Aesthetic Theory*

I want to explore further the notion of *correspondence* in an over-arching, or big-picture, way—hence, metaphysics. The key to the case that I want to put forward is given by the Adorno quotation just above: that there is no *valid* artwork without longing. I shall explain this metaphysics in two ways: Platonic and anti-Platonic. While the Platonic is relatively easy to understand, the anti-Platonic is much harder as it coheres less with conventional understandings and is not so amenable to a commonsense explanation. Neither explanation however is common sense in fact; each depends, in different ways, on faith. By faith I do not mean belief (with which faith is commonly mistakenly equated); I mean our *stance toward death* and how we act (and think) as a result of this stance. The Platonic and anti-Platonic are two dominant stances toward death, both of which denote a nostalgia. We might not think of ourselves as having a stance toward death, but everybody has one, not necessarily held consciously. Baudelaire's aesthetic pertains to both the Platonic and anti-Platonic and both of these stances toward death are also (by the same token) stances within and toward life and art.

Platonism

I said that between the terms of the correspondence is a *longing*, which the artwork brings to life, and which only the artwork itself can assuage. The longing which joins to the two terms of Baudelaire's aesthetic, this sense of correspondence between a timeless or eternal element, and an element made from the day—from historical contingency—is the subject of this chapter. What Adorno called longing in saying that "there is no valid artwork without longing"[1] we will call *nostalgia*. The modern poet and literary critic Jean-Michel Maulpoix puts it like this:

> Poetry is torn between the desire for a land which does not exist and the need for a common ground, between its two contradictory genii: that somewhere else and the commonplace.[2]

Here Maulpoix restates Baudelaire's aesthetic. The "two contradictory genii" are the two terms of Baudelaire's correspondence. The longing occurs between one and the other. In our life (not just our mind) nostalgia arises out of a relation to the past, real and imagined, but more profoundly, therefore needing to be said philosophically, out of a relation to the primordial. Nostalgia in the first sense is a longing or hankering after what we know we have lost, for example, childhood, homeland. Primordial longing is otherwise, it is different in kind, it longs after what it *does not* know, has never known and cannot know. In psychoanalytical terms, we might speak of the womb, of the mother, of the breast, of the umbilical cord, which was irrevocably cut off. In religious terms we might talk of lost paradises. In cultural and literary and archetypal terms, we may talk of Odysseus finding his way through the world and its vicissitudes to Ithaca—whether we speak of this in terms of Homer or of James Joyce. We may talk philosophically about the infinitude of desire—as Spinoza and Freud and others have done. And these ways of imagining and the symbolic orders which govern them may or may not be different ways of thinking and talking about the same thing, or trying to talk about it. We do not know. We cannot know. But we *do* know that these stories—psychoanalytical or religious, or cultural and artistic—are not meaningless, because our emotional intelligence tells us so, and our reflective intellect tells us so, even if we do not know *what exactly* it is that we miss and long for. This is primordial longing—longing for the origin, or rather, more exactly, the longing that is *given with* the origin, given to begin with. The philosopher Martin Heidegger and his commentators have made this thought of origin known to us as "primordiality" to refer to what is originary in our culture, in Greece; for instance, primordial words from which culture arises: *philosophia*, *logos* (word, reason) and *poesis* (creating).

Another modern German philosopher, Martin Buber (1878–1965), called our state of being human one of exile, precisely in this primordial sense. As a German *Jewish* philosopher who survived the Holocaust, he knew about exile and so he has some authority on the subject. As a philosopher of religion, Buber called religions themselves *houses of exile*:

"each religion is a house of the human soul longing for God, a house with windows and without a door ... Each religion is an exile into which man is driven ... but the religions know that they are bound together in a common expectation; they can call to one another greetings from exile to exile, from house to house, through the open windows." I have always thought this a beautiful picture of the metaphysics of nostalgia.[3]

While the Greek world of culture and the Jewish world of culture are each quite singular and different, yet we can see that both have within their different idioms what we are calling the metaphysics of nostalgia. Nostalgia is equally Greek as it is Jewish as it is Christian.

The Bible, the book that has influenced Western culture more than any other book and thereby had a follow-on influence on secular and global culture, is shot through with nostalgia. The Bible begins with the words, *Bereshit bara Elohim et hashamayim ve'et ha'arets* ("In the beginning God created heaven and earth")—there is nostalgia: God's nostalgia for a creation to fill his primordial *lack*. The Hebrew word *tshuvah* (return) means more than simply something similar to repentance in Christianity, or *aliyah*, return to the Land of Israel, although it can have these connotations. Abraham Isaac Kook (1865–1935), a genius and one of the greatest Jewish spiritual teachers of the twentieth century, explains the concept in terms of the metaphysics of nostalgia:

> *Tshuvah*—return is inspired by the yearning of all existence to be better, purer, more vigorous and on a higher plane than it is. Within this yearning is a hidden life-force overcoming every factor that limits and weakens existence. (*Orot Ha Tshuva* [*Lights of Return*], 6:1)
>
> (...)
>
> All our endeavors must be directed toward disclosing the *or hashalom hacalali*, the light of universal harmony, which derives not from suppressing any power, any thought, any tendency, but bringing each of them within the vast ocean of infinite light, where all things find their unity, where all is ennobled and exalted, all is hallowed. (*Notebook* 8:429)
>
> (...)
>
> We must liberate ourselves from confinement within our private concerns ... It is necessary for us to raise our thought and will and our basic preoccupations toward universality, to the inclusion of all, to the whole world, to humankind, to the Jewish people, to all existence ... The firmer our vision of universality, the greater joy we will experience and the more we will merit divine illumination. (*Orot Hakodesh* [Lights of the Holy Spirit] 3:147)[4]

Even the prophetic sense of hope and future here echoes the metaphysics of nostalgia. It is a teaching ingrained in the Jewish transmission and, as in the root, so in the branch: first in Christian culture East and West, then in wider occidental culture. Secular culture that disregards the metaphysics of nostalgia is forgetting its own soul. French culture since the French Revolution has tried to get away from its own past with a vengeance; Anglo culture with its utilitarian pragmatism is apt to forget the metaphysics of nostalgia as well and be too intent on business and short-term goals and objectives. Even so, the secular goal of ethical universalism is a longing itself and Rav Kook reiterates it in his religious idiom.

Primordial longing or the metaphysics of nostalgia comes from the past—from the origins themselves—yet it is not a yearning for what was, but rather for what is yet to be. This is the strange thing about it: it is a longing for what we do not know *but can imagine*. Imagination has its own way of knowing that informs our faculty of knowledge, telling it to get busy. Rav Kook's own longing towards an *harmony*—which in a critically secular register we hear already iterated in Kant's ethical universalism in the late eighteenth century, or, nearer our time, in the philosophy of Levinas—we hear too in a popular register in the speeches and teachings of people such as Martin Luther King, Nelson Mandela, the Dalai Lama, Chief Rabbi Jonathan Sacks, Hans Küng, and Pope John Paul II and from artists and young people from every part of the world. None of this is a yearning for what was, but for what we can *imagine*, and more and more people are realizing it must be so and are working to that end. The metaphysics of nostalgia cuts across the divides of culture and religion, yet in a way that involves them in it. Of course that is part of harmony, that is presupposes different and odd notes. And against this is the voice of reason that eschews imagination and has none. Wherever culture ebbs imagination fails.

Musically, and epiphanically, the notes of a new universal age, the post-secular age, what some have called *the age of world religions*, are perhaps first heard in Beethoven's Fifth Symphony. In this symphony, we hear, in Wagner's words, that "melody is an absolute tongue,"[5] an insight that we shall have to come back to in another chapter. We hear in Beethoven's Fifth Symphony elemental notes of freedom sounded, and the majesty of equality, and the vision of one world, for to hear is also to see; and we hear much else—perhaps, most importantly, we hear something *soul-sustaining*, which will be needed in the time of overcoming that must be crossed in order to reach these goals, if we ever shall. For the rule of quantitative reason must be made to serve, rather than to rule as now. This will involve revolution of some description. Retrospectively, I would say that even the tumults of the twentieth century do not drown out this music of Beethoven, as István Szabó showed so well in his film *Taking Sides* (2001), but rather the tumults of the twentieth century make this music of Beethoven *all the more audible* and all the more necessary to us; in other words, all the killing of the twentieth century has only brought this music *closer to us*, rather than estranged it from us, as has happened with much other music of the past.

In Western culture, as we go back into it, the word for what I am calling the metaphysics of nostalgia is Platonism, or neo-Platonism, referring to that form of Platonism associated with the name of Plotinus (205–270) and the posthumous compilation of his writings, *The Enneads* (*The Nines*, referring to the structure in which the treatises are placed). Christianity was influenced by Platonism and by neo-Platonism in its early development. Christianity is even fundamentally Platonic because it is Platonic in its roots: John's Gospel and Paul's theology in the New Testament are *already Platonic*, despite whatever transpositions they make in order for their Platonism to assume a Christian character. And at our end of Christian history, we have already noted the association of Platonism with Baudelaire's aesthetics. I said as well that Baudelaire's aesthetic imitates the sacramental idea central to Catholic and Orthodox Christianity[6] —that invisible things are understood by things that are made.[7] In other words, the timeless and eternal element of Baudelaire's correspondence is understood by the historical, social and time-bound *objet d'art*. In religion Christ is understood by this bread and this cup at a particular gathering. The human and divine come together or cannot be told apart. In sacramental sensibility something *comes to presence*. In Baudelaire's *Flowers of Evil*, what comes to presence is not evil, or flowers, or poems: what comes to presence with the poems and in them, as Christ comes to presence with this bread and this cup, is *art*.

Just as only false religion is made up, true religion must fall like a revelation or an inspiration from some Nowhere above, and so with art. Bad art is contrived and there is no aesthetic experience, but great art brings art to presence so that we experience it. Just as true religion is atoning, so is such art. In aesthetic experience the presence of art takes one's own presence into it as one. We experience artwork as an experience of self-knowledge.

For Christian mythology and the doctrines that conceptualize it, there is an equivocation between this life and another life after death—an equivocation between two worlds, the seen and the unseen, one present, the other absent. Between the two issues in the heart is a sense of loss and nostalgia. Such nostalgia is a central reverberation within Western culture—and not just Western culture, I may add. Not only does the one who sees and is seen long for the unseen and what she can idealize, in Christian culture the unseen itself comes to life and dwells among us. In every form of Christianity the words of prayer "on earth as it is in heaven" evoke the nostalgia sensed between what is changeless and of timeless value, and what is impermanent and changing, and the coming (advent) of the one into the other for redemptive purposes, to raise it up to all it can be. The words also state that what is seen—the world with all its groanings—will shape and remodel itself after the fashion of the unseen. As the Christian myth has it, "God so loved the world," in other words, from heaven God *yearns after* the world and so much so that he sends his "only Son" to live there, and indeed, to suffer and die there, so that he could feel more connected with this world in his far-off heaven. From the outside one can acknowledge the fact, and from the inside the Christian can experience here, the metaphysics of nostalgia between two worlds. This metaphysics of nostalgia is part of Western culture and religion and, therefore, as Baudelaire clearly realized, integral to any valid artwork within such a civilization.

Let me recapitulate Platonic longing in easier language then move on to discuss anti-Platonism, its shadow form, and the metaphysics of nostalgia. In the late fourth century, the Latin church father, Augustine, Bishop of Hippo, a Roman province in North Africa, in the first paragraph of his *Confessions*, wrote: "Lord, you have made us for yourself and our hearts are restless until they rest in You." These words connote the metaphysics of nostalgia. Augustine addresses his words to what he believes is a being completely outside this world, but who he believes nevertheless loves it as his own handiwork, and Augustine expresses his unassuageable longing for God, a longing so great that nothing less than God can satisfy it. This longing is *essentially* desiring, an unbearable desire just like Jacques Lacan's psychoanalytical *jouissance*, —unbearable because, as Wordsworth says, it is *too much with us, late and soon*. Augustine experienced the beauty in proximity of God as *so ancient and so new;*[8] God as always having been there invisible to his eyes, but now suddenly made visible as if the scales had fallen off his eyes; precisely the biblical metaphor and the one Jesus used to distinguish what we see from what we *could* see, with the same going for experience.

The *Confessions* of Augustine have been translated out of Latin into more languages than any other Christian work, and more than any other *Latin* work, except Virgil's *Aeneid*. This is because its sentiments, summed up aptly in the sentence just quoted, reverberate within the soul of our culture. If we do not share Augustine's belief, we still share that sense of *lack* beyond need. That sense that "I desire" (*desidero*) runs into modernity right through the art of the Renaissance and the desire for art and knowledge, interweaves with the *cogito* (I think) of scientific reason in the logic of Spinoza and Locke, enters recent thought, after Kant and Schopenhauer, and is found in Freud and recognized as central in psychoanalysis. For example, in Freud's *Civilization and its Discontents*, it is precisely desire that needs civilizing and that gives rise to the "discontents" within civilization. Jacques Lacan pins desire down with his delta symbol. According to his eccentric, algebraic notation, delta stands for deep, dark, unassuageable desire, offset within his psychoanalytical account by the imaginary and symbolic registers of our soul's being, like keynotes, which further untune it. Lacan presumes our exile. Comparing Freud's discovery of the unconscious with discoveries by Newton, Einstein and others, Lacan says "the Freudian field is a field which, of its nature, is lost."[9] The whole of analysis takes place in the wilderness. As in Freud, so in Lacan, the unconscious emerges in analysis, a certain situation; it is not there for philosophical conceptualization or hermeneutical interpretation, like something known, "but lacuna, cut, rupture inscribed in a certain lack."[10] If desire constellates the metaphysics of nostalgia, nostalgia itself is "an enchantment of desire" (Jankélévitch) activated by certain "localizations" in time and space, while nostalgia always stretches beyond.[11] The topography of desire announced by nostalgia is always symbolic[12], and the strength of the ancient writers is that they understood this better than we do in our time when we take everything so literally and personally.

Plato himself, 800 years before Augustine, at the end of the fourth century BCE writes, in the Myth of the Cave in Book VII of *The Republic*, of the soul's need to be free of illusion if it is not to die, and if the soul is to behold the truth of the realm in which it *exists*. The metaphor is one of sight and of sharing, or partaking, with our being *in* a power like the light of the sun that is life-giving. This tips over into the Christian tradition: in *Acts*, where God is described as the One in whom we live and move and have our being; and in *the most quoted sayings of the church fathers*—who are crucial cultural figures because it was their authority that decided what texts really belonged to the Christian communities, and it was they who, eventually, when the oral tradition was under assault by fraudulent writings and wayward teachers and teachings in the fourth century, compiled what came to be known and widely circulated as the New Testament. We read there from St. Peter that "we are partakers of the divine nature."[13] This was the saying so often on the lips of the church fathers, as a hermeneutical key to the New Testament. The saying means that, by living in a certain manner, by a certain "light," we partake of the divine nature, that is, we partake of the greatest—indeed, transcendent—*height* of being, above and beyond our mortal nature. To partake of something is to be caught up in its reality. This is what Christians believed: that, as Christians, they were caught up in the reality of God without their being Jews—although, to begin with, they were all Jews. There is a sense in this saying (that we are partakers of the divine nature) that the exile is over—and that this is good news, which is what the church fathers believed. However, despite the Good News, the sense of exile remained, as we heard in the quotation given from Augustine: "our hearts are restless." But this restlessness of the heart, that is, of *being*, predates Augustine and is to be found in ancient liturgy that traces back to the melancholy chants of the old synagogues and, because of the destruction of the temple in Jerusalem in 70 CE, continues into Diaspora Judaism as a beautiful lament. On the Christian side, the restlessness of heart and lament continued out of the old synagogues, well beyond the time of Augustine, into the medieval liturgies, Eastern and Western—particularly the Western liturgies, which were always more melancholy, with their despondency, yet with their hope of heaven.

> Jerusalem my happy home,
> When shall I come to thee?
> When shall my sorrows have an end?
> They joys when shall I see?

This is the opening verse of an ancient processional.[14] It is associated with the name of Augustine—not just the name of a man, but of a whole spiritual ethos of yearning. Twenty-six verses later the processional concludes:

> Jerusalem my happy home,
> Would God I were in thee![15]

We note the tension between "there," Jerusalem, the "City of God" or Heavenly City, and "here," where we are now, in the Earthly City. Between the two is a correspondence that is *held* in the inner sensibility and sensitivity, which is in the soul. Van Morrison reechoes this in *Astral Weeks* (1968) where he sings, "I'm nothing but a stranger in this world, I got a home on high."

Anti-Plato

Having said all this, we should remember that the notion of correspondence is *not* tied to being Platonic and religious. Let us examine the non-Platonic and non-religious interpretation in this section with the help of the French poet, Yves Bonnefoy. In order to keep the discussion neat and orderly, I shall use Baudelaire again as our starting point. Conveniently, Bonnefoy, a poet of enormous authority as an artist, one who understands longing, I would say, beyond my own sense (hence I defer to him), has written about Baudelaire. As a modern French poet of course his spiritual roots could hardly be anywhere else.

Anti-Plato was the title of Bonnefoy's first volume of poems, in 1947. Bonnefoy's own anti-Platonism was allied with the surrealist movement in the arts. The anti-Plato approach is what, from a philosophical and cultural studies point of view, has been called "post-metaphysical" thought, or "non-obectifying thinking" (Heidegger).

According to Bonnefoy, correspondence is not metaphysical, but *enunciative*. That means correspondence is not a conception, but something we meet in words (or music) at the level of their *saying*. The correspondence is, in Bonnefoy's words, "a truth of speech."[16]

When Baudelaire speaks, as he does everywhere in his poetry, something is *intoned*. That is to say, something is brought out from within. What Baudelaire intones in speech is what Bonnefoy calls "his longing," which "was for the universal."[17] This longing for the universal is what, in Adorno's epigraph to this chapter, validates the artwork, we recall. And what characterizes this longing is not faith on one hand or heresy on the other, Bonnefoy goes on, but *lack*—or loss.

Let us consider this lack. Lack or loss is marked in Baudelaire's fundamental ground-mood of *spleen*, and what this mood constellates, the ideal. We recall that the central section of *Les Fleurs du mal* is entitled "Spleen and the Ideal." The two go together: loss and that which has been lost. If the loss is universal (the experience of the death of God, as in Nietzsche, for example; or simply the shriveling away of conventional Christian religious faith to non-existence, as in Lou Andreas-Salomé and as a common experience in our time) then the lack will be correspondingly universal, and what is enunciated— Baudelaire's poetry, in this instance—will be caught in this double bind (regarded existentially) or double negative (regarded conceptually). But the art and the greatness of the art arise precisely out of the ability to enunciate this beautifully. This is Baudelaire's "double passion." His desire, his lack of desire, and his suffering are coordinated and constituted by the correspondence of the double negative, which is, looked at philosophically, anti-Plato. He is the founding modern poet for this reason more than any other.

Bonnefoy does indeed describe lack or loss in Baudelaire's work as "a double passion."[18] By making flowers of evil, Bonnefoy says (perhaps rather over-poetically for an Anglo-Saxon reader) Baudelaire *gives death back its purity*.

This idea of giving death back its purity is a subject that we will consider and I shall try to explain in the remainder of this section. Baudelaire's enunciative notion of correspondence has precisely, and more than anything else, to do with giving back death its purity. This is the starting point of our proceeding.

This starting point exists within an enunciative idiom in Western culture: that of Christianity, and particularly its traditionally conceived, ontotheological explanation of itself. In this theological idiom, death *lacked* the purity that Baudelaire (and Bonnefoy, in his wake) would salvage for it. In the Christian mythological metaphysic (or ontotheology), death equates with sin and punishment. This is how the story of Adam and Eve is classically interpreted within Christianity: disobedience leads to punishment, death, and hard labor, and the subjugation of the feminine. When we say that Baudelaire's enunciative acts (poetry) aim to give death back its purity, we mean he wants to redeem death from the Christian enunciation where it is trapped and untrue.

This old Christian theology, half myth, half metaphysics, each blending unselfconsciously and uncritically into the other, elaborated an undermining of the sense of life this side of the grave at the expense of life after death. Life was divided between before and after death and a logic of obedience and punishment (ostensibly ethics) validated the distinction. This became unbelievable and distasteful in the secular milieu, and philosophically after Kant and Hegel. However, in seeing this life on earth as a "vale of tears" and nothing more or better, and the next life as the place of truth and justice and God, Christianity is not just complicit with Platonism, but implicitly Platonistic. Baudelaire's art is a testimony to an *other truth* in which life and death are two sides of one reality. It is this that I want to explore in a preliminary way. Let me begin with these quotations from Bonnefoy about Baudelaire:

> When God had ceased to exist for many, he invented the idea that death can be efficacious. That death alone will re-form the unity of lost being. And, in fact, through the work of Mallarmé or Proust, of Artaud and Jouve—all spiritual heirs of *Les Fleurs du mal*—we can well imagine death as a servant of souls: in a world at last free and pure.

> Death would fulfill the destiny of the word. It would open to religious feeling—at the end of its long wandering—the dwelling place of poetry.[19]

The key phrase here, to my mind (and that unlocks what is being said as a whole), is "the unity of lost being." Platonism and Christianity divide the world between "here" and "there," "above" and "below," "God" and "man," and so on. The desire to restore the unity of lost being is a non-traditionally-Christian stance, an "anti-Platonic" stance. It is a stance that reasserted itself in the West in the nineteenth century in the arts and philosophy, although not in the mainstream academic traditions of these, and the stance has still not entered the mainstream academic Humanities where shallow rationalism and its shadow, nihilism, still rub shoulders.

The nineteenth-century philosopher, Arthur Schopenhauer, not only encapsulates but sets out and explains this stance that wants to restore the unity of day/night or life/death in his great work, *The World as Will and Representation* (1818, 1844). He wants to restore the *lost sensibility* for the unity of life and death. Schopenhauer's reasoning therefore must be one *inclusive* of sensibility (rather than devoid of it like so much philosophy of his day and ours). Schopenhauer's is a *rare* book of philosophy by modern Western standards, harking back, as it does, above all, to Meister Eckhart and a wisdom tradition lost by Medieval Scholasticism, a loss symbolically ratified by the Church's official condemnation of Meister Eckhart in 1329. Schopenhauer spent a lifetime writing his great work, which shows complete respect for the achievement of his predecessor, Kant, but which adds to that achievement in ways Kant would surely have marveled at.

Schopenhauer writes, "Birth and death belong equally to life, and hold the balance as mutual conditions of each other—poles of the whole phenomenon of life."[20] Schopenhauer reminds us that Indian mythology, in its wisdom, depicts Shiva, who symbolizes death and destruction, not only with a necklace of skulls, but with the lingam, a phallic symbol of generation "which appears as the counterpart of death." "In this way it is intimated that generation and death are essential correlatives which reciprocally neutralize and eliminate each other."[21] Schopenhauer goes on to say that something along the same lines is found in Greek mythology too. Or, as Paul Valéry succinctly puts it in the *Analects*: "Death is the union of soul and body—whose consciousness, waking state, and suffering are disunion."[22] This is the insight of Baudelaire, but poetically; and it is this that Bonnefoy draws to our attention.

Now to further elaborate and clarify what we have just established. Two writers coming in the wake of Baudelaire clarify Schopenhauer. The first is Nietzsche (1844–1900), the erstwhile student of Schopenhauer and Wagner. Nietzsche makes an imaginative (rather than historical or factual) case for an "Apollonian art" of clarity and proportion and light, and a "Dionysian art," which is orgiastic. The love of beauty can lead in either direction, and tragedy, Nietzsche argues, is born of the Dionysian, for there is an orgiastic side to beauty, and a lover succumbs to it with tragic consequences. It is a fascinating thesis, which Nietzsche characterizes, in his post-metaphysical way, as "pre-Socratic" (that is, "anti-Plato"). We can see both sides—the Apollonian and the Dionysian—in Baudelaire's art, and the Dionysian even more apparently in his life, which was in many ways tragic, but in a positive sense, because completely artistic. Says Nietzsche, "Dionysian art, too" no less than Apollonian, "wishes to convince us of the eternal delight of existence."[23] Nietzsche's thesis about the birth of tragedy from the spirit of music exemplifies Schopenhauer's principle that "Birth and death belong equally to life, and hold the balance as mutual conditions of each other—poles of the whole phenomenon of life."[24]

Further, Nietzsche, in his book *Thus Spoke Zarathustra* (1884, 1892) writes: "Many die too late, and a few die too early. The doctrine still sounds strange: 'Die at the right time!'"[25] Like Baudelaire, Nietzsche is not just talking about death in the old Platonic and Christian sense, opposed to life or "after" it, but he is actually talking *about life* in a way that includes life and death together: "Die at the right time—thus teaches Zarathustra. Of course, how could those who never live at the right time die at the right time?"[26]

It is not certain what Nietzsche means about those "who never live at the right time" but it makes sense to believe he refers to those whom he calls earlier in the same book "the last men." He hates these last men, and much of *Thus Spoke Zarathustra* remonstrates against them. The "last men" are basically the bourgeoisie, the middle class, or at least those among them who seek happiness in material advantage and comforts, and who develop a culture around this—the culture of modern commodity capitalism and consumerism, we now realize.

To die at the right time, to die a free death, means—Nietzsche goes on to say—"the death that consummates—a spur and a promise to survivors."[27] This is akin to the Christian idea, in fact, which is perhaps one reason why Nietzsche is so bitter about bourgeoisie who are only nominally Christian—and who, he says, because of the Sunday sanity of their logic and lives, have "killed God."[28] But here we can see that the founder of Christianity meets the criteria for having died the free death, as the saints and martyrs in his name have also done. But these, as far as Nietzsche is concerned, stand over and against "established" Christianity, which has more to do with temporal power and real estate. Nietzsche, in this same passage of *Thus Spoke Zarathustra*, goes on to speak of a possible future culture in which there are new festivals that hallow death, in the sense of its being part of a *wholeness*.

Another writer I might mention in clarifying this point of Bonnefoy's about art purifying death is the poet, Rainer Maria Rilke (1875–1926). In *The Book of Hours* (1905) Rilke writes:

> For what makes dying strange and difficult
> is that it isn't our own death; it's the one which only
> harvests us in the end because we never ripened:
> that's why there's a storm, to shake us all down.[29]

We are shaken down by the storm because we cannot fall from our own ripening; in other words, our lives are unripe within and so we will be taken from without. For Rilke, here, death is inside us, ripening, ripening *with* life, death is the ripening *of* life—in the end, its dark fruit. In an earlier image Rilke said that our birth is also the birth of a death which we carry and ripen through our life and which we carry within us differently at different stages of life.

> O Lord, give each of them their own death,
> the dying that belongs to that particular life
> in which they once had love, meaning and need.

For we are nothing but the shell and leaf.
The great death each of us has within us—
that is kernel round which it all revolves.[30]

Later, in 1910, in Paris, Rilke wrote in the *alter ego* of Malte Laurids Brigge:

> When I go back in thought to my home, where there is no-one left now . . . Formerly we knew (or perhaps we just guessed) that we carried our death within us, as a fruit bears its kernel. Children had a little death within them, older people a large one. Women had theirs in their womb, men theirs in their breast. One had it, and that gave one a singular dignity, a quiet pride. And when I think of those others . . . They all had a death of their own. Those men who carried theirs within their armour, like a prisoner; those women who grew very old and small, and then on a huge bed, as on a stage, passed away, discreet and dignified, in the presence of the whole family, the servants and the dogs. Children too, even the very little ones, did not die just any kind of childish death; they gathered themselves together and died as that which they already were, and as that which they would have become. And what a melancholy beauty came to women when they were pregnant, and stood, their slender hands involuntarily resting on their big bodies which bore two fruits: a child and a death.[31]

Here, then, through Nietzsche and Rilke, we can clarify Baudelaire's non-Platonic sense of philosophy or poetry or art as the practice of dying. To say this is to talk about life as an arts lifestyle; certainly this is so if we say this in the present era of commodity capitalism and its ruinous consumerist culture. Poetry in this age is not Platonic; it cannot be. This is Bonnefoy's point. He says, regarding the truth of Baudelaire's speech: "Death in its chosen place and attentive speech together compose the profound voice that is capable of poetry."[32]

In this non-Platonic view of Baudelaire, *Les Fleurs du mal* is Baudelaire's death as a metaphor of a limit point to which he gave birth in his life. Baudelaire succumbed to his orgiastic side and died the sort of death that is not surprised. Nietzsche went mad, but his madness was like a great accumulation of after-life from his written works which his sanity could not support. Rilke, after the great outpouring of the *Duino Elegies* and *Sonnets to Orpheus* in 1922, changed languages, from German to French, and poured out five volumes of French poetry, but he was dead within three years. Such creative lives are indicative of the relationship between the procreative truth of art, and death.

Symbols as Sites of Longing

We have looked so far at the metaphysics of nostalgia from Platonic and anti-Platonic points of view, and seen both operative in the artist's notion of correspondence—and have seen that this notion can be read religiously (Platonically) or non-religiously. In this last section I want to reflect in a preliminary way about the disjunction between ethics and aesthetics. They are both "good," but it is not the same good. But to start with I will return once again briefly to consider the longing that links the two terms of correspondence: the eternal, unchanging element, or what we shall call therefore the *indeterminate*, on one hand, and the fashionable, amusing, appetizing "icing on the divine cake," or the *determinate* element, on the other. Further I want to outline in a sketchy (but reflective and not haphazard manner) some of the dynamics that arise from the correspondence.

Timeless, in Baudelaire's aesthetic, does not mean "forever." The word timeless usually indicates stasis, as in the theological idea of eternity and the static thinking of Scholastic metaphysics that supports it. What Baudelaire means by an eternal, unchanging element in art is its complete removal from the *reign of quantity* in experience. The reign of quantity is ever more about us now in our Western, teletechnoscientific culture. At least the Medieval period had a sense of the transcendent. Modern people even lack this. The reign of quantity over our lives today is total. The quantification of everything (everything has its price) is what Max Weber described at the beginning of the twentieth century as disenchanting the world. The disenchantment of the world starts with the inner world of sensibility and sensitivity, with the soul. What matters more are external counters, numbers, signs, atoms. Science brings gains in knowledge and technology and losses in sensibility and sensitivity. But we will never know the latter because it is by means of inner sensibility and sensitivity that we would register them in the first place. This unrecognized loss of sensibility gives rise to the illusion of worldly progress. Schopenhauer, the early Nietzsche (the later Nietzsche was already mad) and Rilke were all aware of this and tried to recall their reader to inner sensibility and sensitivity. But opposed to them was a rampant Hegelianism that reified thinking, and believed in the progress of thinking that quickly got confused with the progress of science and even of society, according to extrinsic coordinates of course. So now everything is politics and economics and science, our world is Hegelian in one way or another and it is hard to even imagine sensibility otherwise than in these terms of reference. It is almost impossible to imagine what *timeless* could mean in these Hegelian terms of reference, which is why some (many even) would regard *timeless* as a meaningless word. Yet, the timeless waits on, while we fool ourselves with our projections and objectivity; the timeless can bide its time while we run with the time, for the timeless has not to do with time in our clock-bound sense, our big city sense, the timeless has to do with cycles and seasons, with the qualitative sense of *now*, with living in *the day*, with *contact with the depths*.[33]

The longing which validates the artwork and the experience of it is between two moments of correspondence: a *moment* into which all time is absorbed, and a *momentariness*—of fashion, of the passing parade, of the time we live in. The moment that captures our being stands in time as a memory that is not *just* a memory: *it is a symbol*—individually, for some of us who have had such moments, and corporately, for groups of people who have shared such moments, for example, the feeling (felt experience) that, as at a great concert, something *momentous* has taken place which will stand, henceforth, for us, for who we are. The great artwork stands for who we are, and we know it.

There are famous examples of such social symbols, such as the exhibition of Manet's *Déjeuner sur l'herbe*; or the first performance in Paris of Stravinsky's *Le sacré du printemps*, with choreography by Nijinsky, costume design by Roerich and direction by Diaghilev; or one's first reading of *Les Fleurs du mal* or Rimbaud's *Illuminations*. Experiences like this have been and continue to be symbolic in the lives of countless people. As a result, works have "gone down in history," which is to say they have attained a cultural symbolic value. This is not the same as becoming a cultural icon or gaining cultural status, which have to do with something becoming a "national treasure" or "literary treasure" and, to that extent, a museum piece or a marker of identity.

These symbols we could also say are marks of true culture, despite the culture industry's re-evaluation of all values, including "truth" in this regard, along commercial lines of the market and profit. Great works are symbols and symbols are not just "signifiers," although truly they do speak with significance, and of more than just what they say: great works are apertures through which, and only through which, the eternal and unchanging, which is *in the moment*, can be tasted for oneself. In great works we do indeed *taste* the eternal and unchanging, not for just that measured moment or "for the duration," but *for our whole life*, and perhaps for the lives of our children and their children. And when it comes to music and listening, as we shall see in due course, there is an added factor that the power of now is sustained *across* time, across the time it takes to perform the piece and for it to be heard as a whole, which we cannot accomplish until the last note of the last sequence. The meaning of the correspondence is that at any time, in every moment, there is that "drop-out" point where we acquiesce and are lulled, and where we *fall* for the work. This happens on a completely individual basis, just like love, where the work transports us, and where we exist in the moment and for the moment; this is "the eternal unchanging" element Baudelaire is referring to and that pertains to all true art and to which artists aspire in their work—or used to.

Baudelaire was the first artist and *The Flowers of Evil* the first work of capital importance (a symbol itself therefore) to put the good which is beauty *before* the ethical good—to prioritize beauty, in fact. Baudelaire was hardly to concern himself with the good in any way that might hinder his creative concerns. That the good is not ethical, but beautiful, is a conundrum for our existence, because it means there is some kind of gap or cut between one kind of basic good and another, one kind of truth and another: the truth of the good, which is humanitarian, and the truth of the beautiful, which is not, and which in fact is *oblivious* to human suffering and *allergic* to "dignity," a word favored by "empty-headed moralists" according to Schopenhauer (and he was not referring to Kant, but to churchmen). While we can say that the ethical good is not to murder, not to steal, not to covet and so on, the aesthetic good, which is beautiful, is harder to pin down and codify. A list of prohibitions may well be "good" in an ethical sense. But *art* cannot be like this, and in that sense, therefore, neither can *life*. Adorno comments that "the art of absolute responsibility terminates in sterility."[34] Art cannot be essentially reducible to sociological explanation therefore, as even a great soulful sensibility like Ernst Bloch, tends to do when it comes to understanding music, although more generally his discussion aligns with our account here, as indicated already by its title: "venturing beyond and most intense world of man in music."[35] Bloch while steeped in the metaphysics of nostalgia - in his philosophy nostalgia is not the past but the utopia (which I would agree with)—yet writes: "No Brahms without the bourgeois concert society and even no music of 'new objectivity,' of supposed expressionlessness, without the gigantic rise of alienation, objectification and reification in late capitalism."[36] True, but these social factors are merely correlations, not explanations. The dogma that only by changing the means of production or economy will the music change is Marxian and a betrayal of the human spirit, and in this we agree more with Nietzsche that a single teacher can transform the world, we have witnessed this in the Jewish world in our time with Rabbi Schneerson; the Jewish world in central Europe and Russia saw it not so long ago with the Baal Shem Tov and his followers. The teaching of St. Francis de Sales (and of course the knock-on effect it had) transformed the Catholic culture in Europe in the 17th and 18th centuries; or we can think of the changes wrought in South Africa by Nelson Mandela, that no other man could accomplish. In short change is not materialist; energy follows thought. Art follows inspiration and inspiration lands upon the one capable of receiving it and doing something with it.

Moral supervision is bad for art, but on the other hand, absolute irresponsibility degrades art to fun, or to the sort of rubbish that is passed off as art in many newspapers and arts magazines today. Art and the sensibility to which it belongs must navigate these extremes—sterility on one side, entertainment or government by the concept on the other—and therein *good* will be found. The ethical good lends itself to codification; the aesthetic good certainly does not: it gives in to the artist if, and only if, the artist is a lover, that is, one who will give his or her all for beauty, or for art. But both ethics and beauty are good, in their different ways; both are true. Any systematic philosophy has to confuse (literally con-fuse) this difference.

Hardly to concern oneself with ethics in any way that might hinder one's creative concerns is normative for all creators. Kant, who was certainly a creator, struggled with this doubling of the good and tried to capture the sense of beauty by calling it, in terms of his system of cognitive faculties, "free," and by defining the ethical good outside any specifics, but in purely formal terms. In this way he overcame the problem. Hegel described beauty in his vocabulary as disclosure of "the idea" to the senses and our apprehension of it. Hegel's view ties the beautiful in well with the good—beautifully, in fact. But we have to subscribe to Hegel's whole system to make this appreciation, which is a tall order. Adorno says, "The idea of beauty draws attention to something essential to art without, however, articulating it directly."[37] For the English poet John Keats, who studied these same questions in poetry, "Beauty is truth; truth beauty" (*Ode on a Grecian Urn*). As simple as that. Beauty may be various for Baudelaire,[38] but beauty nevertheless comes to him from above, given by the muse. Baudelaire's muse might be Jeanne Duval, Marie Dubrun or Mme Sabatier in the flesh, but his inspiration is not *from* them as such, but *through* them. They are not the cause, but the conduit or channel. Beauty for Baudelaire indicates a dimension of height—as for Keats it indicated a depth that was Greek in time and eternity.

With regard to Beauty's modishness, we saw in the previous chapter that "*Le Printemps adorable a perdu son odeur!*" ("The adorable springtime has lost its scentedness!") This loss is what is "absolutely modern." In the age of industrialization then, of teletechnoscience now, of the defeat of the earth by the maximization of human self-interest by the creation of "needs" and inflation of desire, protected by the democratic manufacture of consent, the adorable springtime has lost its scentedness. That art could restore or revivify the times in which we live! Indeed, this is a nostalgic thought. And Adorno says that, for art to bring back *le parfum* to our days, "strikes only the artless as possible."[39] Given the state we are in—the enslavement of increasing masses of people to the global marketplace and "economic forces" that ostensibly rule it, no wonder Baudelaire's art is that of a dark enchantment. Adorno says, "Radical art today is *synonymous* with dark art."[40] Art *noir* is the obverse of art as commodity and entertainment—the products of the culture industry. It will be a dark beauty that pertains to an art *noir*, as we find in Baudelaire—a satanic inspiration by which Baudelaire wills to divide the kingdom against itself.[41] Adorno puts it that "The injustice committed by all cheerful art, especially by entertainment, is probably an injustice to the dead; to accumulated, speechless pain. Still, an art *noir* bears features that would, if they were definitive, set their seal on historical despair."[42]

The transient element of the correspondence must navigate between the culture industry and its products, and historical despair. Between these antitheses of overripe cheer and manufactured happiness, and the seal of despair, runs nostalgia. Art grasps this all as a whole and, as such, as unsaid and unsayable. And it gives us comfort that there is understanding. Take, for example, painting. Monet's water lilies are beautiful and ephemeral, but I see those paintings and I see actually they are about light, the beauty of the light beyond the beauty of the lilies, through which the beauty of each water lily is more easily beheld, and I see the care and the little Japanese bridge across the pond that lends stability, a human touch, the familiarity of wood, and I hear the words "wood" and "bridge," with their Ds, and "water" and "light," with their soft Ts, and I realize where I live and how I live and who I am and that these things are beyond me and more than I am, and I see things in perspective, but not the things that can be seen, not the water or the bridge in the painting, but those things which are not in the painting, which cannot be painted, but which the soul knows, and which in the lily pond Monet paints.

Nostalgia at the level of the transient in art is for what is lost, what is remembered, loved, mourned, whether the loss is in the *religious* register, expressed in terms of, for example, the loss of Eden; the loss of God's glory, the right relationship with God that only the Law can resolve; the nostalgia of a St. Paul for a "yonder" where "I can know even as I am known,"[43] or, in Plotinus' words, where the seeker of true being can be "alone with the Alone,"[44] or, in terms of St. Augustine's iteration of such being in the next life: "There we shall rest and we shall see; we shall see and we shall love; we shall love and we shall praise. Behold what shall be in the end and shall not end"[45]; or whether the loss is expressed in the *modern, subjective* register, such as the loss of oneness that was the womb, having been pushed kicking and screaming into the world; the cut of the umbilical cord; and, as we grow older, the *stages on life's way*,[46] the accumulation of memories, everyone of which marks a loss, and the loss of all that is forgotten and not remembered; and then the bigger losses, of relatives and friends to death, of youth, of money, of love and so on to the final loss, of health of body, of gradual weakening, until the last loss, of our personality itself.

We can rightly say that art is a work of mourning. Always perhaps all serious seeking of truth is an attempt to recoup something of this loss and our word "eternity" is the greatest symbol of that. Art marks our original loss. We equate beauty with *death*, not just with impermanence or transience. The soul, says John Keats, "dwells with Beauty—Beauty that must die" (*Ode on Melancholy*). The soul loves beauty, loves flowers, and loves rain after sun. Beauty belongs to both ends of the correspondence between here and there, heaven and earth, now and then, transience and eternity. Beauty will never stay, and so we remain in our nostalgia. Only the unimaginative do not get this nostalgia, do not feel it, and have scant regard for beauty; the big meat-eaters. Beauty is always related to delicacy, intricacy, harmlessness, vulnerability, purity, invisibility—she shies away from coarseness, vulgarity, smell, consensus, publicity, money-raising, and glamour. Beauty is always a matter of sensibility, as Baudelaire, in his adulation of women, reminds us. Beauty is the most ephemeral and indefinite of qualities and so it calls most of all on our inner sensibility and sensitivity. This is why aesthetics differs so much from ethics, which is strong, definite and definitively patriarchal. And this is why we mourn: for life *is* so ephemeral, and beauty along with grace cannot be grasped or had by patriarchal religion or culture, except insofar as they *protect* the feminine. The feminine has to be protected like modesty, it cannot be liberated, that is only to lose it, nor may it be possessed (the opposite side of the illusion), as Goethe famously shows in *Faust*.[47] For the one who protects the feminine is redeemed and led upward (the dimension of height again, that we want to discuss next).

A final point, which is somewhat incidental, but nonetheless remarks what is foundational to Western culture: In Chapter 8 of John's Gospel a woman is brought by religious authorities before Jesus, accused with adultery, the penalty for which is death. What does Jesus do, faced with religious fanaticism and persecution? He turns to art.[48] He begins to draw in the sand. Sand drawing is an ancient, venerable art. The impermanence of sand, shifting sand, blown away by the wind, makes it a performance art essentially. But what Jesus is doing by his turn to art here is defusing the machismo of ethical fanaticism. We find the greatest religious fanaticism of this kind precisely where the cultural conditions for art are poor, repressed, or restricted, and where women are likewise; but Jesus turned away from "God's Law" to the *disarming* truth in art, and this is perhaps a lesson for all of us.

3

The Ladder of *Eros*

The quality of indetermination is the key to music's magic.
—Paul Valéry, *Analects*

The *dimension of height* is essentially what links or joins the ultimate two terms of correspondence: the eternal unchanging element on one hand and the momentary or time-bound on the other. Between them we have what we call *aesthetic experience*. Art should give us aesthetic experience. If it does not, it is something else. The crucial point though is that, to give us aesthetic experience, art must have some dimension of height. The dimension of height is integral to the experience of artwork and the subject of this chapter, enlarging therefore on our discussion so far in the previous chapters.

The French poet Paul Valéry refers, in his essay "The Creation of Art," to some words of the composer Richard Wagner that struck him forcefully and stayed with him as words indicative of the whole creative process of art in general. Wagner had written in connection with his operatic drama, *Tristan and Isolde*:

> I composed *Tristan* under the stress of great passion and after several months of theoretical meditation.[1]

There are two important points to note here. The first is the "stress of great passion" and the second is the "months of theoretical meditation." These are the two sides of creativity. For art, the creator needs both, and they are needed at the same time, in the work, to *correspond*.

As artists, we know that something stands over and above us, a power greater than us. Religions will each have their own interpretation of this. But, for the secular artist, the sense is not very dissimilar. A secular artist will think it hubris to speak of "God" in this regard, but may well speak of the muses, as Goethe did; inspiration, as Nietzsche did; "the venal muse," as Baudelaire did; or abstractly as "melody," as Jean-Michel Maulpoix has done. What is meant, and what Wagner testifies to, is a power as it *bears down* on us. There is a sense in which we are *impelled* to write or paint or compose; and we may make ourselves ill or bring bad luck to ourselves if we try to do otherwise or to avert this course of nature. And this exceeds art as such in being much more generally a part of the human condition. Let us call it a sense of *destiny* too, or a sense of destiny *instead* of an impulsion. This is a sense that is personal and intimate and that no one else can discover for us and that only we can detect, discover and know for ourselves; it is a task which can take the better part of a lifetime. And what do we find when we find this destiny? Well, we find the way to stand *under the sway*—of power—and we find what it is to *be in it*; in other words, you come to "Know Thyself," the words of the Delphic Oracle in the ancient mysteries of initiation. To Know Thyself means to know your *genius*. But we must acknowledge of course that, sociologically speaking, some people live in such abject, poor or tragic personal circumstances that their life is lived on quite another footing. If they break through—like Baudelaire or Dostoyevsky (or a thousand other examples)—it is because of their genius, given that most people we admire for their genius come from modest and not particularly privileged backgrounds. As well, genius conjures up what we call luck in our lives. Following your genius or your destiny will make you lucky—luckier than otherwise would have been the case. Luck is distinct from what we call a fluke—winning in gambling for instance is a fluke, not luck: flukes are not tied to destiny in any soulful way; luck is. Wagner was often down on his luck, but had amazing lucky breaks—and all this is significantly part of his genius.

We should not underestimate Wagner's words that something bore down on him which he experienced as being in thrall to a great passion. But we should also note, *he was prepared*. This is the other side of the pact. This is the other term of the correspondence. He had done the training in his months of "theoretical meditation." Probably he understates it, not realizing that these words that he jotted down would one day be taken as seriously as we are now taking them. On the matter of his preparation for his great outbursts of creativity, I would say his whole life was a run-up—the false starts, wrong turns and all; for while something may seem like a false start or a wrong avenue, nothing is actually lost. Wagner did not think very highly of his first successful opera, *Rienzi*, but it helped him see what he did *not* want more clearly than before. This is exactly how false starts and wasted time and being led astray can be an advantage in the long run and make us wiser. Valéry himself, before writing *La Jeune Parque* (*The Young Fate*), one of his most famous poems, wrote nothing for twenty years—surely he was preparing himself, getting a long run-up, as it were; and then there was *the leap*, the productive, creative time when *the passion fell*. When the passion falls, it falls from *on high*.

Plato wrote about the genius that accompanies us in the tale of Er at the end of *The Republic*, his most ambitious work. Er is a figure of legend who came back from the dead, after being killed in battle: his body was discovered incorrupt on the battlefield, then, after twelve days, while actually lying on the funeral pyre, he returned to life. Socrates recounts the tale and, according to Er, there is life after death—life rather like the experience of being in someone else's dream, in the sense that time is all different (a thousand years is like a day), yet the sense of reality is as strong as in waking consciousness. As of necessity, like a law of moral nature, after death follow penalties, retributions or blessings, after which (metaphorically speaking in terms of time) one can enter a new cycle of life. One of the things Er recounts is that each soul which comes to earth is accompanied by a genius, a daemon, which it chooses, and that to choose this daemon (he calls it) is the same as to choose one's destiny.[2] When we are born our memory of all this is erased, as the soul necessarily, in its new life, must become different,[3] but the genius that accompanies the soul *remembers the destiny it chose in "heaven"* before it was completely altered in being born on earth. Er (or Plato) does not say the soul is simply reborn, for every soul is new and unique at birth. But what he means to say is that *birth is not its origin*. That means the soul is not essentially biological, which means *we* are not. This is an important point in an age like ours that is dominated by materialist explanations, a materialist mentality and theoretical reductionism on every side. From Plato's point of view a materialist explanation is an oxymoron. For the soul, memory of its origin is keyed to its sense of destiny, that is, to what it has forgotten, and what it is here for.

We do not have to believe a story like this to see that it nevertheless says something true about *experience* from the point of view of the soul. It points to an aspect of experience that is not time-bound but a *given* and is, as such, bound up with us as individuals—indeed, it is *constitutive* of our individuality and uniqueness. The story does not provide us with something to believe, which may frustrate our religious (or anti-religious) habit, for we are many of us addicted to believing things; nor does the story offer us an explanation, which may frustrate our tendency to lean toward the authority of science, or toward any authority, for an explanation. Instead, the story provides a perspective that is neither religious nor scientific, but is *poetic*. Wordsworth is another who could see what Plato saw. In a verse from his ode, *Intimations of Immortality*, which he completed in 1804, Wordsworth says:

> Our birth is but a sleep and a forgetting:
> The Soul that rises with us, our life's Star,
> Hath had elsewhere its setting,
> And cometh from afar:
> Nor in entire forgetfulness,
> And not in utter nakedness.[4]

Somehow, as we come in to land, that is, as we begin to grow older, and to take root in the world, something of what we are here for is recalled. Anyone who, like Wordsworth (whose daughter by Annette Vallon by this time would have been twelve years old), knows (because they have seen) that while we say the child "develops," this is merely conventional speech,[5] and what one witnesses with any child is that, as the body develops, the soul in Wordsworth's sense—as that part of us with a higher origin, which is much older than our body—shines through. We realize the child has a "wisdom beyond its years," which is a common expression, or else we could say, the child has a God-given uniqueness and destiny all of their own. Parents know they care for what is only partially theirs. The child is their flesh and blood, but the life is not theirs. It is completely other. The life, as Wordsworth eloquently puts it, has come from afar; the parents discover what it is and what it means (for them) only as it manifests itself, and they realize their child was not born in entire forgetfulness or utter nakedness. As Schopenhauer says (I amplify), the child's personality may be a social formation of time and place, but a child's character is innate. Sometimes the personality blocks out the character for most of life, especially during the first half of life. But sometimes, very often even, particularly in "old souls" as they say, the character dominates the personality from the start, and the personality never gets domination of the *persona*. It is incredible how little psychology has had to say about all this and how much it has had to say about "development." The problem with the colloquial idea of "development" that has been ideologically foisted upon our language and culture is that it presumes a child is some kind of *thing*, and there are experts on every side who purport to inform us about exactly what *kind* of thing: biologists, neurologists, behaviorists, psychiatrists, all exoteric materialists who understand organism in terms of mechanism. Such science is thought to be devoid of spiritual lights.[6]

Book 10 of *The Republic*, at the end of which we find the tale of Er, is the book in which Plato—through his protagonist, Socrates—says that *poetry ought to be banned*. What Plato has his finger on is the equivocal nature of all art.[7] Plato would ban what he calls "imitative art," that is, *representational* art. This is because, to him, it is art of a lower order. The placement of the story of Er just before the ban is not simply coincidental. Poetry ought to be banned if it is poetry—as, presumably, most poetry of Plato's day (as ours) was—without cognizance of our real being as souls. Hence, the flip side of Plato's argument is what he would *not* ban. He would not ban art that draws something down from the "other" world,[8] or that has landed here from the other world in the shape of the artist (as it were) and his or her work and that sheds the light of wisdom or redemption—as with Wordsworth's ode that we have just quoted, or Plato's writing (his philosophy being an exemplary case). Plato's work is philosophy as poetry, poetry as philosophy. He, like Wordsworth, like Wagner, is inspired.

The story of Er orients us with respect to *who we are* as human beings. We need to wonder what we have brought with us into this world. This is the question of our genius. We prefer to say "our gifts," but this is slightly deceptive because it assumes we are the subject of them; rather, we are the recipients. Our gifts accompany us, but they are not ours. That is Plato's point, and Wordsworth's. If we do not know *this*, all our other learning, however knowledgeable, will avail us nothing.

True art is not representational, but actual, in that it *is* the act of conception made present, which is why, for the artist, making the art is not *like* giving birth: it *is* giving birth, it is the *soul's* giving birth to itself in the form of the artwork. What Plato is saying is hardly any different from Baudelaire—that the timeless element (that element, in Plato's terms, that we brought into the world with us) is made manifest in time, in the dress of the time, and in a time-bound manner.[9]

What we find then is that the story of Er is tied to *the truth in art*. This today is an almost lost truth.

When I come to see or hear an artwork such as Plato speaks of and the true artist produces, in its immediacy, not as a representation, but as a work of genius, and not merely as the work of such-and-such, I do not merely see it with my eyes, or hear it with my ears, but *I apprehend it with my soul.*[10] It apprehends me! It touches me. It moves me. When I see, read or listen to something birthed out of the soul—that is, a proper artwork—then I connect *at that level* with it. Any *other* level is not a connection. The genius in the artwork speaks to the genius *in me.* In other words I am not really looking at an artwork by this or that artist; if I am reduced to doing that then there is no art in the work. It is a mock-up. The artwork "speaks" only in a metaphorical sense, of course, without in fact speaking. The artwork "speaks" soul to soul, and, in great work, as a purveyor of art, my soul is *raised*: it gains from the artwork what it cannot get from itself, or from religion or from science, or from any other source in any other way.

When I say "my soul is raised," I mean it is raised in my *being.* Heights and depths of being are what *experience* is all about, and *aesthetic* experience presumes this to be the case. When Wagner's immense passion "from above" and years of preparation "from below" come together in his work, through his genius, something is wrought in time and space that he alone could accomplish, but which I—and many like me—can benefit from because it *succors* our soul. For our soul is succored when it is raised. For my soul—my being—to be succored in this way, is to be fed. As human beings we starve without art—our souls starve. This is our condition today for many of us. This condition is increasing in proportion to the increase in commodification and the rule of culture by fiscal policy and corporations and mass media.

When our soul is raised in aesthetic experience it means we recognize the artist's genius. It is a moment of recognition in which we can recognize the genius of Schubert or Ravel. This is not the recognition of the cognitive faculty of understanding, but of imagination; it is a discernment of sensibility in which we recognize genius. When intellectuals deny the existence of genius (and it is normally intellectuals who do this because no one with common sense is in such denial, and I wonder if it is the *envy* of the intellectuals, brainy but uninspired, the academic norm), it is indicative of a situation of art's occlusion. Art in our day *is* occluded; it is a simple fact. Let me not risk saying *why* again, lest I bore my reader with repetition. But those who recognize genius when they see or hear it *become awakened to their own genius.* Destiny speaks to destiny, soul to soul. And this is why machines do not make art, because they have no destiny and no soul. And this is what true artists aspire to: to unleash their genius—within the intimacy of their solitude, but then on the world—in their work. And this is what true art is: just such work.

When I look at art in the world, it is dominated by what in Platonic terms is called "representation," or by the cheap notion of "meaning," of which the work is ostensibly an expression and which traces back to the artist's intention, or, if not there, to the interpreter's "take" on it (tarted up of course to be "meaningful"). But in real art, such as we are talking about, which is not to do with "meaning" except in a secondary sense (therefore putting art beyond hermeneutics and theory, where it is reduced to academic discourse, ultimately), what we have is aesthetic experience. We have already seen this. In aesthetic experience my sensibility is made by the artwork to *accord with* its genius, its overriding inspiration. It is this that I experience aesthetically, and which I call beautiful. Great art is always beautiful, remembering that "free beauty" is not conditioned by rules. This is why, in Baudelaire's aesthetic—or any one of a number of other authorities I could list, Hanslick as a famous example—he equates aesthetic experience with beauty and therefore art with beauty. This follows from what I have outlined above.

The Ladder of *Eros* is an image of the *longing* that binds the two ends of the Baudelairean correspondence to one another. It is the longing *between* the two separate ends of the correspondence that validates the artwork. If we cannot apprehend this longing at once, we can learn to do so, and this is what it would mean to learn to love art.

Between the two terms of Baudelaire's correspondence, the two terms of which are necessary for art and beauty, is the Ladder of *Eros*. On the ladder, sensibility can run up or down from the height to the ground of sensibility, or from the ground to the height.

Eros is the name for the longing based on the myth of *Eros* and *Psyche*, love and soul. *Eros* and *Psyche* are *personifications* of love and soul. There are two kinds of beauty as far as *Eros* is concerned. *Psyche* personifies the sweetness and innocence and simple loveliness of beauty. *Eros* and *Psyche* are usually represented as a young man (*Eros*) and a beautiful young girl (*Psyche*). But *Aphrodite* is the goddess of beauty in Greek myth, not *Psyche*. *Aphrodite* is the ultimate personification of beauty in its female power. *Aphrodite* was jealous of *Psyche*'s beauty, as an older woman may envy a young girl and wish to acquire her complexion and fresh look. *Aphrodite* is beautiful in a way that is magisterial and imposing, like a great waterfall. Her beauty is a sovereign beauty. She is hieratic, austere and domineering like the beauty of a desert sunset over the Mountains of Moab, or of the Southern Cross in the night sky from the Blue Mountains, or of the

45

white, fishtailed Mount Annapurna from a rowing boat adrift on Lake Pokhara. These are beautiful, but daunting and impersonal. *Psyche's* beauty is not of this kind: hers is a beauty of intimacy and relation. The English poet Laurence Binyon characterizes *Psyche* by her *shyness*, and I think he is right:

The Shyness of Beauty[11]

> I think of a flower that no eye has ever seen,
> That springs in a solitary air.
> Is it no one's joy? It is beautiful as a queen
> Without a kingdom's care.
>
> We have built houses for Beauty, and costly shrines,
> And a throne in all men's view;
> But she was afar on a hill where the morning shines
> And her steps were lost in dew.

A young girl's natural modesty is a picture of *Psyche*. She is the most soulful creature on earth and the most beautiful. The lines "as beautiful as a queen/ without a kingdom's care" mark the difference between *Aphrodite* and *Psyche*. One heart is *Psyche's* dominion. But our age has confused these two kinds of beauty and tried to build temples befitting *Aphrodite*, which she might have inhabited, for *Psyche*, from which she shrinks. *Aphrodite* is the beauty of the mother and grandmother; *Psyche* the beauty of *un petit fille*, as in Valéry's poem *La fileuse* (*The Spinner*), or Ottilie, in Goethe's *Elective Affinities,* Mignon or Natalie in *Wilhelm Meister* and Gretchen in *Faust*, all figures of the feminine soul that give a man life through love.[12]

Modesty befits *Psyche*, as does interiority, and the spinning we do within and the things we make. Hers is a secretive beauty, a soft and silken beauty best beheld close up, and it is the beauty that reveals our sexuality and all its ambiguities. *Aphrodite's* beauty is like a moral beauty (as per Kant, who discussed only this kind of beauty and who seemed to have no *Eros* for *Psyche* at all, but only an Apollonian regard for *Aphrodite*). We must remember that in the story of *Psyche* she has her longing too. Longing (the metaphysics of nostalgia) is not singular but various. *Eros* desires *Psyche*, and she desires him. Desire is split. The boy's desire is different in its being and doing from the desire of the girl. Their separate desires will never merge or be one—but they will intertwine. If in addition it has the god's blessing there will be a third thread that binds it to eternity—that therefore makes it three times as strong. *Aphrodite's* magisterial beauty is unattainable and will not be bound. According to Kant, it mirrors the moral law within. Not surprisingly, given that the gods are only human, she is jealous and angry with *Psyche*, whose beauty surpasses her own—at least *Eros* seems to think so. The beauty of *Psyche* trespasses on the beauty of *Aphrodite*. In other words, the two kinds of beauty are not mutually exclusive. *Psyche* does not mean to trespass, but she cannot help it. It is the nature of love to know no rules.

If we look more closely at soul and beauty in terms of their heights and depths in our soul we can use the analogy of the Ladder of *Eros*. This is the ladder of our longing, and each rung is a new threshold. The rungs do not measure our sensibility for it is no doubt infinite, and we may be on several rungs at any one time. The Ladder of *Eros* is a ladder of love as desire, and we all know that such love knows no bounds. I shall describe the Ladder of *Eros* as it pertains to listening, as it will help us to become listeners and to attune to the creativity of listening, which is bound to soulfulness.

The Ladder of Listening

We can describe ten degrees of listening. Of course, in referring to a ladder we do not mean it literally. We mean it in such a way as to describe the dimension of *inner height*, and the ladder is a traditional metaphor, a way of enabling talk of the structure and form of inner height and of our ability to raise our sensibility accordingly. The ladder metaphor dates back to Jacob's ladder, in his dream in the book of *Genesis*, on which angels ascended and descended: one of the originary stories of Jewish religion, a metaphor (not just a motif, I would say) that carries forward through the ascetical and mystical literature of the religious traditions of the West to describe something that goes on in the human soul that is rightly attuned. To cite some famous examples: the tradition of the ladder between heaven and earth goes from St. John Climacus (St. John of the Ladder), who lived at the monastery on Mount Sinai in the seventh century, now St. Catherine's monastery; to Walter Hilton at Ely Cathedral in England about 800 years later; to Martin Buber's *Ten Rungs*, published in Jerusalem in 1945, another 800 years later.

The rungs are not necessarily reached in the numerical order described below. However, the point as far as a poetics of sensibility is concerned—or a psychology of it (for we are about both in fact)—is to know your "up" from your "down," and consequently to orient the "lost soul" in the madness of a world that *denies* this sense of height out of sheer ignorance, or from ideological motives, or from simple lack of intuition into oneself (unconsciousness)—so easy in our age of totalistic commodity capitalism, where one man's unconsciousness is the essence of another man's profiteering. And if the powers that be (that finance the politicians, as though they were mere lackeys) can work this into the education system, as they are succeeding in doing, then all the better for them, for then people can be *taught* to be unconscious. The ladder of divine ascent and descent, as it is known in tradition, has always belonged to the activists and those opting out of the madness that history books are made of.

The first degree of listening is *interest*. It is that initial degree of openness to art, to genius in art, to greatness in art, which is attractive. It may be this attraction, directly or vicariously, through another, which arouses interest. Interest is arousal. It is interest in that which is beyond ourselves and which we intuitively sense will call us even further beyond, into uncharted waters, as far as we are concerned. It is awakening: the awakening of the desire of the senses, and of a care for that desire. There may also be a technical interest, which is also a care for things and about how they are done. It is interest in the culture that envelops us, in which, awakened, we are aware of finding ourselves somewhere strange, somewhere we had previously taken for granted. Interest is curiosity therefore. Interest is the unspoken acknowledgment that "it matters." Nearly all such interest is "below the surface": people just go to the art gallery, seemingly, for "something to do," to occupy the children, to see what everyone is talking about, and so on. They are hardly aware of their interest, but underlying it is the first rung on the Ladder of *Eros*, interest. Interest, as it equates with care, equates with the ground-mood of melancholy, which we will come to. Care includes love of the kind of art Plato disparaged: representative art, which might show us a scene, a face. In music, this clearly works on our emotions to serve a story. On this first rung, we are interested in the skill of the artist, and to see that skill and be amazed by it. On this rung, we are impressionable and easily impressed. This is the openness and purity of our untrained sensibility at work. Although at subliminal levels we would have already learnt more than we are aware, this is what will orient us one way or another.

The second rung or degree is *tuché*, a concept from Aristotle, the chance touch, the fortunate encounter, by which we "come upon" art, or it comes upon us; a work surprises us, takes us, "grabs us," and we connect viscerally with it. We want to go back to it. We say it "means something" to us. It is not a physical touch, therefore, but a touch from without that reaches to somewhere within us. Jacques Lacan defines this *tuché* as "the encounter with the Real."[13] Aristotle uses the term *tuché* in his search for cause.[14] The cause in Aristotle is the account of what *is* behind what appears, that is to say, the noumenal ground that is hidden or veiled by the symbolic. Lacan says, "The real is beyond the *automaton*, the return, the coming-back, the insistence of the signs by which we see ourselves governed by the pleasure principle."[15] This encounter can happen at all different levels of listening, when we hear something *in* the music, but we do not know what. Suddenly the music is not wallpaper. It affects us. This can happen at an immature level when, among all the din of fashionable, manufactured music put out by the popular music industry, a particular sound strikes us. Musicians whose life takes a completely different turn musically will be able to think back to some music they no longer like, but how, once, it affected them and helped them, and led them forward. This level once reached haunts the other levels and repeats itself on other rungs. The *tuché* is precisely recognition of sensibility by our sensitivity, in the first place; an awakening. Our imagination is released and set free and once this happens it is apt to happen again in subsequent encounters.

The third step concerns *symbolism*. It might be that this step comes before the previous step; whether the real or the symbolic come first cannot be determined, in any case, this step is our social ear, when we listen and hear what "They"—the public—hear. The symbolic rung is concert music that draws crowds, that creates a fashion. The Viennese waltzes of Strauss, the ritual music of the church, brass band music, and the music of pomp and circumstance are examples—music that shows a shared taste and acknowledges the structures in which the music is lodged, which it represents and, indeed, upholds. On the symbolic rung we can understand, even if we do not like the dutiful quality of the music. Music on this rung is also documentary; it documents shared time or shared memory. It can be popular music then: disco, reminiscent of a time. On this rung our sense of identity is caught up with the music and defined by it. The music stands for values, for what we believe, for who we think we are, for the way we dress; it is the music of our subculture and so on. The music not only represents and expresses and symbolizes who I am, but it symbolizes who I want people to see that I am: who I want to be in their eyes, whoever "They" may be in this instance. On this rung music can be a place to hide, to pretend, to shelter. On this rung music is like a code. We can judge people by their music because, for us, the music is indicative of their identity and what they stand for.

The fourth degree of listening is *individual taste*. This is where our sensibility binds the real into the symbolic under the name or this or that piece of music. There is no accounting for taste, they say, thereby affirming essential aesthetic freedom—the impossibility of rules governing taste. The social and psychological factors governing taste of course exist but do not reduce to rules.

Initiation is a feature of this rung. This is where the encounter with, or experience of, the real dominates over the symbolic, but no one can say how or why or even *that* it is so, with any certainty. Initiation is an intimate consciousness of something about the music one loves that cannot be described and cannot be heard in every performance. Only great music is able initiate people into it, for that is its true substance. Wagner's music is of this type. Bach's music is of this type. All subsequent rungs mark levels of initiation, but initiation is mentioned early on at this lower level as the *watershed moment* with regard to listening, the moment of realization when we experience the truth of the music (to borrow a metaphor from philosophy); perhaps we experience music as truth. We move from being an outsider to art music, to being an insider. It is not that we *know* something we did not know before, or that we have obtained helpful information *about* something. Rather we have *undergone* something that has altered our relation to it; it does not necessarily mean that we know anything more about it. One of the purposes of this book is to help move readers from the outsider to the insider position; once again, these are not positions of knowledge, but of sensibility. One knows one is on the inside by the way music touches the sensibility in a way it never did before. How this happens is uncertain. It happens individually, in the sense of *for me alone*, even if, *when* it happens, I am in a crowd.

At the fifth rung the difference between good and bad taste becomes audible, whereas this *audibility in taste* is unclear at the rungs beneath it. On the lower rungs, good versus bad taste is a matter of opinion, but, at the fifth level, the difference between aesthetic experience and the impossibility of such experience may be *heard*. Such hearing comes from reflection on listening and learning to listen, neither of which happens in a vacuum. And it takes a measure of humility to get onto this rung for we must have a sense of our musical sensibility's wanting it , rather than an arrogant and dogmatic view that our taste is as good as anyone else's. Arrogance and dogmatism are forms of deafness. On this rung we learn from the past, and, in terms of culture and its transmission, we learn about melody, harmony, musical "feeling" and musical "language." To try to ascertain aesthetic experience in language without recourse to culture and tradition is to merely foist our own ignorance upon art; this is a form of contempt. On this rung we know what aesthetic experience is and what it is not.

At the sixth rung we begin to make *aesthetic differentiations* and gain discernment. In this way we become discriminating and we learn more about *who we are* as individuals. The uniqueness of our authentic taste, given by aesthetic experience, reveals us to ourselves. Taste therefore becomes something more than what it was. Previously, taste was aligned with opinion and was equally as groundless as it, but now taste becomes revelatory and augurs a way of self-knowledge, a way of soul. This is different from "connoisseurship," which is seigniorial and governed by social affect, public reputation and status anxiety. Soul-making listening has an essential aspect that indicates a break from a love for something being governed by any utilitarian motive or purpose. An expert "uses" knowledge that has been acquired: it is *for* something; a connoisseur simply enjoys it. A connoisseur of cigars enjoys smoking them; an expert may even be a non-smoker. The opinion of the connoisseur of music is different from that of the expert, and that of the soul-maker is different again.

On this rung therefore listening can tend to replace the conventional modes of self-knowledge: philosophy and religion. In art generally, and in art music in particular, we learn about ourselves in terms of aesthetic experience, and the art allows us to explore ourselves in this way, through our enjoyment. Text-based philosophy and religion by contrast have become less and less enjoyable, and more and more belief-based and alienated from art and culture. This has happened particularly since the Reformation of the sixteenth century—although it is not confined to the Protestant spirit any more but is general in nature and general in Western religion and culture.

This is the rung of the nineteenth-century concertgoer in Europe, who, in many respects, was above us today. The composers of the nineteenth century pushed the boundaries of this self-knowledge—in other words, the boundaries of what audiences could appreciate, and, together, they changed the soul of Europe as taste changed. For the public this was an unconscious process that we recognize only with hindsight; but their musical faculties, before the industrialization of culture really took hold (in the twentieth century), were far better developed than ours: they had a culture of taste, rather than the debased musical culture of commodification. It is hard for us to reach this rung in our day and it is getting more and more difficult, which is all the more reason why we need to know this teaching and to make the right effort.

The seventh rung of listening is that of *understanding*. This is where individual taste is accompanied by knowledge of why we like something. We could then describe it in terms of sensibility, as on the fourth rung, or in technical terms. At this level one might be an expert on musical aesthetics, or a music student at a conservatorium. On this rung we can probably count ourselves, in some respect, an "insider" in the music world. Roger Scruton would be well known as someone on this rung (although he may be on the rung above). His works, *The Aesthetics of Music* (1997) and *Understanding Music* (2009), are those of a philosopher and musicologist—in other words, someone who understands music at a higher level than the average concertgoer. At the sixth rung we might be able to enjoy the music and talk about it well, but at the seventh rung, we might be like Bruckner, who, at a Wagner opera, followed the musical score in his lap and missed the drama on stage.

The danger at this level is that we can hear the music at a technical level, but not any more in a soul sense. Technical considerations can govern our taste and it may be that the music becomes an experience of the cognitive recognition of technical matters rather than an aesthetic experience. The musicologist may no longer hear the music essentially. Taking a non-musical example, I remember at a film festival sitting behind two film students and overhearing their conversation about the film as we watched it in terms of shots and angles and edits; but they could not see the film as an artwork (assuming that was possible anyway). Understanding should be at the behest of sensibility, and complement, strengthen, and extend it, rather than block it out.

At the eighth level of listening one is not just *theoretically* proficient, as at the seventh level, but has *practical proficiency*. The listener who is practically proficient as well as technically versed is on this rung. The practitioner knows the piece from the inside and knows it from experience. Their knowledge is more authoritative than mine if I cannot play it. Questions of taste on the sixth rung, of soul sensibility, are decided on this eighth rung, not on the seventh, which is why technical and theoretical challenges from the seventh rung are sometimes repudiated on the rung beneath. For example, many intellectuals (on the seventh rung, some of whom were at the eighth) tried to convince the public (at the sixth rung) about atonal music in the mid-twentieth century, but it simply failed to catch on. In retrospect it is easy to see why. The atonal music was intellectually and ideologically driven by composers (backed by the music industry) who were uninspired; they were clever but devoid of genius like that of those who had gone before. In the reign of technical cleverness and ideological posturing in music, the music died. And so did the audiences for it. The music became merely an allegory of some idea, not something intrinsically musical. Music true to itself is melodious and harmonious. Ultimately taste is not decided in theory, but in practice, and in lives.

The ninth rung on the ladder of listening is that of *accomplishment*. The eighth level is that of the practitioner, the ninth of the real maestro. The difference is largely that of experience. In our time an example of someone on the ninth rung would be Daniel Barenboim. His master classes with the world's greatest pianists of the younger generation show the difference between the two rungs. The younger pianists can play Beethoven's piano sonatas perfectly—they may have won the world's most prestigious musical awards; but in the presence of Barenboim they have something to learn, and they know it. Barenboim does not just *represent* the wisdom of the past: he actually has it *to grant* and pass on. It is not represented: it is *real*.

The tenth and last rung is that of the *composer*. This is the top of the ladder. It may be the deafness of Beethoven, or the silence of Wagner during the years before his great outpouring. In other words, the ability to hear the music interiorly without having heard it exteriorly, and then to write it down. This is the top rung.

The Ladder of *Eros* runs in two directions. *Inspiration descends; aspiration ascends.* The art is in the correspondence and in *cooperation*.

As listeners at the sixth rung, where we seek to develop our individual taste and judgment, we need to be able to feel the inspiration of the music. Sensibility is precisely the activity of intuitively feeling into the music and receptively taking the affect of it. It is a possessing and a being possessed. We need to be able to let something *fall* into our soul. At the same time, we need to have done the preparatory *work of listening*. The work of listening is our apprenticeship in which we as listeners aspire to enjoy the music and receive its inspiration.

This needs time and in our society it needs money. It is not enough to listen to only *recorded* performances (CDs). These can be inspiring, but they are only recordings and we should strive to *hear performances live*. Only in performance do we experience the real presence of the music; this is important because all recording is grounded in the real presence of actual musicians *making* the music. No machine can replace this real encounter of *actual sound*. And it is a great danger to art in the age of technology that this can easily be forgotten.

Getting to live performances is the best way into art music. *Being there* one can experience much more than is possible with a recording, however perfect. Music that I have not liked in recording, live I can enjoy. Music is essentially something actual, and its virtual or vicarious technological transposition only keeps it the way it was in quantifiable terms. The qualitative will communicate too, insofar as the qualitative is reducible to the quantifiable, but not everything is. For the actual space in which the original music is played, which is important if you are there, cannot be digitized, and when the digital recording is replayed, it is in a different space. The ritual side of attendance, too, is wholly missing from the recording. To go to a concert in the evening at one of the great concert halls of Europe is the kind of event someone from the New World will never forget and will tell of for many years to come, if not for the rest of their life; but listening to a recording of the same concert will not be so significant. The atmosphere can be captured on the recording to some extent, but I am sure every reader has experienced the paradigmatic difference between the atmosphere in a recording and the actual atmosphere when you are *there*. With a recording you are never *in* the atmosphere or aura of being there, but by definition *outside* it. Recording is wonderful, but actual reality is natural, not technological; yet the technological may become habitual—and has become so in our time. But the natural will always outstrip the technological and be superior to it simply because electronic technology is by definition never *real presence*.[16] Electronic music is really an oxymoron, but like so many of the other euphemisms of our age, due to lack of sensibility, goes totally unnoticed and unremarked – "social media" is one of the most hilarious and self-contradictory of these euphemisms, and surfing the internet one of the most tragic (here in Australia we know about the surf), twittering is apt and not a euphemism, as only twits twitter, it marks the latest symbolic edge of superficiality and lack of real presence. All this aside, to heighten one's sensibility for real music, we have to attune to the natural voice, to actual instruments, not recordings of them (by instruments here I do not count machines, by definition) and experience of music in real time and space (given we can have the one without the other today)—or at least, if our artwork is fundamentally within the technological sphere, we should not forget we are working in a dependent medium and are in a sense are musically handicapped by the soulless machine and not really engaged in music at all, but in mechanical sound effects, which is another subject altogether, even though many people spiritually sucked into consumer culture today cannot tell the difference.

The Ladder of *Eros*

The ten levels of listening roughly correspond to the eight rungs on the Ladder of *Eros*. This is the ladder of height in desire. The first rung on the ladder is *a lack*. This is our sense of something missing, a hole inside us needing to be filled, an aching longing, or what we called exile or nostalgia for something unnamed and unnameable. The roots of *eros* are here and this lack gives rise to *eros*.

The second rung on the Ladder of *Eros* is *connection*. Our desire connects with something that feeds it, which gives it—and us—life. This will be some tradition, something that is already underway, which other people we know are part of, and we join them. We are seeking our home. What we join in with might not be what we are looking for, but it will be where we start. *Eros* will know if it is wrong, for our desire is ever awoken by lack.

The third rung is that of *learning*. We get to know about things. We see other avenues. We wonder, speculate and imagine. This may be where some disillusionment sinks in and we feel our lack again. Sometimes people can stay on this rung a long time, always pretending to be learning; but proper learning involves unlearning too. This rung may involve some false initiations, where desire seeks and finds itself thwarted.

The fourth rung is *initiation* proper; a threshold is crossed from which we cannot go back—or not easily. A commitment has been made, a direction established; we have found our course. Our desire has found its belonging. We are established in our desire and in inner group connection. This is the rung of awakening.

The fifth rung is time-bound: *perseverance, commitment*. This is the stilling of the desire, or its peaking, or its consummation, or contentment, that is, proper happiness. This is the rung of the work of *eros*.

55

The sixth rung is *reflection*. Mature, ripening and ageing desire are indicative of this rung. On this rung *eros* basks in glory. It is autumnal. Keats speaks of it with respect to soul and soulfulness in his ode, *To Autumn*. Freud and Jung speak of it in their writings on soul and death.[17]

The seventh rung is *wisdom*, where our desire is to serve, where *eros* is sacrifice. Wisdom is not really something we know, but a sense of bearings amidst our sense of everything we *do not* know. Wisdom at the other end of the ladder is actually a *lack* of knowledge, and the wisdom resides in this lack, in *not knowing* what the clever person or the expert knows and so therefore we are able to see by the light that their knowledge blocks out. On this rung we can insight what expertise or cleverness cannot teach, for example, as Dostoyevsky put it: "Each person is responsible for all, each before all, and I before the rest."[18] One does not arrive at this judgment because one is an expert in something, or because one is clever and can see what the propositions *mean*. The judgment is an insight which puts words to an attunement that if we get it we *recognize*. The insight or intuition is a recognition. For Plato and for Eastern religions, it is literally a re-cognition of something we knew in an existence of consciousness before our present bodily incarnation. For Christianity it is recognition in the natural sphere of the divine law or command. Religions symbolize the divine in different ways in accord with this saying of Dostoyovsky, because representation of it is symbolic, and in religion the symbolic is tied to the systematic, as often as not (less so in Judaism than in Christianity). But one may be transfixed by symbols rather than transfigured. The saying of Dostoyevsky is not a categorical imperative but an insight into reality and the fact that the individual soul inter-is with every other living and, for that matter, with the soul of the world, as the higher perspective from which all this is opens out as if self-evident.

The eighth rung is that of *the dark interval*, an expression of the poet Rilke, where the initial lack flowers finally in death. This is the top rung of *innocence*, a subject I shall enlarge upon with respect to beauty in Chapter 11. But the dark interval is the level of which Rilke speaks in his poetry of the unity of life and death: a central insight of his poetry. As we have already quoted Schopenhauer as saying, "Birth and death belong equally to life, and hold the balance as mutual conditions of each other, or, if the expression be preferred, as poles of the whole phenomenon of life."[19] Life is their movement of

oscillation we might say. Rilke says it this way—the way only poetry
can say with adequacy:

> My life is not this steep hour
> down which you see me hurrying so fast.
> I am a tree against my own background,
> I am only one of my many mouths—
> the one that closes first.
> I am the rest between two notes
> that cannot properly get used to each other;
> for the death-note insists on rising—
>
> Yet they are reconciled in the dark interval,
> both of them trembling.
> And the song remains beautiful.[20]

4

Shades of Melancholy

But when the melancholy fit shall fall
Sudden from heaven, like a weeping cloud . . .
—John Keats, *Ode on Melancholy*

In this chapter and the next we want to move from a philosophical consideration of art to saying something about the aesthetic experience of music as soul-making. Melancholy is the soulful starting place for such a consideration.

In Keats' *Ode on Melancholy* (quoted above) he does not say *if* the melancholy fit shall fall, as if it might be only a possibility, a chance, an accident, but *when*, because it will happen for sure. Melancholy is a natural shade of what it means to be. In the most immediate sense melancholy is musical, as I will show in this chapter.

But we will enter the musical via the poetical. Keats' odes are each extremely finely psychologically attuned. Keats was well aware of the age of industrialism and the new types of slavery—inner and outer—that the new social conditions would create. His poetry—and particularly his five great odes, which are his most powerful poems— is a challenge to the age and a countervoice saying (as ancient bards once spoke on behalf of the gods) something contrary to the spirit of the times. This spirit is still unfolding in our times. Keats' poems are misunderstood altogether if they are taken merely as a reaction; and they are totally mistaken if we dismiss the poet as "romantic." Keats was a realist if ever there was one. But his language was not that of the new realism of industrialism and technology, which is the phony realism of utilitarianism, the ideology (it is not a proper philosophy by any stretch of the imagination) whereby the ends justify the means and which seeks the manufactured happiness of the greatest number; an ideology whereby the ends become the short-terms gains of consumer pleasure-seeking, in other words, of plain greed and selfishness.

And so in our age of teletechnoscience, the dominance of the "free world" by corporate interests, and the fiscalization of every aspect of life and social conduct to the point of bondage, *it is hard to be melancholy*: it is hard to find the time and the inner space and freedom! Keats' *when* has been pressed out of existence and for some of us melancholy is not a *when* but instead a *never*. We are too distracted to be melancholy—too easily distracted—and there is too much to distract us. Even while distraction and its glamour assault us on all sides, like God said of creation: it is good. Technology is good. Technology is progress. And belief sucks in our mind. Today we are distracted and deluded by glamour to the point where new psychological disturbances and psychoses—albeit at a low, but nevertheless symptomatic, level— are almost a norm and affect a considerable portion of citizens. As for the failures and fallout from all this efficiency and forward marching progress, psychotherapy can clean it up. Because of this state of affairs, instead of melancholy we have depression, which is quite different.[1] We have a lot of suicidal despair as well.

There is nothing melancholy about depression. Depression is a shut-in experience where people cannot get through to us and we feel cut off from life by an invisible wall enclosing us. Depression is a fearful experience and the mainstream practice is to medicate people and to treat it as a medical condition rather than a soul condition.

But when the melancholy fit *falls*, it does not smother our sensibility and sensitivity like depression: it falls like rain on parched earth, the parched earth of our soul, our inner desert or drought—it falls "from heaven." Keats was not particularly religious in any conventional sense. He could already see conventional Christianity in England had had its day. By "heaven" he means what we all mean—somewhere good in the sense of blissful. Melancholy comes from heaven; in other words, it is a blessing and blesses our life.

To be without melancholy is to be (in a sense) damned—or at least condemned. Not to feel melancholy is to be out of touch with oneself and unable to get in touch with oneself—with one's soul that is: one's selflessness. The "self" in the ordinary sense is by and large a construct, our selfishness—which all (or most of us) can recognize in ourselves and others. But the soul pertains to what is *behind* the façade, the role, the defense mechanisms, the machinations of self-seeking; the soul relates to the wisdom-dimension of our being, which, in some people, has absolutely no connection to their self at all—and if this is the case, it is not a healthy state to be in.

When we are melancholy, our selfish side of our being is low on fuel and energy. We are "out of gas"—or we would be if we were cars. We feel idle and dormant: important feelings. Then the melancholy "fit" shall fall. It is a "fit" because it grabs us and takes us over. But it is a beautiful fit. We sing about it when we sing the blues, or sing along with someone singing the blues. Melancholy is being blue. Melancholy is when our soul opens out to others; we can share and want to share, and we can feel others' pain more than usual because we can feel our own pain more than usual. Singing the blues, we almost feel better. We certainly feel "in touch" with ourselves, with our true condition; we can "see things how they are" for once; we can get some perspective on the whole of our life; we've got no illusions—at least for the moment.

Melancholy is the ground-mood of the soul.[2] A ground-mood lies back of the ego; it is not egoic. Rather, our being in which the ego swims, "is always disclosed moodwise" (Heidegger).[3] This is a teaching of critical importance for listening, soul and society. A main purpose of this chapter, aside from speaking about the music itself, is to give some outline of what is at issue in a non-technical but philosophical manner.

We always only ever know ourselves *in* some mood or other. From this the ego derives its own moods, or hides its mood. "A mood makes manifest how one 'is' and 'how one is faring.'"[4] Our mood is who we are in our being, not who we are in our roles and on the surface of our life, although the two can equate. "A mood assails us. It comes from the 'outside' not from the 'inside', but arises out of our being-in-the-world as a way of Being."[5] We *find ourselves* in a mood to begin with as the ego's starting point.

Melancholy is the mood between the highs and lows that opens us to either direction. Melancholy is between content and discontent, joy and gloom. True openness is its distinctive characteristic, for melancholy as a mood opens our whole being, and therefore our potential for being and for truth—for being true to others and ourselves. Incorrigibly happy people are rarely either. Melancholy is not the starting place of self-knowledge: self-knowledge can start anywhere. But melancholy *is* the starting place for any *wisdom* in self-knowledge, for any ability to *discern* correctly on the basis of self-knowledge, and for soul-making, that is for the formation of the sensibility and sensitivity that comprise soul and lift it out of the mess of illusion in which, in this life, it is so often and so easily mired.

So if you want to listen, it is not enough only to hear. *You must first find your melancholy.* And music is the best of all possible means to do this. And so it is to the music of melancholy that we must turn first.

Keats said in 1819, in a letter to his brother, Tom, that "if we call the world a vale of soul-making, then we will find out the use of the world."[6] Keats is deliberately contrasting the world as a vale of soul-making, which is a hopeful idea and faithful to the earth, with the traditional Christian idea of the world as a vale of tears, which is both tragic and otherworldly.[7]

Melancholy grounds our *being*. Our being grounds our doing. This is why we call melancholy a ground-mood of the soul. Melancholy grounds all other moods and ways of being—and it is itself grounding, for melancholy gives perspective. From our melancholy we find out *what the world is for.* This is something we need to find out and that is not taught in technical colleges, nor can it be taught in any case in technical language. It belongs to art and, above all, to music.

To call the world a vale of soul-making is to see life not as an ascent—whether spiritual (the ascent of Mount Carmel) or worldly (being upwardly mobile)—but as idling in the valley, as taking the easy route, which does not involve climbing (or its contrary, coming back down). From the valley we can see the mountains all around; we will regard them from afar; we are not going to climb them; they are severe, stony and dry and have thin air. But down in the valley, everything is fertile, green, rich, beautiful, and there are colorful animals and birds. Walking through life, to Keats—who had a short, tortured and wretched life, but obviously a marvelous inner life—was like walking through a valley, where the soul finds pastures and the world comes alive to us. But to find the entrance to the valley way of the soul, melancholy is key, not contentedness. Happiness, which expresses contentedness, closes us off from others; it is naturally selfish rather than soulful; it cocoons us in our own happy little world. Not that contentment and happiness are bad things, if we are prepared for them—but melancholy *opens* rather to soul and soulfulness, and is obstructed by selfishness. Soulfulness means our being is open to those around us and to the world around us, and soulfulness makes us sensate and sensitive. Melancholy is soulful, and when it accompanies our joy and our contentment, it is soul-making.

Melancholy is lush. But when we turn to listen to it, we find different people find different music melancholy and that *melancholy* indicates a surprisingly wide range of mood, some parts of which will be beyond our own bandwidth. And so we need to start listening and practicing listening. For this extends our inner sensitivity, our bandwidth. Listening is the exercise of the soul. Listening is a practice, not merely an activity. By listening, our melancholy can be attuned. Our melancholy, our ground-mood, needs to be set or calibrated. For we are not just natural creatures, we are not ready-mades. We have to find ourselves. We have to find ourselves in the world. We have to find out what the world is for. And the music of melancholy will attune us in the first place so that we can do all these things.

Dowland: *Lachrymae*, "Dances of Dowland"

Let us not come to this music "knowing" about it except that it is English, from the early 1600s. Let us just listen. How do we do that? Well, we concentrate and try to attune. But how do we do this? What are we trying to attune to? To listen, we listen for the pure sound— here, the sound being made by the plucking of strings. And we attune ourselves to the music by letting ourselves become attuned, letting ourselves be passive, letting the music "pour over us," or, more likely here, letting it permeate us. Attunement is a receptive activity; it is in fact a form of idle activity; we precisely try not to do anything when we attune, but allow something to be done to us—this is what the music will do to us. Attunement is a matter, then, of letting the music have its way.

This piece on the Play List is track 12 on the album. In any case, we listen to the sound of *plucking*. We cannot see it happening, but that does not matter. Seeing it will not inform our listening any better. Were we to be at a live performance, sitting right in front of Julian Bream, we might close our eyes in any case, to hear better. And what are we supposed to hear? This is the question we suspend while we listen, note by note. The piece goes for five minutes and has three sections, or *movements*, which have different rhythms. What we hear and how we hear will depend upon who we are, right down to the last detail. We are like other people, but when it comes to the details, we become more and more unlike them. We are unlike everyone with different parents from our own, for example—but if we have siblings, which makes them more like us than others in many ways, when it gets down to the details, we may find our siblings less like us than our friends, who are unlike us in other respects too. And so we are unique. And my point is that our listening will be unique. Consciousness of this fact will help our focus. *Every listening is unique* because today we are not the same—not quite the same anyway—as last week or last year or ten years ago. I am hungrier now than I was an hour ago; this would affect my listening now to something I heard an hour ago. Every listening is unique because we are unique and because the moment in which we hear it is unique. And so we *stand in* our attunement, *we stand in that absolute*; it is a form of stillness in which, standing in it, we let the music take us with it.

Now these short movements by John Dowland may not be the kind of music we would normally listen to. It may not be the kind of music we would say that we like. So we have, as listeners, to realize that across time and place this music *stands*. Innumerable unique listeners and every temperament and sphere of society have kept this music alive. To not like it is only to release the possibility that this music will turn our thinking inside out and our judgment on its head. And the same may be said for music we will come to in the pages ahead. We have to be prepared for this. In opening ourselves to the music, we are opening ourselves to more than just music in the sense we may be accustomed to, but to big changes happening in our life from now on: changes in our thinking, in our judgment, in our relating to things and people, and in ourselves: an attunement of mood.

If (worst-case scenario) the music sounds like "just a bunch of notes" to start with, this will change. We must listen very carefully, like someone handling something of incredible fragility. A wandering mind will be enough to shatter it.

What will strike many listeners, I have found, is the sense that this piece of music *is not melancholy*. Having said this music *is* melancholy, many people cannot hear it that way. There is a reason for this. It is that we expect the music to evoke emotion—at least more than it does. We hold this wrong expectation because we are habituated to film music, from cinema and television, music written to call forth certain emotions that underscore what is happening in the film. When we hear therefore a piece of music called melancholy, we expect the feeling to be evoked in us and here we find this is not the case—or it may not be the case—and so we blame the music.

But the music of attunement, such as this piece by Dowland, will show us, if we cannot hear it, how *un-attuned* we are to begin with. To listen to this piece of music and to not hear the melancholy is to have to acknowledge, if you are honest, that you are "out of tune." You need this music, therefore, *in order to* attune, and so that you can hear music in other registers. If you cannot attune to melancholy, you will never attune to delight, which we will come to in the next chapter.

Let the music of Dowland search out and find your melancholy. To listen means to let the music do this.

The music is very careful, it is studied, and it is graceful. We can hear every note distinctly. Although the notes succeed each other in quick succession in places, each is "thought about," that is to say each, musically, is right. Each is in place and not out of place; we would hear if a note were out of place. There is stability about the piece, we recognize as we listen. Music that would evoke melancholy would have to be sad and drooping, dispirited music; but not so here. The notes here form a firm but gentle pattern within our sensibility. At the end, after we finish listening, we find the piece has had a settling effect on our soul without being what we would call soothing. Settling but not soothing, this is our recognition. This settling effect, like a rest position, we realize, must be the melancholy. This must be *real* melancholy! Such is our recognition. And so we start our listening journey through time.

The simplicity of this piece strikes our ear. It is a regressive simplicity, in the sense that it "takes us back." We are not taken back in memory, but in sensibility. This is something we are not used to. We are used to music bringing back memories, but not sensibilities, and we do not have much language for the latter, or much experience of talking about it the way most of us have, at one time or another, shared memories. As I think of the piece after listening to it, I turn over the memory of it, what I recall of it, the impression it made on me. What I discover is that my memory always tries to complicate it. My thought tries to enrich it or embellish it. The simplicity of the music foils my sensibility and my attempts to embellish it through memory are compensations. But the fact is that I do not need these compensations and I am better off without them—at least, as a listener, I am. And so what I am saying is that this piece is very *clean* or *pure*. When I listen to it, I find, each time, the notes have a cleansing *effect* on me. It is as if layers of memory and amusement and thought are removed, or rather that *I* remove them all, these layers, with an inner shrug, upon hearing the music. Now, as soon as I hear it and make this inner shrug then I am able to listen.

There are two kinds of listening in this respect. The first, which we do in order to "hear something," as when someone asks us, "Have you heard a song by such-and-such?" and we say, "I have heard that." We may hear it again, but basically as far as listening goes, to have heard it is to have done with it. That is why no song lasts for long at No. 1 or anywhere in the charts for that matter. It is all utterly dispensable but for sentiment hanging on to it, like those characters in Elvis outfits. The second kind of listening is when we know what is to be heard, for instance something clear and pure, we can hear it, and respond and listen. Or we may not know what is to be heard and may have to keep on listening until we hear it and then hearing is not the end of the story, but merely the start of listening. It is the move from the first kind of purposive listening, to the second kind of receptive listening that we want to accomplish, and that is the practical application of this book. It is not an easy transition to make. Living in a society ruled by the interests of commercial capitalism, with its redefinition of people as customers and consumers in every sphere of life, including even the inner life of religion and culture, the ability to listen in the receptive sense—if it has ever been developed—atrophies and dies. The ability to listen in the first, purposive sense, for what we can get, abounds and takes us over, taking over our whole sensibility, not just our ears. We should not forget then that to listen is a libertarian activity; it is countercultural; melancholy is countercultural: it is neither sad (and so in need of drugs or counseling) nor is it happy (and therefore deserving of publicity and everybody's interest). By listening receptively, we actively free ourselves (yet by doing nothing) from the consumerist definition of listening, which, from our point of view, is actually a failure and *inability* to listen.

Melancholy is not always blue. We hear this in Dowland. This is how we know "the blues" are self-pitying very often. There are cheering notes and turns of phrase in this piece. If we are a little on the despondent or overworked side already, the music will even cheer us. The music will bring us "up." This does not mean it is not melancholy, as some listeners may suppose, believing therefore that they "cannot hear it." We must go into reverse if this is the case, that is, let this music tell our sensibility of melancholy rather than let our emotional prejudice tell us whether the music is melancholy or not. For the latter is the subjective illusion to which consumerism has habituated us. The truth is the reverse: when we have acquired the taste, when we know what melancholy is, as musical fact, *then* we can judge, then we can tell that self-pitying sentiment is not melancholy, but self-pitying sentiment; but when, as has happened in our time, taste collapses into the mere exercise of judgment, all we are doing is fooling ourselves.

Let *this music* tell you what melancholy is.

Let us turn briefly to review some basic information. According to a fine recent study by Peter Holman simply entitled *Lachrimae*, he says this composition of 1604 is perhaps the greatest but most enigmatic publication of instrumental music from before the eighteenth century.[8] The word "lachrymae" means tears. There are seven tears in the cycle. *Lachrymae Christi* were the tears of Christ (lest we get confused with the Italian wine). They are based around types of dance.[9] Melancholy was a fashionable malady of the late Elizabethan age, Holman tells us. It must have been a *soulful age* and a great age of arts, and we know it was.

John Dowland (1563–1626), born after the Protestant Reformation, which took off from the pen of Luther in Wittenberg in 1517, became a Catholic, perhaps for music's sake and his own. Dowland was by no means confined to Britain; he visited France and Italy to study the madrigal form. He worked for many years in the court in Denmark.

The lute, the instrument played in the piece, was the aristocratic instrument of its day, and John Dowland one of its outstanding virtuosos. Interestingly, "virtuoso" did not then chiefly mean "fast fingers." Like all his confreres, Dowland picked up popular songs from every walk of life and arranged them; his *Lachrymae* became so famous that others then arranged his arrangements for other instruments (virginals, viols, etc.). These pieces would originally have been played in a semi-improvised manner, much as in early jazz, where there is a basic tune and the musician elaborates and plays on it. "What was new about the piece and probably ensured its popularity, was the concise richness of its melodic and motivic writing," says Holman, "in 'Lachrimae' the listener is immediately struck by the number of meaningful ideas, and gradually becomes aware that they are tightly and economically controlled."[10]

Each of the tears has a Latin title. David Pinto has recently interpreted the Latin titles of Dowland, which have never been convincingly interpreted together, in terms of Orthodox liturgy: "the tears are those of the penitent, starting with those caused by original sin (*Antiquae*), and the subsequent sins of fallen mankind (*Antiquae Novae*). His woes (*Gementes*), and grief (*Tristes*) force him into apostasy (*Coatae* lit. "enforced tears"). But his penitent soul wakes to the love of God (*Amantis*) and is redeemed by divine compassion (*Verae*)."[11]

It is well known that for Elizabethans melancholy specifically referred to black bile, one of the four liquids or humors thought to exist in the body, according to the ancient Greeks. The melancholy humor was depressive and heavy, like black bile, which dragged one down into the pits. Normally, music was regarded as a cure for melancholy—what we might call "a lift." Robert Burton in his *Anatomy of Melancholy* (1621) followed this tack too, but he also wrote: "Many men are melancholy from hearing Musicke, but it is a pleasing melancholy that it causes, and therefore to such as are discontent, in woe, fear, sorrow, or dejected, it is a most present remedy, it expels cares, alters their grieved minds, and eases in an instant."[12] It is a remedial melancholy that Burton describes here. Dowland echoes this in his dedication to *Lachrymae*. He writes, "though the title does promise tears, unfit guests in these joyful times, yet no doubt pleasant are the tears which Musicke weeps, neither are tears shed always in sorrow, but sometimes in joy and gladness."[13]

It is this "pleasing melancholy" that we are interested in and that in the music I think we can clearly experience. Holman says of Dowland's *Lachrymae* that they both evoke melancholy and cure the melancholy that they evoke.[14]

Vivaldi: Concerto for Lute and Viola d'Amore

Antonio Vivaldi is a very well known composer. This music is melancholy. Again, as with Dowland, let us suspend our view of what is melancholy and say to ourselves, "I do not know what melancholy is, this music is telling me." Of course the music does not literally *tell* us, as if it is speaking; I am using a metaphor (this is actually an important source of confusion that I shall come back to clear up later in the book). The music is not telling us; we are *experiencing* the music. The music is acting on our sensitivity and sensibility, that is, *our soul*. We listen from that same place—a place with no location either—for, we recall, soul is what we *are*, not something we *have* or something "in us" as such.

You can hear from the beginning, before the viola comes in, that melancholy is not unrelated to joy. Melancholy and joy are deeply related here. This is the secret of melancholy, which links it to enchantment, as what the soul wants, rather than, as the rational tradition of philosophy (from Aristotle to St. Thomas, to Kant) has it, namely, that happiness is what we all want. This is only derivatively the case if seen through reason. Desire exceeds happiness (Freud, Lacan) and the only thing that will stop it is enchantment. Desire does not seek enchantment because it has no presentiment of it, but enchantment can keep desire under its spell. Enchantment appeals directly to our understanding, bypassing reason: we immediately know when we are enchanted and the reflections of reason hardly come into it, for enchantment we will be happy to suffer, for joy is beyond the rational goal of happiness and surpasses it. This is what we are beginning to hear and unconsciously acknowledge in hearing melancholy and joy in concert with one another.

The tone of the viola when it first comes in is melancholy. This is precise. There can be no mistaking it. But it is joyful too in a tentative, very modest way and always with delicacy. Listen to the lute and viola play so exquisitely, escorted by the orchestra like an enchanted moment that bears them along. The viola speaks with two voices (there are two violas), one more cautious than the other; one goes forward with light feet, one shows hesitancy and is withdrawing. Only briefly can they consort and revel in one another's presence, some unknown force (parents? social mores?) calling them on their separate ways.

We can hear the melancholy as the ground-mood for the levity. Words can stumble to explain it, but when we hear it, we do not need any explanation; the music is the explanation. Music is direct; words are not. This music will tell us a thousand things about love that we could never say. The melancholy here is *exquisite*.

The piece is in three movements. Dreariness is absent from the melancholy. The second movement *aches* the soul with its delicacy of feeling. When I say the viola is exquisite I mean this is what "exquisite" means; no dictionary can say it like this with a synonym. The exquisite is what makes us ache. In it we attain something of the unattainable— whatever that is; here clearly beauty, in its plain simplicity and joy, and prescience of separation, gives the music an edge, like death is an edge of life so that we experience it in its *passing*. Music is superb at giving us a sense of separation indicative of death as every note *dies*. And so does the whole piece as it *subsides*. Whereas, with the printed word, the words *abide*; which has made some religions believe words and even books are *holy*—or at least, certain words, certain books. It is only a lovely illusion. Words however do stay with us. And they can empower us or they can rot our soul. But music disappears. Nevertheless music leaves a residue. But the residue itself, like an aftertaste on the soul's lips, leaves nostalgia. While all the more immediate to experience than the communicative word, music is at a remove from reality as it persists only in the memory. But this makes the music all the more nostalgic and personal, while words are forever bandied back and forth in an everlasting noise. And so with music we get caught in an inexpressible circle of presence and absence. But this is one of the wonders of the soul: our inexpressible circles.

In the last part of the middle movement, the lute and viola are so sedate, so reconciled, so distant, but all the more intimate in their distance; like couples who hardly need talk because they can read each other's thoughts, compared to young lovers who have everything to talk about and never enough time to say it all. In the third movement some musical parts from the first two movements are taken up again and developed very slightly with the purpose of harmonically resolving them, so that the whole piece can end with a musically harmonious sense. I would say the third movement belongs to the musical impetus of the piece and the need to accomplish something toward resolution of the sounds and accompaniments. Whatever the technical explanations for this might be, from the point of view of musical sensibility—the soul's perspective—we can enjoy the resolution as fitting. We hear the fittingness of it. We understand by this what "fitting" is. We felt the real soulfulness of the music was in the first two movements, although we can feel (without having to know the technical reasons "why") that the movement that finishes off is suitable and unifying. Soul seeks unity, for unity is its most primordial memory—of the soul's ground luminosity.

This concerto was composed in 1729. Antonio Vivaldi (1678–1741) was a resident of Venice, the capital of the Venetian Republic during the so-called Baroque era, the term used for the period of music from about 1600 to 1750. The Catholic Church encouraged baroque after the Council of Trent (1545–63) as a way of communicating the truths of the faith by art that was emotionally involving; baroque can extend to be dramatic and triumphant or opulent. The connotation when people say of something that it is baroque is usually that it is highly decorative and detailed in a way that is laudatory.

The concerto was a new form in Vivaldi's day. It had started in the church, where the organ supported voice parts, and then developed to where the lead instruments replaced the voice and were supported by instrumental orchestration. Lute and viola d'amore went out of fashion shortly after this; the viola d'amore was so called because of its especially sweet sound.

Vivaldi's father, originally a barber, who turned musician, with success, taught his son Antonio—one of nine children—violin from a young age. In 1703 Vivaldi was ordained to the priesthood, aged twenty-five, but was freed from ever having to say Mass as a priest, except for the very odd occasion, due to his propensity to asthma, and general poor health. Vivaldi worked in an orphanage in Venice—the *Pio Ospedale della Pietà* (Devout Hospital of Mercy)—for over thirty years and composed most of his major work while engaged there. The *ospedale* was basically what we could call a children's refuge or an orphanage, and there were four such refuges in Venice in Vivaldi's day, indicative, I would think, of the fabric of society: formed not just by early death from disease, but by the abandonment, on a fairly significant scale, of unwanted children. The *ospedale* had its own orchestra and choir. And so these unwanted children had Vivaldi scoring music for them that they then performed around Europe. He wrote concertos, cantatas and sacred vocal music for them. These sacred works, which number over sixty, are varied: they include solo motets and large-scale choral works for soloists, double chorus, and orchestra. *The Four Seasons* (1723) is Vivaldi's best-known work. Another thing: Vivaldi was on renewable one-year contracts at the orphanage, so he never had the job on a permanent basis and, some years, the board would put him off, then re-employ him the next year, according to their power games. Vivaldi also taught violin to the children at the orphanage, and he was technically one of the most gifted violinists of his day.[15]

Because the pay at the orphanage was not great, Vivaldi wrote operas for the popular theaters, of which there were several big ones in Venice working on a competitive, commercial basis. In this way Vivaldi supplemented his income and funded some of his projects, such as travel with the orchestra, which the board of the *ospedale* could not always afford to fund—or would not. Vivaldi says in a letter to his patron, Marchese Bentivoglio, that he had written ninety-four operas, but apparently only fifty of these have survived.

Schubert: Piano Sonata in G Major, D894

We do not change the melancholy mood with this work, but to show melancholy under another aspect. This is a twenty-minute piano sonata by Franz Schubert (1797–1828), from 1826. It is certainly a work on a par with the mature Beethoven, in the ease with which the sonata form is developed and broadened, "that might blind one to the newness of its thinking."[16] Leo Black, author of *Franz Schubert: Music and Belief* (2005), says the D major melody in the andante (second) movement "gains a special color from being played for the most part in octaves; its texture, tempo (slowish triple time), outline and rhythm all recall a very beautiful song to an equally beautiful Goethe poem, *An den Mond* (To the Moon, 2nd setting, D. 296, date contentious) . . . [philosopher of comparative religion, Rudolf] Otto, however, found in its lines the principle Immanuel Kant called 'aesthetic perception' and granted no less objective validity than any principle derived from logic."[17] All this is very well, if we can hear it! The point of this here is probably for most readers at best informative, but what matters is to find that the sensibility can be knowing and, together with the faculty of knowledge, we can enter further into the music. Goethe was not alone in writing about the moon. How does his poem compare with one on the moon by Li Po, or Tu Fu, given that Goethe was not only interested in Eastern poetry, but his creativity was *en rapport* with that of the Eastern masters of poetry? And so we can extend Black's analysis further. These will no longer be "literary" sources, but aesthetic *affinities*. Experience with listening will give us these affinities. Ultimately, though, the affinities of music of this caliber go beyond those that can tie it to words. The names Goethe and Kant are very grand, but it is something beyond them and ultimately different from them that we will hear.

Schubert was a prolific composer, producing new work continually. We acknowledge him (perhaps revere him is better) as the master of melancholy. The opening notes of this sonata drench the soul in melancholy. The melancholy is different from the other two works by Dowland and Vivaldi; it carries much more silence, much more knowledge.

The silence sounds with the notes. The silence sounds even louder and more musically than the music, and accentuates it, so that the notes soak into the soul like great cool raindrops.

As the piano winds you in to the work, it begins to remind you of something—of something you cannot remember. Other memories will fill the vacancy instead, but none of these can remind you of what the music is reminding you of, which you cannot remember. This is to experience the eternal and timeless element of Baudelaire's aesthetic: that this music begins to indefinitely reminisce.

The music itself is helpless, unsupported; just pure notes on the silence—as near to Being as can be. In the opening of this work, the first notes play a little refrain, which is the like the core musical idea and which will be elaborated upon. But the work gives you its beautiful heart first. This is its innocence. This is its loveliness.

The work stays innocent, without becoming "sweet," which would spoil it. The piano ambles, sometimes runs tiptoe, sometimes with a bit of drama, but never for long, and it never becomes overly dramatic or strident. Melancholy has its crises, it would appear; but they are short-lived, and the balance is quickly restored. Melancholy is a balancing mood, in the sense that it is at home with itself, and in the sense that it is *the* point of view from which to see everything else in proper perspective. The piece is restrained and, as listeners, we enter its restraint and feel the freedom in it.

In his book, *Understanding Music: Philosophy and Interpretation*, the philosopher and musicologist Robert Scruton quotes a review of Schubert by the English composer and critic Robin Holloway as follows:

> Schubert is at the very heart of music. More: definition of what he is, account of what he did, in music, are tantamount to a description of music itself, in its most normative and widely shared sense—what it is, how it works, what it is *for*. No composer is less dispensable, more essential and intrinsic. 'Essential' meaning closest to the art's grammar, syntax, language, which he employs with extraordinary purity and exactness even while they undergo in his hands the most radical extensions ever made by one individual. Their purpose of course, to expand, to deepen, intensify expression: to which the same superlative applies—no other single composer has added so largely to what music, in its innate nature, not foisted upon it, can *say*. This is just as essential and intrinsic as the linguistic usage. They cannot be separated: the wider key-relationships, the major/minor ambiguity, the enharmonics, the enhanced dissonances, equally with the exploration of the most basic facts of diatonicism, and every motive, melodic, rhythmic, textural element; all this is in such perfect fusion with the affective ends that he has to be called Apollonian, whatsoever is being expressed—amiable-convivial, frenzied, doom-laden, *angstvoll*, erotic, pantheistic, radiant, desolate, God-forsaken, weary-unto-death, furious, frustrated, fragmented, nihilistic, nostalgic, or just *cold*! Many more words could thus be adduced, for Schubert covers a wider range of emotion than any other composer and most other artists in any medium; but they would be mere signs and ciphers apart from the way their every nuance within the comprehensive coverage is imprinted into the notes.[18]

To this hymn of praise, Scruton adds the comment: "The passage is written from the heart, and I doubt there is a musical person who will not be disposed to agree with it. This *is* the genius of Schubert, that he is able to express the whole range of human emotions, and to do so by 'imprinting' those emotions 'into the notes.'"[19]

Let us consider this idea for a moment: *emotions imprinted into the notes*. This is how it seems. Is this right? Is this how music works? When we hear the notes, should we be able to "tell" the emotion expressed in the way we can tell what someone is feeling by looking at their face? *Can* we do this? How do we know we hear aright? Of course, if we are professionally trained we can assume we hear aright, but, for the rest of us, how do we know? Are we then left out of this charmed circle of listeners? But surely recognizing emotions is universal? It does not depend on musical training - or does it? Emotion like music culture: laughing, weeping, grieving, longing, seeking, loving and being loved are natural to being human, they are not linguistic or cultural to begin with, although language and culture may channel them or characterize them in special ways. But is this quality of humanity itself, this natality, imprinted into the notes of the music?

In his book, *The Aesthetics of Music* (1996), Scruton writes at length on this question of emotion and expression. He argues that, for the emotions to be imprinted into the notes, as Holloway says of Schubert, the music needs to pass certain tests, and he reviews these same tests in his chapter on expression in his book, *Understanding Music.*[20]

Proper emotion is encompassing of our whole being—and sometimes that of others in our proximity as well. For these states of mind to be imprinted *authentically* on the notes, four tests must be passed: the semaphore test, the understanding test, the value test, and the structure test.[21] If these four tests can be passed, then we can talk about musical expression, as in the statement, "Schubert . . . is able to express the whole range of human emotions,"[22] which no keen listener would disagree with—at least this is our presupposition, believing only a fool would claim otherwise. According to Scruton, then, the *semaphore* test is passed if the music is not established by convention.

Scruton writes: "The meaning of a work of music is given only in the aesthetic experience."[23] The application of rules (as in a semaphore system) will not make the music connect with us.

The *understanding* test is passed, Scruton says, "if a piece of music is what we understand when we understand it as music." One can understand the music in three ways: technically, or purely within sensibility, or both. What matters to aesthetic experience however is the sensibility, to which technical understanding is *post facto*. When we understand a piece of music we are not saying we understand the emotion *behind it* that it expresses, but that it *is* the expression. This would seem to be Scruton's point, although his reliance upon the likes of the mathematician Frege and the logician Wittgenstein to make it is confusing and philosophically misplaced.

The *value* test is passed if the music expresses something, for then it is of value. Music that expresses nothing is empty; it is bad music. Lastly, the *structure* test is passed if "the expressive quality of the musical work is developed through the music . . . [Expression] is brought into being through the musical line, and worked into the musical structure."[24]

The understanding of the music lies with the listener, who may be in the audience or involved in performing the music. Aesthetic experience is *given* by the music, but *happens* in the soul. According to Scruton, what is supposed to happen is *understanding*, but is this not one of the tests? Scruton reverts to the cerebral category that is characteristic of his musicology, but not of love and that which is loved, or of beauty and that which is beautiful or characteristic particularly of Baudelaire's aesthetic. We agree that music must pass his four tests, but not so that we *understand* it, or so that aesthetic experience can *mean* understanding or necessarily cohere with understanding. Music that passes these tests is *art* music. What happens when we listen to music that passes these tests is not understanding, but awakening (or reawakening). What awakes in us is sensibility and at the same time the soul is sensitized. This is to do with being, not understanding.

We want to agree with Holloway. We would not say from listening to Schubert that we *understand* his music, but that his music *awakens* in us an expression "imprinted in the notes," because musical expression is *not* a result of the composer's intention: when a composer is expressing a musical intention we have only academic music, not inspired music, or music *per se* without the idea of it or idea governing it. Imprinted in the notes is Schubert's inspiration that he called upon but did not control. His gift was in being able to call upon inspiration so readily. Many artists have to wait years, calling upon inspiration by the inner pitch of their life and their activity, and not all these artists receive as much as they would like or expect. Schubert's music is not an expression of inspiration: the expression *is* the inspiration. This is because music is an immediate art. The aesthetic experience is that of the inspiration that the music occasions, which is why we speak of being *moved*. The inspiration moved Schubert and, hearing it, it moves us. Feeling or emotion accompany all this in the sensibility. There is a sympathy in the sensibility between listener and the music, and in this way music has a power to unite us. Words come only afterward, in order to talk with one another about the power of the aesthetic experience, its power to unmask us and lay us bare.

Our feelings are like our "antennae" when it comes to music, rather than our thoughts, which interfere and are of use only afterward, for reflection. Music does not *speak* to our feelings or *try* to speak to our feelings, unless it is bad music which is in tow to other, pecuniary interests, such as movie music, which sets out to speak to our feelings in order to manipulate them. This is not art music, but music ceded to sentimental purposes. Real music speaks to our *condition*. This is one way we know it is *art* music, not movie music or background music, or music of mere academic interest or just pretentious music, recognizable because it is always *cerebral* before it is anything else. We receive music with our feelings, but music is not *about* our feelings any more than music expresses feelings. We said feelings accompany music and that aesthetic experience is occasioned by music. Music is about our human condition. Great music really opens out our being in our time and place; it "fills the world," as it were, and, reciprocally, it establishes itself as a condition of that time and place.

Adorno, in an essay on Schubert that he wrote on the hundredth anniversary of Schubert's death in 1928 and collected in *Moments Musicaux* (1964), speaks of truth and feeling: "The poet does not offer an immediate representation of his feeling; rather, his feeling is the means of drawing truth, in its incomparable tiny crystallization, into the creation."[25] Truth is a spectral presence because it does not stand *in* the work itself (the work is not the truth) but truth is represented *through* the work, by means of the work: the work offers a *way* to the truth, in a sense. This way, Adorno says, "always stands within history,"[26] and therefore it speaks to our condition. Adorno has a sociological explanation of what in any other language we would wish to speak of as inspiration. Even so, we should still wish to say with him that "the force that strikes them [what I consider to be inspiration] is human, not artistic."

"Truth itself does not enter the creation; it represents itself within it,"[27] and this is what we feel: the proximity of truth, of something true, the presence of something true; and the music as far as we are concerned is this presence: it is a musical presence. This is the ineffable condition of music (its timelessness) that corresponds with our own fragile condition (subject to old age, sickness, and eventually to every loss, even that of our selves). Thus we describe, once again, the Baudelairean correspondence through Adorno's melancholy perspective with its Hegelian idiomatic highlights.[28] Let us read the whole quotation of Adorno on the truth in art, as he heard it in Schubert and expressed it at this early stage of his notable career:

> Truth itself does not enter the creation; it represents itself within it, and the unveiling of its image remains the work of humans. The artist unveils the image. The image of truth, however, always stands within history. The history of the image is its disintegration: the disintegration of the illusion of truth with reference to all aspects of its intended substance, and a revelation of its transparency for the aspects of truth content which it implicitly invokes, and which emerge in their pure form only through its disintegration. The disintegration of the lyrical creation is above all the disintegration of its subjective substance. The subjective content of the lyrical work, in fact, consists only of its material content. The aspects of truth content depicted are merely touched on by them; the unity between the two belongs to the historical moment and dissolves. Thus the lasting aspect of lyrical creations is not, as static natural superstition would have us believe, that of unchanging, basic human emotions but, rather, the objective characters that, at the origin of each work of art, were touched upon by those emotions which are ephemeral. The subjectively intended and reproduced essences, however, suffer the same fate as only the great materially determined forms which are softened by time. The dialectical collision of the two forces—the forms, which are found among the stars in deceptive timelessness, and the materials of consciousness's immanence, which posit themselves as the ultimate inderivable givens—shatters both, and with them the provisional unity of the work: it opens up the work as the scene of its own transience, and finally reveals what images of truth have risen to its crumbling ceiling.[29]

For Adorno, the height of sensibility will ever be a melancholy "crumbling" spectacle. The lyrical for him—as for all those laden with intellectualism (dialectical materialism)—will always house consciousness above the stars, a perverse reversal of reality, for consciousness reaches the stars, but is subject to their cycles and energies, not the other way around. And yet Adorno is surely right not to allow us to reify our emotions or our subjectivity, and he is surely right to avoid the cerebral analytic tendency of Scruton, where we always stand outside life, looking on; and Adorno is surely right to preserve the transcendental (and for him redemptive) nature of truth as *outside* the order of representation and expression, but to all intents and purposes representing itself within the order of representation and thereby drawing us on into the future. It was Schubert's music that got Adorno talking along these lines and his is what I mean by the music addressing our condition—or having our condition imprinted in the notes—and music having the power to unmask us and lay us bare. Adorno's melancholy words are an indication of this too. Adorno lived long enough to experience that crumbling ceiling he refers to fall on his head—and not only on *his* head, but on the world. He lived to see and hear of terrors that surpassed his worst fears all realized (from the crimes of the Nazis and then the Communists to the capitalist commodification of culture). What Adorno did not reckon on, as Hegelianism is a blind, is that the music of the nineteenth century would speak *beyond* its time and speak *not* of its time, but of that *truth*. And we can hear it still. What we hear can enable us to build a new ceiling. Adorno thought that the crumbling ceiling was cultural, and associated culture with ideas, but he did not reckon on what he did not believe: something completely beyond Hegel, not to do with politics, but with sensibility and inspiration, something that is *not an idea* and that is higher, beyond *logos*, the realm of reason and ideas. This is a subject that we shall come back to later in the book and around which, I wish to show, the whole subject of art music is caught up. We shall have to use words to talk about what is not words—music—but this shall not prevent us from speaking; rather I shall use words differently, as I have already started to do, from poetry, the kinds of words most akin to music. Baudelaire's aesthetic is not a theory: it is poetry and that was where we began. We shall continue to share Adorno's melancholy and redemptive sensibility, expressed so philosophically and truthfully throughout his writing, as we can already see from the quotation above. That our acceptance of Adorno's "dialectic" (or any dialectic) cannot be wholehearted is part of the melancholy we feel about the incompleteness of relationships, philosophy, and their illusions.

To sum up: the meaning *is* the music. It is not a form with content. The form *is* the content; the content *is* sound, which is not form *or* content as such. These are not the right categories for it. This is why (one reason why) music is so direct and immediate and penetrating. The great musical interpreter of our time, Daniel Barenboim, writes: "The content of music can only be articulated through sound. As we have seen, any verbalization is nothing but a description of our subjective—maybe even haphazard—reaction to the music."[30] But he goes on to say: "The fact that the content of music cannot be articulated in words does not of course, mean that it has no content; if that were the case musical performances would be totally unnecessary . . . we must never stop asking ourselves what exactly the content of music is, this intangible substance that is expressible only through sound."[31]

Listening again to Schubert, we might ask: is this a melancholy work? or is it gently serene? It is arguable I think. The serenity of melancholy is perhaps the purest kind, but only our ears will tell us, not words.

We *hear* the music. We hear the melancholy. Let us notice something (Scruton points this out): to understand the music means to *hear* it, but to *describe* it is something else. To talk about music, we must *translate* our understanding (or lack of it) into description.[32] Scruton's point is that, no matter how beautifully described a piece of music may be, it does not represent and cannot represent an *understanding* of it (our sensibility for it, I would say). It is a *translation* of our understanding (or sensibility). This is why we struggle for words: we are translating!

5

Gardens of Delight

How pure it is, how graceful, the little temple
they now form—a rosy round—
turning slowly as the night! . . . it resolves into girls, tunics fly,
and the gods seem to be changing their minds!
—Paul Valéry: Phaedrus, in *Dance and the Soul*

This chapter continues the discussion of the aesthetic experience of listening to art music. Melancholy opens the soul, we have learned. And here we shall be saying that melancholy opens the soul above all to delight. Delight—or we might call it *enchantment*—is the counterpoise to melancholy to which melancholy opens up. Delight then captures our heart, or enraptures us. The melancholy soul if it is not too *sunk* in melancholy, will be delighted, or so says the poet.

Melancholy Delight

In his *Ode on Melancholy* Keats says that melancholy opens to delight. "In the very temple of Delight/Veil'd Melancholy has her sovran shrine." Melancholy has shrines everywhere in the valley of the soul, but her "sovran" shrine, her most important place, is in the temple of Delight. For listening, this is important, because it means that melancholy has immediate access to delight. Melancholy is not a mood like depression, which is shut out and alienated. Depression is not in fact a mood at all. It is a social and cultural disease that can take on clinical proportions in some people, quite involuntarily. We are social creatures after all. Melancholy is a mood and no mood is negative. Positive and negative are electrical metaphors, not soulful metaphors. Speaking of melancholy, the verse goes as follows:

> She dwells with Beauty—Beauty that must die;
> And Joy, whose hand is ever at his lips
> Bidding adieu; and aching Pleasure nigh,
> Turning to poison while the bee mouth sips:
> Ay, in the very temple of Delight

> Veil'd Melancholy has her sovran shrine,
> Though seen of none save him whose strenuous tongue
> Can burst Joy's grape against his palate fine;
> His soul shall taste the sadness of her might,
> And be among her cloudy trophies hung.[1]

Melancholy is a sacred presence or way of being within Delight and belongs to Delight. Delight shelters and protects melancholy, for she is vulnerable. Joy, Pleasure, Delight (dignified with capital letters so that we should not just think of them in the way society accustoms us to as being *about me*) are ways of being and gathering. The first person singular is not at the origin or end of Joy, Pleasure, Delight. They are ends in themselves. Melancholy is their ground-mood. Every way of being is a way of gathering, of drawing together, of being in togetherness.

Baudelaire's *volupté* is his sense of this binding between melancholy and joy: spleen and the ideal. In this equation death is not a simple noun such as names a *thing*, like Gertrude Stein's "A rose is a rose is a rose." Death in this verse of Keats about melancholy and in the *Flowers of Evil* and, most importantly of all, *in our soul*, has a metaphorical register by which it names a Land of Shades, a land *là bas* (down there) that our soul, in its unconscious roots, grows down to and touches in sleep and trance; and always we tend toward it. Death does not *happen*, except from an extrinsic materialistic perspective. Rather, the body is only the material or physical limit of soul and is never really alive, which is what Freud meant by the death drive: our propensity to become ashes and dust does not happen to us it is inbuilt and constitutive of us. What we call "death" has to do with the *continuing life of the soul*. Now death is a sensibility that accompanies the moment and *is* part of its absolute. Our melancholy is at the juncture of this double life of ours: inward and outward, day world and night world, consciousness and oblivion. The forces of illusion pull the soul out of itself into the maelstrom of what it prides itself to be life and what everyone caught up in the same illusion calls "life"; we light up the night with neon and try to call the night day; but the soul, if we listen to her, knows better.

Our unconscious is not a part of our mind, but an obliviousness we fall prey to. When we are lost in thought, furrow-browed, or when we are acting out emotions, we are oblivious to the moment, to the soul, to eternity, to the universe. Unconsciousness is obliviousness or mind-lessness. Consciousness is mindfulness. I disagree with egoists that I am a self-evident substance. I agree with Kant and the psychoanalytic discovery that there is no subject as such. Kant said the subject is apperceptive, by which he meant that "I" accompany my perceptions and experiences. I am not constitutive of them. Another way of saying this is to say that we take ourselves too personally. The problem with personalism is that it contrives a sense of self that blocks the sense of soul from experience. We have selfishness, not soulfulness, abounding. Self ends up replacing soul; the cult of personality replaces any real character; and clever experts replace wisdom figures.

Melancholy would not be melancholy and Delight would not be delight without death's ambience. Melancholy and Delight are not afraid of death nor have they made an enemy of death (the last enemy, according to St. Paul). Being melancholy is being aware of death's ambience. Being joyful is being aware of the soul-consciousness that dies over and over from the realm of the senses, but does not die in its own realm. We shall come back to this subject in the next chapter with Schophenhauer on the immortality of the soul. There is a timeless connection with the soul that art testifies to and in music we can hear. The timeless connection is greater than any one of us and our connection with it is what makes us great or not and wise or not. Death *with life* calls us to the dimension of height. Death and life come together in height, which is transcendental. At the level of height soul does not die. We do not find this level; we only have to remember it and return to it. The music calls us back. It is a metaphysics of nostalgia.

To remember, to return to life, we must indulge. Keats speaks of bursting "Joy's grape against his palate fine." This is a metaphor of *jouissance*, of pleasure and indulgence in which life and death are caught up together. Who has not felt a grape burst within their mouth, releasing all its cool, sweet juice? To die of this pleasure, to die in the temple of Delight and be "among her cloudy trophies hung," is what Keats extols. It is what in his art in the work of reading that we can vicariously experience through words. Words awaken our imagination of reality. It is in this sensibility described by Keats that Baudelaire is able to run the gauntlet with *The Flowers of Evil*.

Decadence renders itself incapable of Delight and is the canker of real joy or delight or, in our glamour culture, the simulacrum. The failing on the other side of Delight is of reason. Again Kant pointed this out. He was the first philosopher to see the limits of reason and to see that taste does not start with it. In our culture we oscillate between decadence and rationalism, missing the middle term of soul and soulfulness. Physical worship and materialism and personalism on one hand, scientism, rationalism (as in economics and policy making) and cognitivism, on the other hand. Utilitarianism is the pitiless philosophy that has managed to join decadence and rationalism. Pragmatism is its soulless servant. On either hand, with decadence and rationalism we pitch out of balance and chase the fiasco, surprising ourselves more and more by the fact with every increasing disaster. Instead of melancholy there is increasing horror. Nineteenth-century artists in different arts and named by art historians and experts under different labels and groupings have this in common, many of them: that they have tried to make us see and hear and feel and so to avert the fiasco. Judging with the wisdom of hindsight, we might say that we have hardly begun to appreciate nineteenth-century art, but we can say, I venture, *it is growing on us.*

With melancholy, we are already in the precinct of Delight, for it is all about. We have but to *awaken to it.* Delight is always innocent. Delight is the sign of innocence. Delight is an inspiration—you cannot get it. You certainly cannot buy it. Delight must befall us. Listening will bring delight. Listening will bring awakening.

Purcell: *The Fairy Queen*

Henry Purcell was an English composer, born in 1659, who died young and unexpectedly in his midthirties, in 1695. He worked on composition from a young age, and was prolific. His *Fairy Queen* is delightful. But how to listen to it? Ought we know the story or legend behind it, of which it is a musical setting? Or ought we listen to it without knowing the story? Purcell, in writing this score, would have supposed his audience would know the background to the story. If they did not, someone else would tell them, or today it would be in the program notes at a performance. Does this mean then that, as listeners, we try to fit the music to the story, and that is what we do when we listen to it? Is the music an allegory? Does it mean that the more familiar with the story we are, the more details of it we know, the better we will be able to "hear" the music?—that as we listen, we "hear" because we recognize what is being "said"? This would be to suppose that the music is saying the same thing as the story but in another language; rather than words, music is spoken. But do we listen as to a language, with comprehension? Is listening a skill dependent upon the texts? Surely Purcell would not have imagined this? *Does it matter* what Purcell expected of the listener? Perhaps it does not matter very much what Purcell expected of an audience, not any more, for we take the music on our terms, not his; but even so, the question remains as to what to do as listeners, how to approach the music, when there is a story, as in this case, so the question always arises, then, as to the story's relation to the music, and our relation to both.

At one level the story is a "pretext." It was perhaps an excuse for writing this work, or perhaps it unlocked Purcell's inspiration; or maybe it was given to him as a job which he succeeded in doing admirably well; in any case, Purcell succeeds in reversing the usual order in which a text is central to the music, as in church liturgy, and he makes the music central to the text. The music is not an allegory. For an allegory is never an artwork: an allegory always falls short because of its dependency upon that of which it is an allegory. It can still be a wonderful allegory, but that does not lift it beyond the status of an allegory. So to listen to the music as illustrative of the text is not to listen to *the music*, but to listen to the music *as* allegory, as something other than it is. Can we then, on the other hand, listen to the music without regard to the story? Those listening with a technical ear will listen like this. This is professional listening. In one way it can hear more, but, in another, it gets stuck in the same problem of allegory again. This time the music is an allegory of musicology. How well does the music illustrate this or that technicality of music theory? it asks. How well does the music illustrate musical technique for its period? And it would ask other such questions, as if the music were about the theory, when in fact it is the other way round: *the theory is about the music*. In this techno-allegorical listening, music gets theory-driven, as happened in the twentieth century with the development of so-called serious music by Schoenberg and those who composed music in the styles of what Adorno roughly called the "New Music." Such music was really only a politicization of music and an intellectualization of a theoretical and experimental type, and the rejection of jazz at that time (and later) as music—on political grounds essentially. It was also a rejection of spontaneous music, and of the listener. Theory music does not care a dime about the listener: that is how we know it. But then, music thus intellectualized is not properly music any more, but the allegory of an idea, and probably not a very good idea—as non-theoreticians listening to much of this music will tell you. Here it is *the music* that we need to listen for. It is *the music* that gets repressed by allegorization, of which intellectualization and conceptual music is the latest type. Conceptual music is a typical child of the Enlightenment—of the age of reason.

Now that age is over. The age of rational humanism ended with the Second World War. We have entered a new age.

We call Purcell's age "the Baroque." Music was under rapid development, as were all the arts at this time. Later we shall come to talk of "absolute music," but, for the Baroque, that is the unknown future. It was a period of great activity in the arts, patronized by the Catholic Church across Europe, but also in the newly emerging secular sphere, for royal families now could choose between more than one type of Christianity, and this gave them a new sense of themselves as separate from or outside religion, and of being free to choose, to accept the best on offer, or to do what was in the best interest, and so on. The court thus had its own sense of the baroque, which paralleled the church's, but it was a more luxurious and this-worldly opulence. Naturally Protestantism, and particularly the puritanical end of it, regarded the baroque as an extravagance and an evil, as it would have so regarded any kind of theater and dance. But while the English are characteristically sober, Puritanism never got a grip on the English soul, and neither did pietism. Purcell's day was a turning point in English history. In 1688, when Purcell would have been in his late twenties, the Glorious Revolution—or Bloodless Revolution, as it is sometimes called—established England as a democracy, with a bill of rights allowing for the rule of parliament of the people. This was signed by William of Orange (King William III from 1689) and Queen Mary II, who shared rule. *The Fairy Queen* was written for their fifteenth wedding anniversary, in 1692 (Mary was to die two years hence and William to reign alone until 1702). In a sense, then, it was an historic occasion. If it was a personal achievement for Purcell to be composing for an occasion like this, then the occasion itself, in the pink freshness of English democracy, was an exciting and surely prescient moment. It followed centuries of war and strife between the people and their rulers and between different religious camps, Catholic and Protestant, and different kinds of Protestant—conflicts all caught up in a fabric of family loyalties, remembering that bloodlines crossed national boundaries and formed a complicated web of loyalty; so, for Purcell, such a moment as this was an achievement, and he would have known it.

The text—or libretto—behind *The Fairy Queen* is that of Shakespeare's comedy, *A Midsummer Night's Dream*. Shakespeare (d. 1616) had written *A Midsummer Night's Dream* at the end of the sixteenth century, so the play was about a hundred years old by the time of *The*

Fairy Queen. Shakespeare's play was a romantic fantasy-comedy, so it fitted the masque, which is a court entertainment, with its love of fashion, disguise, misdemeanor, the odd crudity and flash of farce, but all in the spirit of festivity. Purcell does not even attempt to do justice to Shakespeare's unequalled plotting, character and great language, but sets a series of masques overlaying it through which the story might be glimpsed, but need not be followed. Skipping act 1, there is one masque per act. Purcell makes the play almost an occasion for the music, itself only an occasion for *a wedding.*

And so we have the music of delight.

The item in the Play List is a chaconne, which was originally a type of Spanish dance. We can hear the dance, as we listen to this music, and we might wish we could see it too—even that we might join in! As music of delight, we may have expected, with our more contemporary sensibilities, something more "carried away" with itself, something "higher" spirited, more enthused emotionally; but this is our misplaced sense of delight. As with melancholy, so with delight: we need to attune our sensibility to the mood. It is from correct attunement of our sensibility that we can recognize music that is not really delightful because it is too high-spirited and, perhaps for that reason, overindulgent; for indulgence is never delightful. Delight is about other people. We all share in it.

Consumer culture tries to manufacture things for our delight and get us to delight in possession of replaceable things. It is a culture of false delight. The music of delight will turn our sensibility around from anticulture and attune us to the reality of delight, which is not "out there" but in our soul.

The short chorus, "They Shall Be Happy," which follows, refers to the characters in the masque, but of course to the king and queen in real life. It is very rich with heartfelt strains in the depths and the joining together of all the voices in unison, dominated by the upper registers, but fulsome at the bottom end, giving a sense of grandeur. This is like a sung blessing. Again the delight is in each other, as all delight should be. We are to imagine the stage set in a stately London garden and to envisage therein created, "a transparent prospect of a Chinese garden, the architecture, the trees, the plants, the fruits, the birds, the beasts, quite different to what we have in this part of the world."[2] The chaconne is to be danced by a Chinese man and woman as part of a string of what a biographer calls "Purcellian show stoppers."[3] Tea drinking had just come into fashion in England and a cup of tea is still delightful in anyone's language. Decorative *chinoiserie* was modish in Purcell's time, and no less delightful than it is now.

Debussy: *Fêtes* (Nocturnes for Orchestra, No. 2)

Claude Debussy wrote an "introductory note" to the Nocturnes as follows:

> The title Nocturnes is to be interpreted here in a general and, more particularly, in a decorative sense. Therefore, it is not meant to designate the usual form of the Nocturne, but rather all the various impressions and the special effects of light that the word suggests. 'Nuages' ["Clouds," the first of the Nocturnes] renders the immutable aspect of the sky and the slow, solemn motion of the clouds, fading away in grey tones lightly tinged with white. 'Fêtes' ["Festivals"] gives us the vibrating, dancing rhythm of the atmosphere with sudden flashes of light. There is also the episode of the procession (a dazzling fantastic vision), which passes through the festive scene and becomes merged in it. But the background remains resistantly the same: the festival with its blending of music and luminous dust participating in the cosmic rhythm. 'Sirènes' ["Sirens," the third of the Nocturnes] depicts the sea and its countless rhythms and presently, amongst the waves silvered by the moonlight, is heard the mysterious song of the Sirens as they laugh and pass on.[4]

The Nocturnes premiered in Paris in 1900.

This is "Impressionist" music. *Fêtes* . . . the impression of a fair . . . To listen is to mingle with the crowd. You can hear the conviviality. The piece starts with trills of anticipation and excitement, reminding one of the way children work themselves into excited states of anticipation by degrees from their talking. The circular rhythms are dances, and one hears the carousel and the whoops of delight from the tower of the helter-skelter. Here comes the march, announced with a fanfare of trumpets. All the musicians in the march are dressed in white suits with peaked hats; but they are accompanied by young people dressed as huge animals, and men on stilts. Suddenly, Here Comes Everybody! The drums! The huge crowd forces you forward with it as everything moves together with the drums. Along you are carried. But back over to the side, on the edge of the *melée*, something else altogether is going on that looks more interesting, with hardly anyone watching it. What is that? The music records impressions, imagined or real—it hardly matters. The music records impressions and creates impressions in us, along its theme.

What to Listen for in Impressionist Music

I am quoting this from Charles Hoffer's book entitled, *Music Listening Today* (2008):[5]

- A generally lighter timbre and tone than heard in the music of Brahms and Wagner. The size of the orchestra is somewhat smaller. The harp and the flute are more prominent, and less use is made of the brass instruments.
- Subtle tonal colors, including chords with notes added simply because the composer wanted that particular sonority. The C E G chord sometimes is a C E G A chord.
- Harmonies with a less functional role in favor of a more tonally colorful role. Sometimes chords move in parallel motion, something that was not allowed in tonal harmony.
- More subtle and blurred rhythm. The metrical pattern is not easily felt.
- A weaker tonal center, especially when a whole-tone scale is used.
- Limited use of the forms developed in the Classical period and little development of themes; many works are rather short and programmatic.
- Sensual, somewhat subtle, music that does not attempt to project any message. Rather, expect sensitive, subtle musical works that are simply to be enjoyed.

Impressionism as a Style

A great many contemporary art critics regard (and want us to regard) Impressionism as bridging two periods, the romantic style of the late nineteenth century and the modern styles of the twentieth. However this is not to say what Impressionism is *in itself*, but merely to historicize it. Impressionism is in fact a shift from Germany to France, from the small city with a local courtly culture to the big city of Paris with a bourgeois culture. Impressionism is a geographical relocation of the center of music, and it is a reaction to formalism in society— in French society and in the French academies of arts. Moreover, Impressionism is in itself a new awareness of the artist as a person, or *persona*, who is more or less at odds with society, and something of an eccentric or outsider in the large city. Impressionism is less social, less from a milieu and for a milieu, than individually expressive and it is even often very personal. It is a further interiorization of music and musical understanding. Furthermore, Impressionism is a reaction to the encroachment of industrialization and its threatening social totalization, where art is pushed aside by a rising tide of commerce combined with technology. Impressionism can be seen as the last bright glow of art before the crushing weight of business and technology completely overwhelm musical art altogether, causing it to either retreat to the academy or become part of pop culture on the radio and concert circuit, having sold out to it.

Liszt: *Les Jeux d'eau à la villa d'Este*

Another sample of Impressionist music is this piano piece by Franz Liszt, which is not to be confused with the piece, *Jeux d'eau,* by Ravel.[6] Liszt (1811–1886) was nationally Hungarian, but of German culture, as Hungarians of his day were. The sound of fountains at the famous and exquisitely beautiful Renaissance garden of the Villa d'Este, situated at Tivoli, outside Rome, inspired Liszt to write this piano piece in 1877. It foreshadows the Impressionist movement.

Liszt was an awesome virtuoso performer.

This piece of music is normally an instant "hit." The beginning listener will be musically delighted by it. The expert, at a technical level, will also be delighted, hearing all the incompletion in every direction, as Liszt keeps building the music, only to sharply turn in another direction before bringing a musical resolution.

The piece starts as if someone has thrown a huge handful of tiny diamonds into the air and they are showering down all over us and spilling across the piazza. See the sparkling of diamonds, and feel the water trickling, old stones—the coolness of one, the warmth of another. There is some showing off, some self-display in this piece, yet this does not spoil but indicates excess, exuberance, overabundance, a spilling-over. Left and right hands on the keyboard play at different depths. If I think of delight, which of course I do, I think of *sheer* delight. This is a precipitous piece, turning water into music, and music into water. It is not just a shower. The fluidity and the modulation allow you to sink into it. The music does not just keep you on the surface. Two-thirds of the way through there is quite some turbulence, to the point of damming the source, but the water slowly leaks out in little tinkling droplets, gradually refilling all the spaces left empty by the stomping chords.

It must be that there is something more easily delightful about Impressionist music—perhaps because it is pictorial, rather than abstract. As a listener you do not feel as if intellectual demands are being made of you—as you may often feel with Beethoven, Bruckner or, indeed, other works by Liszt. Rather, the music is very sensate. The music seems to *want* you to take delight in it as well as to delight in it *with* you. And this is not just because of the music, but also because of Delight. As we said with the Purcell, delight is something shared.

Only children delight selfishly, but their innocence protects them from its really being selfishness at all. For adults, delight—if it *is* delight—is equalizing. Delighted people come together to share their delight; social imbalances and pretensions fall away (although in some societies it would take more than music to remove them). Delight moves in social circles too, with a certain "social set" being delighted by certain music. There is something binding and confirming about delight. When Natasha comes downstairs to her debutante ball in Tolstoy's *War and Peace* she knows the music and it confirms her in her identity. All her relatives, friends of the family (and Levin) are there too, to "receive" her; they know the music and it confirms their group identity. But this is not just a matter of identity (another mysterious abstraction); rather it is a matter of *sensibility*, and of the *recognition* of a sensibility—of the recognition of one by the other in and through a sensibility, which is a sensibility *for this*. In Natasha's case, it is her acceptance, and initiation by the event, into Russian high society.

The thing with delight is that it is never served in half measures: it is delight*ful*. Not many things in life are like this, except sorrow. We can be sorrow*ful* too. Many moods of the soul are equivocal because the soul is strange, never quite at home with the body or with the world, always searching, always wondering, always with something to find out, always bound for somewhere new. The soul is a strangeness. The soul wants delight, ecstasy, rapture, awe, and horror even. Strong souls (slightly mad souls) prefer to suffer than be happy.

Ravel: *Daphnis and Chloe* (Suite No. 2 with Chorus)

The *Daphnis and Chloe* story derives from a third-century CE romance by the Greek, Longus. It is told as an Arcadian myth in which lesbian lovers, Daphnis and Chloe, both shepherdesses on the Greek island of Lesbos, fall in love. Daphnis is a shepherd in our version. It is very sensual; they are both so innocent that they do not know how to consummate their love. Chloe gets abducted by pirates, is rescued by Pan, and eventually (after various misadventures) reunites with Daphnis, her love. The nineteenth century had some affinity—even if only imagined and projected—with late antiquity, with its decadence, nonchalance, eroticism, and the arts that went along with these dramas, poems, novels and amusements. The affinity is based on the fact that the arts at that period too were wholly secular; the old Greco-Roman mythology had become merely the stuff of legend and the new Christian mythology had not yet installed itself.

Maurice Ravel composed two suites for the ballet of the Daphnis and Chloe story in 1910.[7] For the ballet the story concerns a shepherd and shepherdess. Charles Hoffer says, "Today the ballet's music is most often heard in the form of two suites. Suite No. 2 contains some of Ravel's most impressionistic music, especially the opening section called 'Lever du jour' (Daybreak)."[8] Of "Daybreak" Hoffer continues, "The woodwinds and then the strings provide a rich accompaniment of rippling notes. One can almost sense the glow of the sunrise in the melody. The recording includes a part for chorus in which the singers vocalize on a neutral syllable."[9]

Daphnis and Chloe is scored for a large orchestra. Played as two suites the piece runs for about forty minutes, and as the musical setting of the ballet, for about an hour. We shall focus on *Pantomime* and *Dance générale*, the last two parts of Suite no. 2. Because the ballet lasts longer, the two pieces of music are not exactly equivalent. In the ballet, *Pantomime* is entitled *Chloe figure la jeune nymphe errant dans la prairie*. We may expect some fairly spacious orchestration from the title, and we get it. Chloe's "errance" is indicated, I take it, by the leading piccolo. The last piece, *Danse générale*, is how both the suites and the ballet end. Here we have some extremely vigorous orchestration. Why this should be so is not clear from listening to a snippet, which we may find rowdy. Musically Ravel has the task in the *Dance générale* of bringing together the music of a dramatically and emotionally complicated set of stage scenarios, "a tangle of roused emotions" as Scott Goddard puts it.[10] Goddard says:

> He [Ravel] must frame such utterances as will give the clue to what has passed and settle the mind so securely, on that score, that the merry-making which ends the work may seem not out of place as a too-rapid change from the horrors and terrors of the drama, but a truly inspired thanksgiving for liberation from those past troubles. In order that those happenings may be felt to be past and over, something more than even a divine appearance is needed to straighten out matters. And it is this spacious sweeping melody that supplies the need and crowns the architecture of the tale with a shapely line. By that tune the ballet will live in men's memories. Enclosed within it lies the germ of the complete work. It is fashioned wholly on melodic material that has previously been heard. In itself it has beauty and strength. Fully to realize its significance it is necessary to know the complete composition and to see how exquisitely all the themes are dependent on each other and how in this last ample melody all the threads are gathered together and all problems solved.[11]

Igor Stravinsky called *Daphnis and Chloe* "not only one of Ravel's best works but one of the most beautiful products of French music."[12] I am quoting Lawrence Kramer from his excellent chapter on this ballet, aptly entitled "Consuming the Exotic," in *Classical Music and Postmodern Knowledge* (1995), where he continues as follows: "Ravel's best friend and pupil, Roland-Maurice, agreed; to illustrate 'the secret power which gives the calculated graces of [Ravel's] art an angelic charm which is at its freest in the world of the supernatural,' as he turns to the nocturne and daybreak episodes of the ballet. 'Here,' he writes of the latter, 'at the limit of effort and calculation, [Ravel] attains ... that pure beauty which is at one with the apparent simplicity of nature.' These remarks should be understood, not only as an index of Ravel's aesthetic success, but also as a description of his expressive intentions."[13] Kramer describes this beauty in terms of the narrative of art history: "It is a beauty sensuous and urgent, and hypnotic but at the same time lucid and artificial. It is a type of beauty much sought after by French artists and writers during the second half of the nineteenth century: the beauty of Symbolist poetry and of art nouveau. It is at once ornamental and organic, part frozen urban artifice, part metamorphic natural growth."[14]

The *Dance générale* starts gently with piccolo and orchestra in an Arcadian setting and moves toward a crashing climax that is very loud. At a performance, or listening at home to a recording, it is always difficult for an inexperienced listener of art music to interpret or "take" very loud music because it is not noise; the inexperienced listener is often overwhelmed and lost by it. Loud music can seem to the listener to propel them outside of it. Rather than enjoyment, one experiences ejection. The fact is that, at these climatic points, the music evacuates itself. We know the storm will subside and the sensibility has to "surf" it. Stillness comes next. Listening to loud or "bold" music actually strengthens the sensibility and empowers it. Softer music is transparent or translucent in quality, which it why it is easier on the sensibility for it makes the soul translucent to itself. Strident, bold, aggressive or conflictual music has a darker depth, like deeper turbulent water that puts us out of our depth; the sensibility has to manoeuvre within it, but we can trust the music to bring us back to shore.

Bach: "Goldberg" Variations: Nos. 1 and 25

There is so much music worthy of mention under any heading we can think of, but it would be particularly remiss to leave Delight without having mentioned Bach before we go. Johann Sebastian Bach (1685–1750) did not live in an age in which the individual artist could act in the independent way a musician might today, producing pretty well what they like. Bach worked for the Lutheran Church and his was an age of the patronage of the arts, largely by the church but also by the various courts. At that time (and for a long time to come), what we now call Germany was divided into hundreds of small kingdoms and, in each, culture was separately promoted. Prior to that, in the Renaissance, there was a similar situation, with various Italian cities, most notably Florence, which developed their arts in order to beautify and bring prestige to the city. Still, in Bach's time, the great age of nationalisms was not yet upon us.

It is said that Bach changed every form of music he touched upon. And he touched upon them all. He was prolific. Music was like a family business. As the Kapellmeister (director of music) at Weimar, and later at Leipzig, he produced new music for church on Sunday week by week for years. This was his cantatas, hundreds of which we have, but hundreds of which are now lost. Bach was an organist and harpsichordist, but he could write for any instrument, orchestra, or choir. His name is associated with contrapuntal music and he was a leader at it in his day and probably the greatest master of it in the history of music. Contrapuntal music is where two different and independent lines of music are "counterpointed" or still manage to work in harmony. Normally, if I were to write three different beautiful songs and have them all sung at the same time, it would be a cacophony. What Bach created was polyphony, where the separate songs, in this example, not only sound well together but sound even more magnificent as a whole than they do individually. You can imagine how complicated this could get if you add different instruments, and so on. Technical and musical ability have to be in equal measures here. Counterpoint in Bach's compositions was governed by harmony, which you could hear, and the counterpoint was the texture or fabric of the harmony. This then, is what we listen for in Bach.

Of all composers, Bach is one of the most consistently delightful, only outshone, perhaps, by Mozart. In the case of both composers, what strikes us when listening is the absolute *ease* of delight in the music. One can *hear* the effortlessness.

An example might be the first of the "Goldberg" Variations. These need to be played not overintellectually, not overseriously. The trouble with contrapuntal music is that people can be very grim and technical about it, and this can come across to the listener. But these variations should be played with a twinkle—at least that way it is much pleasanter to listen to. On the Play List I recommend the recordings of Canadian pianist Angela Hewitt. There is a single line of development to follow with the ear and it is so gentle, so light, so brimming with quiet delight, not spilling over but perfectly contained—effortlessly; and Angela Hewitt lets the sound smile. Listen to the twenty-fifth variation, with its slightly faster tempo (not "upbeat") but the same calm composure, a combination of sobriety and pleasure: warm, gentle and soothing—in a word quietly *delightful*.

6

Listening across Time

Music is the revelation of the inmost dream image of the world.
—Arthur Schopenhauer

Having examined the aesthetic experience in soulful terms of melancholy and delight, in this chapter we shall consider the factor of *time*. Life is like a "dance to the music of time," as in the title of Anthony Powell's great English multivolume novel. The great philosopher of time, Henri Bergson, regarded time as identical with the continuity of our inner life. In this chapter I shall present the question of time in soul and music from three different but intersecting perspectives: first, from that of the ancient Greek philosopher, Plato; secondly, from that of the most musically oriented of all European philosophers, Arthur Schopenhauer; and thirdly, from that of the contemporary philosopher and musicologist, Jürgen Lawrenz.

Plato

Time matters in listening. Music takes up time and takes its own time. Not just its rhythm, or the "time it takes" to play, but its own inner time: the time of sensibility—of *our* sensibility. Pieces of music stay with us over time, lingering like an aftertaste—or like the old-fashioned notion of the "stain of sin" on the soul, which you cannot rid yourself of without confession and absolution. But unlike sin, you have to do it again—*listen*, that is. And with listening too, you must disgorge it; you do this by talking about it, ventilating it, releasing the music or tying the music up in clumsy words and language which are incapable of doing it justice. What "They" say about music only matters before we develop a sensibility of our own. Whether we listen like "They" do or listen ourselves, a current of speech—inaudibly—accompanies all the music of all time so as not to let it slip away. A good piece of music is always superior to the speech about it; the music takes us *up* the Ladder of *Eros*, while the speech just keeps us on the rung. "Great works" are those which constellate the most lavish talk about them, they are talk-inducing; we cannot stay silent in response but have to speak out. At a performance, the audience will jump up and shout at the end. Music sends words spinning.

Music changes time because it has its own timing, which is more important than that of the precise regularity of the measuring clock. Music ignores this most unmusical of tools. And to think that, once, Christians in Europe—the so-called deists—compared the wonder of the universe to a clock that God had setting ticking. The lack of imagination is quite amazing to us now. How superior were the ancients who heard music and, through it, the music of the spheres; even medieval folk could hear the *harmonium mundi* as the background orchestration of life.

Listening starts with an interdiction upon it. Just as ethics begins with "Thou shalt not . . ." so aesthetics begins with the interdiction to *not listen*. Not to listen means a discipline, and also a practice, is enjoined upon the listener which will form a habit and in-form a character, in the long run. Ethical negations are in the interests of the community and it is likewise with aesthetical negations. We find this aesthetic negation at the origin of, Western culture. For Plato, because music affects sensibility, it molds character. It does this by imitating emotion and thereby having an impact on people's character as we imitatively respond. Jürgen Lawrenz in *Art and the Platonic Matrix* (2011) makes the point about culture generally, that: "mimetic practice is the authentic source of what much later falls under the rubric of art."[1] And: "Mimetic behavior is indeed our principal heuristic strategy and precedes conceptualizing."[2] Desire at the origin of religion and society is mimetic in René Girard's anthropology. The mirror stage at the origin of the account of psychological growth in Lacan's psychology could also be said to be the moment of discovery of the imitative rival.

Whitehead is often quoted as having said that all philosophy consists of footnotes to Plato; this may be truer of thinking about music.[3] What does music imitate? Emotion? Or what do we who listen to music imitate in it? It is this binding imitative factor that is implicitly presumed upon when people equate Wagner's music with the Nazi phenomenon, despite the time and history between Wagner's death in Venice and the election of Hitler and his cohorts to power. Art music attunes our sensibility for good or ill is Plato's point, and society needs to be conscious of the fact and take account of it. Some musical modes put the times out of joint by their power to disaffect people, or else they are a signal that the times are already out of joint—and I mean 'modes' here in a more generic sense. The power of music on sensibility was true of music in Plato's day, and the church in the Middle Ages was aware of the power of music in the life of virtue and vice that it adjudicated before eternity. The power of music over sensibility is no less true today in a secular age such as our own. Where materialism is the dominant fount of various ideologies, when lavish greed is both overtly and tacitly acknowledged all around us as the central component of being, of politics and the global economy, then music is found to be without art, taken over by our technological toys, and not just played *on* them, but *by* them. What can wake us up short of massive catastrophe? This is the question for philosophy today, a question that (strange as it may sound to materialistically attuned ears) puts the philosophy of music at the center of philosophy, from where it might trickle down into culture (for it is philosophical ideas that trickle down, not wealth!). The question "What can wake us up short of massive catastrophe (the catastrophe that is guiltily expected in rich nations)?" is not a question that can be asked aside from new therapeutic and activist agendas: even much of religion that gave birth to such agendas in the first place is locked out of them and stuck in its own fundamentalism, giving all the more call to the agendas in their own right, even in their fragmented and perhaps not fully conscious or coherent forms.

For Plato, because music impacts on our inner being and makes us imitate its feeling, some music is good for society and some is not. The old Greek modes have their technical description, but they are also adumbrations of various sensibilities. These old modes—to name the symbolic seven and the most important in subsequent development—were the Phrygian, Dorian, Lydian, Mixolydian, Ionian, Aeolian, and Locrian modes. These modes are groupings of pitches that create distinctive tonal environments. The modes of Western sensibility developed from these, more or less. From these modes we derived the major and minor scales that musicians use today, based on the division of the octave into twelve pitches in which successive pitches are separated by intervals of equal size. This system of musical organization operates as a system of tuning and began to be used in the early sixteenth century. Bach's *Well Tempered Clavier* (1722) is a late rationalization of the system, specifically for keyboard instruments. There are other modes associated with other cultures, for instance, India and China, but these overlap with Western modes, so they are not totally alien. To proscribe one mode is to proscribe that sensibility and, conversely, to advocate and advance a mode is prescriptive. Thus we affect sensibility. Or so Plato has it, where in *The Republic* he writes: "For a change to a new type of music is something to beware of as a hazard of all our fortunes. For the modes of music are never disturbed without unsettling of the most fundamental political and social conventions."[4]

Part of the famous conversation about music between Socrates and Glaucon from Book 3 of *The Republic* goes as follows:

—We said we did not require dirges and lamentations in words.
—We do not.
—What, then, are the dirge-like modes of music? Tell me, for you are a musician.
The mixed Lydian, he said, and the tense or higher Lydian, and similar modes.
These, then, said I, we must do away with. But again, drunkenness is a thing most unbefitting guardians, and so is softness and sloth.
—Yes.
—What, then, are the soft and convivial modes?
—There are certain Ionian and also Lydian modes that are called lax.
—Will you make any use of them for warriors?
—None at all, he said, but it would seem that you have left the Dorian and the Phrygian.
—I do not know the musical modes, I said, but leave us the mode that would fittingly imitate the utterances and the accents of a brave man who is engaged in warfare or in any enforced business, and who, when he has failed, either meeting wounds or death or having fallen into some other mishap, in all these conditions confronts fortune with steadfast endurance and repels her strokes. And another for such a man engaged in works of peace, not enforced but voluntary, either trying to persuade somebody of something and imploring him—whether it be a god, through prayer, or a man, by teaching and admonition—or contrariwise yielding himself to another who is petitioning him or teaching him or trying to change his opinions, and in consequence fairing according to his wish, and not bearing himself arrogantly, but in all this acting modestly and moderately and acquiescing in the outcome. Leave us these two modes—the enforced and the voluntary—which will best imitate the utterances of men failing or succeeding, the temperate, and the brave—leave us these.
—Well, said he, you are asking me to leave none other than those I just spoke of.[5]

What Plato is indicating through this dialogue is that certain tonalities found in different modes affect our mood, our character, our bearing—and therefore, collectively, our society. Not only Plato, but also poets such as Tyrtaios of Sparta and Kallinos of Ephesus (both seventh century BCE), provide evidence to us that the Greeks were inordinately sensitive to these intervals of succession in pitch. That is why Plato singled out some tonalities as "lax" or lascivious, others as "military," and so on. Because of the fact that instruments in classical Greece were fixed to play in certain modes and could not be tuned to other modes (unlike modern instruments), Plato was forced to ban certain instruments from his republic.

These modes are basically the precursors of our own major and minor modes, for example, Aeolian mode approximates our A minor, differing from the latter by just one interval. What these tonalities denote today is largely academic, because modern instruments can reach virtually all tonalities.

Today, when violinists tune up, they must choose a mode (tonality) that is, so to speak, the "foundation" for their instruments' intervals. Because of its build, the violin has a tonal "dead center"; but other tonal centers of a modality can be reached by retuning the strings. The violin sounds best and most sweet at its own "native" tonality, that is, D major, which is why most violin concertos are written in that key; the other tonalities produce stresses on the strings (the way they vibrate) that sensitive people perceive in emotional terms as predominantly "sad," or "strident," or "ecstatic," etc. A plain four-note tune in D minor sounds different from the same notes played in E major. Today, sensitivity to tonalities has virtually disappeared. But this is also because our sense of harmony has changed. Nearly a thousand years ago our listening changed when, instead of attending to harmony "horizontally" (melody), we began to enjoy it "vertically" (as chords). Human voices can reach any tonality, so chords posed no problems to choristers; hence this is when "chromatic" harmony and the new systems of tonality came to be established. But instruments lagged far behind, so, for example, all music for horns until the nineteenth century was written in E flat major; all music for trumpets in D major etc. Horns had a problem in the nineteenth century, like the lyre of Plato's days, in that they had a fixed modality or tonality. The native tonality of the horn is E flat; but, with the invention of valves, horns were able to play all the tonalities in their range simply by pushing the right buttons. Before Beethoven, you rarely find an orchestra with all the instruments we know today playing together because trumpets and horns could not reach the same notes as the strings. Like Handel in his Fireworks Music you had to write the music in a tonality

101

common to them both. For Bach, and even for Beethoven, modalities were still a living concern. For example, in Bach's Mass, the jubilant choruses are all set in D major, the grief of the crucifixion in B minor. Beethoven wrote his "Pathétique" (piano sonata) in C minor (pathos), his "Eroica" (symphony) in E flat major (heroic), his "Appassionata" (piano sonata) in F minor (despair), his "Pastoral" (symphony) in F major (rustic), and so on. In this sense, music and sensibility are keyed together and the origin disappears in the mists of time, which means our sensibility gets lost there too. We cannot tear ourselves away, or detach ourselves, from this sensibility: it is who and what we are at a constitutive level. What we can do though is assault the sensibility with continuous noise and musical monotony or keep the sensibility at an immature level, which is what happens today when people just listen to commercial music and know nothing beyond it, so their taste (for what it is worth) is totally formed (deformed in fact) by it. If "culture" connotes cultivation, this non-cultivating process must be anticulture.

The basic point about modality and sensibility is still with us. It is an *aesthetic* question prior to the pious chatter about ethics. For example, almost all American films and dramas revolve around gun violence. Almost the only respite is pornography, but which is worse? It is all *aesthetically* impoverished and impoverishing. This is culture as anti-culture. But where is the academic critique of any of it? What you find rather is academic legitimation. At the consumption end you have to get used to it, to make yourself immune to gruesome murders in the living room every night brightened by loud advertisements every couple of minutes or interspersed with ham-acted comedies. If the continuous consumption and promoted fashionableness of violent media are aesthetically "OK" with parents and mentors, it will be ethically "OK" with society too. The ethics will follow the aesthetics. The bind is however that, with a "tasteless" (moronic) sensibility in the dominant, decision-makers are in no position to make aesthetic judgments, and are thereby ethically disoriented; look at the "gun debate" in the United States, for example, and at the confusion between violence and freedom. This is why Plato, thousands of years ago, cautioned that "The rulers must be watchful the neglect does not creep in to things musical and gymnastic."[6] (By "gymnastic" is meant something more akin to what today we would think of as yoga.) Socrates' daemon tells him that *our foundations in music* actually guard our society from inner corruption and lawlessness.

Good music calibrates the soul. This is one of the underlying propositions of this book. I mean by that: good music calibrates *the inner sensibility and sensitivity* so that our feeling is right, by which I mean it is *attuned*. Inner and outer worlds, inner height and depth, past and future are calibrated and attuned by good music, that is why it is good. On this basis of attuned sensibility we can have the judgment to recognize bad music or bad noise pretending to be music when we hear it. At the moment it is everywhere.

Schopenhauer

The power of listening and the power of music mirror each other. They are one power. There is no philosopher from Plato's day to our own who has understood the power of music better than Arthur Schopenhauer (1788–1860), and no one has understood better than Schopenhauer why Plato took the attitude to music—and dance—that he did. Schopenhauer was a philosopher with an enormous influence on music and the arts generally. He had notable disciples. Wagner was a devout follower who admired his work so greatly that he was frightened to meet him when he had the chance because he stood so in awe of him. In 1854 Wagner is supposed to have read Schopenhauer's *The World as Will and Representation* four times. Tolstoy was another follower. He wrote *War and Peace* with a great portrait of Schopenhauer on the wall facing him. Nietzsche, Wittgenstein, Freud, Thomas Mann, Karl Jasper, and Heidegger owe much to Schopenhauer.

Schopenhauer was neither beloved nor feted by the academy in his day, and has not been since. Academic philosophy had its head turned by Hegel and Hegelianism (which is to say all politicized philosophy that pays scant or no regard for religion). Marx married the political philosophy inherent in Hegelian idealism and phenomenology to economics. Specters of Marxism have not abated since the collapse of ideological Marxism in Eastern Europe; they abound just as harmfully as ever in the rule of economics over the whole of society, even including governments. By the same token, too few people have been able to see through this insane state of affairs. We still live in Hegelian times, we might say. Marxism has not had its day, as many suppose; rather we live in its heyday in our age of the stock exchange, dominated by the false thinking of economics, propounded by Marx, as the meaning of history and happiness. We can trace this back to the political implications of totally false ways of thinking in Hegel. This is why we can say Hegel, rather than Schopenhauer, turned people's heads. That moment between Hegel and Schopenhauer was a moment of opportunity and crisis in the west of Europe and we missed it. And energy follows thought. The thought was Hegel's, and the world followed it.

Apart from being critical of Hegel, Schopenhauer also stands apart from neo-Kantian scholasticism and from those other types of phenomenology associated with the names of Husserl and his student Heidegger, two of the twentieth century's preeminent philosophers. Husserl's phenomenology is a form of abstract cognitivism. This blinkered stance was corrected by Heidegger's existential phenomenology in *Being and Time* (1927). Heidegger however soon found himself bogged down in terminology and intellectualism and not, in fact, as methodologically separated from Husserl as he had imagined. In his later work he turned toward art, and his idea of Being owes a lot to what Schopenhauer had to say about the will. With the dominance of other forms of phenomenology, Hegelian, Husserlian and Heideggerian, Schopenhauer remains a hidden or covert presence in philosophy right up until our time. But even so, it is a Hegelian world of humanism and hubris we live in, not a Schopenhauerian one, which sees humankind as deeply fallible, misguided by the folly of thinking, and need of salvation, of which people individually are capable, had they the sensibility in the first place to "turn and be healed." (Isaiah 6: 10)

Schopenhauer is unique in the annals of modern philosophy for not identifying philosophy fully with thinking. He did not locate his freedom within the realm of thinking or—as Heidegger did later (like Hegel in this regard)—collapse thinking and being together. Schopenhauer was at odds with his contemporary Hegel, who not only identified being and thinking, philosophy and thinking, the spirit and reason, but he equated them with the Absolute. Schopenhauer followed Kant who differentiated reason from understanding, allowing that reason could far outstrip understanding on all sides if allowed to roam, and Kant fore-fronted what he called practical reason, that Schopenhauer developed in terms of what he called *will*, meaning the act of pure self-presence or the individual in his or her self-presence. Schopenhauer developed a theory of the significance of pure self-presence as the basis of religion and truth and culture in a redemptive sense, given the fallibility (if not stupidity) of so much of our thinking. His philosophy had strong correlates with Eastern religion, insofar as he understood it (being the Western philosopher by whom Eastern thinking first came West) and its correlate in the teaching of Meister Eckhart and his followers in Christendom. It was to the will that *music* directly related, Schopenhauer taught.

Schopenhauer wrote his main work, *The World as Will and Representation*, in 1817, but he expanded it over the following twenty-five years to twice its original size. The main idea that the book elaborates in analytical detail is that life as we know it has two sides: one side is relative, impermanent and passes away. This side is that of the world. It is a world conditioned by time and space and causality (following Kant), to which Schopenhauer adds a fourth condition: consciousness. All of this comes and goes. And thought is always fragmentary—even the most systematic thinking. Thoughts are only ever part of a shattered unity. Thinking (philosophy, as it has been conceived) will never restore the shattered unity. But the world has a second, an inner side, the Schopenhauerean *wille* or will, which we might be more inclined to call energy or life force, or *Prana*, given our greater knowledge of Eastern religion today. This then is not the will as we ordinarily think of it, as, for example, when we speak of our willpower, or of God's will. The world of time, space, causality, and consciousness is a manifestation or exteriorization of this will or life-force. The human being inhabits both realms – the inner (noumenal) and outer (phenomenal) at *one and the same time*: hence, the world as will and representation.

The Indestructibility of the Human Soul

Schopenhauer is often called a pessimistic philosopher, but this label is commonly misunderstood in terms of his merely not being cheery on the same terms as everyone else. Given what I have already said, that Schopenhauer's starting point is the observation that human beings are flawed by their fallibility and their hubris, his pessimism is understandable, but it is characteristic only of his starting point, not his philosophy, which is redemptive. His teaching had to do with moving people from being psychologically unconscious. In their unconsciousness people lead heedless lives governed by ideas and thinking, or by emotion, or by what others think and say and do, that is to say they lead reactive lives. Awakened consciousness is one that realizes that it is able to be present to itself and dwell in self-presence or mindfulness, unlike the state of a person sunk in their own thinking—if not already sunk in the traditional triumvirate of greed, lust and illusion. Schopenhauer's philosophy is the philosophy of awakening. The essence of the personal will—the ground of identity—is indestructible, Schopenhauer argues. It is this that we need to discover for ourselves, in ourselves, and his philosophy directs us to do so; in this his philosophy is redemptive. The discovery of our indestructible nature is carried out in the first instance by what religious traditions have called detachment, or what psychology calls the withdrawal of projections. First we have to see that we are making projections all the time and that our thinking is caught up in these projections, and that our "self," our identity, is identified with them and even *dependent upon them*—and not merely dependent upon them but utterly and totally *tangled up* in them in our thinking. To this entanglement in projections, philosophers are no exception, Hegel being a landmark example (and, similarly, Hegelians in his wake). In the minds of people unconscious about thoughts and thinking arise fear and protective strategies that they act out individually and that are acted out socially through culture. Schopenhauer's philosophy is a philosophy of insight into this state of affairs, which starts in the hearts and minds of individuals.

Schopenhauer was one of the few heavyweight philosophers who, without religious convictions to back him up, or the use of Christian theology to hedge his bets with, argued persuasively in defense of the indestructibility of the human soul. His argument is basically quite simple: the world has these two aspects, conditioned and unconditioned, but while the conditioned or manifest passes away, that which is unconditioned and unmanifest does not. It either never passes away or it lives to see another day. Because human being inhabits the world in both senses, while part of our being passes away, *life itself* does not die and each of us *is* part of life itself, participating in the being of life itself, of the whole of what was, is and will be. These arguments, Schopenhauer later discovered (and incorporated into later editions of his major work) correlated with Buddhist and Vedantic teachings, as well as with what the best Christian mystics had thought. So for example, in Christian idiom, "life itself" is the image and likeness of God in which we are made, our little self passes away, but that part of us joined, as it were, to the image and likeness of God does not pass away. A Christian mystic, however, does not just believe this: a mystic is one who starts with *experience* and takes up religious teachings in an experiential sense, rather than in the ideological sense that believers take up religion, or in a merely infantile sense that many who identify as being religious adopt when they rely upon the supposed authority or divinity of certain teachings. But the aim is not more experience but to be *beyond* what might be termed "experience" by natural lights.

Schopenhauer's central intuition was that "The more clearly one is conscious of the transience, nothingness and dream-like nature of all things, by so much the more clearly is one conscious also of the eternity of one's own inner nature."[7] Schopenhauer tries to show his reader that we are not just physical objects (that is obvious) but metaphysical beings, and we need metaphysical truth like we need food at the physical level. The latter feeds our body, which will die, but the former feeds our inner nature, which is not subject to death. "By metaphysics," Schopenhauer writes, "I understand all so-called knowledge that goes beyond the possibility of experience, and so beyond nature or the given phenomenal appearance of things, in order to give information about that which, in some sense or other, this experience or nature is conditioned, or in popular language, about that which is hidden behind nature, and renders nature possible."[8]

There are two kinds of metaphysics, Schopenhauer goes on to say. One kind has its verification and its credentials *in itself,* the other *outside itself.* "As the metaphysical systems of the first kind require reflection, culture, leisure, and judgment for the recognition of their credentials, they can be accessible only to an extremely small number of persons; moreover they can arise and maintain themselves only in the case of an advanced civilization. The systems of the second kind, on the other hand, are exclusively for the great majority of people who are not capable of thinking but only of believing, and are susceptible not to arguments but only to authority. These systems may therefore be described as popular metaphysics, on the analogy of popular poetry and popular wisdom."[9] Religions based on authority and externally conceived gods or God, and divine revelation, are examples of popular metaphysics. Experiential, meditation-based, mystical traditions exemplified and transmitted by masters are examples of Schopenauer's first kind.

A master is one who does not just teach religion but who would, for example with Christianity, not just teach *about* Christ or teach christology, but would be christified, transfigured from within like Jesus to the eyes of his disciples on Mt. Tabor. Consider, for example, the masters John Cassian met in the Egyptian wilderness and wrote about in his *Conferences,* the masters such as John Climacus at Mt. Sinai, or the hesychasts on Mt. Athos in Greece. For examples of such people are well known in every century of Christian history, despite the fame or folly of the exoteric history of the church. Within major exoteric religions such as the great world religions we have both types of metaphysics that Schopenhauer describes existing together, and not side by side but inextricably bound up with each other. The exoteric religion is usually found sheltering the esoteric tradition, and the two will be found sharing the same idioms: so kabbalah within Judaism, mysticism within Christianity, Sufism or the kind of esotericism Henry Corbin has written about within Islam, and so on; the same goes for Buddhist and Hindu traditions.

Schopenhauer goes beyond any Christian mystic in holding that music is philosophically superior to language. Language can state metaphysical propositions, but music *is* metaphysical. This is where Schopenhauer's philosophy takes us to, a point forgotten even within esoteric traditions themselves very often, particularly Christian one. Music is metaphysics because it is *a copy of the will itself.*[10]

Philosophy of Music

Schopenhauer says, "We could just as well call the world embodied music as embodied will."[11] And: "I have been trying [throughout his whole book and life] to make it clear that music expresses in an exceedingly universal language, in a homogenous material, that is, in mere tones, and with the greatest distinctness and truth, the inner being, the in-itself, of the world, which we think under the concept of the will according to its most distinct manifestation."[12]

Music, or at least what we shall call "absolute music," (and explain in the next chapter) speaks for this unconditioned and unmanifest side of life and our being, and it *sounds into* our conditioned existence, the world that is of our thinking and doing and making. Absolute music does not just sound into our conditioned existence: it *sounds us out.* Music reaches into areas of our being that we did not know we had. We experience this by means of our inner sensibility and sensitivity, or soul as it used to be called. Absolute music makes us more soulful. Absolute music is the music of the metaphysics of nostalgia: it calls us back in the direction from which it sounds. In mythological language we could say that it calls from heaven and it calls us to heaven. Absolute music metaphysically attunes us to the dimension of height. Absolute music sounds from beyond the grave, because it comes from what is undying and cannot die. Absolute music attunes sensibility to the power and beauty and goodness of that unmanifest and unconditioned side of our own being that we were previously hardly aware of. Absolute music aids to awaken us to ourselves—and not just human beings, but animals and plants and all living creatures. For we are all interconnected, and listening to absolute music can help us to realize this. Ultimately what Schopenhauer is talking about is great cause for celebration and the laying down of all arms.

Absolute music is music pure and simple, music that is not for any other purpose than to be itself: *melos*. Schopenhauer's philosophy, unlike every Western philosophy since the neo-Platonists, is not based in *logos* (reason, thought, conceptualizing) but in *melos* (harmony, melody). The philosopher is essentially a person of *melos*, and only then of *logos*. This is a teaching of Schopenhauer completely unrealized by Western philosophy that Schopenhauer adds to Kant, his master. Schopenhauer believes the teaching coheres with Kant's critique of pure reason. (To Kant's critique of practical reason, Schopenhauer has rather more changes to offer, but we need not concern ourselves with those here.)

As Schopenhauer puts it: "Philosophy is nothing but a complete and accurate repetition and expression of the inner nature of the world, in very general concepts, for only in these is it possible to obtain a view of that entire inner nature which is everywhere adequate and applicable."[13] What in our objective sphere of representation we would consider "great music," Schopenhauer says is music that is the best analogy "to the inner spirit of a given phenomenon."[14] The philosophical concepts coin an extrinsic truth while music gives the intrinsic reality. The concepts of philosophy are abstractions from perception (including intuitive apprehensions) and are therefore like kernels "stripped [of] the outer shell of things"; while music (*melos*) gives "the innermost kernel preceding all form, or the heart of things."[15] "The relation could very well be expressed in the language of the scholastics by saying that the concepts are the *universalia post rem*, but music gives the *universalia ante rem*, and reality in *universalia in re*."[16] This little scholastic encapsulation *analytically* describes the relation of *logos* to *melos*.

The Three Ages

Logos and *melos* stand side by side like two different sensibilities; the one is rational, the other is musical. Prior to both is *mythos* (story). We find in our own culture that it began with *mythos*—with Greek and biblical mythology—as the primary factor in knowledge. With Plato and Aristotle we see a shift into a new age with the birth of philosophy as a discourse of reason and with Philo of Alexandria in Judaism and later the logic of the Talmudic rabbis and the historically

109

corresponding different logic of the Church Fathers in the start of the second millennium. In Christianity, the dominant religion of the second millennium, God is called *logos* (word or reason) but associated with a person, Jesus the Christ; and this deification of language is not much different in Islam in its wake, where God actually takes to writing. The linguistic turn (as it is known) in twentieth century philosophy, which affected philosophy from top to bottom, in European philosophy and in British analytical and American pragmatic philosophy is a secular reiteration of this Christian sensibility, even if by means of it it talks about the death of God and the end of metanarrative and so on.

Christian theology as the normative discourse of Christian self-reflection or philosophy tends to mix and confuse *mythos* and *logos*. Hence the notion of Jesus the Christ as ascended into heaven (as if this could be a place) and as the Second Person of the Trinity is a mythologism, a combination of two ways of thinking, one mythical, the other rational. Mythologisms such as these (and Christian theology is wholly constructed from them) are partially dependent on conceptualization and partially dependent on naive, representational thinking of myths, legends and fairy tales; so, for example, heaven as a place is naive representational thinking, as is Jesus' bodily ascension there and his sitting at the right hand of the Father, but the idea that Jesus ascended, the idea of the heavenly nature of the body, and the idea of Jesus' intimacy with God like Father and son are all conceptually and philosophically meaningful. Creation, revelation and redemption are complex mythologisms, that is, they compress whole sets of different mythologisms. They involve rational conceptualization (*logos*) but they depend totally on story thinking (*mythos*) behind them for their proper understanding and explanation.

The new age (which we might associate with the new millennium, more or less), according to Schopenhauer's continuation of Kant's philosophy, is marked by *a shift from* logos *to* melos, just as Christianity marked a shift from *mythos* to *logos*. The age of *melos* is the age we are coming into, marked by consciousness of the limits of reason, and of human consciousness's *being beyond* reasoning, while of course still dependent upon it, in the same way that *logos* is beyond *mythos* in Christianity, but also dependent upon it. So in a simile that is often used of this, the change we are speaking of is like growing up from infancy to childhood, to adolescence, to young adulthood, and so on.

Freud, the founder of psychoanalysis, although very rational in many ways, in his discovery of the unconscious and of the whole psychological domain of being, was among the first major post-Schopenhauerian figures to move beyond the "age of reason" of Enlightenment thinking and Western religious mythologisms. Jung, more mythologically inclined than his old colleague, Freud, was another Schopenhauerian figure. Adorno was another. His melancholy *Minima Moralia* is the opposite of Nietzsche's mad humanism in *The Gay Science*. In *The Dialectic of Enlightenment* (1947) Adorno and Horkheimer (who co-wrote it) show how rationality pushed to its logical conclusion flips into the irrational. There is hardly anyone alive in Western society today who would not have been a witness themselves to this fact, which Kafka famously lampooned in his stifling novels. We all know today that what starts out as sensible legislation soon becomes red tape and endless bureaucracy, and then patches to the red tape, and justice commissions, and so on and so forth, spawning more of the same tape and so on, endlessly, until we have a great tangle and in some places a *culture* of lawsuits. It all started out rationally but, before long, became cleverly mad. The French Revolution preached equality, liberty and fraternity for all, and within a decade it was chopping heads off. This is the "dialectic of Enlightenment." I mention this as evidence from philosophy (though this may not be a privileged place) of a few of the many figures who work beyond reason, but not yet in the time of *melos*; although some may argue otherwise with respect to Adorno, the student of the composer Alban Berg as well as a philosopher.

With our newfound disillusion with reason (not that it is bad but it has to work within limits that reason itself cannot give, and reason is certainly not God nor are we, we realize, essentially rational animals), we are then at the end of an age. Hence (with our jaded sensibility), we no longer call ourselves "modern," or believe ourselves capable of bringing about a Brave New World; rather we call ourselves postmodern or postsecular. We are "post-," which is to say we are "over it" or "passed it." This is a mark of uncertainty. Certainty and clarity were hallmarks of the old age of reason that set itself apart from the Christian *mythos* from the seventeenth century. Uncertainty is a hallmark of the new age. Uncertainty is not such a bad thing we realize; it is fanatics and madmen who are most certain. Psychologically, "I don't know" is a sign of mental and inner health.[17]

Schopenhauer's philosophy, which moves beyond reason, but which is not "dialectic" so not irrational, teaches that ours is a time for *melos* and therefore, *listening*. And if we listen we will wake up from our submergence in the philosophies tied to *logos* and (by virtue of that) to the logocentric age. So we say, *all meditation is a form of listening*. When we wake up we awaken from the sleep of reason, as once we did from the dream of *mythos*. Awake, we realize that we cannot be slaves to stories, and we cannot be slaves to thinking; we are beyond our stories (if they are only stories) and we *are not* our thinking (Descartes was wrong). Awake, we realize that our reason *must serve us*, and if we are in service to reason, or if our thoughts are merely servicing reason to allow it to become more widespread, more embedded in the soul of the world, it will only lead to violence and fragmentation, as it has been doing. Thinking does not lead the way, as Hegel taught, and as twentieth-century "intellectuals" believed and as Hegelians and intellectuals still hold strongly.[18]

The three ages—*mythos, logos, melos*—are not sequential. Let us not forget that the old religions that remember *mythos* and *logos* also remember *melos*. For example, the Talmud, one would have thought, belonged quintessentially to the age of *logos* as an enormous body of religious text; but this is not so because, in the little study houses dating from ancient Babylon and Palestine, where Talmud/Torah was studied—study houses which still exist today in Israel and New York and elsewhere—*the texts were, and are, sung*. Melody is the essence of Talmud, not halakah (law-*logos*) or haggadah (lore-*mythos*).[19] Or, for example in Islam: from when I lived in Jerusalem, one of my unforgettable memories was hearing the Koran sung, and it was beautiful. I lived in earshot of several muezzin and heard all the prayers day and night, year after year. Or, for example, Eastern Orthodox Christian theology: it is essentially *liturgical*, and so *sung*. Or, for example, the Catholic Church: it has been the greatest sponsor of music, and Western art music finds its origin within its heart.

On the other hand, scientism and rationalism cannot be sung: they have no *melos*, no soul, scarcely any *mythos*. They are *logos* alone, a chip off the old block of the Protestant spirit, of "faith alone" and "Scripture only." In the first millennium the *De Fide Orthodoxa* by St. John of Damascus (650–754), a huge synthesis of Christian patristic theology, was able to be rewritten by him as hymns. But the *Summa Theologica* of St. Thomas Aquinas (1225–1274), the equivalent text in the West, could not be set to music or sung, and there is a symbolism in this difference: a loss of *melos*. St. Thomas's work, while seeming to sum up the past, was also a precursor of the dominant rationalism and scientism of the age to come, the second millennium.

According to Schopenhauer, the keynote of the new cultural consciousness of *melos* will be *harmony*. The metaphysics of nostalgia is a prevision of the metaphysics of harmony. Harmony is perfectly reasonable, but it is *beyond reason* as well, because *harmony cannot be syllogized*. Given the criteria of the angels—"peace and goodwill on earth"[20]—the furthest spiritual reaches of the old *logos* culture are *communio* and *concilium*, but these fall short of harmony. They only prefigure it, the way the Old Testament is interpreted as prefiguring the New. In Latin *communio* and *concilium* could be syllogized down to fine theological detail and Christianity was perfectly "watertight" in the catechisms; but a new age has to do, as Jesus said, not with old wine in new skins, but *new wine* in new wineskins.[21] Schopenhauer saw this new wine as made in the East (India and the Far East) and coming west; he tasted new wine already in Kant and developed it in his own work that builds upon Kant.

We still judge the new wine on the taste of the old. When it comes to metaphysics, Schopenhauer writes, "those who stood considerably nearer to the beginning of the human race and to the original source of organic nature than do we, also possessed both greater energy of the intuitive faculty of knowledge and a more genuine disposition of mind. They were thus capable of a purer and more direct comprehension of the inner essence of nature, and were thus in a position to satisfy the need for metaphysics in a more estimable manner."[22] Thus Lao Tzu had said earlier: "On the decline of the great Tao, the doctrines of 'humanity' and 'justice' arose. When knowledge and cleverness appeared, great hypocrisy followed in its wake."[23] He said this because he knew—as we are rediscovering after an age of *logos*—that justice and humanity as values already signify a loss of harmony, a loss of the power of music and a loss of the ability to hear it.

Schopenhauer had ancient high culture in mind when he spoke of "those who stood considerably nearer to the beginning of the human race and to the original source of organic nature than do we." He did not have in mind the archaic dark cruelty beneath the skein of civilization, which is itself not free from primitive motives and lies, such as depicted by Joseph Conrad's *The Heart of Darkness* (1899), set in London and the Congo, or by Werner Herzog's *Fitzcarraldo* (1982), where the main character unforgettably played by Klaus Kinski hopes to redeem the deadly reaches of the savage Peruvian jungle with the glorious Italian opera singing of Caruso, as if to prove that the human emotional depths plumbed by Caruso runs deeper than the eponymous heart of darkness.

In this regard we might better think of *mythos*, *logos* and *melos* as three hedges around the heart of darkness, that protect us from ourselves and bar us from such descents as that described by Conrad's narrator, Marlowe. From this more Spenglerian point of view *melos* would never be more than another way of keeping head above water.

Wagner's Continuation of Schopenhauer

"Art," Schopenhauer wrote as a young man, "is not, like science [i.e. extrinsic forms of knowledge], merely concerned with the reasoning powers, but with the innermost nature of man, in which each must count merely for what he is in reality. Now this will be the case with my philosophy, *for it is intended to be philosophy as art*."[24] We need to remember this, reading Schopenhauer—and I think artistic souls are drawn to him. His philosophy, like an artwork is more akin to a revelation than a treatise, although it is methodically set out and argued as a conventional treatise might be. But as Schopenhauer would be the first to warn us, *do not be deceived by appearances*.

Wagner, talking in a letter of 1854 of his *Ring* cycle, wrote:

> We must learn to die, and to die in the fullest sense of the word . . . The fear of the end is the source of all lovelessness, and this fear is generated only when love itself begins to wane. How came it that this feeling which imparts the highest blessedness to all things living was so far lost sight of by the human race that at last it came to this: all that mankind did, ordered, and established was conceived only in fear of the end. My poem sets this forth.[25]

To die "and to die in the fullest sense of the word" is to put soul before self, soulfulness before selfishness. Soulfulness enjoins the whole world. Wagner's music is the absolute drama music of soulfulness in this sense. It eschews all lovelessness and fear. His music dramas convey the wholeness of life and death, their intimacy with each other and their different kind of blessings. Their difficulties we know already.

In music drama, Wagner affirmed what Schopenhauer set forth philosophically: the realization that music is at the heart of the world, at the heart of our inner life and at the heart of the culture to come, in a world that is dawning. Of course, we know with hindsight the new age to come got stopped in its tracks and Western culture got knocked off course. Schopenhauer and Wagner could not have foreseen this. They have however left their work, by which we can reorient and reattune ourselves and find our way back to where we were before the disaster.

In *The Art-Work of the Future* (1849), Wagner described his dream of the future of culture with art at the center. But the dream was lost by the disastrous events of the twentieth century. Even now, it is as if people deliberately misread Wagner, as if they do not want to see what he foresaw. The artist of the future will not be a lone ranger. The arts of the future will be collaborative. This will be the difference between the age of classical music and the new art, of which art music will be a core participant. Wagner's music dramas are not the end of the classical tradition or the culmination of something: they are the seed of the new, a primitive and quite rudimentary seed compared to what we will do, so he thought. But his works nevertheless give us pointers in several respects. They are rooted in folk consciousness—what we today would call popular consciousness. That is to say they are fundamentally *inclusive* in extent and intent and in gathering up *mythos* and *logos* into a heavy bundle to begin with. His art of the future is replete with the holiness of the past. The art will in this sense collaborate with the audience.

This new art consciousness that speaks of the people is quite different from our idea of popular in terms of mass audience. By "folk" in the future sense given to the term by Wagner, he meant people whose sensibility is awoken to art, one soul at a time. This is not a mass audience, but a collective participation: people held together by a sense of the common good and led by artists, not politicians, who are not creative, whose job is subservient. However, more of this anon, in Chapter 8, "Wagner and World Music." For the present, we must return to the theme of time and our experience of it, which is history.

The Aesthetic Turn

Between Bach (1685–1750) and Beethoven (1770–1827) one would have thought there would be a continuity and development in music, and usually we think of music history in these terms, but there is as much if not more truth in the theory of discontinuity. Jürgen Lawrenz identifies a break, or what he calls a "Copernican revolution of aesthetics," between the time of Bach and the time of Beethoven, in the second half of the eighteenth century. He would not be alone in perceiving the facts of the history of music—that there was a development of the art in the latter part of the eighteenth century, around the time of Rameau and Rousseau. What Lawrenz is saying, however, goes a step further. He equates the changes in music in the late eighteenth century in regard to aesthetics with the changes in philosophy (associated with Kant) in regard to epistemology (the theory of knowledge). The name of Copernicus is associated with a shift of perspective from one where the earth is the center of the universe, to a perspective in which the sun is the center of our solar system—in other words, a relativization of the overly human-centered Christian perspective of the Middle Ages. Revelation is shown as wrong with respect to truth and reality in a major way, and this proved a problem for religion of the time. Kant did something similar for knowledge in the *Critique of Pure Reason* (1781), for scientific and normative thinking in showing that space, time and causality are not "things" we can know about "out there," but they are the conditions of knowledge and belong to our cognitive constitution. Kant did not mean to suggest knowledge is "subjective," given that the conditions for knowledge are the same for everyone (space, time and causality); rather, knowledge, he argued, is what he called "transcendental," neither subjectively "in here" nor objectively "out there," neither immanent (in us) nor transcendent (over and above us and therefore "despite" us). Kant's discoveries are still an intellectual event on the way, coming to us out of the future, given that his discoveries seem not to have fully bedded down into our language yet—but then we still happily talk of sunrise and sunset as well, knowing full well there is no such thing any more, only metaphorically. But that aside, Lawrenz's argument is that, in the late eighteenth century, our ears changed due to music, just like the conditions of knowledge changed due to philosophy—and at the same time—and music has not been the same since.

Lawrenz summarizes the shift in the following breakdown:

- From an understanding of music as primarily vocal to primarily instrumental;
- From mimetic/representational to "absolute";
- From entertainment and service to "work of art" status;
- From harmonic innocence to harmonic density (harmony as an integrated semantic feature);
- From imitative/accumulative structuring to structuring in dynamic contrasts;
- From the nature of a musical "theme" to a "subject."[26]

Let us have just a brief look at these, one by one. Western art music started in the Catholic Church, to accompany the voice. The "Copernican turn" of aesthetics was prefigured in the fifteenth century by Burgundian choristers who developed skills in counterpoint with voices, treating the voices more like instruments, and embedding all kinds of esoteric meanings for the initiated, rather than by seeing the words as important. Here *melos* exceeds *logos* for the first time in history, but it will not be the last time. For example, Lawrenz notes, the *cantus firmus* of Ockeghem's *Ecce ancilla Domini* "contained 662 notes and 993 rests; and the whole work is presented as a musical image of the cross by the divisibility of all its structured elements by 5. The relationship between words and music is planned in a similarly exacting manner, their coincidence displaying a ratio of 2:3." Ultimately, with the demise of the Burgundian empire—which, in the midfifteenth century stretched from the Low Countries in the north, all the way south through the German lands to Italy—and with the reforming Catholic Council of Trent (given that Rome had just lost the whole of the north of Europe to the Protestants), *logos* came to be reasserted over *melos* (word over music) so that words had to go back to being distinguishable in liturgical worship. The Roman composer Palestrina went some way on behalf of *melos* to restore a balance by having richly textured voices in which the words were perfectly "transparent."

In the latter part of the eighteenth century there were two views of music vis-à-vis words, summed up here by the composers Gluck and Mozart. Gluck: "I have endeavored to return music to its true vocation, which is to serve poetry." Mozart: "In an opera, poetry can be none other than the obedient daughter of music."[27] Here I quote at length from one of Lawrenz's unpublished manuscripts:

> The roots of this problem emanate from Greek culture. Their idea of music (e.g. tragedy, dithyrambus) comprised an integrated unity of *harmonia, rhythmos* and *logos*. The latter was *included in music* as the expression of human reason, without which music was conceived to be incomplete.[28] We can see that this is a different emphasis from what we are used to in modern times, where the usual practice is to 'set' a text and where accordingly music has the function of accompaniment, illustration or comment. But the deeper problem was that despite the Greeks' theoretical affirmation of unity, in practice the three elements are detachable from each other; and in this segregation the *logos* claimed the upper hand and eventually exclusive privilege as the communications faculty par excellence. We have testimony from the later career of tragedy that this divorce was already accomplished by the time of Euripides, when music was used as entr'actes purely for entertainment and choral singing partially or wholly dispensed with.[29]

> One insalubrious consequence was the need to 'save' music *qua* music for aesthetics by asserting its mimetic function. This tradition has a millennia-long history that need not concern us here, except to note that Kant's arguments are firmly ensconced in it.

117

Thus, as late as 1798 (when the Copernican revolution in music was already a *fait accompli*), Kant still maintained, "it is only because music serves as an instrument for poetry that it is a fine art".[30] In the *Critique of Judgment*, Kant sought to analyze the 'representational content', arriving eventually at the notion that music reproduces in an 'enhanced' way our "passionate speech." Such speech naturally inclines towards musical pitching and modulation and thus music brings an "unutterable wealth" of expression into it that is denied to the placid forms of verbal discourse.[31] The next step, however, which goes on from here to the recognition that a music that can communicate such "unutterable wealth" must have a richer content than the verbal skeleton that ostensibly it 'enhances', eluded him. The very words he used already point compellingly to music as an autonomous realm of communication, leaving us with little more to surmise than unexamined prejudices keeping his eyes and mind closed.

It is strange indeed that the German philosophers of that era, who lived and worked in the midst of the finest flowering of German music demonstrate so little affinity for it. A generation later Hegel ostensibly scuttled 'representation' and placed 'expressivity' into the driver's seat of musical aesthetics. But eventually he must define what he conceives to be the content of this expressivity, and at that moment we are rudely jolted back to a position that effectively retreats back beyond even Kant and Rousseau:

Music must, on account of its one-sidedness, call on the help of the more exact meaning of words and, in order to become more firmly conjoined with the detail and characteristic expression of the subject-matter, it demands a text which alone gives fuller content to the subjective life's outpouring . . .[32]

In short, for both Kant and Hegel it remained axiomatic that a verbal content is laid into the fabric of musical expression.[33] That music has other potential was, however, the *point of departure* for the theory that grew out of the innovations of the Copernican revolutionaries.

But from these points, a natural division of the subject matter suggests itself. For under the aegis of aesthetics a claim on behalf of music as an independent art can only arise from the concept of an *absolute music*—that is: music unpolluted by any semantics beyond itself. It must be independent not only of words, but of association with dance, theatre and even sacred services.

This substantial quotation describes the confusion and conflict between *logos* and *melos*, and how *logos* was first thought to be included in music. Even the great Kant followed Gluck. What Lawrenz does not mention are nineteen centuries of Christian theology in which *logos is deified.*[34] The millennial and religious subjugation of *melos* by *logos* is the primary reason for the confusion. *Melos* was forgotten. Theologians knew all about *logos* and *mythos*, but that was all. Absolute music is the reassertion of *melos*, pure and beautiful. Schopenhauer alone among Western philosophers—still alone among them—put *melos* before *logos* in the order of Being and knowing. And it is notable how backward is Hegel's philosophy in this regard.

The quotation from Lawrenz provides some brief account of his description of the Copernican revolution in aesthetics and of the consequential rise of absolute music. In terms of the discontinuity I mentioned previously, and which I believe to be important in understanding Lawrenz's text, absolute music is not a development on one hand or a throw-back on the other, but picks up from where the Burgundian composers broke off 300 years previously. Absolute music marks a discontinuity.

Absolute music is not like the court music of the couple of hundred years preceding it. Absolute music is not music for a purpose—and therefore *it is like* Kant's notion of the beautiful; and we have seen in Baudelaire's aesthetic, applying it now to music, that absolute music is beautiful. But *absolute music is not beautiful on the basis of some prior notion based in logos.* It is the music that attunes us to the beautiful, not some discourse that establishes it and which we then hear "evidence" of when we listen to some music. Rather, music is absolutely beautiful—*if* it is beautiful—of its own accord. If it is not beautiful, the composer has failed his or her muse, has failed *melos*, the *presence* of *melos*, because music presences *melos*. Therefore we do not know what *melos* means as a word and we cannot *say*. We can know *melos* only as music. It is music that most absolutely decides what is beautiful and what is not in this regard.

If we use music for entertainment purposes (we could include here music used in movies to titillate the emotions), then it is not absolute music, where alone, *melos* is free; or in Schopenhauer's terms, the universal will is free. With popular music today music is in thrall to lyrics and what we call music is actually words with a tune. *Melos* under the sway of *logos* again. Just as once the Church submitted *melos* to *logos* when it said that music had to support the words and the words needed to be discernible, so today in most commodity or popular music, it is all about the lyrics and most of the time there is scarcely any music present at all, or only a bare minimum. This is a much more oppressive circumstance today under secular commodity capitalist rule with their record companies than under the Medieval Church, but hardly anyone sees the comparison. Absolute music stands aside from one as from the other, in an epistemological break.

Another notable feature of listening across time is that when we listen to classical art music, we listen from the other side—our side— of the Copernican turn of aesthetics, and we listen as if the music *before* the turn were absolute music. We do not hear baroque music like people of that age would have done, even if it is played on replica instruments, and we can hardly even imagine how they would have heard it. Unless we enjoy it for some particular specialist or technical reason, one piece by Telemann or Scarlatti sounds much like any other. Lawrenz notes in his unpublished manuscript:

> The output of e.g. Vivaldi, Couperin, Tiedemann, Scarlatti, Bach, Handel is stupendous, ranging from 500 to over 1000 compositions; Beethoven in a comparable life span produced 130 works. The point made [in the text] is that post-Bach composers worked under different presuppositions. Noble patronage, on account of the servile status of music in their society, rarely challenged composers to reach for the greatest heights, being mostly content with the aural adornment of their environment. Bourgeoise patronage on the contrary arrived eventually at the point where the utmost exertion was expected from practitioners of the art. The best yardstick for this trend after 1750 is furnished by the genre of string quartet, which was considered the most prestigious in terms of 'absolute music', and here the figures speak eloquently. Thus Haydn produced 70-odd, Mozart 23, Beethoven 16, Mendelssohn less than 10, Brahms just three.

The fact here adduced is that, "Beginning with Haydn, on the contrary, a discernible trend is in evidence towards a greater emphasis on 'art' as the *mainstay* of a composer's production and accordingly the emphasis on quantity went down. That this relates in great part also to changing perceptions among their audiences goes without saying." With the voice we now know, from the research and subsequent performances of Cecilia Bartoli, that Vivaldi, before anyone, in Venice in the early eighteenth century, pushed through the baroque into absolute music, using the voice purely musically, with an utter abandon and dexterity that in fact no one has come anywhere near rivaling since.

The move from harmonic innocence to harmonic density indicates a wholly new consciousness of what music is: music has come out of servitude and into its own, no longer playing "on a theme" but according to the reality of its own subjectivity as *music*, of a score as musical, of a composer as a creator. There are a lot of technical changes that go along with all this, as might be well imagined. We might mention one major change as an example. Works became more "individuated" by the discovery of instrumental melody and, along with that, the harmonic field of a melody was found to have immense power if it were musically explored. Rosen writes, "The two principal sources of musical energy are dissonance and sequence—the first because it demands resolution, the second because it implies continuation. The classical style immeasurably increased the power of dissonance, raising it from an unresolved interval to an unresolved chord and then to an unresolved key."[35] Citing Rosen, Lawrenz compares the dissonances in a Bach overture with the dissonances in a Haydn quartet. Dissonances occur in each but only to give interest to the sections that are all, otherwise, in the same key. And this is *Bach*, a supreme master musician, while lesser composers (everyone else) would have avoided dissonance and stuck to the known modes, indebted to the intervallic schemata of the Greeks (Dorian, Lydian, etc.). "In a Haydn quartet, on the other hand, the directional impulse arises from the propulsive force of an *exposed* dissonance, whose strength is such that it cannot be resolved at once, but requires modulation into another key; and this procedure, applied repeatedly, is precisely the element which conveys the sense of dramatic action."[36]

Lawrenz finishes the unpublished manuscript I have been quoting with these words:

> Today, this 'Copernican' turn has become part of the unseen furniture of aesthetic theories. All present-day suppositions derive ultimately from that era; and significantly none refers beyond it to an earlier theoretical platform. Acknowledgement of the men who pioneered that spirit is grudging at best, and in any case reserved almost entirely to music historical literature. But as philosophers we should cultivate an awareness of this genesis, for if we philosophize about music and art today in an historical vacuum, we put ourselves at the mercy of (at least) incognizance of the roots of modern aesthetic thinking.[37]

Schopenhauer Reprise

What is not clear in Schopenhauer, with his equation of will and music, is that it is not the music in itself or "as such" that is "metaphysical," but that the music *gives*. What the music gives—*if* it gives—is what matters. It is only art music that gives. Its greatness is *in its giving.* Much old religious music is great in this respect, as the secular lovers of Bach will tell you. First of all, music gives peace of heart—and in a thousand ways. Every way pertains in one way or another to harmony—and I mean harmony in the most developed sense to include all the seeming departures "beyond" harmony, but which actually only confirm it by presupposing it. Musical spontaneity and spontaneous music are only artificially distinguished from art music.

What we hear in the music that quells the tumult of the soul is beautiful, true and good, in terms of *melos;* these are not three but are harmonized as one and may be heard note by note and verified by the soul. The music *is* this truth, goodness and beauty; they are not *qualities* of the music. As qualities of the music, the beauty and goodness of it may be technically verified, and then the truth of them is technical and harmony domesticated; but harmony is essentially free and tied to the creative capacity for inspiration in the composer *and in the listener.* Therefore the truth, good and beauty of music, whatever else these three may be, are free and irreducible. What we *listen for* however can vary, depending on our sensibility. But however we listen, in whichever of the seven sensibilities or combination of them,[38] we always listen in the moment. Listening is the way that the power of the present moment *opens up.* The music happens in the moment, moment by moment; the listener listens between two spaces: that of the awareness of the present moment and her self-presence in it, and *the all-moment,* which is how our soul feels the eternity to which the moment is bound. It may be harder to hear if we are being swept around by the notes in inner space; quieter music might be better in this regard, as it is naturally closer to stillness. But in Beethoven's symphonies, for example, for all the welter and conflict, the all-moment is there. The musical key is *keyed to* it.

It is from the key point or the power point of the moment that harmonies, melodies, and dissonances flow and assail our ears and we receive what is true, good and beautiful, which is what music gives. This is why music *makes* peace, as if a spell is poured over us. We are spellbound. We need to be so in this life. This is how we experience (and therefore learn) about the peace that passes all understanding. In the Gospel, Jesus speaks of this peace in the first person singular: "I give you peace, *my peace* I give you."[39] He associates this peace with himself, and he can because he knows it and the kind of love that is bound up in it—but Jesus never said this love and peace was *agape* (which is the Greek translation).[40] We actually *do not have the word for it. No logos!*

We can hear it. Across time, this is what we listeners listen to. It comes to us as music, when music is metaphysics, which it is not always. We listen to and we hear the peace that the world needs, to which words do not suffice, and that *as action* is related to *good will.* And behind this peace, in the innermost inaccessible recesses of the music, further back, a whole other horizon of wisdom and love. In the *mythos* of the Gospel, Jesus speaks of this as his Father's house and as the place that therefore we do not know yet, but that we will know: he goes before us, he says, to prepare a place.

It is ironic that the age we live in speaks so much and so highly of connectivity, yet it is the most unconnected of all ages. But that is not because it is a dark age (Heidegger) or an age in irredeemable decline (Spengler) but because it is *an age of transition.* Many people have a sense of this. And so in music we have musicians who bridge the three ages of *mythos, logos* and *melos.* Musically ours is the most exciting time.

> *We have called Music the revelation of the*
> *inner vision of the Essence of the world.*
> —Richard Wagner, "Beethoven"

7

Beethoven and Absolute Music

It is an enchanted state we fall into
when listening to a genuine work of Beethoven's.
—Richard Wagner, "Beethoven"

Our accent in this chapter on some of Beethoven's music is on exaltation and rapture. Exaltation and rapture extend our feel for soul's sensibilities. Religion has much to say on exaltation and rapture, for we seem to feel our divinity in these states. "God," as Meister Eckhart says, is "the heaven of the soul,"[1] and surely that signifies exaltation and rapture. We recall that we are thinking of the soul here not as some supernatural entity or some mysterious bit of us such as the pineal gland, such as some philosophers have imagined, but rather we are thinking of the soul as the unison of our inner sensibilities and sensitivity. The height of sensibility—musically speaking—is divine human experience. As human, I am not divine by definition; however, as a listener I can hear what is divine. Eckhart says, "The highest power of the soul is called an inextinguishable light because of the vision the soul has in his power."[2] The lower soul attuned to the greed body is emotionally keyed to the world round about and to foraging for possessions there; only through sensibility will lower soul grow into higher soul. The greed body is what holds the soul in thrall to bad taste. We experience the greed body as incessantly wanting this or that object to satisfy desire.[3]

In Western (basically Christian) culture, the higher soul has been associated with rational thought-forms and people have been utterly possessed by these thought-forms, as if there is nothing higher than what they think. For example, the thought-form called "God." But sensibility can go beyond the objectification of thought-forms, and what we have seen called *melos* marks the next height of the soul against the backdrop of the absolute. Eckhart, following Eriugena and St. Dionysius and others, called this height, above the stream of thinking and its objectifications, "nothingness." But this "nothingness" is not that of the calculative thinker, where nothing is "no thing," for example, a zero bank balance. Nothingness here refers to the Angel of the Presence, or, in plainer English, to what we might call *pure Presence*— what simply *is* here and now; in Kant's language, *apperception*. This is the consciousness that accompanies being, but is beyond being as such. Sensibility reaches up into this height of nothingness as into the human absolute, for the present moment is absolute in its hereness and nowness; it is timeless; it is still. When sensibility touches into the timeless Presence, it sees the dogmas of rational reason and beliefs for what they are: time-bound, *relative*.

Knowledge is relative—always relative to the world and values and desire, and so on. Sensibility reaches into the pure Presence of the absolute *melos*. "Absolute music," a term that came to be used in the nineteenth century by those who understood what we are saying here (but was thought to be "romantic" by those who did not understand) is *melos set free*—*melos* set free from *logos*—music that is the form of itself, not the form of something else. *Absolute music is music that sounds the inner being of the world.* Absolute music is music as metaphysics. Absolute music has its precursors: famously, Bach, Haydn, and Mozart, but music becomes absolute music in no uncertain terms through the genius of Beethoven. And that is what we are going to discuss in an introductory way.

Here we will discuss Beethoven's symphonies in the particular light of sensibility, with an accent on *learning sensibility*. We will talk of Beethoven's symphonies not because they are his musical credo, or "last word" musically, for they are not; but because of how, through them, we can learn to listen absolutely, which means wakefully, watchfully, in an otherworldly or inspired way.

Exaltation and Rapture

In what follows we shall listen to Beethoven as aesthetic experience and try to chart this happening. Overall the mood is one of exaltation and rapture. There are two kinds of exaltation or rapture. One of enjoyment that is intimate, which is not writ large, but writ small, and winds inward, and savors of *anima*. The other kind is an exuberant and out-thrusting *animus*. Listening to Beethoven's nine symphonies is a way of sensibility for exaltation and rapture; taken together they comprise a showing of Music herself (*melos*), and of human greatness or genius in this regard.

Beethoven's nine symphonies form a ladder for the development of height in sensibility.[4] Listening to them in order, the inner sensibility and sensitivity heighten, and listening to these symphonies as a sequence and life work of Beethoven is a way of soulfulness. My explanation therefore will not be technical—there are plenty of technical accounts available already—but our account shall be, as I say, in terms of *aesthetic experience*, because, as far as listening goes, this will suffice. The end is exaltation and rapture, or, in Beethoven's words, "joy through suffering."[5]

The arts and music critic W. J. Turner has said:

> It is a peculiarity of Beethoven that he can use the words "best" and "noblest" without making an intelligent man laugh up his sleeve . . . The very words "good," "noble," "spiritual," "sublime," have all become in our time synonymous with humbug. In Beethoven's music they take on a new and tremendous significance and not all the corrosive acid of the most powerful intellect and the profoundest skepticism can burn through them into any leaden substratum. They are gold throughout.[6]

To get the power of the aesthetic experience this music offers, we have to come to the symphonies with fresh ears. We should abstain from listening to any other music for a day or two in order to clean the inner ears, as it were, and so to approach our listening with expectation, as we would approach something with proven healing properties that would restore us were we unwell.

Many of us would have heard all or parts of these symphonies before, and know portions of them well; or possibly we have heard snatches of them in advertisements for products or television shows, and so on. However, we will try to listen properly, as if for the first time, as if we did not know the subsequent changes in music, soul, and society.

Roman Rolland, like Berlioz, another great listener of Beethoven, provides beginners with some orientation about how to listen to symphonic music like this.

> Let me remind the reader who has not much technical knowledge of music what the *Durchführung* of a sonata or a symphony is. It signifies the "Middle Empire,"—the section between the first exposi-

tion (and repeat) of the themes and their final conclusive return. It is here that the creative imagination gives itself up to the constructive manipulation of the stated motives which it transposes and combines in twenty different ways. Ever since the *Eroica* [Beethoven's Third Symphony] this section has been the peculiar field of genius (often it remains unoccupied!). There the composer lives and moves at the very centre of the cosmos of his thought, like the God who takes in his hand the substance of the worlds and projects it into moving architectures, suspended above the void.[7]

The term *Durchfürung* means "development section." The music invariably starts introducing a theme, recapitulates it in another key with a bit of variation, returns to the original key (tonic), and then the development section starts. This is what we are listening for, as Rolland suggests. Here is where the greatness of musical imagination lies. Here is where *melos* is explored and here is where sensibility is developed through listening. Beethoven is the subject of this chapter because he was the experimenter and master of development *par excellence*. Of course he harks back to his own master, Bach, who was of the same stature but lived in a different world musically.[8] Bach composed before the Copernican revolution of aesthetic experience that we spoke of in the last chapter, and Beethoven belongs after it, to our period essentially. So that even when we listen to Bach today, we listen with "Beethovian ears," even if we do not mean to, because the aesthetic shift has entered our culture and is constitutive of our capacity for aesthetic experience.

What in particular we listen for happens to us over time. It is possible to listen to Beethoven's *Durchfürung* repeatedly; it never becomes banal. It is like living with a view of Sydney Harbour from the north; one never gets tired or bored of it. One never takes it for granted. Other views from a window, however, we can stop really seeing after a while. People can have paintings worth millions hanging in their living room and if they are bad art you will not notice them after a while, unless they are really atrocious. Someone I knew had a huge David Hockney painting of a Californian swimming pool in his living room in Belgravia in London and you had to look at it every time you went into the room. The painting demanded it. And every time I saw it, it was like the first time. Even now, almost thirty years later, I can still see it in my mind's eye. The painting had an aura and a gaze. With great developments within a piece it is just the same: each time you hear it you rediscover it. That is why it is great; "great" is not an empty word at all, as ideologues and clever people suppose. With mediocre music it is different. With second-rank music—even if it is still esteemed and valued—you become accustomed to it; Grieg, for example, is like this. He is a good composer but with repeated listening you ascertain the belts and pulleys.

First Symphony, in C Major

It is 1800, the dawn of a new century; you are hearing this for the first time. Up until now, the music of Haydn and Mozart is the most progressive you have ever heard—some of it in fact, for this reason, is not to your taste.

But to get into this imaginative space (and, at some stage, this listening space) and to listen to Beethoven, as I have indicated already, we need to sanitize our ears from modern music and modern culture. Our ears are accustomed—*glutted* even—with emotionally provocative music, beat- and drum-driven music, post-Romantic harmonies, background music, and television noise. We have music going on all around us, nearly all of it to accompany something else, be it shopping or driving, having fun, being entertained, waiting somewhere, or wandering around the mall in a daze. We have to practice some silence and withdrawal from the surrounding assault on our senses to become sensitive to the spring water of this symphony. Then we will hear the thing that startled audiences out of their seats in 1800.

If we listen to the start of the symphony, the first bar or two, what do we hear? These are the first notes, before taking the key of C Major, we might reply. Perhaps this is a musical "signature" stamp Beethoven is making at the start. It is true, we hear a few notes before Beethoven picks up the key, but *what kind of notes?* If we were technical we might say a discord. But we are not technical and that answer does not speak to our sensibility. What our sensibility tells us is that these notes *open something up*. Technically, if there is a discord, what follows needs to resolve it by finding the right key; and for the sensibility, if something is opened up, then something is establishing itself as being opened: in other words, the notes *pique our curiosity straight away*. But what do they "tell" us? What do they communicate? If we knew the answer, we would say: The symphony does not begin with a statement: it begins with a *question*.[9] The notes ask a question or, put another way, wear a quizzical expression on their face. The first notes get us wondering. The music is *as if* we were opening a fairy tale book for the first time, or gently pushing an open door ajar for us to peek inside. What is

129

there? In the next few bars, the next few notes, the door opens a little wider, and then finally the door fully opens. Note that, just before that last push, the curiosity is intensified by a fourfold repetition of the chord that demands to be resolved into C major. A musician would say (simplifying): Beethoven does not commence with a statement of the tonality, but with chords that *lead into* a tonality—into the book, or into the room. And so, in a sense, he is claiming a new world for himself that he will conquer, a new story of the soul that he will unfold. What brazen confidence of a youngster, who had by no means the technical wherewithal at that stage to make good on his promise! But we know that he went on to do just that!

The rest is very Haydnesque. It is vivacious and full of interest. There is a freshness and hopefulness about it, a fluency of musical ideas, a continuous unabated flow of melodies, phrases and contrasts, and undoubted talent in this new composer. It is natural that the symphony should be Haydnesque: Haydn was Beethoven's teacher; this symphony represents, so to speak, his "masterpiece" in the old craftsman's tradition, denoting that he was now a fully grown member of the fraternity as whose head Haydn was universally acknowledged.

The symphony stands on the past and points to the future—at least retrospectively we know this and I think we can hear it. This work is a first flower; "this is not Beethoven," says Berlioz, "but we are shortly to discover him."[10] For the present, we can only guess what this first revelation hides. In 1800 Beethoven was thirty years old. This is mature work if we remember how much Mozart had written by the time he was that age, and that Schubert was dead at the age of thirty-one.

Second Symphony, in D Major

If the First Symphony sounds Haydnesque, the Second sounds Mozartian. It has a tenderness and verve. It is clear and bright from start to finish. The spirit of this symphony is freer than that of the First.

The Second was composed in the year when Beethoven was forced to recognize the symptoms that would point, ten years later, to complete deafness. The Mozartian melancholy is mingled, in the two last movements, with an occasional grim resolve. Beethoven could be quite raucous; and there are passages here suggestive of him throwing a rock through a window, even a shadow of that famous utterance, "I will grab fate by the throat!"

Ostensibly, Beethoven wrote this symphony in a very depressed state, such that he wrote a will; "I would have put an end to my life, only art it was that withheld me. Ah! It seemed impossible to leave this world until I had produced all that I felt called upon to produce, and so I endured this wretched existence."[11] Though he felt he walked through the shadow of the valley of death, Beethoven had joy deeper in his soul.

> His old style no longer contented him. Conventional religion Beethoven had none, but his mind was beginning to search into the deeper mysteries of the universe at the same time as he recognized the mission within himself which he must fulfill. The musician must be a liberator of mankind from sorrow.[12]

This redemptive theme is what listening to Beethoven's nine symphonies, one by one, gradually brings us as by a Ladder of *Melos*, for it is in a dimension of height in sensibility here that we move. The symphony shows that *biography* is no guide at all to understanding *inspiration*. "In this work everything is noble, energetic and stately," writes Hector Berlioz.[13]

The polarity we hear right through Beethoven's symphonies, but especially here, between the active and energetic, and the idyllic, is like a male/female polarity. It makes for "realism." The work starts, Emil Ludwig writes, "with a gesture of regal self-confidence."[14] The first movement is long and "masculine," to be followed by the beautiful, tender larghetto, "the pastoral character of which takes on the character of a dialogue between the strings and wind instruments." This is of "such heartfelt meaning," Ludwig goes on, "that the English used it for a psalm and put it in their hymnals."[15] "In the gruff Scherzo [third movement], with an inserted peasant dance in Haydn's best manner, the listener is startled by the novel contrast between fortissimo and pianissimo."[16] The male/female polarity and relation plays out further in the last movement.

Berlioz says, "everything in this symphony is genial, even the warlike sallies of the first allegro being exempt from violence."[17]

Third Symphony, in E Flat Major ("Eroica")

Beethoven's first two symphonies have eased us into the concert milieu of the new century. A young man, headstrong and ambitious, rattles at the doors and windows of the aristocratic musical establishment; but although his noble sponsors complain of his unruliness, his bad taste and his ill manners, the music remains within the bounds of tradition.

Everyone recognizes that the "Eroica" Symphony is something different. This is the new era, as Wagner would recognize. Rather as we are in this book, in *A Happy Evening* he and his friend R. discuss "the innermost questions of art."[18]

Wagner holds, as we do, to the dimension of height. Our Ladder of *Eros* as far as music is concerned is a Ladder of *Melos*. Perhaps the Ladder of *Eros* is essentially a Ladder of *Melos*; however, *these "essentials" are just metaphors*. The friend "R." and Wagner compare Beethoven and Mozart. They do not argue or "engage in dialogue"; they enlarge upon one another's insights, each adding to each. R. says:

> Beethoven immensely enlarged the form of symphony when he discarded the proportions of the older musical 'period,' which had attained their utmost beauty in Mozart, and followed his impatient genius with bolder but ever more conclusive freedom to regions reachable by *him* alone; as he also knew to give these soaring flights a philosophical coherence, it is undeniable that upon the basis of the Mozartian symphony he reared a wholly new artistic genre, which he at like time perfected in every point.[19]

The "Eroica" is music at a next level up from Mozart and enjoins listening at a new height. This is not to say it is "better" in the sense of our preference for one or the other: in the human spirit higher can mean of greater service, and this is the sense here. At the level of taste, Mozart and Beethoven are different; with regard to height, Beethoven is the more imposing. R. goes on:

> Beethoven would have been unable to achieve all this, had Mozart not previously addressed his conquering genius to the symphony too; had his animating, idealizing breath not breathed a spiritual warmth into the soulless forms and diagrams accepted until then.[20]

The key to the difference is intrinsic; with respect to inspiration:

> Mozart's music flowed from none but a musical source, that his inspiration started from an indefinite inner feeling, which, even had he had a poet's faculty, could never have been conveyed in words, but always and exclusively in tones. I am speaking of those inspirations that arise in the musician simultaneously with his melodies, with his tone-figures. Mozart's music bears the characteristic stamp of this instantaneous birth, and it is impossible to suppose that he would ever have drafted the plan of a symphony, for instance, whereof he had not all the themes, and in fact the entire structure as we know it, already in his head. On the other hand, I cannot help thinking that Beethoven first

planned the order of a symphony according to a certain philosophical idea, before he left it to his fantasy to invent the musical themes.[21]

The little door being stealthily opened in the first bars of the first movement reveals a landscape of unprecedented grandeur; and the music unleashes an expressive power of absolute music that has no precedent and has not since been equaled—that is Beethoven's legacy.[22]

It is as if the cosmos had opened itself to Beethoven's gaze.

Firstly, consider his *Durchfürung*. As Rolland points out, it is longer than the first section by as much as two-thirds (250 bars as against 147).[23] The fact is that the first movement is the longest single span of music written up to this date (17 to 20 minutes). Technically and theoretically it is incorrect because of the disproportion it brings to the whole, but creatively it is brilliant and loved, even devotedly. As Rolland points out, even the concept of "development" hardly holds here.[24] Holding such a giant structure together demanded resources of new invention and technique that had not previously existed. Unlike the long movements of later composers (Bruckner, Mahler) wishing to imitate this feat, there is not a moment in this musical flow that is "fill-up" or "padding." Also, unlike subsequent long flows, as in Mahler, who will put in a song or a dance or two, and rely heavily on long repetitions, Beethoven's first movement is part of a *whole*. It all adds up to something and, in that sense, everything "means" something. But we do not realize this until the finale.

The sense that this restless inventiveness conveys is of a torrent carrying you along—a headlong plunge into an outpouring of masculine power glorifying its ecstatic flexing. The listener who can hear this with attention and not be transported, enthused, carried aloft into a brilliant heaven, would have to be deaf to music. So, to open our ears in the right way, we need to be attentive listeners, time-consuming listeners, listeners with nothing better to do. This will give rise to greater musicians and their greater inspiration in *melos* because there is a symbiosis: the two are linked, mysteriously.

To this supreme flight of an incandescent imagination, in the first movement, the perfect counterfoil is the slow, grave tread of a funeral march, in the second movement, in which the profound grief over the mortality of human heroism acquires voice, and physiognomy.

To put this point another way: composers prior to the "Classical era" had basically just one way to keep a momentum going: to write a sequence of repetitive chords designed to change key and then repeat the material from the previous section with floriations. There are thousands of examples of this; it is the element that makes so much Bach, Handel, and earlier music sound "motoric." Around the time of the "Eroica," Beethoven had fully discarded this technique in favor of key changes that have a "physiognomy" of their own and are therefore intrinsically communicative, full of emotional and spiritual impact.

Secondly, before Beethoven, themes "represented" certain states of soul; for example, to express grief, a composer might write a "stepladder" B minor sequence (for example, Bach, *Cruxifixus*; Purcell, *Dido's Lament*), but this was largely formulaic and easily degenerated in the hands of lesser composers into a mere routine. Beethoven's themes are individualized and each appears like a face; and, like a face, they can change the mood infinitely with tiny adjustments to the shape of the melody or tune. Beethoven's "Eroica" is the first fully fledged specimen of this resource of emotion-saturated "variation," and it is of course driven by his new resource of constant modulation.

We can get some insight into Beethoven's skill with modulation. The listener can try this little home-listening experiment: listening to a recording at home, we have the experience where we need to break off for some reason and we listen for a point to stop. Even if you are in a hurry you prefer to go on a little while until a moment arrives when something tells you, "it might have finished here." Most of the time this is a chord at the end of a phrase, when something new begins (or a repetition commences). All Haydn and Mozart symphonies are like that, but many post-Beethoven symphonies are as well.

That "something new" or repetition is usually transposed into another key and therefore brings a different emotional connotation into play. When it ends, there is usually a transposition back into the original key and you feel that something has arrived "at home."

This is the issue that Beethoven surmounted. On some four, five, or six crucial junctures of this kind, he does not give you a plain chord, but a chord that is something other than "home," something that points to a new development being commenced. In itself, this procedure brings about a disequilibrium, heightens tension and expectation, and you intuitively demand the continuity he then actually supplies with new material. This "modulation," the changing of keys in a fluid and continuous way, is brilliantly achieved in this symphony.[25]

The point about Beethoven's inspiration was that it was not prompted by an idea outside the realm of music. In other words, the "thinking" here is under *melos* (music, melody, harmony) rather than *logos* (reason, thinking, conceptuality). What is "planned" is immediately apprehended by the musical imagination, or "perceived," in that language of the Schopenhauer translations for *Anschauung*. In other words, although intangible, the music comes to you as the Real. It comes from within and is perceived with the inner senses, with just as much certainty and promptitude as if some data had come from without and had been perceived through the physical senses. We perceive only *through* the physical senses in any case, not *with* them, because we are not mechanisms but *beings*. Our senses are inner to begin with. Beethoven could hear more perfectly than any of us, even while deaf. But he could hear in the one direction, inwardly, into *melos*.

Making a funeral march the second movement in a "heroic" symphony has struck many as unusual or original. Beethoven's "Eroica" was supposed to have been "planned" to celebrate Napoleon. The composer Berlioz, who was a good listener and always wrote so well about music, such that Baudelaire quotes him as an authority as well, has this to say:

> In this we see that there is no question of battles or triumphal marches such as many people, deceived by mutilations of the title naturally expect; but much in the way of grave and profound thought, of melancholy souvenirs and of ceremonies imposing by their grandeur and sadness—in a word, it is the hero's *funeral rites*. I know few examples in music of a style in which grief has been so consistently able to retain such pure form and such nobleness of expression.[26]

Roman Rolland says of the "Eroica": "let me dream my interpretation of it before you!"[27] Rolland is advocating the work of sensibility. This is the work of listening. What we interpret is "a web of successive and connected emotions" borne out of the tissue of their rhythmic and sonorous combinations in the musical progression. Such receptivity must involve our whole being, ideas and emotions together in words where they cannot be told apart. "*Let us claim the right then, to dream the work of art.*"[28] This is what we are doing in this book: nothing technical: we are claiming our right to dream the work of art. *We are doing dream work.* In the words of our interpretations, the unconscious is made conscious and tied therefore to grammar and formula. The truth of music is ever beyond words though. This is essentially what we mean in saying *melos* goes beyond *logos* and succeeds it. *Logos* can only go so far. From the point of view of *melos*, dogmatism is nearly always a mistake because it is a form of generic shortcoming. And this

135

perception reflects the Christian religion because nearly all of it is tied up in dogmatism, and it has no way out, to the point of delusion that it no longer even seeks something beyond its own ideas.

Like Wagner, Rolland brushes aside the equation of the hero of the symphony with Napoleon Bonaparte. Wagner puts it like this:

> What means the Funeral March, the Scherzo with the hunting-horns, and the Finale with the soft emotional Andante woven in? Where is the bridge of Lodi, where the battle of Arcole, where the victory under the Pyramids, where the 18th Brumaire? Are these not incidents which no composer of our day would have let escape him, if he wanted to write a biographic symphony on Bonaparte?[29]

Let's witness the way Rolland dreams the first section of the first movement:

> The great motive that dominates the symphony is a personality. What matters it to us whether it is a man or an idea, the obscure voice of instinct or the lucid will? It lives and it acts. Who can doubt its existence? Simple and upright it goes forward; for its first step it is marked with the seal of its destiny, that marches to its appointed end and knows no other. The soul into which this order has entered bends, at the fifth bar, under the burden. But the burden itself is its destiny, is a part of its essence; it accepts it with a sigh, and abandons itself to the stream. The overcoming of the first obstacles (bars 25–27) reveals to it its own energy; it takes to spouse the action imposed on it. This resounding "Aye!" (bars 35–45) is answered, by reaction, by the regrets of a tender and weary heart (oboes, clarinets, flutes and violins in alternation). For the moment the heart is subdued by the will (bars 55ff.). The battle is joined between the two souls, a combat with lashing whips, with saber blows (bars 65ff.). The mighty motive gradually raises its head; it transforms itself into fragments, as if by that means to find a way through. But always it is met by the plaint that stays it and troubles its heart (bars 83ff.) Checked in its impulse, it returns, it redoubles. The great off-beat harmonies cut down (bars 123, etc.). It is the confession of defeat, the renunciation of tenderness, of *Sehnsucht* (bars 132ff.). The first section of the allegro closes with a bleeding wound, cruel harmonies that hurt. But the spirit once more plunges into the broil, and now it is as if it has lost its way. The first battle—an inconclusive one—has been joined between the ego of love and the ego of will, in the house at Heiligenstadt [a village not far from Vienna where Beethoven lived for half a year in 1802] enveloped in the night of the fields.[30]

This is just the first section before the *Durchfürung*! The development comes in the second section. Here, "soul's field of battle becomes co-extensive with the universe and the fresco assumes colossal pro-portions," Rolland continues.[31] We can follow Rolland's dream in our listening, as I would probably tend to do myself. There is wisdom in listening, as in good taste, and there is no harm in being guided in one's listening by one wiser. But the reality is that we are talking about *interpreting dreams* and we can dream our own dreams. And this is precisely what music encourages and what listening does. This is why it is soulful and soul-making.

The point of the "Eroica," as for all art music, is therefore to *dream it*. Before the "Eroica" the dream was possible only in more modest and circumspect ways: circumscribed under the aegis of the Catholic reli-gion, modest in the perfected sonata form of Haydn and Mozart. But the "Eroica" plunges into the depths of *music* like a mountain suddenly moved, turned upside down and tumbled into the sea. The "Eroica" is a cataclysm and tidal wave in musical history: a colossus of unheard-of proportions and power, comparable to the similar upheavals brought into their domains by Shakespeare and Michelangelo.

Somehow the essence of Beethoven's innovations have become bur-ied under learned treatises; hence the constant recourse to his life (as, too, in the case of other composers) as if they were inspired *by their lives*, and not by music; as if the composer got his or her music from life, rather than his or her life from music. The life is subservient to the music—at least lives like that of Beethoven and Wagner were. This is a crucial point to be realized by musicians today. Wagner says to R.:

> What Music expresses is eternal, infinite, and ideal; she expresses not the passion, love, desire, of this or that individual in this or that condition, but Passion, Love, Desire itself, and in such infinitely varied phases as lie in her unique possession and are foreign and unknown to any other tongue. Of her let each man taste according to his strength, his faculty and mood, what taste and feel he can.[32]

In the "Eroica" we bask the soul in the power of music. Berlioz specifies of the finale:

> One very curious passage of instrumentation is to be remarked at the commencement; showing what effect can be drawn from the opposition of different timbres. It is a B flat taken by the violins, and repeated immediately by the flutes and oboes, in the style of an echo. Although the repercussion takes place on the same note of the scale, at the same movement and with equal force, so great a difference results from this dialogue that the nuance which distinguishes the

instruments from one another might be compared to that between blue and violet. *Such refinements of tone color were altogether unknown before Beethoven; and it is to him that we owe them.*[33]

In Chapter 11 I shall have more to say on color; we might note here in passing the origin in Beethoven of this musical opening, which is developed by Wagner in the great step in what Wagner calls, "the wondrous process of emancipating Melody [*melos*] from the tyranny of Mode [*techne*, technique]."[34] Truly said, given that each of Wagner's music dramas have their own distinctive color.[35]

Finally, Berlioz again:

> Beethoven has written works more striking perhaps than this symphony; and several of his other compositions impress the public in a more lively way. But it must be allowed, notwithstanding, that the *Sinfonia Eroica* possesses such strength of thought and execution, that its style is so emotional and consistently elevated besides its form being so poetical, that it is entitled to rank as equal to the highest conceptions of its composer.[36]

Fourth Symphony, in B Flat Major

Robert Schumann made some curious misjudgments about other people's music and none worse than referring to Beethoven's Fourth Symphony as the "slender Greek maiden between two Norse Giants."[37] The only excuse for this silly epithet (and its mistaken gender)[38] is that the symphony turns back and continues the gradual ascent marked by no. 2.

The Fourth Symphony was composed two years later than the "Eroica," in the summer of 1806. It begins with a long adagio. Berlioz:

> As for the *adagio*, it seems to elude analysis. Its form is so pure and the expression of its melody so angelic and of such irresistible tenderness that the prodigious art by which this perfection is attained disappears completely. From the very first bars we are overtaken by emotion . . .[39]

Beethoven had first thought he would follow the "Eroica" with a symphony in C minor—but this is, so to speak the *virile* counterpart of that possibility.

In a sense the Fourth Symphony could be looked upon as a harbinger of the "Eroica," except for the historical fact that it followed it. It is the dithyrambic sequel, the *eros* of the limbs and the ecstasy of the senses.

A long, rapt quasi-nocturnal adagio full of questioning and anticipation suddenly erupts into a wild Dionysian dance with brilliant flares
and full to the brim with intoxication. This episode, which fills most of
the first movement, has its own ecstatic dimension – not as Olympian
as the "Eroica," but which listener would not wish to stand up and
gyrate with abandon to the sound of this music and its compulsive
rhythms? . . . Those driving rhythms return after the slow movement.
Not as reckless as earlier, perhaps, but more as sonorous images of
an immense vitality. The individuation of thematic material, however,
is already a legacy from the achievements of the "Eroica." We might
put it this way: Beethoven here explored the rhythmical resources of
absolute music in a way that had not been accomplished before; and
rhythm is a vital, indispensable trigger to rapture and ecstasy. In our
time this is something we know only too well.

Fifth Symphony, in C Minor

"The most celebrated [symphony] of all," says Berlioz, "is also, without question, in our opinion, the one in which Beethoven gives free
scope to his vast imagination; without electing to be either guided or
supported by any outside thought."[40]

This then is "absolute music"—*melos* let loose.

"The C minor symphony seems to arise directly and solely from
Beethoven's own genius . . ." Now what the music is "about," whether
it is deeply personal, as Berlioz imagines, or not, in any case, as Berlioz
rightly says, "the melodic, harmonic, rhythmic and orchestral forms are
there delineated with an essential novelty and individuality, endowing
them also with considerable power and nobleness."[41]

The Fifth is Beethoven's most characteristic work, were we to
choose one work that best characterizes him overall. It was the work
Mendelssohn chose to introduce Beethoven's music to Goethe in
Weimar. Goethe, who was an old man at this time, in 1830, straight
away recognized its massive grandeur and could not imaginatively
place it in bourgeois surroundings. His first words though, were
enigmatic: "That causes no emotion," he said.[42] I take this to refer to
Goethe's sense that this music reaches us at quite another level of
sensibility—at a higher rung on our Ladder of *Melos*.

This is music which soars and takes us soaring with it, above the
realm of thinking; this is why it is not "emotional" (because it is
thoughts that trigger emotions); nor, as Berlioz imagined, does it

belong to the psychobiographical. Rather, this music awakens us to freedom, it is quintessential music of freedom, but not in the Hegelian sense, tied to worldly politics, but in Schopenhauer's sense, tied to awakening of our being, a forgetting of our own person and its relations and connections, a release from all representations, but also a release from that *wille* that as a rule holds us to our representations as "reality." This music is music of the power of true freedom; it can put us into that state of pure perception Schopenhauer talks of, where we see "objectively," from no perspective, and our soul becomes, as he puts it, "the clear mirror of the inner nature of the world."[43] This is music about triumph in struggle against all odds, for the awakening to the inner nature of the world is the real struggle going on beneath and before all other struggles, which, ultimately, are merely symptoms of the real struggle.

One could say, slightly sarcastically, in Nietzsche's style: This music is too great for most ordinary mortals; best to make a commodity of it and keep a safe distance. Do not let yourself be engulfed by it. Do not risk touching the divine with your fingertips!

But this is why the Beethoven symphonies, from the Third and the Fifth in particular onwards, are still *the music of the future*. How is it possible for us to surrender to this violence done to our emotions, where we have to leave our suburban comforts behind, and give the soul its authentic nourishment, and then return? How are we to cross back afterwards? Is it already too late? Better to turn this into a commodity on the concert circuit and focus on celebrity orchestras and conductors and dazzling venues that we can look at and read about in magazines on the way to work in the air-conditioned office block. How do the comforts and conveniences and manufactured consent birthed in us by consumer culture and commodity capitalism cope with this larger-than-life upheaval in our spiritual nature? As Nietzsche would have said, we have not grown up to a fully human stature, which indeed music such as this demands.

The first four notes of this symphony Beethoven himself explained as: "'*So pocht das Schicksal an die Pforte*' (So Fate knocks at the door)."[44] Berlioz:

> From this tiny germ the whole of this fierce stormy movement is evolved. Not even the beautiful tender second subject, nor the lovely little unbarred oboe cadenza can win it away from this rugged fierce mood. When this second subject appears in the recapitulation, still in the minor, the atoning major outburst which immediately follows

is quickly brushed aside by the impatience of the reinstated first theme. Even the limitations of the old-fashioned horns and trumpets in those days seemed to be turned to advantage in the colossal bare thirds and fourths of the "Fate" notes.[45]

Fate is that which cannot be avoided and will not be avoided. This is what Berlioz hears too, in the first movement.

The pastoral scene of the second movement is followed by a somber and mysterious intermezzo, like a witches' dance at midnight (and note how this thematic material is very similar to the opening of the symphony! But the mood is totally different), which ends in a sudden, huge crescendo when the full blast of the sun illuminates the landscape. Beethoven's Fifth is the first of his "Finale-Symphonien." The sheer exuberance and grandeur, and the blindingly bright light of this long and massive C major movement, represent one of the peaks of symphonic writing. Never before or since has a musician made such inexorable, such ecstatic good sense of the slogan *ad astra per aspera*, which might congenially be rendered "from Hell to the Light of the Great Star in Heaven." This music overwhelms—totally, utterly; it opens the gates to Elysium in such fulminant colors that few can swim with the tide. We are awestruck, thunderstruck; and, as often happens, we feel we must escape it, and save our sanity by uttering platitudes (or falling back on technical analyses).

Sixth Symphony, in F Major ("Pastoral")

This symphony is what is usually called "program music" (descriptive music), and was composed in 1808, ostensibly, so the books will tell us, the first example of it from a great master. Yet, composers have always delighted in imitating the sounds of nature and animals and human festivities; it is nothing new, and this symphony is not "program music," imitative of nature. But if that is what we hear, we are *not listening.*

Compared to the Third and the Fifth, this symphony is not a shock to the system, yet it brings another novelty to light, another change in perspective on music that wishes to speak to the soul.

Beethoven, in this work, was first again in vesting the emotional and spiritual aspects of our relationship with nature with the *subject* and the subject's responses—to the music, not to imitative formulas. We do not hear dancing, frolicking, thunder, etc. as pictorial elements but as *musical elements* (pertaining to *melos*) that affect our mood and

141

soul in a certain way that reminds us that we are a part of nature. It is nature sounding *as music*, not as imitated.

The music issues from the same well of inspiration as the second movement of the Fifth, for which no "poetical" or "nature-derived" inspiration was claimed. As Beethoven justly said of the Sixth Symphony: "'*Mehr Ausdruck der Empfindung als Mahlerey*' ('More the expression of feeling than painting.') Notations of the soul, not of the eyes."[46] We should take this evoking of emotions as governing perceptions as well. With this thought we align Beethoven and Schopenhauer's viewpoints on the matter of such evocations. We would not find this same sense in Mozart or Haydn, indeed, for it is beyond the delights of their music.

We listen to the Sixth across the dark gulf of the catastrophes in Western culture. In the first movement, nature comes alive, full of light and strength. In the second movement nature stirs and dreams, nature sleeps, she goes into herself and reemerges out of herself and wells up. Sometimes we are lying on our back looking at the clouds; sometimes we are riding with the clouds for a thousand miles. There are descriptive titles over the four movements, but the music comes from the inside out; it defines the titles, they do not define the music; there is more to each of the movements than the titles suggest. The titles suggest a "feel," and little beyond that.

Beethoven's Sixth speaks to the world of harmoniousness, which is not *of* the world, but which the music externalizes and holds before the world as the essence of nature, and which gives us endless reason to listen to it. In music we seek the higher harmonies in nature, everything is alive, everything is connected.

Seventh Symphony, in A Major

There is a five-year gap between this symphony and the Sixth. This symphony was completed in May 1812 and first performed in December 1813.

What is so startling about the Seventh is the immense variety Beethoven draws from *single notes* in this symphony, opening up another new reservoir of expressivity. Right at the beginning, there are fifteen staccato notes; in the transition from the introduction to the main body, the flute and string exchange *one note* in patterns of eight, four and then two—always just *one note*. The slow movement is completely dominated by a repetitive theme that has three-plus-two notes (up or down). *How does this impinge on our listening?* That is the reflective question to ask, to get us listening more "deeply." Contrast with any modern painter who does a "study" in red - "quiet red", "excited red", "soothing red", "raging red" etc. Threads, knots, curlicues, spots etc. How does this impinge on your seeing? Maybe it embroils your whole nervous system. Or a poet who uses the same rhyme or phrase many times in a row (e.g. Tennyson's Ode on the Death of the Duke of Wellington). In the third movement the chatty wind episode in the middle section keeps repeating the *last note* of a four-note theme eight times. And in the finale, the main theme is one-plus-three notes rushing madly up and down, up and down, dozens of times in a row.

Wagner called this the "apotheosis of the dance"; but it would have been more appropriate to reserve this comment for Symphony no. 4. Because of Wagner's authority, however, experts have waffled endlessly about the movement's "rhythmic vitality," but this is a *constant* in Beethoven's music. Hence, the most apt feature of no. 7, it seems to me, is that Beethoven is squeezing incredible quantities of "spiritual juices" from unbelievably simple, virtually skeletal, thematic material. This is unbelievable too because the symphony sounds rich and grand—like the full panoply of a host of knights on horseback on the march. However, the last movement is unselfconsciously bacchanalian, perhaps Dionysian in the Nietzschean sense . . .

The sportiveness of the music attunes the listener to levity in inner-found freedom. This symphony is not "free spirited" music, but music for a free spirit—in fact, it defines whatever that might mean (for instance, in Nietzsche). But a proper sense of "free spirit" (distinct from Nietzsche's idea of free spirit) will be garnered here, which is why we must listen to it again with as much attentive self-presence as we can bring and sustain. We will find—hidden, in fact—in this sportiveness an exultant mood, which will be fully fledged or allowed full exposition in the Ninth Symphony.

All the other arts, says Wagner, "present us with *that signifies*. But Music says *that is*." The passage continues:

> This lofty property of Music's enables her at last to quite divorce herself from the reasoned word; and the noblest music completed this divorce in measure as religious Dogma became the toy of Jesuitical casuistry or rationalistic pettifogging . . . Only her final severance from the decaying Church could enable the art of Tone to save the noblest heritage of the Christian idea in its purity of the over-worldly reformation.[47]

This is the freedom we mean. In this essay, *Religion and Art*, Wagner goes on to foreshadow the affinities between Beethoven's symphonies and religious—particularly Christian—revelation of peace and justice on earth, which for Wagner, in the judgment of humanity, the church has shown itself incapable of fulfilling. But that does not mean the revelation itself is lost; and despite whatever terrible scenes may unfold, "this alone can be the road conducting to the shore of a new hope for the human race."[48] The new age beckons.

Wagner does not analyze Beethoven's symphonies, but draws upon the principles they evince—principles that are musically implicit, principles with regard to a dimension of height in Being that, in these brief notes, I have been trying to bring to the fore as well. Wagner explains some of the difficult terrain that must be crossed if humanity is to reject greed and materialism, and restore art and religion in a new or post-secular age. And yet his words have stood neglected and uninterpreted by mainstream intellectuals and artists. Even now we are hardly ready to hear Wagner on the arts-led future.

Eighth Symphony, in F Major

The Eighth Symphony is lively, petite, and teasing and, says Berlioz, it "sparkles with life."[49] He said this of the finale by contrast with the preceding minuet which he finds "ordinary" and old fashioned. Of the second movement, Berlioz says, it "is one of those productions for which it would be equally vain to seek either a model or a counterpart; which seem to have fallen from heaven and straight away entered the author's mind; which he therefore writes, as it were, at a stroke; which we can only listen to, amazed."[50] Written in the summer and autumn of 1812, this symphony was first performed in Vienna on February 27, 1814. The Eighth, like the Seventh, supposes a new-found freedom, as its music is founded on the achievement of the symphonies that have gone before it.

This is a more mature, more accomplished counterpiece to the Fourth Symphony. Beethoven might have said of this symphony, apropos our quotation from Beethoven with regard to the Sixth, "More the expression of *joie de vivre* than bacchanalian sensuality" (as in the Fourth). The Eighth looks back to Haydn: *it is a Haydn symphony*, but such a one as Haydn could never have written because it already carries on its back all the melodic, harmonic, rhythmic features and subtleties of expression from the days of the "Eroica." Interestingly, Beethoven said of the long passage of "crazy" fortissimo repetitions near the end of the first statement that he had a "raptus," a kind of divine madness (such as Nietzsche in fact succumbed to); it is indeed the first occurrence of a "signature" that was to recur frequently in his later works (sonatas, string quartets) with increasing intensity and that has led to innumerable discussions about what he might have had "in mind." But the answer can only be the very one that Beethoven gave: quaffing from the cup of divine liquor. . .

The second movement (ticktock, ticktock) is a joke at the expense of Maelzel's new metronome; and the minuet a slightly melancholy "good riddance" to a dance form that has meanwhile grown up and become a scherzo (in most of the other symphonies), waving a last good-bye to Haydn.

The last movement clearly picks up on the whirlwind of the first. This is often played too slowly, especially by the Viennese, depending on which orchestra is being conducted for which audience.

Ninth Symphony, in D Minor ("Choral")

In his last phase, after eight years of silence, Beethoven started anew. Beethoven's absolute music is like the creation of a new language. With the creation of this new language, in five piano sonatas and five string quartets, Beethoven leapt over a whole century of musical evolution. No body of absolute music to match his was written until Shostakovich grew to an equivalent maturity in the 1950s, in his last six quartets. To audiences and experts of the nineteenth century, those Beethoven works remained books with seven seals.

Beethoven wrote this symphony in a state of complete deafness, and yet it is the symphony of symphonies. Even Berlioz baulks before such a daunting task as the analysis of this symphony.

To get what I think is a helpful description of this symphony about which so much has been written and over which dispute remains, let us dream along with Edward Carpenter from his book *Angel's Wings* (1898).[51]

The interest of the symphony as a whole, says Carpenter, "lies in the fact that it is Man (not the composer) who is face to face with the sphinx-problems of life: and the Symphony is the solution of these problems not for one but for all the world."[52]

> The first movement is very tragic; indeed it is truly awful in parts (. . .) Whatever various interpretations may be put on this *Allegro*, no one can fail to feel its restlessness, its strife, its pathos, and (in passages) its heart- rending despair (. . .) But if the first movement

145

represents the ever-lasting strife of the elements (and man in the midst thereof), the second movement, the *Molto Vivace* [2nd movement], may well suggest the endless grace and beauty of Nature. The subject is said to have been suggested to Beethoven by stepping out into a starlight night. It might well be called a dance of suns and stars—so brilliant is it, so vast, so simple, in a kind of monotonous endless-ness, so—exquisitely beautiful in form. The drums and the horns give I know not what air of magic and distance; a mysterious wind rushes through; the background of night spreads behind. The exqui-site daintiness and lightness of touch, combined with such strange deep meanings, make this one of the most wonderful of Beethoven's creations. There is no strife; all is harmony and beauty. Yet here again a great sadness makes itself felt. It is the sadness of human loneliness—the sense which is sometimes so terribly enhanced by the very sight of Natures careless perfection.'[53]

The next movement presents us with the two most human, most lov-ing themes imaginable—the one the more pathetic and full-hearted, the other gayer, but equally true and tender—the one in B flat major, the other in D major. As one listens to the alternating dialogue of these two melodies, it is impossible to resist the image of two lovers conversing, two human hearts, contrasted yet sympathetic, twining with each other in sweetest intimacy. The movement glides on through delicious confidences, and lingers with a kind of lazy grace over its own beauty. Yet here too, strangely enough, it ends in sadness. The coda contains passages of deep dejection and unsatisfied expression. It would almost seem as if the composer had meant to say (in these three movements), "Not in the strife of the world and of life; not in the contemplation of the pure beauty of Nature; not even in the luxury of love, two together apart from the world, is rest to be found;[54]

A violent discord and uproar breaks into the close of the last-mentioned movement. The whole scene changes, as it were, and all is bustle and excitement . . .[55]

[In the final movement Beethoven is to introduce the voices singing words slightly adapting Schiller's Ode to Joy]. "It must be said that he effects this difficult transition with great skill. The orchestra, first dwells for a time on the final subject, working it out in some detail. Then its performance is dismissed by the same violent discord and up-roar as before; and the recitative — this time the bass voice — breaks in, saying, "Not to these tones, O friends, but to sweeter and more joyful ones, let us attune our voices." The way is now open, and the whole chorus, supported by the orchestra, takes up Schiller's Ode.[56]

This air with its absolute simplicity of structure (the first five notes of the scale in plain diatonic succession), the fruit of long meditation and labor, has that quality which we have already noticed in many of Beethoven's late subjects, especially in that last Arietta of the piano Sonata, Op. 111.[57]

Carpenter footnotes a point of Wagner here:

Melody (says Wagner) has by Beethoven been freed from the influence of Fashion and changing Taste, and raised to an ever-valid, purely human type. Beethoven's music will be understood to all time, while that of his predecessors will for the most part only remain intelligible to us through the medium of reflection on the history of Art [58]

The air by which Beethoven takes up Schiller's Ode has the sense of perfect rest, of virginal and grateful gladness, conjoined with a sense, partly produced by the arrangement of the harmonies, of infinite experience (and even sorrow) outlived and transmuted. If it has (as it has) that character of naïvety and childlike innocence which Wagner attributes to it, it has also the character of a return to childlike innocence. The round of all experience has been circled. This- is our surrender again to Nature, to simplicity, to the human heart, to Love, to Joy itself; for after all else has been tasted, there is nothing better than these.[59]

But the words help us of course. While the music gives the *Stimmung*—the deep mood which is thus common to much of his late work—the words give us its special application here. It is curious to find that so early as 1793, when Beethoven was but twenty-two or twenty-three years of age, a friend writes of him (Thayer, *Leben*, i. 237). "He intends to compose Schiller's Freude verse by verse;" and from that time onward in his Sketch-books at intervals occur Schiller s words with musical setting, down to 1822, when the theme takes its present form. For thirty years these words—embodying in a kind of joint human and religious fervor the strongly revolutionary sentiments of 1785 when they were written—had been floating in Beethoven's mind; for thirty years he had tried to find music adequate to their expression.[60]

Returning from this biographical anecdote, interesting for what it tells us about the working of inspiration at this level, to the fourth movement.

In many respects it may be allowed that the vocal conclusion is not altogether satisfactory. Notwithstanding Wagner's dictum (in his monograph on Beethoven) that it was one of the great triumphs of B.'s genius to treat the voices in this and in the Mass in D as human instruments, and their combination with the ordinary instruments as forming merely "an orchestra of increased capabilities," there is a very general consensus of feeling that it was just because of this treatment of the voice "as a human instrument" that the result is not quite satisfactory. Somehow it would seem that Beethoven had not quite the *feeling for the human voice*; seldom does he treat it with absolute sympathy. This choral movement is after all not quite sympathetic. There is a strain and a tension throughout, an activity and a restlessness, which are not quite natural to a great body of voices; twelve bars on the high A natural is a tyrannical demand. Brilliant, intense, giantesque, and displaying endless resource, as the variations vocal and instrumental are, in this great concluding movement, one misses the absolute beauty, repose, and unity which are shown for instance in the concluding variations of his last piano Sonata. There is a sense each time that the composer has not quite attained the effect he wanted, and is *trying again*.[61]

The use of voice and word as Wagner points out is under *melos*, and exemplifies what I said in the last chapter with regard to the discontinuity of absolute music, that it does not develop from the music immediately preceding it, but the inspiration jumps, as it were, and Beethoven picks up from where the Burgundian choristers left off, when they subsumed the words of Catholic liturgy beneath the sway of melody.

Of the melody here Wagner himself writes in his *Beethoven* (1870):

> Never has the highest art produced a thing more artistically simple than this strain, whose childlike innocence as though breathes into us a holy awe when first we hear the theme in unaccented whispers from the bass instruments of the string-orchestra in unison. It then becomes the *cantus firmus*, the Chorale of the new communion, round which, as round S. Bach's own church-chorales, the harmonic voices group themselves in counterpoint. There is nothing to equal the sweet intensity of life this primal strain of spotless innocence acquires from every new-arising voice; till each adornment, every added gem of passion, unites with it and in it, like the breathing world around a final proclamation of divinest love.[62]

Beethoven said, "Whoever understands my music will henceforth be free of the misery of the world." Quoting this, W. J. Turner, at the end of his long book on Beethoven, writes:

> We discover this freedom is only obtained by the recognition that life is a tragedy to be played out to the last drop of blood. It may be true that if we properly understood this tragedy we would not change our tragic destiny for any other, and since it is Beethoven more than any other artist who has revealed this destiny to us, his claim to have set

us free is to some extent justified. But we have the will to demand in art and in life a creation of concrete happiness and delight. It is from this aspect only that Beethoven is open to criticism, for he has not given us, as an artist, all the concrete joy for which we long. He has indeed revealed to us a New World, but it is a tragic world, a world whose beauty breaks the heart that perceives it.[63]

These words summarize the sensibility of the Ladder of *Melos* in Beethoven's symphonies, listened to as a set, from melancholy to tragedy, energetic and idyllic by turns. And herein is his heroism: playing out his own lifework, against all odds, "to the last drop of blood." Hearing the dream, *perhaps we will wake from it*. In the end, he points beyond himself. Perhaps this is the Beethoven we hear in the late piano sonatas and string quartets; or perhaps it is he who sets the basis upon which, and the yardstick against which, the true music of joy, of exaltation and rapture is to be written.

8

Wagner and World Music

It seemed to me that this was my music, and I recognized it as every person recognizes the things he is destined to love . . . You have led me back to myself in my hours of melancholy, to that which it great.
—Charles Baudelaire, "Richard Wagner et *Tannhäuser* à Paris"

My passion for the Wagnerian enchantment has accompanied my life ever since I was first conscious of it and began to make it my own and penetrate it with my understanding. All that I owe to him, of enjoyment and instruction, I can never forget: the hours of deep and single bliss . . . of nervous and intellectual transport and rapture.
—Thomas Mann, "Richard Wagner and The *Ring*"

Wagner is a fraught topic, given that the Nazis enlisted his music on their side. Much has been written on Wagner and Nazism and I have desisted from going into the subject as so many others—to no real end—have already done this. Wagner's music (and musical conceptions that go along with it) grow in popularity and influence with audiences around the globe, despite everything. Daniel Barenboim has done more than anyone to present Wagner, knowing both sides of the story—about what happened to his people in Europe during the Holocaust—and knowing the music of Wagner perhaps better than anyone alive today. In a humanitarian and peacemaking gesture, Barenboim founded his West-Eastern Divan Orchestra of Jews and Palestinians. He writes: "Music teaches us that there is nothing that does not include its parallel or opposite as the case may be; therefore no element is entirely independent because the relationship is by definition interdependent. It is my belief that although music cannot solve any problems, since it is, as Busoni said, 'sonorous air', it can teach us to think in a way that is a school for life. In music we know and accept the hierarchy of a main subject, we accept the permanent

presence of an opposite and sometimes even of subversive accompanying rhythms."[1] Wagner's name is associated with Nazism and that
is a fact, but I will be talking about Wagner in terms of philosophy
(Schopenhauer and Hegel), the terms in which he thought about his
music, and I shall be wanting to show how Wagner points forward to
our day, and to all those genres and sub-genres associated with what
we call, somewhat inchoately perhaps, world music.

Wagner's opera is not opera in the Italian sense at all; it is transcendental rather than emotional. Wagner used operatic elements to
try to achieve a new collaborative art, beyond opera, that included
drama, poetry, psychology, liturgy and a new kind of harmonics in
music. In this chapter I want to talk about this crossroad between
philosophy and music that is more explicit in Wagner than anywhere
else before his time, and possibly since. The chief idea is that of the
transformation of the world into music, as Werner Herzog entitled
his 1994 documentary on Wagner. The transformation of the world
into music is the exteriorization for our ears, for audiences, of what is
implicit in the universe, inside us and outside us, the Implicate Order,
in David Bohm's phrase, which is to say, what the ancients called matter
or substance is energy and that energy has levels (thought is energy
at one level, leading energy at the lower level), and all of what we call
space, "outer space," however far we can see with whatever telescope,
or calculate spatially with whatever math, that space is full of energy,
and energy is vibration and vibration is sound, and the sound of all
together is the music of the spheres, the sound of the One. This is what
Schopenhauer thought metaphysically, and Wagner tried to bring
some of that sound "out there," of the universe, within earshot. On this
note, Michael Eigen, after a lifetime of psychoanalytical case studies,
writes: "Perhaps music is even the basic structure of our bodies, our
rhythms, timing of processes. Perhaps there is a special ear that 'hears'
body times and rhythms, tonalities, and builds on them, with them,
an inaudible kind of hearing that feeds sound."[2]

Such a hunch as this augurs a new age for science if science starts
to discover the sonic nature of reality or energy, as it is beginning
to do, and it marks a new age for music, beyond the entertainment
industry, of music that is transcendentally attuned and has therapeutic
properties recognized straight away by their beauty. Schopenhauer
was enabled to gain his insight into music as metaphysics thanks
to Kant, and Wagner got Schopenhauer's real meaning, beyond the
cliché of Schopenhauer as a pessimist. Schopenhauer, for us, was a

world philosopher and as well as his iteration of the metaphysics of music, which we will develop here, Schopenhauer's philosophy marks the moment when Eastern philosophy came west. Schopenhauer moves beyond religious parochialism (and its ideological trademark, exclusivism), as Kant had already done. Eastern philosophy comes west and that does not just mean change to Western philosophy (and religion with it) but Schopenhauer's guess is that it will give birth to something beyond either, something new—and Wagner follows and develops this drift of thought. Schopenhauer's main work *is* this juncture of East coming west. Wagner's works are Schopenhauer's philosophy *as* art, principally as music. And it is the inner logic of Schopenhauer that Wagner correctly worked out along the lines of his own inspiration.

The materialist philosopher Alain Badiou writes in a recent book on Wagner that, "We are on the cusp of a revival of high art and it is here that Wagner should be invoked."[3] Badiou may be overly precipitate in his judgment (a *cusp*?); however, insofar as we want to connect art music in its inspired forms (rather than academic pretensions) with world music, it is true that Wagner's name stands to the fore. 'World music' is a term like 'world literature' that is difficult to define. I take the term to mean music that contributes to diversity in unity; to do this the music must have an appeal with an especially wide reach. Some of the music of Bach, Mozart, Schubert and Beethoven and of a few others is of this kind. To consider the works of Beethoven and Schubert as world music means that they are recognized wherever they are heard, not for their provenance, which is secondary, but for their *music*, which people feel the truth of just as well in Beijing or Seoul or Tokyo as in Vienna. Their music is world music—the inception of world music. They are *world-class* for a start. This is perhaps the basic criterion for world music, that the composers and musicians are acknowledged as being world-class. This must be done according to the criteria given in Chapter 2, because nowadays the publicity machine and big money can raise someone to the seeming height of being world-class when in fact they are far from it.

Since the days of Schubert and Beethoven, world music has become more and more culturally diverse and integral, but to the same end, now as then, it is world music because it *makes melos present* everywhere it is played and heard. The names Schubert and Beethoven might be German, but *melos* is transcendental and that is what the music of these composers presences: something out of this world.

153

Between Beethoven and Wagner there is a continuity of musical transmission, just as there also is continuity *philosophically* between Kant and Schopenhauer and Wagner. This transmission continues into psychoanalysis and literature and then disperses widely into all sorts of fields outside music, including religion and the whole movement of Eastern religious ways of thinking into Western discourses that is the mark of our time. We live in the age of world religions, world literature, and world music.

Wagner continues the exultant sensibility we find in Beethoven, sweeping up love and suffering toward a further horizon. The nineteenth century was peculiarly predisposed to ecstasy and rapture, and Wagner, with his amazing orchestration skills, sent the latter part of the century literally into ecstasies. In the nineteenth century audiences reacted to this music with screams. Women became hysterical, men had palpitations as the tension within the music dramas was sustained for such a duration that it became unbearable for men and women groomed on order and its rationality. This was not just music—nor quite opera—but a music drama, by which people's senses were further engrossed and bothered by the stage action, a story (as we might guess) of the pain of love and of the trials it has to bear.

The ecstasies are exacerbated in Wagner through a strong elaboration of their dark side, not just their heights. In a sense their depths become their heights, as if Wagner upturned the very order of being people were used to as the only one they ever knew. The start of act 3 of *Tristan* is an example of such an upturning. There are many grave passages and crises, and great mourning, desolation, and despair as the other side of the ecstasy and rapture. The cheapening of this is of course melodrama. Many composers who came after Wagner tried to reduce the eruption from volcanic genius into a technique. The next generation, inspired by Wagner, found his music *did not resolve into technique*. It was high in that indeterminate quality which we called the "timeless" or "eternal" earlier in the book. The unstable harmonic field, so edgy in Wagner, even when unwieldy, imitated methodically by a later composer, for example Schoenberg in *Pelleas and Melisande*, simply sounds repetitive, even somewhat mechanical. In the *Poem of Ecstasy* by Scriabin, we have a work that is *intentionally* ecstatic; of course this backfires. The eternal is non-intentional. Wagner captures this non-intentionality, not with his technique, with his art, but by his genius and the hard work of preparation that went into both, but to which neither is reducible.

Once again it is hard to turn our ears back.[4] To our contemporary ears, when we play some Wagner it has a tendency to sound like film music from old Hollywood movies. This is of course not the same if we attend a performance, when we become engulfed—and we surface at the end to wonder where we are, even double-checking if we are still *who* we are. With recordings, though, some of his pieces call to mind images of oceanic scenes, sunrise on the prairie, and suchlike from the movies and television that we naturally tend to make such free associations. Our manufactured entertainments have schooled us into this way of sensibility. This is not by accident at all. Max Steiner and Erich Wolfgang Korngold, both from Vienna, influenced musically by Wagner, basically invented the idea of the classic Hollywood music score. Wagner's music dramas had given them the model: the music was engineered not just to suit the action, but also and especially to key up the audience emotionally to it.

Nineteenth-century audiences had the opposite experience. Brought up on Viennese classicism by and large—Haydn, Mendelssohn, Beethoven—they were used to order, to music with a beginning, a middle, and an end, or, in musical terms, a tonal center out from which the music moves and back to which it inevitably returns. Music was always music with form and they had never heard or, presumably ever imagined, music without form. Even if they were unaware of this and of "tonal centers," and so on, unconsciously, in their natural sensibility, this is what they understood and this is what their aesthetic experience of music was and all it could be. Then along came Wagner.

"Born out of the spirit of music"

It is important to realize that Wagner was the musical heir of Beethoven. Wagner took from Beethoven what he called "unending melody," which is to say the *continuity* of musical argument such as I commented upon in discussing the "Eroica." Unending melody means nonstop variation and modulation, not in the old (Bach and pre-Bach) sense of adding to a theme, encircling it with external filigree,[5] but in the sense of a *unique physiognomy* by which other themes arising from it may be recognized as its "children." For instance, the way the arpeggio of the horns at the opening of *Rheingold* (E flat major) recurs in the opening of *Götterdämmerung* as a chordal sequence in E flat minor, this tiny change of one note (major arpeggio to minor) transforms the motif (the parent into its offspring) from a seminal, creative, hopeful "opening of the eyes to the light" to a dark, destructive,

155

evil, scheming grimace. Thanks to the work of Derryck Cooke, it is possible to identify countless other examples of how Wagner weaves a seamless texture of many motifs to produce a colossal variety of moods: dark premonitions, jubilation, and so on.

Apropos Beethoven, this is where they are geniuses of a similar kind. Here's a good example: Beethoven's initial inspiration for the adagio of the "Hammerklavier" Sonata[6] was a rupture in a tonal texture (not in a theme or a melody, but a breakage or collapse in a musical flow); and this was such a luminous image for him that he took it on board, knowing full well that it would stretch out like an endless bridge between two shores. He had to "discover" a thread of melody that would lead to this rupture; and then another stretch that would take it "home." The point about that image was a huge tension needing to be built up, and a long, calmer flow needing to reach out to the other side. The result was one of his "massive" movements, about twenty minutes of continuous invention.

Nietzsche once derided Wagner as "our greatest miniaturist . . . who crowds into the smallest space an infinity of meaning,"[7] which might make us think of chemistry and how a grain of one chemical can change the potency of a whole brew. Nietzsche must have forgotten that the epic scale (as in, for example, Homer, Tolstoy) is precisely the same thing: miniaturism multiplied, the sweep of hundreds of details, driven along as by a majestic river (the Rhine, in Wagner!). Unlike, for example, Brahms, Wagner was not afraid of designing a huge span of story line, always confident he would discover the resources necessary to fill out every moment along the way with meaningful music.

If audiences reacted strongly to Wagner, musicians reacted even more strongly. The musician and conductor, Hans von Bülow, who first conducted *Tristan and Isolde*, was driven to the brink of madness by it. Possibly his madness was helped by Wagner when, in 1868, von Bülow's wife, who had been having an affair with Wagner, ran off with him (taking two of their four daughters with her). Earlier, in the 1860s, when *Tristan* was to be premiered by the Vienna Court Opera, the musicians and singers—the best in the world—had seventy-seven rehearsals and gave up! They could not get it right. It was too different from anything that even musicians had known or could imagine. Their difficulty was with adjusting to the fact that all the "white notes" in the score are offset by "chromatic" harmony, making it difficult for musicians to stick to their fingering routines. As well, the bass players, who were used to following certain patterns and hardly having to think about it, were suddenly having to master what seemed to be impossible fingering while having to read every note as they went because the harmony kept moving into unexpected, uncharted terrain.

Wagner was a unique talent. He was a man of volcanic inspiration. He could work sixteen or eighteen hours a day for months at a time, when active; but when he was inactive, he wrote nothing. In 1850 Wagner laid down his pen in the middle of writing *Siegfried*—his hero was in the middle of a forest—and did not pick up his pen again until twelve years later, leaving the project to one side for the time being. On the inside he was working, though, on what would be the whole *Ring* cycle.

Rienzi was Wagner's third opera and first success. It is not what we would call a "Wagnerian" work except perhaps for the start, which I shall briefly recall. If we put on our nineteenth-century ears, imagine the lights going down in the theater, a hush gradually falling, the conductor waiting for complete silence before being willing to start, then, in the silence, the conductor turning to the orchestra, nodding, giving the start with his baton raised, then, in the silence and darkness, *one trumpet sounding a single, long, seemingly endless note* softly out of the silence, and the sound swelling, relapsing—all *on one note*—then this is how *Rienzi* begins. And with our nineteenth-century ears, hearing this, we would wonder: what am I to make of it? Nothing in the world of ordered music I have known would have prepared me for what I am now hearing. In fact, I did not think of the music I am used to as "ordered" at all—until now! Thus would my sensibility speak to my heart and mind. Instantly, with that trumpet call, the listener *does not know where he is.* It is a foretaste of the Wagner to come and the new musical space he would open up. The eerie sound would transport the nineteenth-century theatergoer from their ordered bourgeois world—governed by strict codes of manners, stiff collars and corsets, dinner, dress and moral codes preempting almost their doing and being from the cradle to the grave—to another world, to what would feel like another order of being. This is where the exaltation and rapture come in. And this is the historical uniqueness of Wagner. Hearing that trumpet, the listener would have had no idea what would come next—nor do we today, when hearing it for the first time.

At the start of a piece of classical music before Wagner, the "tonal center" of the piece is introduced and opened up. Everything that is going to happen musically starts here and will come back here by the end. While other musicians before Wagner as far back as Bach,

157

and probably earlier, had played with indeterminate beginnings and endings, it is Wagner who really breaks this "ontology," this order of musical being. An ontology is when a "way it is" is thought natural. But Wagner would alter the musical imagination forever and his name would stand in the breach. And because it is music we are talking about, we can *hear this happen* in recordings now, even if we cannot have been present when it *first* happened.

If we listen to the beginning of the overture to *Tristan and Isolde*, we hear the tonal center opened up. A world of longing is opened up. The music, rather than heading back to a brief, if temporary, resolution, before getting going again, keeps opening up, across greater sonic environments of longing. And it keeps going like this. Like water that is running over and keeps running over and no one has the sense to close the tap off. The overture runs for about seven minutes, but even at the end Wagner leaves it unresolved and the music drama, which subsequently goes for nearly four hours, keeps the music unfolding, sometimes subsiding, as if the tap is being closed off now at last, then gushing forth again more persistently and stronger than ever; and so the tension is unalleviated, stretched out and drawn taut until it is torturous. Not until right at the end, after four hours, does Wagner resolve the music. This is his "Tristan chord," the A minor chord that our soul has craved since the start.[8]

The overture to the *Flying Dutchman* starts with a blast of wind, a storm. The first sound to strike the hearer is the shrieking of high tremolo notes in the violins. The horns break in like a huge wave crashing over a ship: a missing middle note (empty fifth) emphasises the stormy nature of the theme and imparts a hollow, ghostly feel especially in its fifteen-fold manic repetition at the end of the initial phrase. This bleak theme winds its way through the entire opera, an incredibly apt aural depiction not only of the tumultuous black sea, but of the phantom ship and the torture of the Dutchman's soul. Wagner worshipped the Beethoven of the 9th Symphony, which is in the same key of D minor and begins with a stepwise decent from violins into basses on empty fifths - quiet, but with a distinctive sense of menace.

In the nineteenth century, this storm music would have blown people away emotionally, as far as established sensibility was concerned. There is a trick to it, though, and Wagner had a genius for musical techniques—technical gimmicks we might even call them. First, he insisted the horns play without valves. This was a throwback, as, by Wagner's day, all horns were installed with valves, but Wagner wanted the old style. Wagner creates a sound with a big hole in the middle because of the missing note (an empty fifth is a chord with a note missing that affects the pitch); this increases the storm effect by conveying a sense of menace and spiritual torment. In baroque organ music, this device was used to indicate the threat of the devil. For Wagner, it is a coloring device; and Wagner is unique in the annals of music in being able to create a tonal coloring that would carry through the whole of an opera. So in the *Flying Dutchman* this menace carries right through, giving a bleak aspect to all the proceedings until near the end, when Senta, the chaste maiden, gives herself to the Dutchman and redeems him from his eternal punishment through "apotheosis" music.

In the prelude to act 1 of *Lohengrin*, Wagner wants some music that is pure white because a knight will make an entrance on a white swan (again the audience is being transported to another world) and, for this, Wagner needs suitable music. The "trick" here is that the violins are divided (each section plays different music) and all play in the highest register. The risk is that they might "whistle," so this places enormous demands on all the fiddlers to tune their instruments exactly. When the flutes come in, they imitate the old wooden harmoniums in small churches, adding the religious and devotional mood that underlies the miraculous appearance of the knight.[9]

Here we have pure *color* in music, "something that was established for harmony and above all for melody only in contemporary music. The coloristic dimension," says Adorno, is "a realm where Wagner is completely at home."[10] The color here is supposed to be a pure white. It sounds translucently white to me, although others say it sounds silver to them. Color is never one thing. When Wagner wrote and staged this, listeners would have been used to a melody. But rather than have the cello accompany the violins or provide counterpoint and form harmonic padding, Wagner has the violins accompany the violins; he has them divided into groups to provide accompaniment. Violins in counterpoint had been standard fare, but what was not so was the chromatic harmony in the highest register for each of the counterpointing groups. The white or silvery shimmer is the result of the enormous stress on the strings—Wagner knew like no one else how to exploit the physical vibrations of sound to create his magical effects—and he would not have guessed: his musical intuition would have told him.

Wagner used dissonance expressively as well to show the "inside-out" of rapture: the pain, and the pleasure in the pain.

The Music Dramas

A music drama is not an opera, but the "erecting of genuine drama on the basis of absolute music."[11] Beethoven's achievement is a starting point for music drama; this is why Wagner was so passionate about Beethoven. Alain Badiou says:

> If you want to know what the deep connection between music and drama in Wagner ultimately is—the essential question regarding the new opera as he conceived it—the most important thing to remember is the fact that, in Wagner, *dramatic possibilities are created through the music.* The music does not simply reinforce or support a pre-established dramatic situation, even if the text in fact is always already there; it creates dramatic possibilities as such. In other words, the subjective process of the decision or the figure of the emotion as a dramatic possibility is built right into the music.[12]

Baudelaire wrote about his impression of first hearing Wagner's *Tannhäuser*.[13] In the same essay he refers to Wagner's later opera, *Lohengrin*, from which he had heard excerpts the year before, at the Théâtre-Italien. Wagner's music dramas are an aesthetic experience and are, as we hope to be able to appreciate, of the highest order.

> I remember that from the first bars, the impression was given to me of that happiness known to all imaginative people, by dream, in their night-world. I felt set free from the *force pulling me down*, and I felt restored to the memory of the extraordinary voluptuousness (*volupté*) that circulates in *high places* (noting in passing that I had no idea of the program notes at this time). After that, I involuntarily projected the delicious state of a man in the throes of a great reverie in absolute solitude, but a solitude with *an immense horizon* and a *large diffuse light; immensity* with no other décor than itself. Then I experienced the sensation of a more vivid *clarity*, of a rapidly increasing *intensity of light* that the verbal nuances given by the dictionary could not suffice to explain, of ever increasing *heat and whiteness*. Then I became plainly conscious of the idea of a soul that moves in its ground luminosity, and of an ecstatic *voluptuousness (volupté) and knowledge*, soaring above and beyond the natural sphere of habitation.[14]

Baudelaire compares his own aesthetic experience with that of the composer Franz Liszt, whose authority on the matter he trusts as much as his own ears, as found in Liszt's book, *Lohengrin et*

Tannhäuser, which he had on hand. Baudelaire is able to match the aesthetic experience of he and Liszt with Wagner's own description in the program notes. What struck Baudelaire were the correspondences.

> In the three separate transpositions [into thought] we find the sensation of *spiritual and physical beatitude*; of *isolation*; of the contemplation of something *infinitely great and infinitely beautiful*; of an *intense light*, which rejoice the eyes and soul to the point of fainting, and lastly, the sensation of *space extending to the furthest conceivable limits*.[15]

The point of the comparison, Baudelaire explains, is "demonstrating how true music suggests analogous ideas to different minds."[16] In other words, it *unites*.

> No other musician excels like Wagner does in *portraying* space and depth, material and spiritual. This is a kind of remark that a number of the brightest and best minds has been forced to make on more than one occasion.[17]

Listening to Wagner is in fact intoxicating:

> He has the art of translating by subtle gradations, all that is excessive, immense, ambitious, in both spiritual and natural man. It sometimes seems that in listening to this ardent and despotic music that one rediscovers painted in the pit of darkness, torn by daydreams, the vertiginous conceptions of opium.[18]

One of Wagner's ideas was of seamlessness—a seamless flow of music that gives an organic and enveloping feeling; a flow of material with an organic feel, as of a "whole" that expands or contracts. Each of Wagner's music dramas has its own spiritual and emotional temperature and texture. If you compare him to Verdi, for instance, in Verdi, you have a composer with genius who is inventive with melody and situations and dramatic climaxes. But if you listen to *Aida* or *La Traviata*, they all sound recognizably "Verdi"; the arias all have a predictable form and flow. There is at work a craftsman of genius who is very inventive, but you would be unlikely to feel, if you were in the middle of *La Traviata* and you got lifted out and transplanted into the middle of *Aida*, that there would be an awfully significant difference or real *break*, for it is not as if there is a completely different spiritual, emotional or even musical temperature there. It is recognizably the same. You can tell the composer's fin-gerprint. The music has the same texture. But it is different with Wagner. With Wagner, if you hear a couple of minutes of his music, you can tell where it comes from because each of the operas is *different* musically and spiritually. In each of Wagner's works there is a very specific emotional coloring, or *sensibility*—a specific soulful dimension. It is almost like saying that his thirteen different stage works would have been written by different composers because they all have a different color.

Baudelaire also calls Wagner a composer of music drama, which is *not opera*, "that is to say the reunion, the *coincidence* of several arts—by the art *par excellence*, the most integral and the most perfect."[19] "In the early works we see at once how Wagner's art was rooted in Beethoven's and how his progress as original musician was bound up with his progress as music dramatist."[20]

The singular power of each art comes together in Wagner's art. The point here is that the "music dramatist" was to consummate all art; even if Wagner did not achieve it, even in his greatest work, consummation was nevertheless his goal, and he not only conceived this consummation, but got nearer than any other musician ever has. This points to what *still has to be done*, and today we need to imagine as well *how technology could be part of it.* As we have seen more than once before in these pages, unfortunately, just as the assistance of technology arrives, our culture loses all sense of what art is and what music is. This is a reason why it is helpful and fortuitous to go back to Wagner and reconsider him after "Wagnerianism."

One thing Wagner makes clear is that the music does not have a supporting role, as it does in the commodities of the movie industry today. Baudelaire: "Music has its own manner [of conveying certitude] by the way that is proper to it."[21] Listening to Beethoven and Weber had primed him for Wagner, Baudelaire says, but nonetheless he heard in Wagner "something new that I was powerless to define."[22]

Baudelaire quotes Wagner from the latter's open *Letter on Berlioz*, in which he is trying to explain his position on music more clearly: "There [in Ancient Greece] I came across, everywhere, artistic work *par excellence*, drama, in which, the idea, however profound it is, is able to manifest itself with utter clarity and in a universally intelligible way."[23] This is, Wagner says, "the theatre of ancient Athens,"[24] perfect "due to the alliance of all the arts concurrently assembled toward the same end"—to show something, to reveal something, to initiate the listener and viewer in the things of the spirit—"that is to say the production of the most perfect and only true artwork."[25]

Wagner then describes our Ladder of *Eros*—the dimension of height in sensibility—from the composer's point of view: "I recognized, in effect, that there, where one of the arts reached the impasse of its own limits, was precisely the point of commencement for another art with the utmost rigorous exactitude, which consequently, by the intimate union of the two arts, were able to show more with a clarity more satisfying than either of the arts could have succeeded in doing by itself; but, on the contrary, had either of the arts by itself attempted to do what both of them could only do together, it would be fatal, leading to obscurity and confusion, and the degeneration and corruption of each of the particular arts."[26]

Redemption through Love

Redemption through love is the major theme of all Wagner's music dramas. Wagner chose myth because, in his words, "myth is the primitive and anonymous poem of the people" able to be taken up and remodeled in every age.[27] As Baudelaire says, "Myth is a tree that grows everywhere, in every climate, under every sun, spontaneously and without grafting. Of this, religion and poetry from every corner of the globe furnish us with abounding proof. Just as sin is everywhere redemption is everywhere myth is everywhere. *Nothing is more cosmopolitan than the eternal*."[28] Moreover, "Nothing of what is eternal and universal needs to be acclimatized."[29]

We might take *Tannhäuser* as an example of this new age in art and start with the authority of Baudelaire. He describes listening to the overture to *Tannhäuser* as follows:

> From the very first bars our nerves vibrate in unison with the melody; all recollected flesh is made to tremble. Every well-endowed mind conforms by carrying within it two infinites, heaven and hell, and in every image of each of these infinities the person suddenly recognizes half of himself. The satanic titillations of a vague love are now succeeded by the seductions, the dazzlings, the cries of victory, the groans of gratitude, and then the howls of ferocity, the reproaches of the victims and the impious hosannas of the officiating celebrants, as if barbarity were always to have a place in the drama of love, and carnal pleasure were always to lead, by ineluctable satanic logic, to the delights of crime. When the religious theme, making an incursion across the unchained evil, comes little by little, to re-establish

order and take the ascendancy, when it dresses itself anew in all its sound beauty, over and above the chaos of voluptuous agonies, the whole soul finds a refreshment, a redemptive beatitude; ineffable feeling . . .[30]

What matters in all this, above all, is the *musical intelligence* at work. Here are the words of Liszt from his *Lohengrin et Tannhäuser*, with Baudelaire's emphasis:

> The spectator, predisposed to find *nothing but detachable morsels which, strung together, on the thread of some intrigue or other, composes the substance of the operas we are accustomed to*, will certainly have his interest piqued not a little over three acts by the deeply considered, surprisingly skillful and poetically intelligent combination, with which Wagner, *by means of his various principal phrases*, works out in *melodic knots* which are constitutive of the whole drama. The folds that these melodic lines make while binding and interlacing the poetic speech, in effect move us to the end point.[31]

What Liszt is recognizing—and Baudelaire's emphasis shows that he recognizes it as well—is Wagner's uses of *leitmotif*. Liszt describes it as follows:

> By this method which complicates the facile excitements procured by a series of arias rarely connected with each other, he makes hard demands on the attention of the theatre-goer; but, at the same time, he prepares emotional dishes and delicacies for those able to taste them. *These melodies are the personification of ideas*; their recapitulation announces the feelings, which the speech is unable to explicitly indicate; it is to them Wagner entrusts the revelation to us of all the secrets of the heart. There are phrases which, for example, the first scene of the 2nd act, which winds through the whole opera like a venomous snake, coiling around its victims and fleeing their saintly defenders; there are phrases, like that of the introduction, which only return rarely, but then with supreme and divine revelations. Situations or characters of some importance are all musically expressed by a melody, which becomes its constant symbol . . . and these are melodies of rare beauty.[32]

In terms of *melos*, or the metaphysics of music, in Schopenhauer's sense, *Tannhäuser* is the story of *purification* of the soul by music; one might go so far as to say that *Tannhäuser* is designed *as that* purification. In this sense the music drama is *a rite*. Perhaps, as Wagner envisages in *Religion and Art*, rites symbolize and encourage human atonement, their symbolism, "beckoning to the highest pity, to worship of suffering, to imitation of this breaking of all self-seeking Will."[33] It is a religious vision in the past tense, and a secular art ideal in the future tense.

Experiencing the music drama as a rite is an *initiation*. And yet this is neither secular music nor religious but, like the ancient Greek drama, social and inclusive. Such "postreligious" and "postsecular" works were already instanced philosophically by Kant, Hegel, and Schopenhauer. And Wagner instances this postreligious and post-secular ethos of the new music in the first place, not with a political act (as he did in his misspent youth) or with a book (although he was a philosopher too), but with the *music*. Absolute music in Beethoven becomes world music in Wagner.

With *Tannhäuser*, as Baudelaire rightly says, the inner senses can distinguish forces of desire in us which pull us in one or another direction. *Tannhäuser* is a music drama about purification of the soul, pointing toward the possibility of a rite by which the soul may be purified by listening. In *Lohengrin*, Wagner's next music drama, the characters have already worked through the stage of purification on the ladder of listening, and the music drama is about the next stage. Wagner himself describes what we hear in the overture. The music drama *begins* at the level of *rapture* and *exaltation*:

> Out of the blue ether of the sky there seems to condense a wonderful yet at first hardly perceptible vision; and out of this there gradually emerges, ever more and more clearly, an angel host bearing in its midst the sacred Grail. As it approaches earth it pours out exquisite odors, like streams of gold, ravishing the senses of the beholder. The glory of the vision grows and grows until it seems as if the rapture must be shattered and dispersed by the very vehemence of its own expansion. The vision draws nearer, and the climax is reached when at last the Grail is revealed in all its glorious reality, radiating fiery beams and shaking the soul with emotion. The beholder sinks on his knees in adoring self-annihilation. The Grail pours out its light on him like a benediction and consecrates him to its service; then the flames gradually die away, and the angel host soars up again to the ethereal heights in tender joy, having made pure once more the hearts of men by the sacred blessing of the Grail.[34]

Wagner is not using hyperbole. The reality is that, until this overture, such music had never before been heard on earth.

The music of *Lohengrin* comes from that "second world," as Wagner calls it; it is literally a sound-world, which, he says, "bears the same relation to the world as dreaming has to waking."[35] But out of only this world—of harmony, of universal will, of what we have been calling *melos*—"can the Essence of things without be learnt in truth."[36] Wagner had the music come to him one day at noon in Marienbad, where he was recovering from the enormous toll that his creative receptors were imposing on his mortal frame. About to step into an obligatory bath, "I was suddenly overcome by so powerful a longing to commit *Lohengrin* to paper that, unable to stay in the bath the regulation hour, I jumped out impatiently after the first few minutes, and, hardly giving myself time to dress, ran back like a madman to my lodging to write out what was pressing so heavily on my mind. This went on for several days . . ."[37]

In 1845, Wagner had been in dire poverty, his wife had left him, he owed money on all sides, his work was getting him nowhere, he was in a state of ruin and he was on the edge of nervous collapse and trying not to tip over the brink. His doctor sent him to Marienbad for a rest. As holiday reading he had taken the poems of Wolfram von Eschenbach with him and the old book of German legends, which had the *Tannhäuser* legend in it. The same book contained *Lohengrin*, as he would find out. In these circumstances, reading *Lohengrin*, Wagner recalled, "there suddenly sprang up before my eyes a Lohengrin complete in every detail of dramatic form."[38] Maybe. But he did not have the strength to conceive and write it. Nothing in his experience led him to believe it worth doing, in any case. It was only an impulse; the other impulse—the sensible one, which followed doctor's orders—was to forget it. But Wagner, unlike Elsa (in the drama), and even, probably, without all her purity, did not doubt. He wrote the music drama; again it is a monument to that which it reveals, of which there is nothing else like it—except for other surpassing works of Wagner.

If *Tannhäuser* depicts the powers that we are torn between in our natures, powers which, because we are social creatures, can tear the world apart, or bring about peace on it, if they get hold of us, then *Lohengrin* depicts the next stage, that having become established in purity, we must develop our inner senses, for our outer senses are as in a dream; the inner senses are developed through calm and stillness, and, through them, we touch on what we inwardly share in the lives of others. This inward sharing starts with *affinities* of sensibility—of soul—and moves toward the development of inner group consciousness. *Lohengrin* is about inner guidance and Wagner knew about this through his experience of inspiration and through the work he had to do on the mythical material he used, and on the poetry of the librettos he wrote and through his conceptualization of the music-dramas as a whole; in all this guidance had to come from within and not just "from himself" as it were. Those in his outward everyday life often suffered because of his inner preoccupations. But because of this inner work that the composer must do, and every artist has to do, it is so important to be physically and economically well established and free from worry. One does not make art in order to become well-off and established, although people do. If economics becomes an end in itself and an encompassing mirror we all see ourselves in, then even the first step of purification makes no sense.[39]

Elsa, the main female character, is pure and innocent. "The whole interest of *Lohengrin* consists in an inner working within the heart of Elsa, involving every secret of the soul," Wagner tells us.[40] There are still powers of destruction abroad, which, because of Elsa's purity, rather than despite it, fasten their attention on her; Ortrud and her husband Frederic instance this. Elsa has a protector, a knight in shining armor, who is a dream figure. The whole action is pitched at the level of what we would call the unconscious, in which the night world of dream figures is as real—if not more real, because more inward—than the day world, and the consciousness of one transforms into the consciousness of the other. To the naive listener this drama will seem to be more of "fantasy," but that is not the case. Wagner is revealing something about the "straight and narrow" path that leads to life. First, it involves purification, but then, it seems, it involves believing wholeheartedly in your inspiration, personified by a supernatural guardian figure. Elsa is pure and exquisite, but flawed by doubt, which proves her undoing, in a moment of weakness. All of Wagner's work is of this kind: to do with the inner life of the soul. The conceptions become more grand and encompassing as they also become more profound.

As the inspiration took him, Wagner had the habit of working on various projects simultaneously. After *Lohengrin*, there was the period of *Tristan and Isolde* (composed 1857–59) and *Der Ring des Nibelungen*, which he took twenty years to compose (1853–74) and which heard once through takes around fifteen hours. It is here, in this vast and complex work, that Wagner's use of *leitmotif* becomes an important unifying factor, as is famously explained by Derryck Cooke.[41]

The doubt that was deadly for his character Elsa (just as it was for Lot's wife, who looked back and turned into a pillar of salt) was overcome by the magisterially faithful Wagner—faithful, that is, to his daemon, his creative urge.

> All doubt was at last taken from me, when I gave myself up to the *Tristan*. Here, in perfect trustfulness, I plunged into the inner depths of soul events, and from out of this inmost centre of the world I fearlessly built up its outer form . . . Life and death, the whole import and existence of the outer world, here hang on nothing but the inner movements of the soul. The whole affecting action comes about for reason only that the inmost soul demands it, and steps to light with the very shape foretokened in the inner shrine.[42]

In *Tristan*, Wagner achieved—or at least believed that he had at last achieved to his own satisfaction—the wondrous combination of word and music in which each brings the other to life and the whole is poetic. The concepts of the music drama also perfectly synthesize his musical genius with philosophy.

The Ring of the Nibelung

The purpose of Wagner's music—to awaken us to reality and the possibilities, and responsibilities, in our power—continues to be expressed in the *Ring* cycle. Wagner "had been obsessed by the fatality of desire"[43]—"The ring, the talisman of world-power, desirable and therefore accursed." It is in the *Ring* that Wagner's use of leitmotif that I have spoken of already reaches unprecedented and incredible proportions of musical genius.

> The term *leitmotif* is not Wagner's but Wolzogen's [he worked for Wagner at Bayreuth and propagated Wagner's music after the latter's death]. Wagner spoke of *Grundthema* (fundamental theme), thus stressing the role it plays in how the work is structured and its formal aspects, although not denying its place in the drama . . . but insufficient attention has been given to how the difference in terminology reflects a radically different perspective. Wagner speaks as a composer, Wolzogen as someone hearing the music: the *Grundthema* leads to organization, but the *leitmotif* leads to being able to follow the unfolding of the work. The *leitmotifs* are indispensable in a miniaturized sound-world, in which Wagner exasperated Nietzsche, but it is in the minutiae of the writing, in the detailed finesse, that the composer shows himself at his most artistic. The motifs guide the listener ("I have already heard that!") but they also create a complex world of relationships, forcing us after the event to ask "what connec-

tion is there between two completely heterogeneous scenes imbued with one or more motifs that are the same?"[44]

Wolzogen, as I have said, was an apprentice to Wagner, was mentored by him, and worked with him at Bayreuth; indeed, they were near neighbors from 1877, when Wolzogen would have been twenty-nine years old, until the composer's death, in 1883. But Wolzogen stayed on in Bayreuth until 1938.

"A detailed analytical study of the leitmotifs in the *Ring* would show that with the exception of motifs linked to love all of them can be generated from the opening motif of *Das Rheingold*."[45] In other words, the life of the whole thing emerges out of the primeval waters; but this is not the case for love, whose origin is directly divine and not organically derived. But Wagner's creative work imitates the way of nature, proliferating into life-forms from the basic bacterial cells of inspiration.

At the very heart of the *Ring* are Siegfried and his death: *Siegfried's Tod*. Wagner completed the libretto for this in 1848. It would become with little change the libretto for *Gotterdammerung*, which was composed in 1869–74 and premiered at Bayreuth in 1876 as part of the first complete performance of the *Ring*.[46]

Here, by way of summary, is Thomas Mann on the *Ring*:

> This extraordinary revolutionary was just as radical about the past as about the future. The saga was not enough for him, it must be the saga in its most primitive form . . . He must penetrate back to the original sources . . . these alone were the sacred depths of the past, corresponding to his sense of the future. He did not yet know that even within his work he would not be able to bring himself to stop at any beginning already somehow weighed down by history, and to start from that point, as it were *in media res*; that here too he would be by a magnificent compulsion forced back to the beginning and arch-beginning of all things, the primeval cell, the first contra E flat of the prelude to the prelude; that it would be laid upon him to erect a musical cosmogony, yes, a myth-cosmos, himself, and endow it with profound organic *bios*, the singing spectacle-poem of the beginning and end of the world. But so much he did already know, that in his insatiable burrowings into the ultimate depths and dawns he had found the man and hero whom he, like Brünenhilde, loved before he was born, his Siegfried, a figure that enchanted and gratified as well his passion for the past as his avidity for the future, for it was timeless: the human being—they are his own words—"in the most natural, blithest, richness of his sense-endowed manifestation; the

masculine embodiment of the spirit of unique, eternal, procreative instinctiveness; veritable doer of deeds; in the fullness of the highest, most immediate power and most unquestioned loveliness." This unconditioned, untrammeled figure of light, then, this unsafeguarded, independent, self-responsible being, relying upon his own strength alone, radiant with freedom, fearless, guiltless doer and fulfiller of destiny, who by the noble and natural event of his death brought about the twilight of old, worn-out world-powers, redeemed the world by lifting it to a new level of knowledge and morality—him Wagner makes the hero of the drama conceived as belonging to the music, which, no longer in modern verse, but in the alliterative accents of his Old Norse sources, he sketched and called *Siegfried's Death*.[47]

More could not be said in as few words about the whole sense and feeling of this massive artwork—perhaps the greatest ever conceived by a single mind. The search for truth down one of life's infinite avenues is a search for redemption.

Art Religion

Paul Valéry, that master of the soulful in art and life, says:

> Thanks to Richard Wagner music became an instrument of metaphysical delectation, both a stimulant and a builder of illusions, a splendid means of unleashing nonexistent tempests and opening empty chasms. In his art the world is remade, replaced, multiplied, speeded up, and deepened, illuminated by a system of titillations acting on the nervous system—in the same way as an electric current induces a taste in the mouth, artificial warmth, and so forth.
>
> But, when all is said and done, is "reality" other than this?[48]

These are words that cut both ways.

Religion is not an art and art cannot be a religion or provide the substitute, but it is true that they go together, and now more than ever. This is what Wagner, following Schopenhauer, knew. Metaphysics as music has been our interest through this chapter. The operas are dashing conceptions. But not to everyone's taste. In the sung passages, which make up most of the time, the sensibility is large and wildly overwrought. Compared to the purity, simplicity and wonderful straightforwardness of most of the music of Bach, or of the melody in the operas of Puccini or Verdi, Wagnerian opera might be experienced as discordant, even crude in its vocal extravagances. Also, the music accompanying the voices is illustrative and evocative in a manner that many listeners would still hold points forward to its uses in movies and even in Walt Disney cartoons, where the music is the continuous symphonic support to the action. The musical interludes and bookends of Wagner are lovely but the singing lacks grace and above all, *dance.* Oh for music that dances!—for *Swan Lake, The Rite of Spring,* rather than cascading motionlessness and rather clubfooted drama! So might cry out a gentler sensibility.

But it is the *philosophy* in these operas that they carry and marry that is overarching. The works are philosophical as much as they are musical—and in their inspiration too: this is indicated more in the rich symbolism at work than in the musical settings of the librettos. This philosophy is compelling, as Wagner himself found it to be, although it might be more compelling to *read* than to listen to in the incarnation Wagner gave to it. The sung librettos may be hard on the ears and not sweeten the heart, but the beauty perhaps shines all the more brightly where it shines: the Priesleid in *The Mastersingers,* the Liebestod at the end of *Tristan and Isolde,* and the Karfreitagszauber in *Parsifal* come from unheard heights to our world, who could doubt?

Wagner's librettos are poetry and yet the style throughout is that of declamation. Wagner had in mind ancient Greek drama and thought to recreate it. As far as we know, in ancient Greece the style was not declamation but chant. The ancient Greek dramas had a sacred status and import, not just the social political status and import that is accentuated in modernist interpretations; and it is likely that the chants originally employed at the origins of Greek drama, before its secular development from Aeschylus, are closer to Bhakti yoga in *ethos,* something of religious and ritual origin, but with *inner* import to do with states of meditation. The traces of this had already been lost in Greece, and in Wagner the singing is emotionally calibrated (at least it was for nineteenth-century audiences). It is argued in favor of Wagner (Bruckner thought this) that the singing is part of the fabric of the music, but listeners today, used to the twentieth-century development of song and exposure to songs, might find that Wagnerian singing continually rips that musical fabric and does nothing to enhance or enrich it at all—this being why the preludes and interludes are so often regarded as the "best bits."

The relation of chant to states of meditation that are preserved strongly from ancient times to our own in Bhakti yoga, and which survives in old synagogue chanting and in old church plainsong, although without the consciousness of how this works psychospiritually, would suggest a missing ingredient in Wagner. Current research links ancient Greek drama to the Orphic mysteries (devotional and musical mysteries);[49] this would make the chants sacred, and would explain the origin of the meter of the spoken verse in the later dramas; it would also necessitate the invocation of the ancient musical modes (Lydian and so on) that are keyed to states of human being. Wagner's work is too early in the age of *melos* and the future of the artwork that he foresaw to get this right or to advance far in this regard, so the work of tying music back to meditation and inner life is for musicians still to come. There is therefore some credence to the criticism of the operatic side of Wagner which decries that we must listen to relentless declamatory and overwrought emotion; this goes along with the drama's clubfootedness so far as *the spirit of dance* is concerned.

But not only are there tensions *in* Wagner that divide listeners, there are philosophical tensions *with* him that also divide listeners. The real tension with Wagner is between the exteriorized drama on stage and tremendous music and singing, and the fact that the real meaning of it all, the real action is *interior*, going on inside the mind. Some listeners enjoy the trappings, some enjoy the musical technicalities, but the truth of it is psychological, to do with what goes on *is us*, or the *metaphysics* of the music. Wagner is a philosophical composer *and* a psychological one; it is with Wagner's music, prefiguring Freud and Jung in this respect, that the philosophical *becomes* psychological; parallel with Ibsen, therefore, whose plays are both philosophical and psychological (and no coincidence that both artists draw from Shakespeare). This psychological transposition of metaphysics was an event in the life of the culture that Nietzsche picked up from Wagner and tried vainly to capitalize on. However, those who want to concentrate on the interiority of Wagner's music dramas might find them overly drawn out and excessive, parallel to the verbosity for which German academic writing is famous, but which drags it down. We should not forget, in Wagner's day he would invite a few friends over to his house and have someone who could do so sing an act of *Tristan* accompanied by the piano. Obviously in a confined space this would have been sung softly with the high level of inflection and intimacy of expression that we are used to from the popular song. In our age of electronic amplification some listeners to Wagner await a time when the *singing* is revolutionized, and with that, the type of person who we *see* singing might key into the imagination of the drama much better. The real revolutions in Wagnerian productions have perhaps hardly begun.

I posit that what we hear when we hear Wagner, which may take some getting used to, is Wagner's *inspiration* and it is this that matters and continues over time and place, drawing full houses. We hear his inspiration most of all in *the music beneath* the singing, rather than in the singing or drama, and this is what, if we cannot bear the singing, we need to listen for. I would posit that Wagner *met* his inspiration. He had the predisposition and gifts and lived the kind of life that enabled such a meeting. His inspiration was not something he had, but something that *had him*, like love. Hearing his inspiration is like hearing something from another world, which is not merely the world of the nineteenth century. What we hear—as I have wanted to show in this chapter—is music that speaks *over the top* of the moral and existential disasters and disorders of the twentieth century and *over the top* of all the confabulated intellectualist music of the twentieth century, but plays into a new age.[50] Music that speaks over the top of a century like the twentieth to step into a new age has to take a giant leap. Music, not words—what in Chapter 6 I have distinguished from *logos* as *melos*—will be central to such an age: a core argument of this book. And another core argument is that it is philosophy—and *religious* philosophy—married with the music, that will be the enabling factor of any such age. For this is what *metaphysics as music* means.

Bayreuth, Wagner's foundation in stone, is not just a festival hall but his temple to the new ideas and what they stand for: the idea of collaborative arts that will unite people and have a redemptive and uplifting power and influence.[51] Bayreuth was founded as the place where the eternal symbols of a new and different world were to be felt and encountered. Wagner brought together *mythos* and *logos* under the sway and power of *melos* as the hallmark of a world to come.

9

The Work of Mourning

Night does away with colors. It lets blaze the color of the soul.
—Edmund Jabès, *Le livre des questions*

We return in this chapter to the music of the ground-moods of the soul. Previously I discussed melancholy and delight. Now I shall treat of mourning, stillness, and beauty in turn in this and the subsequent two chapters. The soul sounds out these moods or states of being in music and in life. Each of these—mourning, stillness, and beauty— is intrinsically soul-making and that is why I include discussion of them, from a much longer list of the kaleidoscopic colors of the soul.

Mourning comes out of our depth. Mourning is a form of truth without words, and in this it takes as easily to music as to tears. We have seen that music expresses the inner being of the world. Mourning, too, is close to that being then. In this chapter we shall look at several kinds of mourning, and at representative pieces of the music of mourning.

The contemporary performance artist and philosopher, Peter Banki, has pursued the fraught subject of forgiveness, with his comparative readings of texts addressing the problem of forgiveness after the Holocaust.[1] This is a problem, as he shows, which is not just a matter of the history books or a matter that can any longer be contained among Jews and Germans who "remember," although their doing so remains paradigmatic. The upshot of Banki's work is that we realize more sharply that the problem of forgiveness is one that is spreading everywhere in the world today, where, due to ammunition such as bombs, mass death can be conducted "out of sight, out of mind," or with guns and rocket launchers, from a "safe distance." It is not just that violence has been escalating since the Second World War, but that technology escalates the crimes of violence while allowing perpetrators not to "get their hands dirty." In the old days a war could be cathartic, because it involved hand-to-hand combat for the most part; in the nineteenth century, in Wagner's day, men met in the fields and fought; it was still possible to forgive, because the fighting or scrimmage was on a human scale, however brutal. But today *war is technological.* Although we still use the same word and so we think we mean the same thing—war—the phenomenon is not actually the same at all.

The arms industry is one of the biggest and most lucrative in the world, and America, the political system which gives freest reign to the manufacture and exportation of deadly weaponry built to kill human beings "enshrines" the so-called right to bear arms in open society, even to the extent of having a home loaded with automatic weaponry, should one wish. The political and psychological—and religiously endorsed—confusion between freedom and guns is no longer confined to America, where the militarization of civil society started and grows apace. The American-style commercialization and commodification of armaments in which military and civil uses are matters of purchasing power essentially has now spread to other nations all competing for "markets." The difference between war as it once was, everywhere on earth for the whole of history up until the twentieth century, and recent wars, lies precisely in this difference between a world in which armaments is a global profit-based industry and a world in which it was not. The American situation in which the concept of freedom goes together with guns has been normalized by the public relations industry that accompanies every visible move of society, so that in the United States gun ownership is so normal it is regarded even by educated people as anti-American to advocate the total abolition of all weaponry from society, as it would literally be an affront to people's freedom. Too much money is involved to even warrant such an advocacy anyway, and in that kind of culture money is all that really matters and everything is geared to making it. Any threat to money is a threat to freedom and that is when one needs to reach for one's automatic weapon. When big capitalism is producing guns, missiles, bombs, and so on, the problem of forgiveness is not what it was for most of history—or what it *should* be.

Forgiveness is meant to operate on a human scale, if we think of the Christian notion of it, for instance; but today technological war crimes beggar forgiveness. Furthermore, given that forgiveness is supposed to be "the glory of Christianity," the fact that the churches themselves, as organizations, have stood forth so seldom on this issue, particularly in the United States, and said so little about it, is actually part of the scandal, and shows, the *complicity* of the churches with the *manufac-*

ture of violence. When war becomes a technological accomplishment with human and ecological collateral damage, when that is to say the human and cathartic element is removed from war, a *just war is impossible*; combine with this the intentional and concerted manufacture of violence, this absolutely ensures a just war is impossible. I emphasize this because it is a new state of affairs. Even up until the Second World War a just war was possible, but since the Second World War (this is a negative side of the turning I referred to at the end of the previous chapter), and since wars became technological spectaculars that can be televised and draw the prime-time advertising dollar to the newscast, and war can be syndicated and the film sold on, the sense of *decency* which belief in a just war requires is gone. This is why no one looks back at the American war in Vietnam—or the more recent wars in Kuwait or Iraq—as just, although they entertained millions on television and were terrific for broadcasting revenue and commercial advertisers. To the contrary, a peacekeeping role is the only *decent* role for troops and armaments in our time; the manufacture of armaments beyond this is indecent and the large-scale profiteering from the manufacture and sale of armaments is criminal. I do not know why arms manufacturers and governments are not criminally liable if the weaponry used in a conflict is found to have been purchased to make technological warfare possible where once it would not have been.

The technological aspect is what takes the war out of the range of possibility for forgiveness or, at best, it makes forgiveness much harder because the inhuman and catastrophic element of conflict becomes central; consider, for example, the destruction from massive bombs or long-range missiles. Even on a local scale, say of those American schools where someone goes on the rampage, there is a categorical difference between someone who goes on a rampage with a knife in hand, and someone who goes on the rampage with an assault rifle capable of firing dozens of bullets in seconds and killing and maiming a lot of people at a distance with the hair-touch of a trigger. One rampage is on a human scale, the other is not. Where the human is dominated by the inhuman, justice is impossible. Where justice impossible, forgiveness is impossible or not real.

Banki shows that *listening* is at the heart of forgiveness. Reflection on listening leads us to think about the role imagination must play in forgiveness. To start with, listening means being able to listen to one's conscience so that one can admit wrongdoing; this is the first step toward a desire to reform, on the basis of which there is a possibility

177

of presenting oneself for forgiveness to the one you have wronged. To have no remorse, and so not to be able to reform because of a lack of any will to do so or of consciousness of the need to do so, hardly merits forgiveness. The injured party can still forgive, but what meaning can forgiveness have if the attempt at rapprochement is totally one-sided? The person with no remorse is in a sense "deaf" to something—not just to their conscience, but to their own humanity and to the humanity of the other person: "imagination, dead, imagine," as Samuel Beckett stamped the condition in his book of short texts of that title. Where there is no imagination, there is no empathy, and where there is no empathy, there can be no justice—except one imposed on uncomprehending parties (so a "semblance of justice"). While there *can* be forgiveness where there is no justice (the Christian position), without imagination there is no forgiveness, precisely because forgiveness demands empathy, which, in turn, demands imagination, and in this sense the historic Christian position on forgiveness is unimaginative. Blessed are those who mourn, says Christianity, but this is not true if people are condemned to mourn. Rather, the *work of justice* is that of consciousness-raising that will release people from endless mourning, and release humanity. Musicians and composers work to raise consciousness of justice as well on the assumption that there is something *about* music and *in* music that *allows* it. There needs to be justice as the ground in order for the Christian call to "higher justice" of love and forgiveness to become possible.

Banki reexamines the case of Vladimir Jankélévitch (1903–1985) a musician and philosopher. His parents left the evils of Russia and settled in France hoping for a peaceful life, only to become victims in the German invasion of France. Among many other works, Jankélévitch is author of *Le Pardon* (1967), in which he grapples with the reality of trying to forgive the unforgivable.[2] After decades of trying, he decides that, as far as he is concerned, forgiveness is impossible *and immoral*.[3] With emphasis on the musical and performative nature of forgiveness, Banki retells the story of a young German, Wiard Raveling, who in 1980 wrote to Jankélévitch, asking forgiveness, although he was not personally involved in committing the offences requiring forgiveness since he belongs to the young generation. In his letter he expresses obvious genuine remorse for a past he was not involved in, but that, being a German, it nevertheless involves him.[4] Raveling shows strong empathy for Jankélévitch, on the one hand, and for his own people, on the other. Jankélévitch is touched. In his reply he owns up to never—in thirty-five years—having received a letter like this, a letter so open and real and truthful. In his letter Raveling invites Jankélévitch to Germany and says that they will not talk about philosophy, "But I will play a record of Chopin, or if you prefer, Fauré and Debussy [. . .] let it be said in passing: I admire and respect Rubinstein; I like Menuhin."[5] Wearily, but endearingly, Jankélévitch says he is too old now to go to Germany, too old to "inaugurate this new era." He invites Raveling to Paris: "knock on my door, we will sit down at the piano."

And the meeting took place, Raveling took up the invitation and went to Paris to meet Jankélévitch, thirty-five years after the end of the war, and they sat at the piano together. Banki adds: "The allusion on both sides to music, to music played and listened to together, to the sharing of music, is significant to the extent that it designates a realm beyond words which is perhaps required by forgiveness (if it is truly something that happens only between two singular individuals, an event irreducible to any form of generalization or universalization)."[6] If, as we have said, music expresses the inner being of the world, to sit down with another, with an "enemy," to make music, is to engage *together*, at a level before words, in which the one and the other *are not two*.

Much that cannot be forgiven has to be forgotten. Mourning is a forgetting in the form of remembrance. We mourn what we remember, but it helps us recover. We recover who and what we are and a sense of what the world is for. We recover our sanity. Hence the revenge cycle (of some parts of the world today) has not done the work of mourning. In the work of mourning all hostilities cease. In places like the Middle East where there has been such a lot of technological violence for such a long time and so much tit-for-tat, hostilities would have to cease forever for the work of mourning. Like Jankélévitch I believe music is essential to the work of mourning and that is why I have a chapter on it. The work of mourning will be necessary to any new age, and no new age will be entered except through this portal. Mourning we remember in order to forget, it is a foundation stone of sanity and the philosophy of sensibility, such as given in this whole book, must have sanity as its foundation, it cannot start anywhere else. Sanity is a word for our inner ecology and is what normal means: sane. Hardly a totalistic claim either as we can only each be sane in our own way. But sanity is recognizable and is a spectrum concept , like sexuality.

The phrase "the work of mourning" is one associated with the work of Freud, whose psychoanalysis really took off after the First World

War, when it helped the culture cope with the aftershocks of so much violence. Freud's team of psychoanalysts trained doctors, themselves traumatized by what they saw in the aftermath, in how to deal with abnormal, nonphysical disease and pain. Psychoanalysis sensitizes those involved with it to others and to the world in a new way. Part of what it sensitizes us to is our unconsciousness. Mourning comes out of the unconscious, as does delayed mourning, as does inability to mourn. None of it is "intentional." Mourning is not something you choose or initiate; it happens to you. Mourning takes us over and does something with us. The work of mourning is the work of the soul as soul work. The work of mourning is work *in and with* music to heal our individual souls, but, as Wagner had in mind for the future, it is more than that: it is for mending the *anima mundi*, the *soul of the world*.

Mourning has a deep root in the Western musical tradition. Western art music emerges out of the church, of which the symbol is a cross. Mourning the death of Jesus, identifying with his sorrow at his abandonment by his God, identifying with his mother's sorrow as she watches her son beaten and crucified, after all the great hopes his followers had placed in him . . . this mourning predates and undergirds the joy of the resurrection. It is not simply that he has "come back to life" like Lazarus, come back from the grave, but that he testifies to life *beyond* death, to a *form of body* that is inextinguishable and that is human. It is the sadness of mourning the death of the Son of God that we hear at the center of the great plainsong chants. These chants go back in time too. The chants trace back through the synagogues, where communities remembered Jerusalem from the lands of exile: there they remembered Solomon's temple and David's kingdom; there they remembered their sins and failings before the law, recorded in the Bible. The Bible is a great book of mourning; the mourning hardly lets up. The roads to Zion mourn.[7] No wonder *plainchant is the purest sound of the metaphysics of nostalgia*. It sounds the very *essence* of that nostalgia.

Ultimately caught up in the mourning is the yearning for redemption from exile, for the Promised Land, or, for Christians, heaven; yearning for the Messiah or the return of the Messiah—Messianism in either case, Jewish or Christian. Plainchant is the very sound of all this. And the keenest ears will hear the presentiments of the redemption in it. "He who has ears to hear, let him hear!" as the prophets so often declared.

De Morales: *Missa pro Defunctis*

The *Kyrie* from the Mass for the dead (*Missa pro defunctis*) by Cristobal de Morales (c. 1500–1553) must be heard in a Spanish cathedral, or on a great sound system in a large, echoing space. *Kyrie, eleison* of course means "Lord, have mercy" and is sung or said even today at every Catholic Church in the world at every Mass. The sound in this version of the *Kyrie* by de Morales on the Play List is large and assertive, full-blooded, masculine, slow, resonant, expressing joyful sorrow—or sorrowful joy. The sorrow attunes our joy and the joy attunes our sorrow. Either without the other is lopsided and about to collapse our sensibility. The joy that does not remember sorrow is really a kind of euphoria, which, without sorrow, is hollow and collapses into depression or fatigue syndromes. The sorrow in which there are no invisible shadows of joy is only misery and traps us there in a culture of griping, moaning and suffering, such as one may discover in some parts of Europe as part of the local culture (if you have the language). This music—and great chant like it—is a tonic for the soul. All great religious traditions have their equivalent of such chant. Ultimately it is awe-inspiring. It gathers you into a universe of joy and sorrow much greater than one's private world, being both more sorrowful (like drowning in nameless forgotten ancient sorrows that the music alone knows) and more joyous (with the joy of the redeemed who have felt the sorrow and been raised to life—whether this is life everlasting as in Christianity, or life in the eternity of the historic community as in Judaism, or the Oneness of life in oriental religions). In this music you can sink: your sorrow can find its depth and there you find some hope, some faith, some joy.

Not a great deal is known about Cristobal de Morales. The outstanding introductory study is Robert Stevenson's *Spanish Cathedral Music in the Golden Age* (1961), which covers Guerrero and Victoria as well as Morales' life and work. Morales was a Spanish church musician who, in a difficult time, achieved international prestige, as his work in Italy ran to thirteen editions in his century alone and came to be performed as far away from Rome as Peru and Mexico.

Spain was an important region for music and musicians, but the major patronage for music then was to be found in Italy. Juan de Tapia, a Spanish musician, collected sufficient money by going from door to door and asking for offerings that he was able to found the first music school, in Naples, in 1537, the Conservatorio della Madonna di Loreto, the model of all similar schools created since, even our modern conservatories.[8]

Morales began his musical life as a chorister in the Seville cathedral, and went on to a position in Avila (1526–27) and, later, with a number of other Spaniards, to Rome, where he sung tenor in the papal chapel for ten years (1535–45). This was the time of the Medici popes—in other words, a time of religious latitude, openness, commerce, learning and great artistic patronage. Moral corruption then was no greater than in any other age, and a lot less than others, although, to the puritanically-minded like Luther, it seemed otherwise. The Reformation was in full swing in Northern Europe. However, de Morales was the only Catholic composer the Lutherans included in their own music at this time. He returned to Spain in the latter part of his life to take up the position of chapel master at Toledo. He was known then in Spain as its greatest musician. All his music is church music, and all of it is vocal.

Exaltation and rapture we saw before is an overflowing of the soul at an uplifted height of sensibility. Mourning is another kind of overflowing. It is related to the passing over into death of loved ones. We do not need to find words for our mourning: our mourning finds words for itself. Mourning is very particular, like love; it marks an absolute relation between two people, not just a fixed relation. An absolute relation underlines the indissoluble uniqueness of each person which love and empathy bind, as we realize our common human nature, we all bleed, we all mourn. A fixed relation is one that is basically conceptual, fixed by thinking and then by people's identification of themselves with these ideas that they have. The absolute relation is to do with sensibility first and foremost, the fixed relation with words.

Memory and Mourning

We shall briefly consider some different aspects of mourning. First, that to do with love and memory; second, religious mourning; and third, mourning that has to do with "the soul of the world."

Memory is one part of mourning; the other part is dashed hope. In both cases we mourn a loss. This is less the case the older one is, and conversely. The mourning of one who dies unduly young testifies to the strength of expectation that lay like an invisible cloth or screen over that person's life. This expectation can be so strong for those closest to the one who has passed from this life that it can crush the mourner totally. I think this is where mourning becomes grief, which is *abject* mourning. Grief is unalleviated mourning. Grief is dreadful pain and suffering. That we can, by the strength of our expectations on others, be put into such an abject state says much about the strength of those expectations. We have them on ourselves, we have them on others, but they are invisible structures of the life of the soul.

Fear makes mourning harder, because the mourner fears the grief that their mourning might turn into. Others around the mourner may fear for him or her too, that the mourner may become a victim of grief. We become a "victim" of grief, because we are totally overcome and without resistance and the only way onward seems to be down. The serious griever would prefer to be dead, but the mourner desires to call the deceased back to life. Grief is an utter obliteration of the *eros*, which is still with the mourner in the desire for the deceased. The fear around the mourner is the fear that the mourner's flame will go out, that their heart will be extinguished by pain.

Bach's much-loved wife, Maria Barbara, died in 1720. Bach is believed to have started writing unaccompanied violin sonatas, expressive of his grief, from this time, but he wrote them with, naturally, a sense of her continued life in God. This is the case in particular for the famous *Chaconne*, as it is known in French, in D minor for Violin from his fourth partita. A "partita" denotes a suite (composition in successive movements), usually for one instrument.

According to musicologist Professor Helga Thoene of the University of Düsseldorf, behind this partita are various hidden "chorales," which is to say, hymns. Bach quite naturally had these hymns in mind when he was composing because his heart and life were full of them. To expert ears of the musicologist, these chorales can be heard like a very distant echo, evoked by the solo violin like a ghostly accompaniment. Professor Thoene published her findings in a specialist journal in 1994. Of course only a musicological expert would manifestly be able to hear these fractals in an identifiable way. The Hilliard Ensemble, with Christoph Poppen on baroque violin, has reconstructed the haunting hymns alongside the beautiful and eminently noble and eloquent solo violin and recorded it on an album entitled *Morimur*, which means "We die"—"we," that is, all of us. It is taken from the Catholic Latin doxology, *Ex Deo nascimur, In Christo morimur, Per Spiritum reviviscimus* (From God we are born, in Christ we die, by the Spirit we are revived to life). It was in fact around the unheard chorales on this word *morimur* that Professor Thoene heard the partita. When musicology is linked to *listening* like this, you have truly astonishing and exemplary scholarship. The recording of the Hilliard Ensemble has to be something we must listen to before *we die*.

"What we hear," says the tenor John Potter in the liner notes to the CD on the ECM label, "is surely something of what went on inside Bach's head when he composed the pieces."[9]

Brahms wrote to the composer Clara Schumann, wife of Robert Schumann, of this chaconne:

> On one stave, for a small instrument, the man writes a whole world of the deepest thoughts and most powerful feelings. If I imagined that I could have created, even conceived the piece, I am quite certain that the excess of excitement and earth-shattering experience would have driven me out of my mind.[10]

Religious Mourning

Mourning humanizes religion and brings the religious authorities down off their pedestals and out of their caves and hermitages. The destruction of the temple in Jerusalem is mourned by Jews today, who still pray for its restitution. Wearing sackcloth and ashes was the dress of mourning. In Catholic culture there are the Sorrowful Mysteries of the rosary as a way of remembering and mourning. Ancient stories of religious significance and devotional import are imaginatively recalled as the beads are said. Jesus in the Garden of Gethsemane says to those who love him, his disciples, his loyal followers, "Stay, here. Watch and pray." But they fall asleep. And is not this unconsciousness our unconsciousness? Thus we mourn. Jesus prays, "My soul is sorrowful unto death . . ." He sweats blood. Jesus says, "Father, if it is possible let this cup pass from me." But sometimes it is not possible. This is the cup of suffering for which he is praying for deliverance. Finally, his friend, Judas, arrives and kisses him in greeting, which turns out to be a secret signal for a brutal arrest and Jesus' total separation from his followers and loved ones, although his mother follows, as we know, at a distance. In the second Sorrowful Mystery, Jesus is scourged with a whip that tears chunks of flesh from his body. In the third, Jesus is crowned with thorns to mock him as a spiritual king, and Pilate drags him in front of a mob and says, "*Ecce homo*" ("Behold, the man!"), and the mob cry out that he be crucified like an enemy of the empire. Then there is the carrying of the cross, the falling, the jeering, Simon of Cyrene helping Jesus—the fourth Sorrowful Mystery. And the fifth is the agonizing crucifixion itself in which Jesus cries out, "My God, my God, why have you forsaken me?" and it is recorded in Aramaic, "*Eloi, Eloi, lama sabachthani?*"[11] so that the actual sound of the cry still rings in our ears. Remember, this is mourning. The only recompense is that some good came out of it. But the good (the Glorious Mysteries of the rosary) does not efface the sorrow; indeed, single individuals and whole communities are reminded again and again, through history, of the sorrowful mysteries, so that they can never be forgotten.

In religious mourning we mourn for *all* the dead, for the kingdom of the dead. In Judaism we can mourn directly; in Christianity, it is customary to mourn all the dead through the death of one man. The particular name, Jesus, in Christianity, links with the suffering of the nameless, who need our prayers, who need someone to cry out for them, whose cry has not been heard or remembered.

Religious mourning is not a passion, but a com-passion, and empathy, and an opening of the inner sensibility and sensitivity to its optimum extent, where we mourn for "our people." Here, the word "our" assumes the connotations of the oneness of humanity. Humanitarianism is different: it is cerebral and intentional; in it, the feeling and emotion have to follow, are duty-bound to follow, the idea. The idea comes first and leads the way. One has to learn compassion. Compassion reinforces the idea. The result is perhaps the same as in religion, if we regard it in terms of its usefulness, but the principle is different.

Perhaps mourning is *in its essence* religious. Just as melancholy, as I have said, is in its essence soulful. Mourning itself is a state, not a mood. It is a state one can be "in." Like love, one falls into it, suddenly—say, "on hearing the bad news"—but one *remains* in it because of one's truth and one's love. Not that one is trapped in it. To be trapped is grief. Without the meaning of mourning as the religious instinct in all of us, we could not fall, and we would not. The event would leave us "unmoved." But we fall because we are religious. And by that I do not mean believing, but soulful. We are soulful because our mourning for one is a mourning for all *in that one*, and *for one* in that all. This is the *strangeness* of compassion—that it is never simple. Schopenhauer says compassion is the sensibility that best shows the truth that we are one. It is not so much humanitarian as mystical. Identification with the calamities of others is also a true self-identification as *soul*—as including in oneself the other, the basis of soulful relations. Compassion is the manifestation of our intrinsic oneness on the plane of phenomena, and the metaphysical foundation, therefore, of ethics. The event that brings on mourning *jars* our religious instinct, and so *puts us* in mourning; for we need to be *put* in mourning.

185

Geo-Mourning

Many of us are mourning what some of us are doing to the earth. But we need to distinguish artificial, technological disasters from natural disasters as they are two different kinds of disaster and lead to two different kinds of mourning. We can think of natural disasters such as floods or forest fires or a tsunami, and we can also think of artificial, technological disasters such as the ones at Bhopal in India, where Union Carbide's pesticide plant blew up, at Chernobyl, where the nuclear power station blew up, and the oil disasters, such as those of the Exxon Valdez in Alaska and the BP oil spill that, more recently, destroyed life and communities in the Gulf of Mexico.

Steven Picou from the University of South Alabama has studied mourning in communities suffering the effects of technological disaster. He distinguishes surviving and mourning natural disasters from technological (artificial) disasters. He says communities that suffer a natural disaster pull together and form what he calls "therapeutic communities." Whereas communities that suffer from technological disasters form what he calls "corrosive communities." For a natural disaster you always have these identifiable stages: warning, threat, impact, rescue, inventory-taking, restoration and recovery, and these stages reflect the emergence of a therapeutic community and the building of social capital. But for technological disasters, these do not work: the stages go: warning, threat, impact, and blame, and communities get stuck in that cycle. In the case of a natural disaster, there is no one to blame, and there is a consensus that there really was a disaster and people suffered, so then people can respond in a supportive manner. But a technological disaster is preventable, and people had been assured that this *would not* happen, so you have someone to blame, someone to poke the finger at, someone to vent your anger against. This does not help you get over the disaster, because the recourse you have to receive damage payments and be made whole again after the disaster is litigation, and the courts become a secondary disaster or series of continuing uncertainties, with new issues, and the litigation also brings all of the original disaster back to people, and the accused fights the blame, avoids it, rejects it, pours huge sums into mitigating any responsibility, and all this makes things worse. The Exxon Valdez case was twenty years in the courts. The jury verdict was reduced by eighty percent by the US Supreme Court, so people waited twenty years to receive $15,000 on average for their losses, which had been the permanent destruction of their livelihoods for a lot of them, and the ruination of their close-knit communities by internal divisions, mental health problems, and so on. People never recover from technological disasters and the research literature says *recovery is impossible.*[12]

It has been found with the BP disaster in the Gulf of Mexico, which is still unfolding as I write, that suddenly it is hard to get real information. According to Picou, this is a pattern. In cases of technological disaster the company always leaks the information slowly, delaying how bad the situation is until just before it becomes apparent, and then "spins" the information to play it down. In the Gulf of Mexico, at first there was no oil leaking, then it was 1000 barrels a day, then 10,000, then it was estimated it might be as large as a million gallons a day. It is the misinformation that is stressful, and compounds the disaster. The close-knit communities that hunker around the gulf will be completely taken over by the cleanup teams—at least this is what happened in Alaska—and they will stay for years and decades, and set up in the towns and villages, and hold the purse-strings, which every single family relies on, as they cannot work, and then there is favoritism, and so the blame game spirals deep into community and family life. The companies themselves, before such disasters, have no plan or strategy, or even technology, to deal with disaster. For big corporations, disaster is something dealt with by the legal team, and is a matter of litigation, not cleanup.

In the time frame of writing and finalizing this same chapter, in the Australasian region alone there has been an earthquake in New Zealand, devastating floods in Queensland, and a tsunami in Japan, followed by a technological disaster at its Fukushima nuclear plant. The last of these will have permanent effects and may eat at the soul of Japan in a way that will not get in the news services or rather not stay there. The disaster at the nuclear plant follows the pattern of Picou's research, starting with glaring misinformation. It becomes impossible to trust any "official" information. This situation is intrinsic to technological disaster. The news services soon forget. Chernobyl is spoken about in journalism as if it were a thing of the past, but it is *still a disaster.* Bhopal as well is still a disaster and the corporate crimes against humanity, animals and the earth there in India have still not been investigated, or compensated for—as if this were even possible to do. But having a go at it at least is possible. Acts of other multi-national corporations around the world go unreported because they are regarded as normal rather than criminal. War crimes are not the only crimes against humanity and while they are more obvious and brutal they are not the worst crimes. The worst crimes are promulgated among those in boardrooms wearing suits, clean shirts, and ties. Crimes of reason are worse than crimes of passion. Evil is cold-blooded.

Messiaen: *Quartet for the End of Time*: Fifth Movement

When the French composer, Olivier Messiaen, was a prisoner of war of the Nazis, he wrote and co-performed for his captors his chamber piece in eight short movements, the *Quartet for the End of Time*. Messiaen later recalled of the occasion, "Never was I listened to with such rapt attention and comprehension."[13]

The fifth movement, with a violin playing extremely long drawn-out notes and seeming to plead over silence or the beat of a single note or two on the piano, is searingly sorrowful. The long notes on the violin are painful as we ache for them to end: but the pleading note ends only to continue on another string. The violin keeps the ear focused, modulating its pitch upward and downward, while winding ever onward, although to what end, if any, we do not know. The piece, because of its constant pleading, the strident coming and going of the piano note, and the relentless forward-directedness of it all, becomes excruciating, almost unbearable, were it not for the beauty of the sonority of the instruments together. Towards the end the piece softens a little or "lets up," but the muting is perhaps resignation, perhaps exhaustion close to collapse. As the violin fades altogether the gentle insistent beat of the piano goes on.

Messiaen was inspired by an apocalyptic text from the book of Revelation:

> And I saw another mighty angel come down from heaven, clothed with a cloud: and a rainbow was upon his head, and his face was as it were the sun, and his feet as pillars of fire . . . and he set his right foot upon the sea, and his left foot on the earth . . . And the angel which I saw stand upon the sea and upon the earth lifted up his hand to heaven, and swore by him that lives for ever and ever . . . that there should be time no longer: But in the days of the voice of the seventh angel, when he shall begin to sound, the mystery of God should be finished . . .[14]

The fifth movement (see the Play List) is entitled "Praise for the Eternity of Jesus." It is not really the music of mourning, therefore, but of praise. Did my ears deceive me then? Perhaps the praise is of the tears and cries too deep for words that St. Paul speaks of. Perhaps this is yearning poised in praise. But perhaps, at some point, yearning and mourning cannot be told apart. Certainly from a religious perspective I think this is true to say. It is a complex sensibility therefore that this kind of music awakens in us.

Messiaen could not have known about the Holocaust at this time, when he wrote and co-performed this music, but it is as if the music already knows. There is something inconsolable in the violin. But, as the psalmist says, "weeping may endure for a night, but joy comes in the morning."[15] To equate any kind of violence, let alone genocide, with joy is perverse: but the joy arises from the morning and in the morning, not from the night, when there is weeping and gnashing of teeth. Joy comes in the morning because it is another time altogether, the presage of a new age. This is why the psalmist says elsewhere, "I wait for the morning, more than watchmen for the morning."[16]

And so while in mourning, the violin is not desolate, for that would only lose the listener. The violin keeps the listener's ears pricked because there is an *eros* of *longing* in this piece that we may hear in its slight and majestic beauty, in the sonority between the violin and piano, in the instrumental humility, and even while they mourn, in a purity in which is some hint of dawn.

Shostakovich: String Quartet No. 13, in B Flat Minor

The twentieth-century Russian composer, Dmitri Shostakovich, undoubtedly had a hard life. It was expected under the aegis of Soviet Communism that music would emerge as naturally as it had from within any other culture, as in Europe. Why would it not? Was not music to the credit of the society from which it came and reflective of society?—Bach's Leipzig, Mozart's Vienna. Well, Vienna became *the* center of art music before the First World War. Paris, as well, was a name synonymous with art and culture, and still is. Why not Leningrad and Stalingrad? If the church historically could be such a patron of great music and give rise in time even to music beyond its walls, why not the Soviet Communist party? The fact is: *art music cannot come out of a false culture.* This is not just a problem with Communism then, but it is a problem with commodity capitalism now. Communist art was propaganda. Commodified art is kitsch or junk, or if it is to be successful it has to think below the belt, because success is contingent upon conformity to the reign of the blasé. How one can be an artist under a political dictatorship or under the total-izing reign of the blasé boils down to the same question: how can one be an artist?

This was Shostakovich's dilemma. As a high-profile Soviet com-poser with an international reputation, hence representing the Soviet Union (principally Russia in today's terms), the whole country and the Communist system could be judged by him. Shostakovich was not free to express his musical genius, or rather to let his musical genius express itself. In fact he had to repress it and somehow press it into government service, which, for a powerful creative spirit like his, was psychologically and spiritually painful and debilitating. The possibility of suicide always lurked in the shadows for Shostakovich—an "option" which many of those he knew took.

The artistic freedom Shostakovich yearned for came too late for his prime; it came at the end of his life. His late string quartets are his own works. The string quartet, a genre pioneered by Haydn in the eighteenth century, always has the ability, as in Haydn (also a very public composer in his day), to not only *express* the inner person, but to *explore* the inner person. Shostakovich's late string quartets are harrowing works. They are works of mourning in a class of their own. They show the genius of this composer—and his tragedy, his personal tragedy, which was also the tragedy of his times. Political repression had separated him from his own self, his own creative powers and artistry. The end was near. In the quartets, Shostakovich mourns his lost youth, his lost opportunities, his wasted genius, his crippled pur-pose, his lost health; he mourns his old age, sickness, and approach-ing death, which surely cannot be far off; but most of all, perhaps, he mourns *his lost music.*

In the Thirteenth String Quartet, in B flat minor, which runs for just under twenty minutes, we can hear this great old man, this great survivor, mourn his lost music. This is a lonesome and haunting pre-monition of death, with moments of beauty side by side with alarm. It is a quiet piece that settles us into the dark and adjusts our eyes, as it were, to see in the dark. The piece—as sound—is strikingly modern in its discordance and indeterminacy. The beat of the cellos save the piece from disintegration into disharmony (and precocious modern-ism) altogether and suggests a pattern, order, or certainty at a deeper level, one not found in the surface elements: a *gravitas* of absence behind the inaudible tonal center, which is nevertheless *there.* Eleven minutes in, the music falls preternaturally quiet, the violins have us in a holding pattern of uncertainty; the cellos, which eventually come in, do little to resolve the uncertainty, but their tonal depth is some solace, although it is quite unresolved for the ear and heart that listen.

If in beauty and sadness a great composer can put us out of our depth, I think that is the case here. We go back to this music to reattune to those depths of the beauty which is there to be heard. The solo violin in the last few minutes makes a sound literally out-of-this-world, like a sound of music after the end of the world, like the only sound left at that point, and the only thing one could hear in any case. The ultimacy of these sounds seems to me beyond compare. But one cannot bear to listen too often to them: something about them makes one feel that, if one were to listen to them too often, they should be profaned. How you write something that sounds like that beggars belief, but Shostakovich evidently did.

The deep notes, the somber, funereal tone, the slow measure of pace give way to the sudden screech of violins—which makes your hair stand on end and makes me glad no picture in my mind's eye can correspond to what I hear—and the chug-chug-chug of the cellos, which brings the music back to the reality of rhythm, although not right to the end. This is an attunement that can only deepen our sensibility, our empathy, and our imagination—musical and otherwise. To share Shostakovich's mourning is to listen to his music: at least this he is owed. And of course the music does not just stand for the composer's own life, but could perhaps be said to be the music of the victim—the victim who refused to become a scapegoat and "redeem" their victimhood, or someone else's. "Let this be a testimony," the sound seems to suggest. The beauty of the last minutes of this piece, where the violin comes in over the cellos, suggests . . . I would not say a peace . . . but, somehow, I would say, a *private victory*—like Jankélévitch's, when he sat down at the piano with Ravelin, perhaps. It was impossible then to talk about what had passed, about what one of them had lost the capacity to discuss in any case; it was too late, it was impossible to reconcile, or even to bother trying, even, to forgive; but the music was still possible. It is like that here too.

Tchaikovsky: Sixth Symphony, in B Minor ("Pathétique"): Final Movement

Tchaikovsky led the first performance of this piece in Saint Petersburg on October 28, 1893, nine days before his death. It is music of an "inner" mourning, a kind of mourning that we hold inside us.

A single trombone plays outside the brooding main orchestra at the start. Then the orchestra returns gently, swelling—like a heart full of emotion (this is the "pathos"). This is a music that assuages feeling even as it mourns. The dolefulness of the tune builds up to a climactic—perhaps a melodramatically climactic—point. And again the music returns, repeating parts of the melody, like a heart unable to leave—or to forget a memory. Softly the music continues, gently, like a reminiscence, and then, like a force that cannot be held back, the music rises up into to a storm, a climactic crash. And then the music quietly mourns, but calmly now, eventually falling away, as if into sleep, exhaustion, emptiness or consolation.

The symphony is said to be the story of Pyotr Tchaikovsky's soul told for Vladimir Davydov, his nephew, with whom he was madly in love; of course homosexuality in Russia is hardly tolerated today and, in Tchaikovsky's day, it was simply unmentionable. Tchaikovsky's homosexuality has been thoroughly gone into by Alexander Poznansky, a Russian American scholar.[17] He is cautious. To speak, as some musicologists have, of the "Pathétique" in terms of "homoerotic discourse" is patently anachronistic.[18] Edwin Evans writes against the autobiographical interpretation:

> It does not seem to fit in with Tchaikovsky's reserved and retiring nature that he should allow the circumstances of his own life to inspire a symphony . . . a work which, with the single exception of its first performance, has everywhere obtained a hold on the most varied audiences. It is uncharitable to suppose that Tchaikovsky had no greater object than to make the world pity him or to indulge his own self-pity. Thus, regardless of what has been advanced in most other quarters and is almost universally accepted, we will dismiss this idea.[19]

Given that Evan's interpretation is in line with Proust, *contra* Sainte-Beuve, we are even more inclined to believe it, given Proust's artistic authority in these matters of aesthetics.[20] In the same light, Schopenhauer argues to the effect that: "in the composer more than in any other artist, the man is entirely separate and distinct from the artist."[21] It is this sound of the heart, not of biographical self-expression, that we hear in the "Pathétique." A heart in winter.

10

When Time Stands Still

*What lies deepest in you is what is most remote from me and it
extends to that extreme point where lies our absolute identity. For
there is a common zone and an incommunicable depth between us,
and an identical point within us.
But this applies just as well to my relations to myself.*
—Paul Valéry, *Analects*

Kant showed in *The Critique of Pure Reason* that time is not in the
first place an object of knowledge: it is a *condition* of knowledge. He
means, we can *know* only in time and in terms of time and in a timely
way. Kant showed that time, space, and causality are three conditions of knowledge. Therefore, we do not *perceive* time, for time is a
condition of perception. Schopenhauer, in his completion of Kant,
showed in *The World as Will and Representation* that there is something behind what we sense in terms of time, space, and causality a
force that gives rise to them. Kant had little to say about it, Schopenhauer called it will (*wille*), referring to the in-forming energy of
all that is. Will is the *prana* of Indian metaphysics. Actually Indian
metaphysics has a more sophisticated account than Schopenhauer's,
which Schopenhauer only had some early inklings of. Basically it is
an account of the noumenal in terms of energy of which *prana* is a
main term.

We considered the noumenal experientially in Chapter 3 in terms
of the Ladder of *Eros*. On the fourth rung of awakening, for a moment
we are outside of time and time is outside of us. This is the detachment of our sense of *presence* from the persistence and dominance of
our habitual time-bound *thinking*. Soulfulness is not an experience
of thinking, but of the cessation of thinking, a lull in thinking and
feeling and all that we imagine defines us as human. Soulfulness is a
halt. Self-presence (which is different from self-consciousness) is the
gateway. The moment time stands still is a soulful experience. Our

experience is subservient to time most of the time, but not all of the time. When time stands still we experience what we have been calling a height of sensibility, above time anyway, that resonates in the depth of our being, and we may speak of an unforgettable or timeless moment. The music becomes a *symbol* for us, of the timeless moment, and as music is a *transubstantiation* of the timeless into time and therefore the possibility of experience.

What happens in that moment that time stands still is that we touch timelessness or eternity. In the mundane realm we have to remain with this touch as a memory. However, we experience something behind reality. For a moment, in an imaginative flash, we perceive the dream-like nature of ordinary life that most of the time we and the world around us take to be concrete reality. For a moment we see for ourselves what we have heard quoted from Shakespeare a thousand times, that "all the world is a stage" and we are actors on it briefly. Bergson's Duration is not a concept so much the name he accords to the timeless moment in time, of which listening to music is paradigmatic as we hear the whole piece in sequential notes and bars, one at a time; this is our paradoxical situation, caught between two worlds - phenomenal and noumenal in Kant's language; it is Plato's idea of the oneness of time, the illusion of time, that from a real perspective (when time stands still) *there is* no time. Immediately if we try to think this we fall back into mental representations and concepts and it does not make any sense. Plato's idea of eternity as oneness is of a *still image* of time.

It is often said that we have only the present moment and therefore, when time stands still, we might be inclined to believe that we are in a pure present. In a way we are, but not in the way we might be inclined to think. If the past does not exist any more and the future does not exist yet, it is wrong to imagine that the present moment exists simply here and now. On the other hand, while the present moment does not exist simply "here and now," that is not to say that the present moment does not exist in the way that we say the past does not exist and the future does not exist. The present moment does not exist, but it has a different kind of nonexistence from the past and the future. The past has fallen into oblivion, it is irretrievable, and yet it still binds us. The future is never present by definition but our expectations of it still bind us. The present moment is different because we *are not* bound to it. The present moment slips by. For the present moment has always vanished. The present moment is never really there. There is no *consciousness* of the present moment; this is why Goethe said that there is no such thing as consciousness, but only the history of consciousness. He touches a crucial point with respect to time standing still.

What makes a difference in the present is *how we stand* with respect to it. So long as we are living in the past, or are absorbed in the future through plans, dreams, imaginings, fantasies, and in the grip of expectations, we miss the present moment altogether. Missing the moment is the most common way that we stand with respect to it. A less common way of standing with respect to it is in pure presence: being, not doing. This is difficult to accomplish because we are unused to simply being. Even when we are not doing anything, we are thinking. When we are thinking we are "sunk" in our thoughts. That is to say, there is no difference between me and my thoughts. They seem to be absolutely mine. Pure presence however is when we "stand out" from or stand outside our thoughts and witness our thoughts. They are there, but they are not mine. When we make this inner act of consciousness, we stand in pure presence in the moment. This is not a step of self-consciousness, but rather a stepping aside from the self altogether. This is the sense often lauded by poets and mystics. Usually these moments in the lives of a lot of people are rare moments, like a first kiss. Time stands still or, rather, we become present to ourselves in the moment. Sometimes it is a bad and unhappy incident that causes this experience. However, as is commonly known in spiritual practices, this experience may be had while doing anything and at any time, or nearly all the time. It is what is known as "awakened" experience. Being "sunk" in thought is known as unconsciousness because my pure presence is lost in what I am thinking, imagining, believing. In Schopenhauer's terminology, when we are present to the moment, standing in self-presence, we are identified with the one will of all manifestation, not with the little will of the ego or what he calls the principle of sufficient reason.

The possibility of our self-presence defines the moment and makes it "exist." If we could cultivate self-presence then time would stand still for us often. If we read some wise poets, such as the Chinese poet, Han Shan, or the Japanese poet, Basho, or the European poet, Rilke, evidently time stood still a lot of the time for them, and their poetry gives us a glimpse of this way of being. Their poetry helps us absorb their way of being into our own, by reading. It is quite otherwise than our time bound way of being. If time stood still for us often we would be completely different people from whom we are now. Our basic character would not change, but how we manifest it would. All religions teach self-presence and awakening, each religion according to its own idiom keyed to a specific, natural culture. Catholicism speaks of the sacrament of the present moment or the practice of the presence of God. Eastern religion teaches methods of meditation that allow one to get together with others, or to go apart simply by oneself, and *be*. Religious ritual is really a cultivated form of self-presence in which, for the participants, time stands still. Of course it has other devotional complexities as well, but the self-presence in the moment of the devotee is the truth of the devotion as far as being is concerned, otherwise it is an unconscious "going through the motions" or mere performance.

Art arrests time because it arrests our attention and attunes us to the present moment. Reading, listening, and gazing are primary ways into self-presence. This means reading worthwhile literature that time and posterity have marked "great," listening to art music, standing in the gaze of a painting or sculpture, or watching dance. Through the practice of reading, listening, and gazing we will learn to live time which stands still and live in it. The problem is that we need art that corresponds with the importance of such reading, listening, and gazing. This is what is scarce.

The key word in the saying that "time stood still" is not "time" but "still." What one touches in self-presence is not one's self, but stillness. This stillness is not self. Perhaps this is why a lot of people living little, shut-in lives need to shut out stillness: it is instinctively fearful for them. Many intelligent, successful and well-educated people are totally lost in activity and are unable to slow down and stop. A story illustrates this. Joshua Bell, a top-rank American concert violinist, pretended to be a busker or street artist and played his 1713 Stradivarius on a street corner in New York one Friday morning. A total of 1097 people walked by without noticing, seven stopped for more than a minute, twenty-seven tossed him some coins as they passed him by.[1] Multiply this experiment in comparable terms by every street corner in every city in the world and you have some sense of the problem. I would expect the more "first world" the city, the worse the problem would be. This is the problem of soullessness.

On the other hand, there is nothing more soulful than stillness. "Soul" and "still" are two words that are virtually synonymous. To understand stillness, we must realize that it is not a state contiguous with, or opposite to, a state of becoming, or motion, except in the realm of thinking and conceptualization. Conceptualization cannot know stillness, but only a mental representation of it that is tied to the incessant movements of thinking. Stillness generates expansiveness.

We can call it the expansiveness of inner spaciousness. Listening will enable us to fathom or explore this expansiveness. New art music starts here, I think. If Wagner's music dramas lead anywhere, it must be to here as well. This is not just philosophy or psychology but new music theory. When we listen to art music our soul expands with the explorations that the music gives.

In stillness I enter the Oneness of life. The identification of my self-will with the will of All That Is, of cosmic will, which holds everything together in manifestation and being all at once, here, now, requires a higher level of consciousness than belongs just to thinking. Stillness is what the ancients and in Catholic tradition is known as contemplation. Contemplation is the highest kind of philosophy. The universe itself calls us into this consciousness, if we have ears to hear. Schopenhauer: "The great Goethe has given us a distinct and visible description of this denial of the will . . . in his immortal masterpiece *Faust*, in the story of the sufferings of Gretchen."[2] Stillness is a realization of consciousness, because stillness is ultimately what Faust seeks through his tragedy, as told by Goethe.

What the music of stillness does is to explore this region of Being and draw us into it, first by attunement, then by participation. We might expect silence to be closest to stillness, rather than music. Noise disrupts stillness. Music can explore silence. The Debussy and Sibelius entries in the Play List are in their individual ways powerful instances of this. Time can stand still in so many ways when we listen to something beautiful; beauty arrests time.

Debussy: *Des pas sur la neige*

This is the sixth prelude from Debussy's first book of preludes. It was written in Paris the day after Boxing Day, 1909. It was a white Christmas. Debussy continued to write the preludes through January. The snow thawed and the River Seine rose from being seven feet deep to twenty, flooding areas of inner Paris around the Isle de la cité, where Notre Dame stands—hence another prelude entitled *La Cathédrale engloutie* ("The Underwater Cathedral").[3]

These are preludes. They are to accompany something else—our daydreams and musings, perhaps. Debussy did not think it a good idea to hear his preludes as a set, although he planned and published them as such.

I mentioned the musical color of pure white when discussing Wagner and the beginning of *Lohengrin*. The pure white of the snow here in

197

this piece by Debussy is an absence. It is not there musically except as a silence. This is the silence of the snow. If we live in a place where it snows, we know that, when we wake up in the morning in winter, we can tell if it has snowed overnight by the silence—the peculiar silence of snow. And there is the peculiar light in the window glowing through the dark curtain. It is not the light from the sky but from the snow: a charmed light wrapped up in an unearthly silence. All we overtly hear in this music are the steps. But the silence is not nothing. Every silence has its quality for the sensibility. No two silences are ever the same. The silence of this snow is Debussy's snow, Parisian snow, not the snows I know of Oxford, Wolvercote, and Port Meadow. I see the footprints in the snow in my mind's eye marking hollows: dark cavities brutally imprinted on the virgin white surface, showing a trail, a path, a way, morphing in my mind's eye into black musical notations on a white page. Normally our steps are invisible, but in snow they follow us.

The footprints I hear here cross a white garden completely enveloped in snow, where it is piled on every individual branch and leaf and rises high from the ground. The snow is a stark expanse. "The melodic line, delicately woven as it is, still bears the burden of the emotional message of the piece, and sensitive attention must be given to its note-values and pitch line to render truthfully its despairing loneliness."[4] It is a magical, charmed moment, each step so full of the absolute self-presence of the walker, the prescience of the white world all around her, the cold pressing against her jacket and trouser legs and pinching her face. Time stands still. One is a child again.

Sibelius: *Tapiola*: Finale

Tapiola (1926), says Feruccio Tammaro, is the "music of silence."[5] Its opening motif is "the embodiment of stasis." Tammaro would persuade us that Sibelius's music is symptomatic of his withdrawal from the world. His music is neither romantic nor nationalistic (as is often said); it is music, in researcher Glenda Goss's words, that is the result of "immersing himself in an inner sound world."[6]

Listening to great music, such as this piece, does not just necessitate that we stay poised in the moment, attentive, concentrated, recollected, in a word, listening. We must do this, but what the music does is that it *presences* us. The music is the presence and the music presences us in presencing itself. In listening we become conduits. Normally, if we have self-presence, we have inner space, we are detached or dis-inter-esse-ted, which is to say, not identified in our being with what is passing or happening here and now. Listening to music, the music *is* the inner space. It fills as it empties.

A lot of people listen to music to "pass the time" and to "fill" or occupy their mind, because perhaps otherwise time is "heavy" on their hands or "drags" and people do not want to be with their thoughts: better to block them out with some loud music piped from a personal device straight onto the ear drum (a sad sight on our streets and in public places). This sight shows the control that the corporations have. When Sibelius becomes our inner space—or Debussy, or Tchaikovsky, or whoever the composer might be—time will stand still for us because we will experience the spaciousness that is. When time stands still, one is in musical time, which is no longer time, but space: inner space. When time stands still, it becomes pure space and opens in any and every direction, with anywhere able to be seen from any angle. One can discover inner space without the mathematical formulae by listening. This work by Sibelius is a perfect practice piece for listeners searching for inner space.

The piece premiered in New York. The title refers to a wild, dark pine forest, of the sort we might imagine or actually find in Nordic lands, where dwell the god of forests and his wood nymphs. Cecil Gray, in a monograph on Sibelius in 1931, hailed *Tapiola* as "a consummate masterpiece"[7]—an opinion borne out by great conductors such as Beecham and Karajan, who have helped establish the fame of the work.

> Wagner said of the Third Act of *Tristan und Isolde* that if it was properly rendered it would 'make people mad: only bad performance can save me.' If the Cavatina of Beethoven's string quartet in B flat, Opus 130 is really played *adagio molto expressivo*, it can be almost unbearably poignant and we understand why Beethoven said the memory of the emotion it aroused always cost him a bitter tear. So *Tapiola*, when played to its utmost is chilling and devastating that it shakes one to the core. It has been well said that it is scarcely to be endured when one is alone.[8]

The continually interesting abstract surface makes the piece easy to focus on for contemporary listeners.

Tapiola is a fairly long piece, at eighteen minutes' duration. It is a work that is musically complex and not easy for newcomers to art music. Its opening phrases are drear but give immediate access to what one is going to hear. It may be unhelpful with Sibelius to at once think of what we imagine to be the Finnish landscape, given that most listeners will not have been to Finland. The music then has a circling motion, occasionally dancing—prancing, even—and churning. The horn, with a froglike note, sounds a liquid depth. The orchestration holds some tension. We do not know what to expect next, but we half-expect the unexpected. This gives the music a slightly "breathless" quality. The quick phrases repeated on violin, with levity, on horn, softly, make for this breathlessness and tension too, and then the churning that verges on the menacing or the possibility of menace. But it is always recompensed by light tunes that sit above the depth, while depth remains there even when it cannot be heard. The middle of the piece becomes very quiet and still and we are surrounded by trees and taste the clearness of the air. We spin, whirled by some unseen force that we must abandon ourselves to. Time stands still.

The noisy reintroduction of full orchestration breaks the spell. The music does not mellow. It is never mellow. It keeps the listener expectant and on edge. Three minutes from the end the violins race each other with high-pitched screeching like mad birds flying low in a tight formation. One anticipates a crescendo of exciting sound, but the mad birds subside into the murk; then suddenly they are back, like a vision afloat. Magic, not murk, now greets our inner eye. Time stands still. With this the work slowly withdraws itself and disappears back into the night and forest.

The piece has an "immovable" quality that does not carry you with it like a flow, but it is more like a body of water, stirred now and then by a big gust of wind, into which one is immersed and comes out, eighteen minutes later, drenched, if not somewhat bedraggled. But the piece ends in a positive, C major tonality, which suggests all is well at the end, even if we are left a little bewildered.

Sibelius: Fourth Symphony: Introduction

Music historians distinguish Sibelius's Fourth Symphony (1911), which is austere and dissonant, from his more comfortable–sounding Fifth Symphony (1915).[9] Something of the same thing goes on at the beginning of the Fourth Symphony as in *Tapiola*: one note or chord shifting around the different parts of the orchestra: movement, but nothing apparently happening.

The music starts slowly and sedately with thick rich sounds, individually on violin and orchestrally. Everything is irresolute, starting up and breaking off before it develops. Several times, the beautiful, floating violins, translucent and piercing, meet an earth that rises precipitously in front of them led by trombones but with full orchestral backing. It is uncertain throughout if the piece will be heavy or light. The listener switches expectations back and forth, but the piece ends gently, softly, on a light note. But what has been accomplished? What has been "said"? The music has opened a space for hearing, but it is all opening, or all entr'acte, with nothing before or after, so that time stands still. Nothing starts, nothing begins, it is all held in suspense, one supposes it is all yet to come.

Musically something is always happening, there is music *there*, but nothing comes of it, as if the music could be the absence of itself. Visually stated: it is like not being able to distinguish the fog from the tundra. There is a shifting around of fog, but seemingly no ground, as if, behind the fog, but too far away to hear, a voice is calling, as if from a distance, but from more than a distance (in such a landscape): it is as if from *a very ancient time* a voice were trying to make itself heard through the fog. This is what the beginning of the Fourth Symphony is like.

Burnett James says the Fourth Symphony uses the tritone. In medieval times the tritone was said to be of the devil—"*Mi contra fa diabolus in musica est*" ("'*Mi contra fa*' is the devil in music").[10] The tritone was considered diabolical because it was an awkward interval for the voice and the interval sounds dissonant. Another "devilish" aspect James notes is the way Sibelius condenses the symphonic structure. "This is the orchestral symphony stripped to the bone; not one ounce of superfluous flesh is left: some could even call it emaciated."[11] Perhaps it can be called "a reaction to Wagner," which is a very trite way of looking at it, or, given James's metaphor, one might think of it as ascetic music for a time in need of asceticism. Sibelius did not see any good around the corner. His "asceticism"—and perhaps this symphony then—is like the prayer of the desert monk living on honey and termites, praying for a world oblivious to excess or the damage it is causing and the catastrophe it is heading for, but who can do nothing to halt it.

Schubert: Eighth Symphony ("Unfinished"): Second Movement

Schubert composed Symphony no. 8, in B Minor, in 1822. He left it with two movements that run for thirty minutes. It is regarded as the best orchestral music Schubert ever wrote.

Horns, basses and violins croon the introductory melody very softly, holding the last note to raise to draw in the listener and raise anticipation. Then silence and then the violins give us a feathery rhythm with the plucked basses punctuating it, as an introduction to the haunting clarinet tune which begins the symphonic proceedings. The plucked cello in the bass register is often echoed in higher registers by violins, or almost silently implied in the background while the bass is silent; and in the foreground an oboe plays a curlicue or two, or the violins play full tilt with lush melodies. The whole orchestra moves to the rhythm, almost a march, but not quite that insistent because, lacking regimentation, it is more like two lovers who walk hand-in-hand, keeping pace with each other. Like the soul itself (Plato said the soul moves in orbits) the music moves round itself in more of a circular than straightforward motion. (Do lovers walking hand-in-hand really care where they are walking? After all, it is perfect *just to walk*.) Round the music goes, in swathes of gorgeous, rich melodious sound, so naturally and purely it seems a sheer extension of the human spirit that time is stood still and has to wait: love goes first. Softly and slightly (not overdramatically) tempestuous by turns, the rhythm is not lost but affirmed more strongly as true by the heart of the listener each time it recommences. Though musical instruments do not speak verbally, the violin nine and a half minutes into the piece must be the closest an instrument has ever got to doing so. Seldom has a violin sounded more like it is saying something and speaking our language. What dances here are not feet, but the soul, which bobs along with the rhythm like a cork in a stream, completely carried away, in such perfectly judicious combining of the parts of the orchestra, but especially in the symbiosis between the violins and bass, the top and bottom, the rhythm and the harmony. It is hard to get a proper impression of this with a recording unless you can amplify it with state-of-the-art speakers to get the full range and tonality of what is going on—the uplifting, loud orchestral interruptions where the soul is thrown skyward, and the sense of fluttering back down to a soft, therapeutic landing in the rhythm, which you can feel even when it is not actually there but only implied by the other instruments. Time stands still for bliss. This is it. It ends in E major, softly, affirmatively. Active and passive sensibilities are equally engrossed. Simple it seems, utterly masterful it is.

Beethoven: The *Heiliger Dankgesang*

We cannot leave the subject behind without a mention of Beethoven's so-called *Heiliger Dankgesang*, the third movement of his A minor

String Quartet (1825). The title means "Holy Song of Thanksgiving" and is marked in the Lydian mode. Beethoven wrote it upon recovery from what he thought was to be a fatal illness. The Lydian mode that Beethoven used is the medieval church mode, not the old Greek mode, to which however it is related. Church music was mainly vocal while ancient Greek music was mainly instrumental, so the intonation is crucial to the Church in a different way than to the Greeks. When several voices sing simultaneously in different registers (boy soprano, tenor, baritone, bass) as in Gregorian chant some intervals (from note to note in series) are extremely unpleasant on the ear. On instruments however, they sound fine. But it was to circumvent such problems that the Church modified the Greek modes. However, both Church and Greek music was linear—all voices singing the same notes up and down. This was "verticalized" after the 10th century, which gives our modern sense of harmony. In simple practical terms the difference is: you can play a C major scale two ways. Use one finger to play the notes C E G C in succession. This is the Greek/Gregorian way. Or you can play those notes all together with four fingers as one chord. The latter is vertical (harmony). Applied to Beethoven, this means his Lydian mode applies to the tune itself (linear) and to the four instruments maintaining the four harmonic pitches simultaneously (vertical). The emotional range of the old linear modes was narrower than the harmonic, but as this music shows, the old mode takes the listener out their emotional range and by Beethoven slowing the music down, the music gives the impression, it is generally agreed, of "timelessness," because the music has no sense of direction to it and no sense of tension in it. While the piece takes a certain amount of time to play, about fifteen minutes to the calculative mind, the fifteen minutes are *abolished* in listening. It seems to be the music of pure presence.

True listening does not just take time, but abolishes it because *it gives us all the time in the world*. This is what we search for fruitlessly in a thousand ways. The condition for timeless time is listening. Timeless time is what great works yield; this is a reason we acknowledge their greatness. With bad music so often we waste our time instead. The serious musician today is ambitious to make great music that opens time to endless inner space and takes us out into it so that, looking back, as if from the cliff-edge of time, we can see ourselves as a little dwelling faraway below, like a farmhouse seen from an airplane.

In the *Heiliger Dankgesang* the total release from tension that is so unusual for the modern sensibility that is so often "stressed" turns Beethoven's piece into soul therapy and a perfect example of everything we have been saying about time standing still. The recording of the performance by the Alban Berg Quartet is not quite as slow as some other performances, but it captures a sweetness and gentle grace.

11

Beauty and Sadness

Our inner life is not what it is thought to be—it has "ineffables."
—Paul Valéry, *Analects*

There is sadness in every community in the world about the loss of sensibility; it is a sadness of the soul. While beauty is driven out of the world by the indifferent and blind forces of destruction, it is not only habitats that are destroyed, for technology is useful in preserving many habitats; what are destroyed are the inner habitats of the soul that can perceive and find joy in beauty. The destruction of these habitats is invisible and it goes uncommented upon. However, unless these habitats are preserved, outer habitats cannot be preserved either, because we have no inner basis in sensibility to make sound value judgments. We have to make judgments in terms therefore of expediency, efficiency, utility, cost, and the like. We are the first and only culture in history ever to fail and betray beauty, while trying nevertheless to keep up a façade of being "good" and "true." The technical mentality can only confirm us in the destruction of sensibility and beauty; it cannot extricate us or save us from our predicament, or warn us of the disaster.

Beauty is what perfection *is* in being and time. Beauty is always vulnerable and fragile, subject to destruction and death, because otherwise it would not be soulful. The mentality and lack of sensibility that comes against beauty is an *animus*—that is to say, a cruder, more primitive life force that, acting rightly, is sporting, protects, organizes, strategizes, carves out, and builds; but, left to its own devices, it is ignorant, brutal, violent, and apt to fight and wage war.

People love the beautiful. If I were asked, "What is beautiful?" I would point to what people love. A woman showing her baby to her friend: the friend can see the beauty without having to think about it, because she can see what is lovable. There is beauty in all sorts of places too that we might not imagine finding it. Beauty tends to divide taste;

it is a unique quality, not an inclusive one. Beauty evokes sadness as well as love, because it is vulnerable. Beauty is vulnerable because it is innocent. Beauty is innocent because it is without *animus*. Beauty is a phenomenon of *anima*. Power looks after itself and its own, but innocence and beauty need care and protection. *Anima* is the feminine principle and the valley way, the world as vale of soulmaking by which, John Keats said, we find out what world is for; the valley way of the world that keeps it whole. For *animus* carves the world up.[1]

Innocence and Experience

One of the problems with psychoanalytical thought from its inception, as discussed, for example, between Freud and Lou Andreas-Salomé, is the lack of notice taken of the difference between innocence and experience.[2] One of the most important facts about the soul is *purity*, and psychoanalysis, at least as it has developed, has no account of it and hardly even mentions purity.[3] But the most obvious fact about children is their innocence and purity. Freud's theories of infant sexuality, at least in the manner that they have been traditionally interpreted, give insufficient attention to this fact. Freud's word for innocence is "polymorphous," but this has largely been taken as an adjective to describe the noun "perverse" and all the attention has been on the latter, with the polymorphous character of it forgotten. But this is the "original innocence," in plain English. Freud saw the drive to knowledge, as he called it, starting in remotest infancy as a dynamic or destiny that enters into innocence and plays out in terms of it, becoming responsible at some stage, all other things considered, for the switch, which happens at some stage—but certainly not when one is four or five—*from innocence to experience*. This is more important than the oral, anal, and genital stages, if there are such things in this respect as "stages." Anyway, what matters is this first initiation or induction, or second birth, from innocence into experience, because it is from this point on that living really starts, that the person takes on or begins to take on what they have brought with them into the world in terms of the circumstances in which they find themselves surrounded. Life is really all about such births, or initiations, and music can help us to make them and must accompany them. The switch from innocence to experience takes many years. It is gradual, and not complete until the child is about thirteen or fourteen. At any time before this the child may be seriously psychologically handicapped and so fail the initiation. But who would notice this in a culture like ours?—one completely steeped in materialism and economics raised to the status of a metaphysical cult with its totem towers presiding like huge phalluses over our urban domiciles, with us like ants, but without any of their solidarity: rather, like ants at odds with each other, competing and trying to outdo one another. If only we could see ourselves. But to do this, we need innocent eyes, such as those of a William Blake or a Wordsworth.

Vladimir Jankélévitch, who has written an important study on purity, says purity is a *movement*, not an element: purity is intentional (self-grounded), not some kind of cellular entity that analysis can extract from the bosom of neurosis or other complexities where purity is not.[4] Intention in this sense is not psychological, not adjectival; intention is an *event*, but not the event of some thing, not an eventuality. But as I understand it, it is more like Kiekegaard's or, rather, Lacan's notion of repetition,[5] belonging to the moment, or to the duration (in Bergson's sense of a stretched moment, or *qualitative* time). Purity does not commence: it repeats itself. Something commences out of lack, out of "flattened inspiration, chilled verve, failed fate, disappointing continuation!"[6] Purity commences like repetition without precedents excepting itself, or proceedings to follow, but by its own lights.[7]

All innocence is beautiful and needs protection and nurturing and love, yet innocence lights the hearts of the experienced, even those jaded by experience, even those hardened by it. "Purity is an atom in space, a very fugitive occurrence in time," writes Jankélévitch, "it is not just that purity does not endure (alas!), even an instant, but purification, which is to say the only kind of purity accessible to the creature, is itself an instant which comes instantaneously, which does not exist, nor consist, nor subsist and which properly speaking, does not continue for a second without break. Purity is very fragile and labile, it is not a diathesis, not a state, nor a manner of being, not a 'habitus.'"[8] Purity is the *lightness of being* in that case! But not an *unbearable* lightness of being (Kundera), rather a *virtue*, therefore like all virtue resting on self-emptiness (called "humility" in Christian idiom), therefore *presque rien* (next-to-nothing) for Jankélévitch, and for Jankélévitch that which is next-to- nothing—like art music—is most important of all in life and truth. St. Francis de Sales, who Jankélévitch refers to at this point in his discussion, has it that, in the human soul, at the highest point of our faculty of reason, "no light of human reasoning functions there."[9] Allegorically, as St. Francis de Sales explains it, this highest point of the soul beyond reason is signified by the shrine in the Holy of

Holies, in the inner court of the temple of Solomon, which possessed three surrounding courts. "There were no windows to light the inner shrine; no human reasoning lights up the apex of the soul." That means no theology (no propositional truths of faith or exoteric teachings of religion), no philosophy either, because no *logos* rules here. But there is a door through which the light comes. The light is obscured when the high priest sets foot on the threshold, "all the insight gained in the highest point of the soul is dimmed to some extent by what the soul foregoes: there is no concentration on the beauty of God's truth, on the truth of God's beauty; the soul simply strives to accept them."

This is the *beautiful* lightness of being. It is from out of this door that purity comes. It is within this timeless space that purity has its source. Purity does not hark back, for there is no nostalgia where there is no time. The metaphysics of nostalgia derives from the outer courts of Solomon's temple and from exoteric religion symbolized by the priest. It is not reason that enters the shrine, but *sensibility* in its three notes of faith, hope and love, beyond *logos* and the source of inspiration in *melos*. For in all great music a certain purity shines, and this shrine in the Holy of Holies in Solomon's temple is the source in *mythos*, but the direct human source is virtue, which can be only in the *hic et nunc*, having to do with real presence and little to do with thinking, with the light of knowledge, which is not the same light, such that if the soul enters this inner sanctuary of the temple, according to St. Francis de Sales, on approach to its sacred holdings—the ark of the covenant, in which lie the tablets of the law, the heavenly manna in a golden jar, and Aaron's staff—God will bid us *close our eyes*.

Our closed eyes confirm the *innocence* of sensibility in purity. Innocence, like purity, is not a state or substance, but a movement: a movement towards itself by means of *oscillation* between two others. "The movement toward purity is purity itself," attests Jankélévitch.[10] What is characteristic of innocence, Jankélévitch argues, is what is also characteristic of the erotic, personified by the daemon *Eros*, in Plato, the movement of oscillation between *Poros* or Plenty (his father) and *Penia* or Poverty (his mother) symbolizing the governing factors of *Eros*: to have and to have not. It is not that *Eros* is torn between the two, but that he has to bind both together—to bind the world together. The movements of desire and innocence are binding movements and world-significant movements. The space of oscillation is *metaxic*, which means the space *in-between* life (Plenty) and death (Poverty), having and not-having, knowing and not-knowing, neither mortal nor immortal; in a word, not in total self-possession. Originary *lack.* This lack is not to say unstable, but searching. *Eros* is "a philosopher at all times."[11] A philosopher is the name of the one who searches, who seeks wisdom; neither the gods on one hand nor the ignorant on the other hand seek wisdom, *Sophia.* This means that the erotic force *in us* oscillates *between* wisdom and ignorance, knowledge and foolishness, what is and what is not, a force of binding and unbinding heaven and earth. The seeker—and movement of seeking—is neither wise nor foolish. A mean between the two is the lover of wisdom, "for wisdom is the most beautiful thing, and Love is of the beautiful."[12] Innocence is keyed to philosophy and to beauty. The ladder of *Eros* (Chapter 3) is a symbolic description or codification of this searching and oscillation garnered from experience.

Innocence must oscillate with *Eros. Eros* is an innocent; his purity is of double origin and the innocence of purity precisely reflects its double origin. Sometimes the innocent know not what they do. This is the irony and tragedy of innocence. This is how innocence can never be partitioned off from experience "on the other hand." Rather, "the movement towards purity is purity itself . There is for man no other purity but love."[13] Ultimately, this is what music is "about." This is why innocence is the highest step on the ladder of listening in Chapter 3. Music is about nothing but itself, but this "itself" is the innocence we are talking about and that attunes us to it, by means of itself. *Eros* will never find what he seeks, for innocence belongs to the very seeking, which is a movement and a duration; a movement and duration that music renders audible. Innocence gathers experience. We become *listeners* because we experience music (*melos*). *Eros* in his innocence, by means of which he gathers experience, seeks beauty, because "love is of the beautiful."[14] To seek wisdom is philosophical. To seek beauty is erotic, but the seeking of beauty is wise. Innocence that gathers experience is *wise innocence.*

We must answer the question therefore: "*What is given* by the possession of beauty?"[15] You do not necessarily have happiness by the possession of beauty. The man who conceives himself as a rational animal—as in Western rationalist (ontotheological/logocentric) tradition—seeks the good and good things, and he is happy when he possesses them. But this is not the pleasure principle: this is the super-ego. For this individual (*monos*), virtue is *habitus* and can be instilled like any habit and possessed. But the man who seeks beauty is not a rational animal; he or she is an erotic creature, a religious creature too, for *religio* means that which is binding, and *Eros* we said *binds* and what the lover or mad artist seeks is "birth in beauty."[16] The "madness" of love is the "dark interval" between the pleasure principle and the death drive, we could say. The "dark interval" of the top rung on the ladder of listening (Chapter 3) is perhaps the rung of inspiration and the listener's attunement to it. The "dark interval" is the utopia where the soul oscillates—its "madness," in Platonic terms. The listener ultimately seeks what every erotically maddened creature seeks: *birth in beauty*, not "the good life." And birth in beauty means: to bring something into being; in other words: *creativity*. Listening at the top rung *hearkens* to creativity, a status associated with God the Father according to the historic discourse of ontotheology. This hearkening is an awakening of the soul to its creative possibility that will presage giving birth—*to a star*, Nietzsche's Zarathustra said. Birth in beauty touches the womb of life in each of us, for which we must remain faithful to heaven *and* earth (not just earth, as Nietzsche's Zarathustra supposed).

What is given by the search for beauty? Creativity. All music, all art evinces creativity of some degree and this is of the essence. So philosophy, the erotic search, religion lead not to the possession of goods and economy, but to "'poesy' or creation."[17] Poetry actually means creation. "Beauty, then," Diotima the wise woman of authority tells Socrates the philosopher, "is the destiny or goddess of parturition."[18] Creativity is not an activity: it is a destiny, like a birth; it is what our life is for. And all pregnancy is sacred. All parturition or birthing is painful. The creation of art music is painful, and *messy*—bloody, even. Beauty is not pure in the happy man's sense, where it is also clean and hygienic, functional and efficient, turns on and off at the switch, and so on. This is *un*erotic. Our machines and gadgets are merely indicative of commodity fetishism, which is to say displacements of *Eros*. The created is not *designed*: it is begotten or born. What is born may be made without design, or at least without too much design. *Eros*, then, is not love of the beautiful only, which would only be good, but "the love of generation and birth in beauty,"[19] or creativity.

From this discussion the conclusion must be that beauty destabilizes the good, and that the satisfaction of creativity, if such is to be had, is beyond the satisfaction of the happy man, who, as it turns out, is perhaps Nietzsche's "last man," a man ensconced in the complacency of "goodness" and "happiness," the conceit of calculated virtue, with no question of anything beyond possessions and acquisitions and stability and "goodness."[20] Innocence then is dynamic, and experience an extension into life of that dynamism. The impure comes into the picture when experience becomes the *basis* of the dynamic, instead of innocence and *Eros*. Then we talk of "lost innocence" indicating a difference in operation. The difference between innocence and experience is that one extends from the other: experience from innocence. It is possible for innocence and experience to go their own ways and one of such ways is for them to come into opposition. When this happens (and it is all about us) the relation of innocence to experience cedes its place to a plural complexity: from complexity to confusion, Jankélévitch writes, as it becomes awfully hard to disembroil or tell apart. This leads to violence. Psychologically and culturally, lost or destroyed innocence is a primary source of violence and bad *animus*. The violence in our societies and between them and between religions is the abortion of creativity. No wonder then that, culturally and historically, *women and children* are always the first and worst-affected victims; because this is not just a fact but *symbolic* of what is going on and *why* it is going on. At a certain point in the confusion of innocence and experience, "the pure and the impure become one another at the same time in their desires and hatreds; the desire for purity and desire of impurity, the horror of one and the horror of the other bizarrely join in each case . . . To love or hate? Man vacillates."[21]

Sadness accompanies beauty because the nature of the phenomenal realm of time, space and causality is impermanence and it is saddening to see something beautiful die. It is easy to get sentimental, but we should consider the existential side to this sadness in terms of innocence and experience more closely. Innocence and experience are two sides of life. In ethics, this two-sidedness is coded into good and bad, and in religion it is inflated into Good and Evil. But from a soul perspective, the difference is not really ethical, nor is it religious. In the Bible, thinking back to the story of Adam and Eve in the Garden of Eden, we recall that innocence and experience are two sides of the human divide. Christianity has traditionally interpreted this story in terms of a "fall" due to "sin" (the woman Eve disobediently eating the apple and causing the "fall of man"). The "moral of the tale" is obedience and conformity, which religion has capitalized on to legitimate itself and enforce its moral code. But leaving this classic interpretation of the "fall of man" as a moral tale to one side, we can see it otherwise. We can observe from the story that the *continuity* between before and after the apple bite is *human* and what *divides* before from after, innocence from experience, is "knowledge of good and evil." In other words, you do something which causes you to know something, and you cannot go back on what you have done; what you have done is once and for always (and in the story, once for all people); and what you have done changes the relation you have to everything and everyone else. We see from the story that "knowledge of good and evil" is not knowledge as such—in other words, some item of knowledge that you did not know before but now you do, that is, knowledge as information. Rather, knowledge means having been a *subject of experience*; in other words knowledge is self-knowledge, or, in another word, *gnosis*. This is why the serpent, a symbol of wisdom, is a symbol in the Gnostic tradition of that very gnosis. This is a tradition that, as Jung has shown, is psychologically freighted. This tradition therefore differs from Christianity, which has never developed a psychology for all its theology; the lack of a psychological dimension is a deep and thoroughgoing feature of Western philosophy, as a consequence, with its elevation of reason and repression of imagination. Western religious culture (Christianity) has perennially battled over the status of art as a consequence.

The shift from innocence to experience in Western culture has largely been regarded as sexual awakening, as Adam and Eve after they have eaten the apple become aware of their nakedness, as if this is bad; but it is symbolic of a shift from childhood to adulthood. Modern theory is skeptical about the importance of innocence and experience. Rabbi Chanan Morrison, in a commentary on the Torah portion, *Chayei Sarah*, speaks of two views of childhood. The first, which prevails in the world, everywhere, across culture, is where childhood is a time of preparation for adulthood, when one becomes a productive member of society, or, in our context, a cog in the machine. The second, which treats childhood as a saving grace for adults who have lost their innocence, and as a boon for those who have not. "The world endures only for the sake of the breath of school children," says the Talmud (Shabbat 119b) because their Torah is learned in purity. As Rabbi Morrison puts it:

> When children are educated properly, we may discern within their pristine souls untold measures of holiness and innocence, purity and elevated traits. But only if the grace and beauty of these delicate flowers has not been crushed by the spirit-numbing reality of the factory floor and the cynical manipulations of corporate culture.
>
> Childhood is good and holy, but it is too weak to withstand the powerful and complex forces of society. It is our obligation to guard over the simplicity of childhood, to carefully allow our children to

mature without losing their natural innocence. Then they will acquire the physical strength and spiritual resilience that they lack, while retaining the innocent exuberance of childhood.[22]

Rousseau had this sense and our world secretly revolves around the truth of what is said here, but modern theory hardly acknowledges it. All war stands against these truths, that is why the history of humanity is a history of insanity, and in our accelerated world, insanity on speed.

The difference between innocence and experience is primary and primal, but it is not necessarily a "Fall". That experience is "better" than innocence, who can doubt? if it is an extension and outgrowth of that innocence rather than its soul-destroying *animus*. Perhaps the greatest artistic exploration of this subject is Dostoevsky's novel, *The Idiot*, which he finished writing in 1869. The main character of the novel, Prince Myshkin, is often said to be "Christlike," or a "holy fool," but what he is in fact is an innocent. He is holy in the literal sense of "set apart"; innocence is by definition holy in this etymological sense. Also, Charles Dickens, a writer whom Dostoevsky read and greatly admired, could be said to allow the difference between innocence and experience to bifurcate his entire collected works. In almost every novel, a child, often a waif, is crushed by an overbearing "system" of society; not so much by malevolence (although sometimes that is the case, as in *Oliver Twist*) but usually by adults oblivious to circumstances, without "eyes to see" what they are doing and the terrible effects that has, crushing the weak—principally children. Mr. and Mrs. Micawber are Dickens' Prince Myshkin, showing that *innocence can cross into adulthood.* What both Dostoyevsky and Dickens show us is that the difference between innocence and experience is structurally more existential (that is, runs deeper than) the religious concept of "sin," which would divide sinners from "decent" law-abiding religious folk, precisely the divide Jesus himself died trying to break down. It is not that Myshkin or the Micawbers are sinless; that is not the point. The point is that these characters are without malice or conceit. In a sense they are "beyond good and evil," but not in Nietzsche's sense. Nietzsche's character Zarathustra in *Thus Spoke Zarathustra* (1883) is beyond good and evil only in a malicious and mischievous sense, which is not truly *beyond either*, but craftily wrapped up *in both*. The hermit who Zarathustra meets and cheats at the start of the book is closer to the truth of life than Zarathustra who secretly mocks him. Zarathustra is impure and

213

neither innocent like he can see the hermit is, nor experienced in any proper sense either—a bit like Nietzsche! Nietzsche's teaching of the *Übermensch* (Superman) is a perverse caricature of the Christian notion of deification (*theosis*), the idea that the human may undergo transformation toward the divine. The contrast between Dostoyevsky and Nietzsche on innocence and experience runs deep and tellingly and reflects Jankélévitch's sense of how easily they can be confused and the dangers of their confusion.

The poet William Blake, in *Songs of Innocence and Experience* (1794), shows how innocence and experience are both present from birth. If we compare, for example, the poem "Infant Joy" from the *Songs of Innocence*, with the poem "Infant Sorrow" from the *Songs of Experience*, Blake shows us that innocence and experience stretch from the start to the end of life and from earth to heaven; he shows us that God does not reside outside the difference between innocence and experience but is better understood in terms of it. In ontotheological terms of traditional Christian metaphysics, God stands outside the innocence/experience dichotomy as the Creator. This is a mythologism. As far as creative experience goes, the innocence/experience dichotomy cuts right through our consciousness. We may see in the story of Adam and Eve in the Garden of Eden, from *Genesis*, that God is different, as far as the forebears of humanity are concerned, for innocence than for experience. In innocence Adam and Eve are like a happy family, but it is a fool's paradise because God is wise but does not want either of them to become like him, which will occur if they eat of a certain tree. In experience (the state of knowledge, once they have eaten the forbidden fruit), God separates himself from them and shows a more brutal front. They are sprung from the fool's paradise and God shows his "true colors." Or, to put it another way: the human pair see God "as He is" clearly for the first time. Blake shows these two faces of God, according to innocence and experience as well. The poem "On Another's Sorrow" from *Songs of Innocence*, says that God "smiles on all" and cannot stand grief, even the care and hurt of the smallest animal. But in "The School Boy" from *Songs of Experience*, we read:

> How can the bird that is born for joy
> Sit in a cage and sing?
> How can a child when fears annoy
> But droop his tender wing
> And forget his youthful spring?

214

The poem is about the way we organize and carry out education. Ordinarily in our society education spells death for innocence with its joy and levity. Implicit is the suggestion life need not be like this—Blake himself (who had no education to boast of) being a case in point. Blake writes about what he knows about and he knows about both sides of the divide between innocence and experience. Ordinarily we speak of "lost innocence." Blake though has "kept innocence." His poetry that shares his consciousness is crucial reading.[23]

"On Another's Sorrow" from *Songs of Innocence*, typical of the series, is a poem about the naturalness of love that accompanies innocence. There is no reason not to love.

> Can I see another's woe
> And not be in sorrow too?
> Can I see another's grief
> And not seek for kind relief?

This empathy extends from one's kith and kin right out to the smallest creatures of the world. Blake ties the last section of the poem back to Christian thought, rethinking it in terms of innocence. The poems in *The Songs of Experience* denote the opposite (that is, loss of empathy) and the point is that *both innocence and experience are true*. For Blake, as for inner experience, God does not preside over this *difference between* innocence and experience: God is *caught up in it*. God is not the *creator* of this difference, which would be a metaphysical postulate; rather this difference is the *source of creation and creativity*. Our ideas of God come out of this source; our notion of revelation is an experience at this source. This source of creation and creativity is something every artist knows firsthand.

We should note in addition that, within both innocence and experience, there are many levels. The novelist Marcel Proust shows how innocence and experience differ between the sexes.[24] The fact that sensibility is not the same for both sexes is not merely biological or merely socially constructed, although these are dimensions of the difference. It is a *soulful difference*. Rousseau shows this in *Émile* (1762) as well. In fact he retains a strong sense of the difference of innocence and experience that modern theory has completely bypassed in its own obliviousness to the distinction. Proust, the supreme psychological writer, gives many of the coordinates of the soulfulness in sexual difference. For example, in the early volume, *Swann's Way*, while Monsieur Swann is a "man of the world" in every way, the woman with whom

215

he is in love, Odette, he sees as quite innocent. Proust makes this very humorous, for, unbeknownst to Swann, Odette is streets ahead of him (sometimes literally!). Through the whole, circuitous story line the relativity of innocence and experience are shown, not just between the sexes, but within each of them. This is very often dramatized in opera, the first act of Verdi's *La Traviata*, for example. "In the present confusion of the sexes it is a miracle to belong to one's own sex," wrote Rousseau,[25] words even more pertinent now than then; but *La Traviata* like all the great popular operas has no equivocation on such matters and therefore affirms us in the innocence of our humanity.

The words of poetry can sensitize our listening because they can empower the receptive capacity of the soul. Music more than any other art may be the means by which we can best restore the domains of innocence and experience to their mutual interdependence. The music of beauty and sadness allow us to hear innocence and experience most clearly. Both have their own kind of purity.

Schubert: String Quintet in C Major: Second Movement

The second movement of Schubert's String Quintet is a perfect encapsulation of innocence and experience. The sound is governed by a strong musical formality, which may be strictly of technical import, but is in any case of the soul. We hear a slow dance in which a couple dance arm in arm. The music tells of their feeling for each other: the heartstrings are more and more insistently plucked. Some more quiescent passages in the middle take place out on the terrace, where one or other of the dancers stands under the night sky and consults their feelings—and realizes some truths of love in the intimacy of the night by themselves. The delicacy of these feelings requires a sheltering heart. Then it is back to the dance and to rooms and faces transformed. From moonlight to lamplight, the music alternates.

The music goes close to, but pulls back from, and resists the lushness of a Tchaikovsky; exquisite, it stays sociable, its features composed like those of a face, civil—with an outwardness not too obvious, a gentility, a propriety, a sense of circumstance. This is music good for the soul. All these qualities lend the piece a special purity.

In terms of the attunement of the soul to purity, this piece is hard to surpass.

Written the year of Schubert's death, 1828, first performed in 1850 in Vienna, it is written for two violins, a viola and two cellos. Robert

Schauffler, in his book *Franz Schubert: The Ariel of Music*, writes of the quintet:

> It has been wittily characterized by Josephine Braider as "the quintessence of beauty." Cobett, calling it "the most romantically conceived work in all chamber music," declared that "from the lyrical and dramatic point of view, nothing so ideally perfect has ever been written for strings as this inexpressibly lovely work." According to Laciar, it has "all the poetry, romance and inspiration of the G Major Quartet . . . all the intensity of the D Minor and the subdued melancholy of the A Minor; a workmanship never before approached by Schubert and equaled in chamber music only by Mozart, Beethoven and Brahms; in short it crowns Schubert's entire creative life in this field, if not in all forms.[26]

In short, the quintet is not amiable: it is lovable. I do not know if this is overpraising the work, which, historically speaking, has only gradually gained notice, not being published until 1853.

Schubert followed Boccherini in having two cellos—not one—in the ensemble, which changes the "musical force of gravity" of the composition and its "thickness."[27] Of the adagio (second) movement on our Play List, Newbould says: "The slow movement, in the course of which divine peace confronts and dispels human *Angst*, is courageously slow, the theme in the middle three instruments so statuesque as to concede enormous expressive weight to the little first-violin interjections and of the plucked cello. A final trill suddenly raises the level of activity and of tension, leading to a hyperactive and relentlessly burdened middle section in the Neapolitan minor key. Traces of this turbulence, as suppressed as the players choose to imagine, spill over into the reprise of the Elysian first theme; but by the coda serene stillness is restored—threatened but not banished by a cursory if powerful last turn to the Neapolitan minor key (complete with the original upbeat trill), which is Schubert's way of harking back to, and laying to rest, the dark currents of the middle section."[28]

Mozart: Rondo in A Minor, K511

"The apogee of Mozartian melancholy," Julian Rushton calls this, in his book, *Mozart*.[29] Mozart wrote the rondo in 1787. It is a perfect example of purity, and fits perfectly up against what Proust said after hearing Saint-Saëns play it on the piano in 1895 and noticing all the disappointed faces coming out of the concert hall:

Here is the reason: the fact is that it had been truly beautiful. True beauty is indeed the one thing incapable of answering the expectations of an over-romantic imagination. All other things come up to its idea of them: it wonders at skill, is flattered by vulgarity, intoxicated by sensuality, dazzled by histrionics. But beauty having been united with truth since in undying friendship ever since time began, cannot call on these attractions.[30]

Beauty has a purity and transparency about it, as this rondo by Mozart has. Mozart renews lost innocence—such was his genius. Perhaps no other composer achieves this with such ease, such perfection, and such elevation.

Ultimately, if we think of innocence and experience as bifurcating our unconscious worlds *and* our consciousness (at a level prior to intention, or motive, or will), and if we think, as I said above with regard to Proust, of the manifold *levels* within and between each way of being, then we could go so far as to say that they stretch the whole height, the length, and breadth of the Ladder of *Eros*—the ladder, we recall, which marks the stages or gradations within the metaphysics of nostalgia. Having said this, here, now, toward the end of this book, we need to have a sense of where the top of that ladder *is lost*. The bottom is on (or *in*) the ground of our sensibility. The top, we have so far seen, is in the indeterminate "timeless" and "changeless," according to Baudelaire's aesthetic, which has been our guide. But what does this really mean—"timeless," "changeless," "indeterminate"? We can answer in a word. It means the *ineffable*. The top of the ladder is not lost: it is found! The Ladder of *Eros* reaches from our sensibility *into the ineffable*, which comes *down* the ladder in the music, or not really *in* it, but *as* it—*as* music, if not *all* music, and *as this music*—to *touch* us. And this touch is aesthetic experience.

Mozart: Piano Concerto No. 21, in F Major: Second Movement

This is Mozart's greatest piano concerto: it is great among great concertos, full of exuberance and innocent pleasure.

Written in 1785, what we hear and what we should listen for in the second movement (the andante)—in a great performance of the concerto such as that recorded by Geza Anda—is the perfection of *silence* that comes through his timing. This quality of silence as much as of music is *charme* (charm).[31] *Charme* or charm (the connotations are slightly different in the English) dates back in time and music.[32]

In French the word *charme* carries the sense of the word, *enchants*. We use the word synonymously with the *enchantedness* of music and *the work of enchantment*, which is what true listening has to do with. Originally charm had a sober or religious setting in church music and in early classical music, before it became "absolute." Charm is more French than German. The music's charm is defined by its sobriety and vigilance—like a moral watching over of something. The beauty of custom, Jankélévitch says, in Greek, ευηθεια, meaning "good character," sets the standard for acceptable rhythm and harmony, and then we have the music's ευαρμοστια, meaning its "well-composed quality," and finally, ευρυθμια, meaning its graceful movement and order.[33] Of course, when music actually served the church this was much more strictly regulated than later, when music began to find its own wings—in Haydn and Mozart to begin with, and later in Schubert and Chopin and others. Art music became increasingly secular, in the sense of ungoverned by any other authority except the composer's genius; it remains governed by the old order in some senses, as we can hear. We can hear the continuity—and therefore we speak of "the Classical tradition" and hear it with Beethoven's great symphonic works. With Wagner—and of course thereafter—radical *new* concepts come into play, for good or ill (or both, as it turns out). A discontinuity comes into play.

But the emotional life of humanity has meanwhile not changed at all: a smile is still a smile, a tear is still a tear, war still means war, peace still means peace, and love and pathos still bind. The ineffable is still ineffable. But the music that will carry it to us sounds different. At first it sounds strange, perhaps. *Charme* arouses love. When Augustine asks in Book 10 of *The Confessions*, "What is it that I love when I love my God?" we might answer him, *charme*! Since Book 10 is all about *memoria* (the combination of memory and imagination), which is where Augustine finds all the realities of religion, within this collective store of all being, I think he would like our answer.[34] Of course it would be too modern for him, learning as he was at the time of writing his *Confessions* (387) the new theological idiom of his day (and contributing to it). It is well that we recall the name of Augustine here (and no accident either) for Jankélévitch says *charme* belongs to the metaphysics of nostalgia. "*Charme* is far away, like Ithaca. But it is a spiritual Ithaca."[35] Like in Cavafy's poem of that title then. "*Charme* is not a given, it demands we seek it and it will disrobe for us when we find it. And perhaps that for which we search we always find, and that which we find we shall continue searching for, because it is always lost."[36] *Charme* is like our nostalgia for our native place, which is not simply geographical (think of Cavafy's Alexandria in the poem 'The City,' Alexandria is impossible to leave because wherever in the world you go you will take it with you, inside your mind; or think of Van Morrison's 'Cyprus Avenue' or any one of a number of his songs rich in nostalgia). *Charme*, Jankélévitch goes on, is "like the *charme* of Gabriel Fauré, not something inherent or something particular to the harmony, mode or cadence," something therefore that we can put our finger on, "it is something we love to call *charme bergamasque* of the I-do-not-know-what that we cannot assign a place and which is mysteriously omnipresent."[37] The *charme bergamasque* is something that comes from the poet Paul Verlaine from his poem *Clair de lune* (Moonlight) that Debussy famously set to music as the third movement of his *Suite Bergamasque* (1905) that he labored on so long, so lovingly. Verlaine's soulful poem *Claire de lune* starts: "Your soul is a chosen countryside/of charming masques and bergamasques/with lute and dancing and somewhat/sad under their fantastic disguises."[38] The bergamasque refers perhaps to an Italian style of masque. Fauré's *Masques et Bergamasques* (1919) that Jankélévitch is referring to is one of his popular works, originally performed as a modern masque in Monte Carlo for the Prince of Monaco. Like the Debussy work, the Fauré work is inspired by Verlaine's poem in *Fêtes galantes* (1869).

And along with *charme* and the metaphysics of nostalgia we discover the *purity* of innocence, as in the six piano pieces entitled *Charmes* (1920) of Federico Mompou, which Jankélévitch loves. The sadness we speak about when we speak about beauty—as we are doing—is the sadness of innocence. In some sense, for Jankélévitch *melos* belongs to the metaphysics of nostalgia, because music like time is irreversible, and the reiterability of music only doubles the sense of irreversibility, binding us further to nostalgia, the reiteration does not release us, and *charme* is the essence of this—essence as in *parfum*, not as in Aristotle.

In his book, *Le je-en-sais-quoi et le presque-rien* (1980), Jankélévitch defines *charme* like this:

> *Charme* is what makes sure that tedious perfections will not be left as a *dead letter*: when awakened, activated, animated, dead perfections become capable of arousing love, and only then are they alive . . .

> In opposition to every definite thing (*res*), is *charme* not the very operation of beauty, the poetic influx through which beauty—far from remaining exposed, passive and quiescent, like a wax statue under the gaze of the spectator—will enter into a transitive relation with the human? . . . *Charme* makes beauty not only actual but efficacious. Plotinus had a term to indicate inefficacious beauty, perfection that does not act, and that is literally as "perfect" as the passive past participle. He called it [. . .] *lazy beauty*.[39]

Charme is the active ingredient of beauty. *Charme* upon the Ladder of Eros is that which *heightens* sensibility. *Charme* works on us, in us. The "transitivity" that Jankélévitch refers to in the second part of this quotation means that, between the listener and the ineffable, there is a "passing between." What passes between *depends on the music*. From the Play List, we have been hearing what passes between, and naming it: "shades of melancholy," "gardens of delight," "exaltation and rapture," "the work of mourning," "when time stands still," and "beauty and sadness." *Charme* is the transitivity of these to one another. It is not of course just a linguistic transitivity, but one of sensibility to which we, as listeners, are sensitive and makes us soulful. These "ground-moods," we called them, are not of our making, or at least not wholly of our making. They *correspond*—in the Baudelairean sense—with the ineffable. Something from "there" has come to us, *being here now*. This is true realism, not mysticism; it is a description of empirical fact: of what happens when we listen to art music.

"*Charme*" says Jankélévitch in the quotation just cited, "makes beauty not only *actual* but *efficacious*." Efficacious beauty is beauty that *acts*, that does, that affects, that *generates*. As such, beauty is a force for good in the world. But human sensitivity is the antennae which "picks it up"—the "ear," which is to say, the sensibility, is the conduit of this force through which it flows, carrying us with it. This is the "song" that is "existence," according to Rilke's *Sonnets to Orpheus*.

But there are two sides to this *charme*. Paul Valéry's poem *Ébauche d'un serpent* ("Silhouette of a Serpent") from his volume *Charmes* (1922) is written in the voice of the serpent, *the only creature in the Garden of Eden that can cross between the states of innocence and experience*. Wisdom alone speaks on both sides of the divide. From either side, all we really see is the silhouette (*ébauche*). The serpent can see the charm of Eve: the golden sunlight on her naked body, "The soul still stupid, and as it were/Nonplussed on the sill of the flesh."[40]

Valéry captures the beauty of Eve through the serpent's presentiment of the desire she will engender. And the other aspect is the charm of pleasure that the serpent offers her, "that very essence of heaven/To a purpose sweeter than honey."[41] This charm is the *pleasure* that, like God, like love, *you may propose to yourself.* The serpent then calls into the soft ear of Eve to yield her body and appetites and her thirst for metamorphoses, around the Tree of Death. Death is the "All-power of the Nothing," but barring it is this "irresistible Tree of trees."

The ineffable is not confined to one or other side of the Tree of the Knowledge of Good and Evil. In gaining the pleasure, which, like God, she may propose to herself, as the serpent put it to her, Eve loses her grip on something so that from then on she will be only a memory or a vestige of what she was. So she becomes a shadow of herself, the ultimate logic of which is death, where the vestige of herself that she has become itself becomes lost, and then not even that, at least for the one proposing her own pleasure. But the music of the ineffable affirms, in its *fall*, that death is not an end but *a part.* Like innocence and experience, the two sides of desire in *charme* cannot be told apart, and belong to the one story, to the same Tree of the Knowledge of Good and Evil—or to the same poem or music.

> And we, who have always thought
> of happiness as *rising*, would feel
> the emotion that almost overwhelms us
> whenever a happy thing *falls.*[42]

Lassus: *Lagrime di San Pietro*

We finish listening in this chapter in the Renaissance. This madrigal by (de) Lassus (or di Lasso) is one of his settings of the Italian poet Luigi Tansillo (1510–1568) that depict the stages of grief experienced by St. Peter after his denial of Christ and his memory of Christ's admonition:

> Now Peter was sitting outside in the courtyard. A servant-girl came to him and said: "You also were with Jesus the Galilean." But he denied it before all of them saying, "I do not know who you are talking about." When he went out on the porch another servant girl saw him, and said to the bystanders, "This man was with Jesus of Nazareth." Again he denied it with an oath. "I do not know the man." After a while the bystanders came up and said to Peter, "Certainly

you also are one of them, for your accent betrays you." Then he began to curse, and he swore an oath, "I do not know the man!" At that moment the cock crowed. Then Peter remembered what Jesus had said, "Before the cock crows you will deny me three times." And he went out and wept bitterly.[43]

This madrigal is one of a cycle of twenty-one in seven sections for seven voices. There were eight modes—systems that organize the pitch of Gregorian chant in church music—but Lassus used only nos. 1 to 7 of the modes. This seven stands for the seven days of creation. The "Eighth Day" is that of the New Creation, the new age.

If we can access the recommended track on the Play List, we will hear a madrigal written in 1594 and dedicated to Pope Clement VIII on May 24 of that year, just weeks before the composer's death. These are regarded as the greatest spiritual madrigals ever written. The madrigal on the Play List is entitled *Come Falda di Neve*. The English translation of the Italian goes:

> Like a snowflake which, having lain frozen
> and hidden in deep valleys all winter,
> and then in springtime, warmed by the sun,
> melts and flows into streams;
> thus the fear which had lain like ice
> in Peter's heart and made him repress the truth,
> now that Christ turned His eyes on him,
> melted and was changed into tears.

The beauty of these pieces is very pure, almost *sweet*.

(De) Lassus, or di Lasso, was born about 1530 in modern-day Belgium; he was Franco-Flemish, and probably the greatest singer of his day. He worked in Rome for Cosimo de Medici and became the chapel master of St. John Lateran Basilica by the age of twenty-one. He was an itinerant during his career, working throughout Europe.

On a historical note, Pope Clement VIII was a post-Tridentine (and therefore reforming) pope. "Tridentine" refers to the reforms the Catholic Church made to its own institutions, liturgy and theology at the Council of Trent (1545–63), largely as a response to the Protestant Reformation, which began on October 31, 1517, in Wittenberg, Saxony, where the Catholic Augustinian friar, Martin Luther, spoke out against the sale of indulgences, the sale of church offices, and the financial authority of Rome in the German kingdoms. The Saxons—as were all Germans—were a hardworking, thrifty, mercantile people, and when Luther walked all the way to Rome on a pilgrimage, he was shocked to discover something he had never seen before in his life or even imagined possible: people with seemingly no economic sense at all, gathering in money from the whole of Christendom and *wasting* it. The pope excommunicated Luther, but (as they say) he took half of Europe with him, and the split plunged Europe into an almost unending series of religious wars.

It is interesting to note, however, that the Reformation and the troubles that ensued did not stop Lassus moving around Europe and working in various kingdoms. As I have said before, *melos* is intrinsically *not* political and able to move in any camp.

Disinterestedness

If the ineffable falls, or descends the Ladder of *Eros*, while our sensibility for it rises to meet it—to co-respond, which means to *respond together*—then the reason that aesthetic experience cannot be completely *private*, and the basis upon which we *agree* about beauty, is precisely this correspondence *upwards*, "over and above" ourselves. Hence, beauty is always transcendent, just as people have always maintained.

Something of beauty is acquired, but something of beauty is *infused*. Of beauty which is acquired, we *aspire*. Of beauty which is infused, we are *inspired*. Acquisition and infusion, aspiration and inspiration: these are the way the Ladder of *Eros becomes*. For it is ever in motion, like music, or it ceases to exist.

Two things that we learn from Kant may be said of music with respect to beauty. Kant's philosophy brings up the subject of the *disinterestedness* of beauty that has been hovering in the background, behind the word "ineffable." The Greek philosophical word for essence, *esse*, is in the word "interestedness." *Esse* is *interesse*, essence is interestedness, says one philosopher of our time, Emmanuel Levinas.[44] "Disinterestedness" therefore is not meant in the colloquial sense in which I may be *un*interested in something, but in the sense that, of the phenomenon (beauty, in this case), there is not an "essence" fixing it "as such"—in other words, Kant's "free beauty." This is precisely why, though, beauty is ineffable. And we might add, why the soul is ineffable. And why music is ineffable. Taking Levinas out of context, and applying his words to music and to beauty, they are not "things" and have no essence not because they are "inessential," but because they are "otherwise than being." "Transcendence," says Levinas (and we mentioned the word a moment ago) "is passing over to being's *other*, otherwise than being. Not *to be otherwise*, but *otherwise than being*."[45] This is phenomenological description (in Husserl's sense) not conceptual, not therefore appropriately captured in Hegelian or dialectical and materialist terms. Music and beauty pertain to that "inter" of "dis-inter-esse," which means, "in between." The ineffable comes not *as* this or that, but *in between* a number of variants that a work has brought together to form a piece, rather like the "dark interval" of Rilke we referred to at the end of Chapter 3. Genius lies precisely in this "bringing together" and is another reason (if we need another reason) why art requires the human presence and cannot be made by machine or technology. Art is dis-inter-ested in all technology. The best technology can do is to *serve* music and beauty; it can never produce them, but only the *simulacrum* of them. For they are ineffable and a machine can never know what is otherwise than being, *nor can a machine-minded consciousness* know this.

As we have seen, beauty and music and the ineffable are interphenomenal (and we may speak of beauty, music, and the ineffable as coming together; they do not come apart. But they must be *occasioned*. This is a point that Kant labors in the *Critique of Judgment* and that Lawrenz develops in *Art and the Platonic Matrix* (2011).[46]

To take an example, compare a black cat with a long tail, and with shining, soft fur and a silent tread, with one of Baudelaire's poems about a cat, or Rilke's, or Eliot's, or Manet's etching of a cat, or Erik Satie's *Chanson du chat*, or Igor Stravinsky's *Berceuses du chat*, or Andrew Lloyd Weber's musical, *Cats*. The first occasion is natural: the black cat. The other occasions are artistic, where we do not capture the "essence" of the cat, but the ineffable life of it. The last example is popular and occasions rejoicing over cats, and the ineffable enters at that level.

One thing these examples have in common is the disinterestedness of the experience of beauty. There is no capturable essence which makes any of them beautiful; that is why the music must be performed and the etching seen (a reproduction will hardly do). Only the poems are able to circulate—but only insofar as poetic sensibility exists and has not died out.

A counterexample might be Adolph Hitler's watercolor of a cat, which looks more like a bulldog, probably without his meaning it to, but Hitler was no real artist.

The other point about art or music's disinterestedness is that it has no instrumental value. Art music cannot be *for* something, unless that something itself is art, like music is for ballet. But music for a commercial product like a Hollywood film is not art, although it might be very well done and very popular. But it belongs to the category of object, not to that of art.

Along with the occasioning of beauty and ineffability goes the *perfection* of a work. By perfection we understand a work's "finishedness." An experience of beauty or ineffability is also an experience of perfection. "It is perfect as it is," we say; another note would spoil the work. Analogously, we say to one we love: "I love you just as you are." A work, like a person, may not be morally perfect, or even perfect according to the fashionable style of the day, but the judgment of perfection lies further in than these "cheap" judgments. The judgment of perfection is "costly" in that it takes time, indeed, it takes a whole life, for example, Bergotte's love of Vermeer's "View of Delft" in Proust's novel, *Remembrance of Things Past.* Bergotte invested so much of himself in art, just as the lover does in the beloved. Only the lover can see the perfection of the beloved and know it.[47] The judgment that a piece of music is "just as it should be" falls like an inspiration, just as we "fall" in love. We cannot make ourselves love, or train ourselves to do so, no more than we can make ourselves experience beauty, ineffability, or perfection, or train ourselves to do so. In fact, any training is more likely to be obstructive, just as training in "relationship skills" is not the way you make friends.

Perfection or finishedness is a *quality* of our experience. The artist is the one who knows whether a work finished or not, but if he or she is wrong, we may be able to hear it.

Beethoven provides an exemplar of one who knew perfection in art. Beethoven added two notes to his seemingly completed "Hammerklavier" Sonata (No. 29 in B flat major). The Hammerklavier is the longest piano sonata ever written. The adagio alone occupies a pianist for twenty minutes. The famous adagio from the "Moonlight" Sonata takes 56 bars to write out; the Hammerklavier adagio 186. Beethoven's pupil Ferdinand Ries took the autograph with him to London in 1818, four months after its completion, to oversee publication and performance. While the engraving was in process, Ries received a letter from Beethoven, with instructions to ensure that an amendment made by the composer would be implemented. When Ries saw the amendment, he wrote to a friend, "I confess that involuntarily the idea took possession of me that possibly my dear old teacher had gone batty. . . . Two notes added to such a large, immensely carefully crafted work, half a year after its completion? Yet subsequently my greatest astonishment was over the effect of these two notes, which now comprise the first bar . . ."[48]

It does seem extraordinary, indeed, for the two notes do not correct mistakes somewhere, but *change the whole complexion* of the work by being the first two notes we hear! That change, prefacing a vast melodic arch (*adagio appassionato e con molto sentimento*: impassioned and with the utmost feeling), makes that melody sound, in Adorno's words, "as if it had been retrieved from a black chasm."[49] Daniel Barenboim takes fourteen seconds to play the two notes, giving all the reverberation possible to piano strings.[50] Barenboim holds the pedal down for 14 seconds to let the 2 notes breathe out like two drops of water falling into an immense silence. But the most astonishing feature is the variance among the great pianists over the duration required to perform the piece. People comment if one conductor takes two minutes longer than another over a Mahler adagio, but in this sonata the pendulum swings between Alfred Brendel, who takes less than seventeen minutes, and Eschenbach, who takes over twenty-five.

A piece may be a bit rough-hewn and still be an artwork: Impressionism made this very apparent. As critics and public sensibility became more conscious about form in music, and composers and musicians became more self-conscious about form, it resulted in people wanting to alter the form in certain ways. Great art has this finishedness. The greatness of a Michelangelo or a Picasso is that even their jottings have this quality. This is genius at work. If we listen to the andante movement of Mozart's Piano Concerto no. 21, or to the Lassus pieces, belonging to different worlds though they do, they both have that finished quality. They could say of themselves in all truthfulness, "I am what I am." That is their very splendor—lavish or modest as it may be.

To sum up then, disinterestedness and finishedness go together as belonging to *perfection* or music of genius. Disinterestedness is not an attitude but an *aptitude.* We need this aptitude to experience the *disinteressement* of the work, which is given by or in its finishedness. The *disinteressement* or disinterestedness of the work is not a quality of it so much as its *objectivity*, that is, that it stands over against us *as a work*[51]—and not just as a work but as a work which requires an *aptitude* of sensibility to *correspond* with it. Listening to the Mozart andante you would have to be hard of hearing or hard of sensibility *not* to recognize its perfection—and the same may be said of the Lassus, as well as of course of many other works, usually those universally recognized as great according to the criteria I gave in Chapter 1.

Beauty then falls as perfection or finishedness. In recognizing this "fall," we say, whether the artist worked hard or not, that he or she "must have been" *inspired*. This is often said of Mozart.

Composers write for the soul, and for the aspiration of the soul: they want their music to catch the soul of the listener in its aspiration and *take it with it*—to listen to it to get carried away. Would that this were our lifestyle! Would that the world would get so carried away! It would certainly make it a better place!

The Soulful Aspiration

St. Augustine described the aspiration of the soul, the movement of getting carried away, in this description of the degrees of soulfulness, which I outline here for the record:[52]

1. *Animatio* (animation)—We realize that music is life-bringing.
2. *Sensus* (sensation)—We start to listen and "get into" pieces of music. We indulge ourselves (and this is the kind of indulgence you cannot "overdo").
3. *Ars* (art)—We begin to apprehend in hearing the "art" in what we are listening to. In other words, *we connect with melos*. This is the crucial stage, for which this book is written, in order to connect people, and, more broadly (in my dreams), the culture.
4. *Virtus* (virtue)—We become discerning listeners; we do not just hear the art, but our sensibility is alive to how it is operating. This can (and in the first place *should*) be in terms of sensibility and therefore we will describe it. This is what I have done in this book, describing, to the best of my ability, the "art" in the pieces on the Play List.
5. *Tranquilitas* (tranquillity, *apatheia*)—The *melos* enters into the soul and becomes one with it. This is the level of *soulfulness*. The music is beginning to make us soulful. This can happen right from the start in fact. So there is a "secret accord" between this step and step 1. Right from the start, from animation, you might already experience this step as well.
6. *Ingressio* (entrance, initiation)—We are changed by the music. Initiation means (among much else) there is no going back: we have passed the "point of no return." Our *passion* is now connected with *melos*. We know what we like and why we like it and we can "bear witness" to the fact.
7. *Contemplatio* (contemplation)—This is the "temple" state or "meditative" state. *Templum* in Latin means, "from where all perspectives open out." It is not therefore itself a perspective. This is the coming to "height" in sensibility and in music.

In our age of transition we can add one more level, which I have taken the liberty of doing. Contemplation in the old metaphysics of *logos* was an end point, but for *melos*, it is a new starting place, therefore:

8. *Exploratio* (exploration)—If contemplation is characterized by self-presence, by stillness, exploration characterizes the new art music. It is adventurous and *travels* therefore. For example, the absorbing and purifying kirtan chant of Krishna Das that crosses between East and West, traditional and contemporary modes, and within a *religious* work too, since he is chanting the names of God, and we find the music *more*, not less, authentic for that exploratory quality. This he discovered not by seeking but by being sought (something St. Augustine would have appreciated as the way it works). Exploratory work in the new art music or world music is indicated and characterized by the move *beyond the self-presence* to identification *with All of it*. This is why world music is in a new sense religious too, because one needs some religious sensibility, in the philosophical sense, to have a feel for identification with *All of it*. This kind of musical exploration *thanks*, by contrast with religion and philosophy in the age of *logos* that *thinks*, and subsumes music to its ideas. We should be able to see the connection between absolute music and what I have said here.

St. Augustine could not have seen this, but we can.

12

Blue in Green

What is pure art according to the modern idea? It is the creation of
an evocative magic, containing at once the object and the subject, the
world external to the artist and the artist himself.
—Charles Baudelaire, *L'art romantique*

We have remained within the soul sensibility of the nineteenth century throughout this book because it was an axial time for music,
as for much else; whereas unfortunately most of the twentieth century was a period of discontinuity, and soulfulness became a casu-
alty of the turmoil and disaster that struck the German heartlands
of Europe and affected the whole world. Soulless ideology gained the
upper hand, including in music, and ideology still abounds today,
though much more loosely for the most part. But even with the turmoil of the twentieth century there were musicians whose genius
shone nonetheless. And now, in the twenty-first century, as the world
is finding its way clear of all the desuetude of the previous century,
hope is rekindling, more people than ever are working for a better
world and have a sense of a new age in the offing. In this chapter and
the final chapter to follow I examine new art music today in terms of
the aesthetic experience, and the true meaning of aesthetic experience that this book has been all about.

If Adorno is right- -that Wagner discovered "color" in music and
that Wagner's phrase, "in such a way that color becomes action,"[1]
refers to the orchestration of the quality of sound—then color is what
leads art music beyond atonalism, and the overplayed dissonance of
theory music, back to art music. Yet color is elusive in practice and
abstract in thought.

Olivier Messiaen (1908–1992) was one composer who tried, by
means of color, to turn antimusic back into music in works such as
Coleurs des cité céleste ("Colors of the Celestial City") and *Des canyons*
aux étoiles ("From the Canyons to the Stars"). But for many it was an

unmelodious and academic coloring, an intellectual kind of music for musicians; and for the ordinary listener the titles would always sound more entrancing than the jarring sounds: *Vingt regards sur l'enfant Jésus* ("Twenty Gazes on the Infant Jesus"), *Chants de terre det de ciel* ("Songs of Earth and Heaven"), *Trois petit liturgies de la presence divine* ("Three Small Liturgies of the Divine Presence"). Any doubt about whether Messiaen with his difficult music belongs to the New Music crowd of musical allegorists of theory or to the truly musical (as his titles would suggest) is banished by listening to his organ music recordings alongside Jon Gillock's masterful and enlightening, *Performing Messiaen's Organ Music*,[2] which takes the reader through 66 master classes representing each of the works. Gillock learned from the Messiaen himself in Paris and his book is revelatory.

The present chapter is about the art music to come, after the dead-end of atonalism and serialism, and dissonance for dissonance sake have all been recognized as a repudiation of *melos* and the either overt or implicit ridiculing of the metaphysics of nostalgia, of which *melos* partakes.

The rebirth of art music in the twentieth century came from an unexpected quarter, and because of our belief in categorizations, along with loss of sensibility for art music, the story is not widely told.

In 1959 Miles Davis, collaborating with the musician and composer Gil Evans, recorded an album in New York entitled *Sketches of Spain*. The opening track, which runs for sixteen minutes, is "Concierto de Aranjuez," a concerto written for classical guitar and orchestra by Spanish composer, Joaquin Rodrigo, from 1939. This is not the first or the last time a "jazz" musician would play a "classical" piece. The second track on the album is "Will O' the Wisp," which was originally a chamber piece composed by Manuel de Falla in 1915 and then a symphonic suite and ballet. It is from this suite that the piece is taken. Then come three tracks arranged by Gil Evans: "The Pan Piper," "Saeta," and "Solea." In the second of these, "Saeta," something revolutionary took place in twentieth-century art music.

For this moment to have happened it is as well that Davis, while musically literate, was an exponent of spontaneous music, and while he may have known about atonalism, serialism and so on, he was not musically driven by theory or politics nor did he derive inspiration from them, as do those who may be said to come under Adorno's umbrella concept of the "New Music." The New Music is characterized by its contempt for the ordinary listener, which is not merely elitist but part of that mad intelligence that is probably remarkable of any time, but especially of our time. Even to call this antimusic "new" is a bizarre case of wishful thinking, as well as a disassociation from the mythic ground of popular culture and the transmutative power of art within this ground.

"Saeta" starts gently; a small march begins with the trumpets out front. It is not a militaristic march in the least, more of a processional through the dusk, between one Spanish village and the next, the white stone picked out in the half moonlight against the dark earth and the neighboring village. Then the procession stops in its tracks—I have no idea why—and there is just the silence of the night and the stars: a dark silence of beauty falls on all the upturned faces, and then Davis calls out long on his trumpet, softly, longingly. This slightly muted imploring and primordial soul cry goes out, like the single sigh of the people of the warm earth, into the night sky and out across the dry Spanish hillsides, where it can be heard a mile away through the dark desert shadows and where the hard rocky ground cannot even be seen, but only the dark outlines of great trees, here and there, and the stars.

This trumpet call is new and unheard of, although it *symbolically* evokes the horn with which Wagner started his first successful opera, *Rienzi*. Symbolically, the two sounds are linked, as historic stages of the new art music and as the advent in our cultivation of *melos:* music as real presence. We could say, and it would be in the spirit of our earlier chapters to do so: *the two trumpets call to one another, from exile to exile, within the metaphysics of nostalgia.* Just as, absolute music (*melos*), best instanced by Beethoven, harked back, discontinuously with the "development" of music, to the Burgundian choristers, so now, Davis' trumpet harks back across a century of academic theory-driven "new" music to absolute music. And just as Beethoven took up where the Burgundian choristers left off, giving full sway to music *qua* music (without bowing to either church or court, and this time being allowed to get away with it), Davis takes up world music where Wagner left off, with a freedom from classical tradition on one hand and going beyond jazz on the other. Davis' accomplishment is as different from Wagner as Beethoven is from Bugundian choral music, but the philosophical move is matching in both cases; both are inaugural, Beethoven (philosophically picking up from the Burgunidan choristers) of absolute music, Davis (philosophically picking up from Wagner) of world music, the stage beyond absolute music.

We have already seen Wagner's music dramas articulated as pointers toward new world music, as the meaning of absolute music; and now we see it is not the New School Viennese who pick this up, indeed who *hear* it, but Miles Davis, from jazz. What I am alluding to here has nothing to do with "influence." No way would anyone think Davis was influenced by Wagner. Rather, what I am alluding to—and one can only allude and leave it to the reader's intuition—is what we have referred to in these pages, following Schopenhauer, as the metaphysics of music, and following Hegel as an historical progression. Therefore we would say that Davis belongs to the same time body or to use Bergson's term, Duration, as the nineteenth-century European tradition because this is directed toward world music and new cultures.

The track just before "Saeta" on the album is called "The Pan Piper," but Davis does not invoke the pan pipe with his trumpet on that track; but now, in "Saeta," the trumpet might be a pan pipe, or the invocation of one, and we imagine we hear that ancient, indeed mythical, musical instrument. The sound Davis creates by himself, all of a sudden, comes as a shock as it transports us to this legendary space of time immemorial, and the implacable relation between earth and heaven that you get in Spain as night falls after a hot day. It could be a reveille—that is probably what it is—as the processional draws to a halt, from inertia, or sheer wonder at the night, perhaps; but if it is a reveille, then Davis turns it into art, he sustains an improvisation around the holding note, which is the single upward cry of the trumpet, a cry from the deep past, right up out of the earth itself. The drum scratches hesitantly in the background. Davis reaches out and up with a haunting, strange sound. What is this? It is not jazz. It is not classical art music. No, it is not. It is the clarion of the *real* New Music. Beyond jazz, beyond classical. Not a "fusion" (although later Davis invented that genre too), but the next stage of art music. It started with "Saeta," right here in this solo. This is where art music today starts: the first note sounded beyond classical and jazz, in a musical space Davis opens up.

After several minutes, which, because of the sheer intensity of the moment, Davis's trumpet quails and falls silent, the march continues. In the next track, "Soleo," two-thirds of the way through, Davis gets back into the mode of "Saeta," beginning musically, just briefly, with sketchy phrases, to feel this new area beyond jazz and classical.

Davis's own account of recording *Sketches of Spain* in 1959 with Gil Evans is one of the best parts of his *Autobiography.*

The 'Saeta' was an Andalusian song known as the arrow of song, and it was one of the oldest religious types of music in Andalusia. It is a song usually sung alone, without any kind of accompaniment, during the Holy Week religious ceremonies in Seville, and tells about the Passion of Christ. It's a street procession, and the singer, a woman, stands on a balcony grasping the iron railing overlooking the procession, which stops beneath her balcony, while she sings this song. I was supposed to be her voice on trumpet.[3]

Davis recalls that this trumpet part was the hardest part he had to play on the album.

The difficulty came when I tried to do the parts that were in between the words and stuff when the singer is singing. Because you've got all these Arabic musical scales up in there, black African scales that you can hear. And they modulate and bend and twist and snake and move around. It's like being in Morocco. What really made it so hard to do was that I could only do it once or twice. If you do a song like that three of four times you lose the feeling you want to get there.[4]

Davis's recollection here is precisely in terms—wholly in terms—of listening, love and soulfulness. What he could hear in those musical scales made it actually like *being there* in Morocco; it is a song of the earth in a way far beyond the Viennese contrivances in this direction by Mahler. It is a song of heaven too, because it commemorates the passion of Christ, and Davis certainly knew something about passion and woundedness, and that finds its way into his sound and "worlds" it. We might note the importance of spontaneity—a theme of the whole *Autobiography*—and its place in art music. I refute the academic distinction between art music and spontaneous music. Spontaneity, inadvertency, and above all, *feeling*, in a "world" sense that anyone anywhere can feel (if they are not too much caught up in their head) are part of art music as it moves forward in time and body.

Feeling means affinity more than personal emotion when it comes to music and to listening to it. Davis knows and can list his affinities, "like Max Roach, Sonny Rollins, John Coltrane, Bird, Diz, Jack DeJohnette, Philly Joe . . . Monk, Mingus, Freddie Webster and Fat Girl."[5] All of them are dead, but as spiritual affinities they are all alive in the notes Davis gets from his trumpet. "Their spirits are walking around in me, so they're still here and passing it on to others. It's some spiritual shit and part of what I am today is them. It's all in me, the things

I learned to do from them. Music is about the spirit and the spiritual, and about feeling."[6] Feeling as inner affinity rather than as emoting. It is in this affinity, in finding our affinity and in attuning to it that the soul flourishes and death has no dominion.

Davis had been working up to this trumpet part in "Saeta." It takes more than one's whole being: it takes one's affinities and the ability to project them. Ten years before *Sketches*, in late 1949 and into 1950, Davis made some recordings that would appear in 1956. The recordings are usually credited with inventing a new style of jazz, but they are much more than this. In these recordings Davis invented an attitude which would completely dominate popular culture right into our own time, now more than then. The recordings comprise the album, *Birth of the Cool*. Cool was not just a kind of jazz, it was to be a cultural attitude, it would govern people's social personas— especially after Clint Eastwood's performances as *The Man with No Name* in Sergio Leone's spaghetti westerns of the 1960s, where Eastwood exemplified what it meant to be cool. But I will come back to Eastwood shortly.

In 1959, the same time as he made *Sketches of Spain*, Davis recorded the album, *Kind of Blue*, in the cool idiom he had already invented. This is a jazz album. There were five tracks on the original. The first track, "So What," and the second, "Freddie Freeloader," are modern jazz. The third track, "Blue in Green," however, breaks in the same direction as "Saeta," Symbolically, blue is the jazz color, the color of black music (jazz, blues, rhythm), *blue in green* is the new color of world music.

At the beginning there is piano accompaniment and Davis's clean, full, but slightly bereft trumpet sounds. When Davis plays we have a presentiment of new art music. The saxophone comes in and the track is jazz again. Then Davis comes back, and he plays between the two idioms: cool jazz and a new expressivity. We hear this not in the actual notation—the riffs, if you like—but in the *color*, blue in green.

The album's final track, which goes for ten minutes, and of which there is a second take on the fiftieth anniversary re-release of the album, is "Flamenco Sketches." A piano played by Evans provides some very low-key accompaniment to what is basically Davis going out beyond jazz the whole way. Cool is the way he reaches it first. Cool paves the way because jazz is not naturally "cool" music, but hot and for parades and dance halls. The reinvention of jazz under Parker and Gillespie as bebop, where the beat is implied by a drum pattern around it, over the top of which high-speed improvisations run, it hot jazz club music. But in "Flamenco Sketches" we can actually hear Miles Davis in another world that he is beginning to explore all by himself, like someone stepping onto the shore of a previously undiscovered continent. And on this track—unlike "Saeta," that clarion of arrival at the new continent, where the other musicians all stand lined up behind him and stand in reverential silence while Davis goes it alone—Davis takes his musicians with him. Julian "Canonball" Adderly on alto saxophone seems to have an ear to what Davis is doing, beyond jazz, and tries to follow him; and we can hear his steps: almost bemused notes at the limit of jazz and across it. For it is very difficult for an instrument like the saxophone to do more than Lester Young, say, can do with it; he prefigured cool to some extent and played with incredible intimate feeling and expressivity, but Adderly manages it. Then, following Adderly, playing tenor saxophone, comes the jazz legend, musician and composer, John Coltrane.[7]

The line-up on this album is legendary in jazz. But it has to be so: this is jazz becoming something other, less a way of treating musical form than a new, indefinable, and multiple form in its own right. And it manages simply by relying in the solo on *color*. What is so wonderful is that you can play the track and, if you are sufficiently used to listening to jazz, you can actually *hear it happening as it happens*, this move from jazz to a new age in art music. After Coltrane, the piano, played by Gil Evans, follows through the entrance that has been left empty. By the end of track, when Davis comes back in, art music has laid down its first track in the new age, and regardless of the awful sound effects posing as music under the intellectualist umbrella held out for the New Music in the Viennese manner. This is jazz moving into art music. Jazz is a verb; it is a treatment of music rather than a musical form. In short solos based on color, such as "Blue in Green," perhaps it is possible to create jazz form, but hardly yet as a major work.

Coming back to the actor Clint Eastwood in the Sergio Leone *Dollars* Trilogy made in the 1960s in the cool genre invented by Miles Davis: these films would not be what they are if it were not for the musical scores that accompanied them by Leone's friend and collaborator, Ennio Morricone. Morricone's film music is a departure from the Wagner-influenced film music of Hollywood, which tries to emotionally accompany the scenes. Morricone produced art music in the same cool genre as Davis, but without the limitations that jazz manner brings with it. Morricone's compositions are a major force in the kind of world music that I have been positing. The old-fashioned pigeon holes confining classical and pop, sound and vision, classical and contemporary simply no longer hold credibility when we listen to Morricone and look at his career. If Davis moves jazz into art music, Morricone moves classical music and film music—and film with it—into a new age.

Aura

The new art music seeks ambience and color within harmonic and disharmonic ranges. *Aura* is the name of a 1989 album by Miles Davis which uses some formalistic techniques in an experimental way to explore colors musically. The album would not succeed musically because it follows the intellectualist musical theory of serialism, but it is redeemed by Davis's signature trumpet playing. The formalism holds the music down, but Davis's musical genius redeems even formalism and makes the album bear repeated listening. It is a concept album recording, but the concept of aura—as a combination of color and feeling or ambience in a broad sense—is important in new art music and world music, if world music is to be something more than simply an amalgam of styles, which is the danger. Interestingly, in the track, "White," in which Davis is after pristine sound of no color, and in which rhythm and other instruments are muted and in the background, he echoes "Saeta," at the start, his track of forty years before and the whole feel of "Saeta" is momentarily rekindled, in the pause we may almost expect the marching band to come back in.

A home of art music—one of many, but perhaps the most important—would be the recording label ECM, standing for Edition of Contemporary Music but often thought to stand for European Contemporary Music, because of what the label houses. The recording company was founded in München in 1969 by producer Manfred Eicher, who has a background in both jazz and classical, and an ear for new music which is breaking boundaries, but uses spontaneity for truth in music, rather than music theory, as with those associated with Adorno's attempted definition of New Music. Many north European artists have recorded on ECM. One who has achieved worldwide recognition is Arvo Pärt, who composes contemporary sacred music in the Orthodox tradition. Another musician who records with ECM is Keith Jarrett, who tends to switch between classical and jazz, as between genres, and only in his improvisations does he seem to unite them in a single expression; hence the famous recording of his *Köln Concert* (1975), a one-hour piano improvisation, of which one can say only that that night he was inspired.

One of the most important early recordings exploring new inner space is *The Codona Trilogy* (1978–82), made up of Don Cherry, Nana Vasconcelos, and Collin Walcott. They are in the space from the start; they do not move into it from jazz or classical. Their music explores the new spaciousness they find. Sometimes they merely make a noise in the new space, as if confounded somewhat by it. This is not to criticize their musicianship, for at that time, to even *be in* the new space of art music was accomplishment enough; and they were among the first explorers of it. You can hear the spaciousness and it is wonderful and future-reaching. It is completely different from the *closeted* silence and stuffed space of theory music, which is stifling. Theory music is tied in a fraught space; Davis announced what he discovered, which is free space, and this is what Codona avail themselves of. This is acoustic multi-instrumental, experimental transcultural world music. These three musicians are adventurers and explorers. To discuss their works would need another book about musical sensibility.

Another of the many musicians recording with ECM is the American multi-instrumentalist, Ralph Towner. Towner mainly plays classical guitar and piano, instruments that most easily slip between "genres" (jazz/classical) without allegiance to either. Ralph Towner more than anyone has continued the movement Davis began, with reference to neither "jazz" or "classical" as such; and so he has really moved into this new area of world music as art music and established himself as a composer and a musician.

What Miles Davis opened up beyond jazz is huge, because it is the avenue through which all the new music in our culture is coming. It is a good thing that the music is outsmarting the names we try to apply. In the language of this book: *melos* is outsmarting *logos*. Towner has recorded over twenty albums since the early 1970s. I shall talk about a few works from this range where he is at his best.

In *Diary* (1974) Towner accompanies himself by overdubbing his guitar on his piano in the studio. The technical manipulation of sound of course interferes with the art in the sense of saying something is a work of art, because it is an artificial, although hardly a commercial, product aimed at a market. The technical, as in film, becomes part of the work as art. In Towner's case, with *Diary*, although he used technology to do it all himself, one supposes he could quite easily find a pianist or guitarist to co-perform the work, which would allow a performance of it to exist as an artwork. However, if music cannot be performed except technologically, it is more problematic: it may be "arty," but machine productions are soulless.

If the color in jazz is blue, relying on the "blue note," the note played at a lower pitch than the rest of the scale, or "flattened," the color of this new music is, as Miles Davis suggested, *green*. The green refers not to a note, but to the color, and to the *soulfulness as color*. It is the color of the new music, perhaps because it will always be music that remains faithful to the earth and calls upon us to do so. This is all the more important in an age of technology, where we dispossess ourselves by our advances on technological fronts—not out of any necessity, I should add, but because of a will to power. Technologized music or "metal machine music," as Lou Reed bluntly called it in the 1970s, is not green in the sense we mean here to speak of musical color: it is black. Like jazz, techno is a treatment of music, not a form of *melos*. Techno mechanizes *melos*. Techno totally destroys inner space, which is free and non-mechanical. This is the problem with ambient and lounge music today, which are not New Age or artful, as they often like to advertise themselves, but modernistic, contrived, predigested because mechanized and, in that sense, go back to Schoenberg in ethos, but in a way he would not have approved of musically either. However, the idea of musical *ambience* is important and new harmonics need to capture an ambience, as Davis does on *Sketches* much better than most of those working in the ambience industry, which is a computer industry as much as a musical one, and therefore robotic and contrary to any art.

In discussing some works by Ralph Towner we might also consider his "Oceanus," from the album *Solstice*, recorded in Oslo in 1974 and produced by Manfred Eicher. The album runs for just over forty minutes and "Oceanus" is the first track. Towner plays twelve-string and classical guitars, and piano, so it is overdubbed; the other members of the quartet play an ensemble of instruments: tenor and soprano saxophones, and flute (Jan Garbarek), bass and cello (Eberhard Weber) and drums and percussion (Jon Christensen), and there is a synthesizer in there somewhere, from time to time. One can hear all the instruments of "Oceanus," which starts with Towner's twitching guitar in warm, scattered notes and chords, becoming musically accumulative and coagulative with the introduction of the other instruments, led by a tenor sax. It is hard to play a sax and not sound jazzy unless you play in that inner space opened up by Coltrane under the influence of Miles Davis; this is what Garbarek confidently achieves. The sound builds quickly, not eschewing rhythm, into a tumultuous, swelling and heavy or thick nimbus, but it is layered so that one can listen to the depths, from the instrument running across the surface, to the instruments constituting the thickness of the sound, to the percussion at the bottom driving it in this and that direction. I'd love to watch Towner perform those huge cascades of guitar notes that fall down to the swirling waters beneath and emerge out of them, only to shower back down into them, to see how it is done. Each of the instruments—from the guitar to the sax to the bass to the percussion—by turn provides atmospherics, but not in a segmented way, as is the custom in jazz combo solos. Rather the instruments interplay and interconnect and then play across and over one another, at various tempos or none, where a continual, drawn-out note is made like a line of sound, which could be a reverb effect or a synthesizer. The electronics are always in harness to the music and are key to the atmospherics and cohesion. The listener is drawn right into the sound, in the thick of the piece, as into a maelstrom, comprised of instrumentation, but not a noise; there is a harmonics at work and a melody, in the undercurrent or surfacing, which the ear can follow and enjoy. The piece is divided into three sections, or it might be said that the music reaches a point of its own cessation before starting out once more. Each section has its own distinct feel, but is recognizably part of the whole. Of course (it goes without saying) this is beyond jazz or classical music. This music picks up from both genres, within another register of meaning which is beyond naming at present. The music gives a sense of calm elation, although one needs to hear it a few times for this sense to arise, and for it to last on repeated listenings.

Repeated listenings are the test of new art music, as of any music: does it bear them? And of course most music does not, even the most highly regarded rock music of the most progressive kind is only worth rehearing in the end for sentimental reasons. The exception is the song that metamorphoses through multiple rerecordings by different artists, each giving a different version. Out of ten thousand songs we would be lucky to find one like "Mr. Bojangles," say, or "Send in the Clowns": songs which great performers can do justice to and which do justice to great performers. Among examples of modernistic music, music of the atonal school and serialism does not really bear repeated listenings; neither on the whole does highly dissonant music—unless it is done well, as art music, for example, Albeniz's piano music, *Iberia*. Most dissonant music, with repeated listenings, becomes normalized as we become accustomed to it, and at that point it begins to show the cracks, the musical tricks begin to stand out and it starts to sound like something of a *charade*. Ultimately, in the language of this book, for the listener, the music just proves itself *cerebral*, not *soulful*. The music has been worked out like the theory and the muse locked outside the door. Cerebral music is music that, on repeated listenings (perhaps we liked it at first), sounds *contrived* rather than *inspired*. It is possible of course for music to be both contrived and inspired—Bach is like this. The contrapuntal system that dominates his musical "thinking" is contrived, but what he manages musically to accomplish, nevertheless, can be wonderful and entrancing and able to be listened to across a lifetime, as is common knowledge. Cerebral music that most people can hardly bear to listen to once, let alone repeatedly, is propagated by musical academia and aficionados of musical technique, not by anyone listening with their soul.

"Blue Sun," the title track of the 1983 album, starts with Towner's twelve-string guitar and some simple keyboard double-tracked, then the piano, a flicker of tambourine and what will be a mounting refrain is sounded from the background. The intimacy and interplay of instruments, somehow sounding both free and tightly structured like a chamber work, with the repetition of the refrain each time different. The piece achieves clarity, light, and gentle hopefulness. The ability not to overstate, the blend of instrumentation, the detail, and the accomplishment of a whole by the sum of its parts is marvelous and bears repeated listenings.

"New Moon," the first track from *Old Friends, New Friends* (1979) has Kenny Wheeler on trumpet giving a generous, spacious, clear sound softened by Towner's accompanying French horn that opens out the music, and just as the trumpet wistfully begins to jazz up the sound, an electric violin counterposes with warmth and firm melodic touch. All the time the guitar runs underneath like clear stream–water pouring over pebbles.

"Beneath an Evening Sky," the final track from *Old Friends, New Friends*, starts with piano and soft violin together, then the very quiet plucking of the guitar sets up the melody. This is one of Towner's most beautiful and sensitive compositions; "pastoral," one might call it, if such an idea can exist any more in the age of agribusiness and "Food Inc." This piece is soft, gentle and evocative, but tight, structured, melodic, and not wandering or merely ambient. This is music sodden with soulfulness. "The Prince and the Sage," from *Blue Sun*, seems as if to elaborate the previous track. Towner solos on twelve-string guitar with synthesizer keyboard extremely subtly played. The guitar is melodic and exquisitely played. "Nimbus," from *Solstice* builds from the initial plucked twelve-string guitar and then goes into a virtuoso guitar solo, Towner brings in the whole ensemble, gradually intensifying the sound in all "directions" although the "forward" propulsion is strong, then lastly Jan Garbarek's soprano saxophone is let loose, but not allowed to go wild, as all the instruments land the piece together. Complex and accomplished is the feel rather than experimental.

In 2010 Towner released an album called *Chiaroscuro*, which he had recorded the previous year with the Italian trumpeter, Paolo Fresu. It is a work he had been planning to make and was in the offing for fifteen years, according to the notes. Fresu has the clean, clear, atmospheric sound that fits well with Towner's music and compositional practice. The whole album is Towner's twelve-string and baritone guitars on a couple of tracks and Fresu's trumpet and flügelhorn. Trumpet and guitar are instruments that one might not think go easily together, but here it is a perfect contrast and match. The one track not Towner's is "Blue in Green." Paulo Fresu's playing pays homage to Miles Davis, with a touch of that muting that makes the note seem to sob slightly, and right at the end there is that mellowness that has the same ache so characteristic of Davis. Otherwise Fresu and Towner make this track their own, hardly needing to take it out of jazz, because it had already left jazz behind and presaged exactly such music as Towner has been making. The light, serene airiness and elegance of the piece is beautiful. Here is a kind of music able to pay homage to jazz because it is no longer jazz: Towner and Fresu *in free melos*.

Reprise: Baudelaire's Aesthetic

Art music in our time is in a hyperexperimental phase, a phase of enormous creativity. What is called "world music" or "ambient" or "experimental" music (there are a lot of names), or, in another direction, "roots" music, would be evidence of this. Something is in the offing with this music, a new genre in the broad sense, *blue in green* we have called it, and the ingredients are being gathered. In countless areas of music, on every continent, wonderfully gifted and inspired musicians are working with their loved ones and helpers and their audiences and the music in new ways, and if it is not always "art" in a high sense, as given by our aesthetic theory in this book, it is artful, it is artistic, it should be categorized with art, rather than excluded. This is quite different from crass commercial pop poured out by our radio stations and force-fed to us through shopping malls across the world as "music," as big business tries to create a sensibility attuned to their commodification, which they can then—for a price of course—satisfy with their products.

243

I even go so far as to believe—perhaps rather optimistically—that there is a "critical mass" of musicians (real artists) and audiences (authentic listeners to those specific artists) everywhere, that is, in every place. Most of these artists are not billed in the newspapers and mass media or featured on TV and we do not read about them very much, except perhaps in specialist publications. And yet, they work on, regardless, despite the odds against them, often in obscurity, in a totally rationalized and glutted social and political order which would silence them altogether if it could, given the profit to be made in that case. These musicians humbly garner what little publicity they can to keep going, and the internet has been a help so far, though this may be a "window period" of opportunity, not a permanent state, as we may naively believe. Unfortunately, in any book, such artists and their music and what it means to listen to them cannot be adequately mentioned in a discussion of art music now and to come. The only consolation for lovers of such music is that, in discussing classical, I also have been extremely exclusive. Ralph Towner will have to stand in for countless contemporary musicians, and I must leave it to readers to know their names or to find them out.

In a notebook known as *Fusées*, Baudelaire said, "music excavates heaven."[8] These words encapsulate what we saw in the previous chapter about presence and inner space. These words are the aesthetic criteria of the new art music; they are how we recognize it. That is what the new art music is doing: excavating heaven or the skies. The "skies" are not given in advance, but cannot be seen, until the music shows them. To decide whether a new artist is in keeping with our aesthetic or not, suffice it to ask: does this music excavate the skies? Artists can ask this of themselves too to keep themselves on track—*even to find their way into their own art vocation.* Is my work excavating the skies?—musicians may ask themselves. This is the aesthetic and philosophy of culture that I advocate as my core message in this book. All the music I have discussed meets this criterion. Miles Davis is historic in this regard; I cannot guess the length of a list of notable names we could add to his today, knowing at least the criteria for such a list; having the tools to judge, having, in a word, sensibility, so hard to define, so easy to lose, soul and soulfulness.

13

Attunement

How can people talk of Mozart composing "Don Juan"! Composition!
As though it were a piece of biscuit made up of egg, flour and sugar!
It is a creation of the spirit, the part as well as the whole coming from
one source, at one burst, filled with the breath of life; so that it cannot
be said that the creative artist tried first this thing or cut that one into
a certain shape or disposed of anything as he himself willed it; the
divine spirit of his genius so overpowered him that he was forced to
carry out its commands.
—Johann von Goethe, *Conversations with Eckermann*

The New Music

Alain Badiou writes, "My hypothesis is that high art has once again become part of our future—I have no idea how this is so, but I am absolutely sure of it. Greatness is no longer merely part of our past; it is part of our future as well. Needless to say, it is not the same kind of greatness as before."[1] And he surmises that his new kind of greatness will be "high art *uncoupled from totality*."[2]

True, but to uncouple high art from totality means to release art from theory. Twentieth-century music is by and large theory music. Wagner is the ultimate inspired artist working in terms of what we have called Baudelaire's aesthetic—of course it belongs to all real artists. But artists from Baudelaire's time on, and especially in the twentieth century, began to eschew this aesthetic and replace it with theory. Wagner in this sense stands over and against twentieth-century music by and large and, in philosophy, all Nietzcheanism, where art is used for *self-creation*. The Nietzschean Zarathustran artist is the self-proclaimed artist. This kind of artist has been another delusion of twentieth-century art, as in expressionism, where Nietzscheism and theory art come together. Nearly all twentieth-century art is tainted with expressionism to some degree or other. The only salvation of expressionism is if it is in a good cause, as for example with the paintings of Max Beckman; but then it is essentially politically motivated art, which in its lesser lights is merely a form of journalism. A lot of twentieth-century American art and literature suffers from this problem, because of the dominance of commercialism and publicity not just *in* the culture but *as* the culture. While the poet is a celebrity then his or her work remains of interest, but it vanishes with the celebrity status. It never is this way for art, which is nothing to do with celebrity status.

But the point for now is that we need to understand that *melos* has been in thrall to theory during almost the whole of a century. The result has been theory music, and one of the philosophers most associated with this kind of music has been my own master, Theodor Adorno, and so I have to take issue with him.

Adorno theorized the new music associated with the twelve-tone technique developed by Arnold Schoenberg and associated with the names of Alban Berg (Adorno's teacher), Anton Webern, and Hanns Eisler in the first generation, and of course many others since then.[3] This new music has nothing to do with the future of the artwork that Wagner had in mind, or what we mean by art in the new age, or the high art Badiou envisages. Adorno's new music is theory music. It is *melos* in thrall to *logos* in a particularly narrow way, full of interdictions of what can and cannot be the case with it. For a thinker such as Adorno, with the name Auschwitz at the center of his thinking as a touchstone of reality, it is amazing what an authoritarian personality he becomes when it is down to musical taste that he expects people to have. This theory music was the near death of *melos* in the twentieth century.

The nub of the matter is that modernistic music is contrived *aside from Baudelaire's aesthetic.* Theory music is oblivious to the meta-physics of nostalgia. It is not as if Adorno was not cognizant of the metaphysics of nostalgia: we saw earlier in this book that he had a deep sensibility for it. So his disregard for it is a sad lapse in his philoso-phy, it would appear. At the same time his animus against American music, which we have not gone into, but is famous, blocks his ears to the connection we have made between absolute music, especially as practiced in the German tradition, and world music and its explora-tions of inner space.

What matters to theory music is the theory that it is illustrating and the intellectual propagation of the music that goes on hand in hand with such intellectualization. This spells the death of *melos* and it is a death that a whole culture in the twentieth century has been forced against its will and choice to experience, as theory music has been foisted on us both by composers and the music industry that supports them with grants and contracts and the like, and of course the publicity machine which goes along with it all. Most listeners confronted with this prospect of theory music have stayed with music that is easier on the ears—popular music. And who can blame them? Or else they have stuck to "fine" music, the classical music of which the nineteenth century can be most proud.

Theory music is music to illustrate theory and if it accidentally manages to be musical (in the generally recognized sense) at the same time, that is a bonus, but hardly the real meaning of the work. The theory may be inspired, but the music is not, as I think we can hear. This music is driven by the force of intelligence of men such as Schoenberg, Boulez, and Cage, not by their soulfulness. *Theory music is not music that one can attune the soul by.* Therefore, if anything, it makes us less human, more spoilt, more perversely self-indulged, more problematized, and culturally adrift.

If one listens to Schoenberg's *Pelleas and Melisande*, which is an early work before he got serious about atonalism, one can hear the Prelude to Act 3 of Wagner's *Tristan and Isolde* resolved into a technique. In Wagner the music is desolate and gray, Tristan the lover is waiting for Isolde his beloved, the music is chromatic and unstable. In Schoenberg, the chromatic and unstable harmonic field—which was a soulful mood, if ever there was one, in Wagner—becomes a technique, which, as such, can be repeated *ad nauseam*, like patterned wallpaper, which is basically what Schoenberg's music is. In Wagner, when the lovers eventually do meet, about five minutes into the act, the music fizzes up and wells over. This too, can be resolved into technique. If we listen to Scriabin's *Poem of Ecstasy*, we can hear this Wagnerian moment, in which the lovers rapturously meet, as technique carried on for twenty minutes. On first hearing it might seem impressive, but on repeated listening we eventually hear the soulless gesturing, which is all it is. Once something authentically rapturous or beautiful becomes technique, it is dead as art. Technique music is the early manifestation of fully fledged theory music, which reaches its far-fetched consequences in the hands of various charlatans who are held in the highest esteem and who receive all the accolades of important composers, which is how they too regard themselves to be.

If one listens to a recording of Schoenberg's last string quartet (no. 4) sufficiently to get under its skin, or to Arthur Crumb's *Black Angel* (to take two examples only, to derive broadly generalizable criteria therefrom), what do you find? With Schoenberg's last string quartet, once you get over the forbidding harmonic exterior, you begin to recognize the stamp of humanness (in a truncated sense) on the music. Music has to articulate something, and this is done by gestures, rhythms, harmonies, developments, and melody—in a word: *melos*. If we think of music—as the important philosopher of culture, Spengler, might have done, as *having a physiognomy*, which is a good way in fact to think of it—after we have spent time listening we begin at once to recognize the different physiognomies when the music plays. We know that twitch of the lips, that scrutiny of the eye, we know that face, that pretty face and that ugly one, we know that high brow and that smile. And when Schoenberg plays, we can see the lack of character in the face; this is not the king, this is not even a prince, this is a courtier and a pretender to the throne. And after "communicating" several times with a work, we know how deep or shallow it is, by what it expresses and the manner in which it expresses.

There is an additional factor. Human hearing is intensely sensitive. Humanity would not have survived without it. Our hearing equipment is sensitive to the slightest tonal variations. Sounds that are "pleasant" to us, like a euphonious voice, attract us. Rough voices repel. There is a graduated scale from ugly noises to bearable noises to beautiful noises. Composers such as Schubert, Beethoven, and Wagner had a very deep instinct of what kind of mix to give us so we can delve into the depths of this analogue of the spirit. It is an analogue because the spirit does not "speak"; and this is the reason why music can be so deeply spiritual, whereas words cannot be because they carry a freight of explicit meaning.

Listening to the aforementioned pieces by Schoenberg, we find he is constantly preoccupied with *how* to say things. His quartet is an endless exploration of tricks and "snazzy" technical virtuosity. This may be of interest for a while, but sooner or later you come to the point where they tire you. "There must be more to it than all this dancing on knife-edge," you feel. In other words: to justify this dancing on knife-edge, there ought to be some inner compulsion, some extreme of emotional or spiritual anguish that is being conveyed. Well, therein lies the problem. Something similar may be said of Crumb's *Black Angel*. As a performance piece it may be amazing with the amplification, the plucking thimbles, the musical glasses, the violin bow underneath the strings, and so on, but it is not music. What we have are sound effects. Instead of *melos* presencing and inner space we have tedium. These kinds of compositions, of sound effects, ubiquitous in modern music, have a novelty factor, like the new technology of our culture in this regard, but such compositions are contrived, whereas art is never contrived. Contrivance is the sign of a lack of art. These kinds of compositions carry with them an undertow (like what we call a sub-text) that goes "what are the journalists going to say?" These peices are the musical equivalent of literary conceits, but they are big business and that is the crux. A lot of contemporary art has this undertow and for this reason it is not art, but a testimony to a power of self-advertisement; this is a big problem in the United States, where self-made celebrities (the recent transmogrification of the old-fashioned self-made man) pose as important composers and musicians, even with all the attendant trappings and honors of real composers and musicians of importance. And where there is no sensibility there is no way to tell the difference.

If you listen to Schoenberg or Crumb and then, for instance, to Schubert's String Quintet, the difference is massive and ungainsayable: compare the musical artificiality of Schoenberg, and the unmusical tokenism of Crumb, with the mesmerizing inspiration of Schubert, which tingles the nerves and elevates the soul—or indeed may even help us find our soul in the first place. With Schoenberg, the tricks absorb your entire attention with nary a thread of melody: just glissandos, arpeggios, and so on. The "harmony," because it is so unpleasant, detracts for a while from the melodic texture because you respond instinctively by looking for the extreme emotional/spiritual condition that gave rise to it. *But it is not there.* It is exactly the same in countless other works by twentieth-century musicians because they are all theory music or expressivist journalism, even Crumb's *Black Angel*, which pretends to be serious. But this is one of the best among a bad lot, which is why I refer to it. Theory music or expressivist music inevitably "seeks the limelight" in circumstances of commodified and industrialized culture. Perversely, bad publicity can be the best thing for the artist because it leads to celebrity status, which is what the artist needs in order to establish that (as Warhol ironically, one presumes, showed) anything counts as art at the artist's say-so—even nothing. In American success-culture, publicity does not *lead* to success, it is the *same* as success. So if the publicity machine recognizes you as an artist in the commodified system, then you *are* one. Simple as that. It has got nothing to do with genius, nothing to do with soul, as everyone will tell you.

As far as aesthetic experience goes, with this modernistic music, you do not have a soul. After hearing Schoenberg, you feel singularly dissatisfied. It was not an experience, not even a journey, but a kind of static picture show, one image after another, glittering and screeching in turn. But the emptiness underneath becomes more shocking than the harmony. With Crumb, the more you hear of it, the less you feel that it has anything to say. It does not suffice to say this is soulless music for a soulless world, or harsh music for a harsh world, or "black" music for a pointless, unforgivable war that should never have been fought. This novelty-value music has analogues in other arts. For instance, in literature, James Joyce spent years on *Ulysses*, writing each chapter in a different style, but it is stylistics at the expense of everything else. Ultimately it has the style of "damn the reader," a style that, as Joyce predicted (at least he had wit!), would be taken up by po-faced academia; and he was right. Joyce put in the work on *Ulysses* and then spent nineteen years full-time on *Finnegan's Wake*, but the stylistics and virtuosity cannot cover up the black hole in the middle of it!

It is interesting that Adorno, despite his unqualified endorsement of Schoenberg, knew deep down that all this was wrong, dead, with not a shred of spirituality in it. In his *Philosophy of New Music*, he gives himself away so often that even Schoenberg noticed: Schoenberg wrote to another music writer: "I've always known that deep down Adorno hates my music."[4] This was because it was essentially music to illustrate *theory*. Deep down, Adorno's aesthetic judgment disliked theory music, but the theorist in him was so strong that there was no other music he could like instead. This was his unconscious dilemma. Adorno was the major critical theorist of the twentieth century and a real intellectual heavyweight of the top rank, but he had what we might (cheekily) call a "negative dialectical" attitude to musical theory. He was always trying to deny and espouse it at the same time. Although I mean this half-humorously, I think you can hear it in his work, if you listen, especially where (as in all his best work) he is at his most theoretical. The trouble is that Adorno's poor musical taste was completely out of sync with his fierce intellectuality. His intellectual firepower continually mastered and overcame any aesthetic experience he might have had if his thinking had not got there first. This is the little-known secret of his poor musical judgment.

The Question of Technology

I have tried in this book to establish that art music is human, and by human I mean soulful. All music—if it aspires to being art, and is therefore not commercial dross, or pretentious theory music, sound effects, or novelty music such as we have just discussed—is soulful. It is hard for music to be any other way than soulful—until you make machines to make it; then it is *automatic.*

All musical instruments, if we think about it, are plucked, hit, rubbed, or blown into. These are the means by which to communicate through the chosen instrument: soul to soul. It is not the same if a machine makes a sound. That is a sound effect, not music in the sense of *melos.* An instrument is tuned, but the soul is attuned. To attune the soul one must have a model against which to attune it that is of a *higher order* than it. In tuning an instrument we need to find the keynote from which we know what the different notes are. When we tune a musical instrument or check its condition and worthiness for music making, we tune it against the ideal so that it is as it should be. We do not have the ideal note at hand; we hear it in our inner senses. We measure the actual notes the instrument will make against the inner notes that we can hear inwardly, so we know the instrument is tuned correctly. The ideal is an *intellectual* actuality, but it is *empirical* as well in that it can also actually be played on the instrument. There are two kinds of actualities at work here: the one inner and the other outer, the one intrinsic and the other extrinsic, the one pertaining to the thing itself, the other to the phenomenon. Between the two is a correspondence, just as in Baudelaire's aesthetic at the start of this book I spoke of correspondence. Soulfulness will happen in the correspondence if the note is right. For music, inner and outer, ideal and empirical *cooperate* in the literal sense of operating together at one and the same time.

The ideal against which tuning takes place cannot be made up: it is *a given.* It is there to begin with. Socially speaking, it *precedes* the culture and a culture *discovers* it. And yet, this is not to say there is one way of harmony; just as there are more than two ways to read the stars, so too for harmony.

Music as a whole is also an attunement as the composer tries to write down what he or she hears with the inner ear of the musical imagination. Like ideas that (as we say) *come to us,* music must come to us too if we are composing; it is no good chewing the end of our pencil and trying to make it up. This is not to say that composing comes easily. It may take half a life-time of preparation, it may like Wagner enjoin setting down your pen altogether for a while, as he had to halfway through *Siegfried* in the middle of a bar (at the point where Siegfried rests himself beneath the linden tree), lost for music as he said in a letter to Liszt, in 1857, and it would not be for another twelve years, in 1869, that Wagner would pick up from where he had left off and carry on to finish the work. The genius of the music is in a simple sense linked back to that of the composer. But the genius of the composer is not a reference to part of their personality. Genius is something realized by the composer at the *expense* of their personality, at the cost of their social life, and indeed their whole life.

Plato recognized this. The genius of Socrates was his daemon, his angel in Christian mythology, a "divine something" in secular idiom. The daemon would not tell Socrates what to do, but would speak inwardly to him to say No.[5] Plato has the wise woman Diotima, an authoritative voice, tell Socrates (and us) in the *Symposium* that Eros is not a god, as we might believe, but a daemon.[6] The daemon is neither of heaven (metaphysical or transcendent) or of earth (empirical or immanent), Diotima says, and posterity regards this as Plato's teaching. A daemon belongs to the *metaxy* (in-between realm) a figure of imagination that is not imaginary, but *imaginal*, that is to say, indicative of the autochthonous imagination that modern culture no longer believes in, as the imaginary is for us synonymous with the unreal and non-existent. But the notion of having a daemon suggests the imagination has its own kind of reality "in between" empirical and ideal. Kant in this same vein has it that the imagination is *productive* of our reality: the structure of the universe is as much imaginative as it is logical, except that it tends to be pre-modern peoples who are "able to comprehend different planes of reality without confusing them."[7] In Kant, genius is daemon-like, standing alongside the artist's biographical sense of themselves like the synthetic unity of apperception that constitutes the reality of the self in his philosophy. In Kant the essence of self is not-self. Genius, therefore, is not something that belongs to the artist; rather the artist belongs to his or her genius. This works in exactly the same way for our attunement: attunement is not something that we have but something that *has us*. Artistic genius for the composer or artist is something they have to attune to and they do this by seeking their destiny in the world as best they can. Dry periods and writer's block are not merely being out-of-sorts, for they artist it means being out of attunement. And the listener who cannot hear what is great in a piece of great music is also not attuned.

That against which one attunes the soul and spirit is also a given. There are moral keynotes that we must hear. This is why Kant called them universal and categorical imperatives. They are given and discovered; and needless to say these discoveries may be adapted and refined; they are not given in stone; although it may be that in some cultures the core moral attunements *are* given in stone (thinking of the Ten Commandments).

Certainly music is a matter of taste, but *taste is a matter of culture.* Culture is the attunement of a community or society. All these things hang together: culture, soul, genius, music and it is all wrapped up with the faculty of productive imagination, coming "in-between" and shaping our reason, understanding and judgment in all sorts of ways.

Imaginative people may invent and design machines but no machine has any imagination. Not only are machines absolutely soulless but many machines in our culture—television and computer games for example—purvey predigested imagination and suck soul out of us. Spaces filled with "muzac" (machine music) do the same. This is the culture of the simulacrum and simulation celebrated by Jean Baudrillard, who writes, "the era of simulacra and of simulation, in which there is no longer a God to recognize his own, no longer a Last Judgment to separate the false from the true, the real from its artificial resurrection, as everything is already dead and resurrected in advance."[8] As Baudrillard bears witness in his Nietzschean attempt to revaluate all values, reality disappears in a soulless world. Imagination is crucial to reality. Yet in the machine world of virtual realities there is *no imagination* to bring reality about. Samuel Beckett had it right: imagination dead imagine.[9] Baudrillard's clever madness is complicit with the world of simulacra and simulation he describes; the only music left is noise.

Ubiquity and Attunement to the *Real*

The subject of ubiquity arises from the discussion above about technology and the role of the machine in art. In his essay entitled "The Conquest of Ubiquity" (1928), Paul Valéry writes:

> Our fine arts were developed, their types and uses were established, in times very different from the present, by men whose power of action upon things was insignificant in comparison with ours. But the amazing growth of our techniques and adaptability and precision they have attained, the ideas and habits they are creating, make it a certainty that profound changes are impending in the ancient craft of the Beautiful. In all the arts there is a physical component that can no longer be considered or treated as it used to be, which cannot remain unaffected by our modern knowledge and power. For the last twenty years neither matter nor space nor time has been what it was from time immemorial. We must expect great innovations to

transform the entire technique of the arts, thereby affecting artistic invention itself and perhaps even bringing about an amazing change in our very notion of art.[10]

Walter Benjamin quotes this as the epigraph to his famous essay, "The Work of Art in the Age of Mechanical Reproduction," in *Illuminations* (1955). Benjamin discusses art in this essay in purely functional terms—that is to say as the artwork functions in terms of society, mass society in this case—but he does not wonder if it is still "art" or a simulacrum. It is obviously not art in the old-fashioned sense that we might speak of classical music; but is it art according to Baudelaire's aesthetic? Benjamin points out that *the mechanical process comes between the art and the audience.* Valéry goes on in the essay quoted by Benjamin to say that in future we can expect "works of art will acquire a kind of ubiquity." This has now happened.

Technology interferes with art music when recordings are engineered in the studio. What we hear then is not the recording of a performance but something which has been tampered with, perhaps with listeners' best interests at heart, but the reality is that one person, an engineer, or producer, who is not an artist or performer, comes between the music and the listener. This does not just make a big difference: it is a falsifying factor that loses the art. A feel-good factor thanks to the engineer and record producer is merely commercial and has nothing to do with art. A performance of the music that communicates soul to soul happens through art, but it cannot be produced by such a recording: so-called production values negate soul to soul communication. It is on this basis that manufactured music is not art, despite its honest pretensions in this direction. To find proper recordings of art music we need to do our homework as to the reputable recording companies. Even great recording companies under bad management governed by technical and commercial considerations before those of art go through phases when all the music they release is heavily engineered.

We can expect great transformations and innovations in the technique of the arts as Valéry foresaw. Wagner already foresaw it. But art and artists have to be in the pilot seat, not the technicians or sales personnel. If our notion of art is to change as Valéry thinks it could, it can only be on the basis of aesthetic experience and this is soul to soul, not a vicarious experience or, as is being pushed today, virtual experience. Virtual experience is actually a lack of experience and, as far as art and love go, it is not experience at all but the simulacrum covered with glamour and publicity, like so much else in our world.

Valéry goes on in his essay to assert that change in our time is so great that it is undermining the ego's self-certainty and "the pretensions of the self."[11]

> We used to be under the impression that our deepest substance must be some absolute activity, and that in each one of us must reside some strange power to *begin*, a certain quantum of pure independence. But we are living in a prodigious era, an era in which the most widely accredited and seemingly self-evident ideas have been attacked, contradicted, undermined, and put to route by *facts*, so much so that we are witnessing today a kind of bankruptcy of the imagination and corruption of the intellect, for we are no longer capable of forming a self-consistent notion of the world, encompassing all the data, both old and new, of human experience.[12]

Yes, we are learning that the world is not about me but about all of us together. Soul and soulfulness, which I have spoken of throughout this book pertain to the soul and soulfulness of the world, not just to *me*. This is what so many New Age art projects are showing up, raising consciousness about, waking people up to inner space, the dimension of height.

> *One* space spreads through all creatures equally— inner-world-space (*Weltinnenraum*). Birds quietly flying go flying through us.[13]

Such projects—for example, Kenneth White's geopoetics, and Bernard Stiegler and friends' *Ars Industrialis Manifesto*—are so numerous, we could fill a book just listing examples. An example from the world of art music is Duncan Bridgeman and Jamie Catto's "1 Giant Leap" project, *What About Me?* It jumps the false divide between sacred and secular, religion and non-religion, them and us, as music tends to. Their project also shows how technology can be used to serve art (and humanity), rather than the other way around.

Eight Programmatic Conclusions

My conclusions follow out of the central claims of this book, which are in sum as follows. Art generally, and art music in particular, is bound to what I have called, for convenience, Baudelaire's aesthetic; that is to say that great art or real art constellates a correspondence between its time and timelessness, and occasions aesthetic experience of both. This correspondence constellates a dimension of height within aesthetic experience. Height is measured and known in sensibility, not cognition. Sensibility is partly cognitive and partly imaginative, but it is chiefly soulful. Soul is the unison of inner sensibilities and sensitivity, and soulfulness is the receptivity that captures this unity, horizon, or harmonic. The soul has basic attunements—such as melancholy, delight, beauty, sadness, mourning—that music (and real art generally) calibrates and these ground-moods can get way out of calibration with bad music and art. Our time, I have attempted to show, is one of transition, like the transition around 2000 years ago from the age of *mythos* to the age of *logos*, associated with the advent of Christianity. Judaism, the antimythological religion, paved the way for Christianity over the previous period, which was otherwise dominated by myth everywhere. *Mythos* (story) and *logos* (reason, rationality, traditional metaphysics) always shadow one another and are permanently bound up in Christianity and culture, its theology being comprised of a congruence of each (that is, of story and of concept or idea). The Patristic age or the Talmudic age (on the Jewish side, contemporary with the Patristic) was the age of the emergence of *logos* from *mythos*, or, as philosophers say, of ontotheology— in Judaism, the logic of rabbinics. The central claim of this book is that we are moving from an age of *logos* (faith in reason) to an age of *melos* (beyond reason, in which music will speak louder than words), which is correspondingly an age of world religions governed by interests of harmony, rather than communion. The age of world religions began in the nineteenth century, when, symbolically, Tolstoy (who was already postdenominational) was alive and the first Parliament of World Religions was held in Chicago in 1893. Harmony is a higher kind of *communio* and *concilium* and this is something the West will learn (because the West is already beginning to learn it) from the East (India and the Far East). Just as *mythos* is taken up in *logos*, so both *mythos* and *logos* are taken up in *melos*, and Wagner is the first to attempt this modal *transposition*. Thus these "three ages" are not temporal but concern sensibility, soul, and soulfulness. World music is the sound of *melos* in our world today and today's world music is the true transmission of, and inheritance from, the art music from old Europe and its development as absolute music.

1. Taste is not individual but cultural. Culture shows our collective attunement. To become aware of the attunement is a matter of being highly

reflective, which is a task for philosophy—philosophy in Schopenhauer's sapiential sense, that is, not theory, not hermeneutics. Proper philosophy is about a wisdom tradition. Taste as a matter of culture involves the whole of us. We do not have an aesthetic experience with a part of our selves; it is a whole experience. In other words, it is an immersion experience, it is baptismal, it is a soul experience, it involves not just the whole of ourselves but goes deep into us, into a depth we hardly know and, most of all, *it deepens us.* One soul at a time, culture is attuned, not as a project, but in freedom as people are each drawn to the good of their own souls.

2. Science establishes a world of facts and we would be lost in superstition and religious gobbledygook without it. But as Kant first showed, and Schopenhauer followed, reason has its limits and we can get just as lost in scientific gobbledygook as in religious superstition. It is not error that is the problem of reason, but illusion. Art is keyed to the world of reason but not to the illusions of reason.

3. Listening is not about intellectuality but sensuality. Listening is perception. It is direct and immediate. You do not learn to do it: you just do it. You gain experience of it and grow and mature in experience. Listening does not come out of a book: it is something in us that the music taps into and opens up, it opens us up, it unlocks the world, but it starts with listening as act and actualization in real presence. Sensibility then, to make it quite clear, is not an idea of the intellect, but the quintessence of the senses. Sensibility is not a theory but a practice.

4. Art is not divorced from life. That means it is tied up with *how to live,* and how we *should* live, and therefore with philosophy and religion (in their wisdom aspects). Great art, like great philosophy, and religion, calibrates sensibility. "Love your neighbor as yourself" gives us something against which to calibrate and attune sensibility. Art is like ethics and religion in this sense. Art cannot tell us what to do but it can reveal who we are. If I know who I am, I will know what I can do and what I may hope for.

5. Perfection is what all artists work toward. Perfection does not mean being faultless in some sense, because by what criteria could we measure it? Something is perfect if it is what it is supposed to be. Beauty pertains to perfection. We carry a prior sense of it, we know what a father or a mother is supposed to be; these are not just roles but archetypes. We know what love and justice are supposed to be. We carry the measure of them in ourselves. We can lose it or have it distorted and this is the worst thing in the world and how it goes with us. The sense of perfection, of what something is supposed to be, protects us. It gives us back what we have lost, it seeks us out and brings us back to reality. The composer knows perfection when he or she hears their work and knows it is finished.

6. If Wagner is right about the collaborative nature of the artwork of the future then it will be based on each person's unique contribution. It will be based around our difference, not our sameness. Each of us lives on a different footing, and finding who we are means finding that footing. There are hidden laws of the universe; one of them is that of prayer, which contains the law of attraction. The Bible has God say, "to those who are

wise of heart I have given wisdom."[14] You get wisdom if you desire it strongly enough. The Talmud has one of the sages say that "the way a person wishes to go is the way he will be led."[15] The universe conspires with our desires. That is why desire is an electric property and dangerous in a rotten soul or culture. Somehow the artwork of the future will be keyed into prayer in the sense of the law of attraction *in a way that brings vision to the world.* Hope can be for the wrong things; hope needs to be accompanied by a real sense of the new age. Prayer in the sense of the law of attraction worked for Wagner; it is not supposition. Bayreuth is living proof.

7. Good music is something we enjoy, which is not to say it is just entertainment. Enjoyment as I have shown is hierarchical and, at the higher levels, it is more intensely enjoyable because it is more inwardly affecting, just like love. On the other hand, the enjoyment of the artist that has gone into a work is not a feeling of enjoyment, but their whole life; that for them is what enjoyment means. Beethoven may have agonized but the impossibility of *not* agonizing over his work would have been greater, and anyway he never even considered it.

8. One thing Wagner understood is the epochal nature of art and of the great artist. He returned to folk tales precisely because they belonged to an age, to the soul of the world, not to anyone in particular. To work out of such stories would have a unifying power, he believed—a redemptive power. The art of the future is about one world, which means peace and goodwill, "Christmas on Earth," as Rimbaud put it. It is this redemptive calling of art Adorno has in mind at the end of *Minima Moralia* (1951), where he writes: "knowledge has no light but that shed on the world by redemption."[16] Music shows itself in the same light.

I want to end by emphasizing a point too lightly touched upon earlier about the orchestra. The orchestra must not be abandoned. The orchestra remains the crucial organ (in the biological sense) of art music. Many people tend to think of the orchestra historico-culturally and therefore not properly. The orchestra needs to be thought of metaphysically, as Beethoven and Wagner thought of it and as I wish to remind us. Many people, thinking historically, culturally, or sociologically therefore imagine the orchestra as an ensemble of instruments and instrumentalists, a gathering of musicians and their instruments, who then play in concert and "make music." However, the music is already there, inaudible, and the musicians bring it into audibility; this is not just another way of saying the same thing, but captures the fact that the orchestra is perhaps the finest achievement of Western civilization because it (and it alone) has the capacity to capture such sound; machines cannot do it and never will, *because* they are machines. Machines *produce* music, even if it sounds the same to untutored ears, while instruments *capture* the music, through their instrumentalists first, and this difference makes all the difference in the world. Producing the right music is completely qualitatively different from capturing the music and every art music audience knows this without saying it or even having to think it; but no ignoramus knows it, by definition. The difficulty of capturing the music is such that even some orchestras cannot do it. As I mentioned earlier, the Vienna State Orchestra under Hans von Bülow gave up on *Tristan* after over seventy rehearsals between 1862 and 1864, and many said it was unperformable, except that Wagner knew better. It was performed under von Bülow in Munich in 1865 with the husband and wife team of Ludwig and Malvina Schnorr in the leading roles. Great orchestras with great conductors and the right musicians will capture the music. *An orchestra is a spiritual instrument.* The orchestra is only an ensemble of instruments and instrumentalists by default: that is not what it *is* in its being, which must be said in philosophical terms that perhaps only the initiated can understand: *only by means of the orchestra can the One come to presence through the All.* If music excavates the skies, then the symphony orchestra is our divining rod, our instrument of divination. Only an orchestra is fitted to presence *melos* and only an orchestra is really able to do so. This is the greatest achievement of Western culture—one we might easily lose nowadays due to our fixation on machinery, however new and glamorous it is. If this philosophical point speaks only to the initiated, we have to blame what we have done to our education system, for once, not long ago, everyone would have known what I just said and could have explained it. In only a short while this sensibility has been lost—this sensibility, this soulfulness, in which are joined together the spirit of music and the spirit of humanity.

Play List

The works are listed below in the sequence in which they are discussed in the book. Generally entries follow the sequence comprising: composer: work—performer(s).

Chapter 4: Shades of Melancholy
Dowland: *Lachrymosa*, "Dances of Dowland"—Julian Bream
Vivaldi: Concerto for lute and viola d'amore—Solisti di Veneti
Schubert: Piano Sonata in G major, D894—Vladimir Ashkenazy

Chapter 5: Gardens of Delight
Purcell: *The Fairy Queen*—English Chamber Orchestra and Ambrosian Singers conducted by Benjamin Britten
Debussy: *Fêtes* (Nocturnes for orchestra, no. 2)—London Symphony conducted by Leopold Stokowski
Liszt: *Les Jeux d'eau à la villa d'Este*—Stephen Hough
Ravel: *Daphnis and Chloe* (Suite no. 2 with chorus)—Vienna Philharmonic conducted by Lorin Maazel
Bach: "Goldberg" Variations: nos. 1 and 25—Angela Hewitt

Chapter 7: Beethoven and Absolute Music (Exaltation);
Chapter 8: Wagner and World Music (Rapture)
No particular recommendations. Hopefully my discussion will send you to various works of Beethoven and Wagner.

Chapter 9: The Work of Mourning
De Morales: *Missa pro defunctis*—Gabrieli Consort and Paul McCreesh
Messiaen: *Quartet for the End of Time*: fifth movement: *Louange a l'Eternité de Jesus*—Daniel Barenboim, Luben Yordanoff, Albert Tétard, and Claude Desurmont
Shostakovich: String Quartet no. 13, in B flat minor—St. Petersburg String Quartet
Tchaikovsky: Sixth Symphony, in B minor ("Pathétique"): final movement—Philharmonia Orchestra conducted by Carlo Maria Giulini

Chapter 10: When Time Stands Still
Debussy: *Des pas sur la neige*—Walter Gieseking
Sibelius: *Tapiola*: finale
Sibelius: Fourth Symphony: introduction
Schubert: Eighth Symphony ("Unfinished"): second movement—
Berlin Philharmonic conducted by Herbert von Karajan
Beethoven: String Quartet no. 15, in A minor: third movement:
Heiliger Dankgesang—Alban Berg Quartet

Chapter 11: Beauty and Sadness
Schubert: String Quintet in C major: second movement—Borodin
Ensemble
Mozart: Rondo in A minor, K511—Claudio Arrau
Mozart: Piano Concerto no. 21, in F major: second movement—Geza
Anda (pianist and conductor)
Orlando de Lassus: *Lagrime di San Pietro*—Raphael Passaquet ensemble

Chapter 12: Blue in Green
Miles Davis: "Saeta," from *Sketches of Spain*
Ralph Towner and Paolo Fresu: "Blue in Green," from *Chiaroscuro*

Notes

Introduction

1. See her book, Julia Kristeva, *New Maladies of the Soul*, trans. Ross Guberman (New York: Columbia University Press, 1995).
2. Charles Villiers Stanford, "On the Study of Music," *Music and Letters* 7, no. 3 (1926): 234.

Chapter 1: Baudelaires Aesthetic

1. Not without good reason. See Y. Bonnefoy, *L'Alliance de la poésie et de la musique* (Paris: Galilée, 2007).
2. The actual phrase, "interarts theory," I have taken from George P. Landow. See his "Ruskin and Baudelaire's Romantic Interarts Theories," *University of Toronto Quarterly* 37 (1968): 295–308. The comparison with Ruskin is forced and the idea that either of them is "Romantic" is incorrect in my view.
3. Kant, *The Critique of Judgment*, trans. J. H. Bernard (New York, NY: Prometheus, 2000), 64–5.
4. See Elisabeth Prettjohn, *Beauty and Art* (Oxford: Oxford University Press, 2005), 49–50.
5. Theodor Adorno, *Aesthetic Theory*, trans. Robert Hullot-Kentor (Minneapolis, MN: University of Minnesota Press, 1997), 114.
6. Baudelaire, *Journaux intimes* (Paris: Livres Généraux, 2010), Section X. [Translation by the author unless otherwise stated.]
7. *"Comme tu me plairais, ô nuit! Sans ces étoiles/Dont la lumière parle un langage connu!"*
8. On Baudelaire and the Renaissance, see Charles Taylor, *Sources of the Self* (Cambridge, MA: Harvard University Press), 427. On Baudelaire and Swedenborg, see Baudelaire, "The Poem of Hashish," in *My Heart Laid Bare and Other Prose Writings*, trans. Norman Cameron (London: Soho, 1986), 110.
9. Walter Benjamin, *The Arcades Project*, trans. Howard Eiland and Kevin McLaughlin (Cambridge, MA: Harvard University Press, 1999), 240.
10. Although I do not think I'd go as far as Walter Benjamin, who makes this same point and goes on to say: "His most important subjects are hardly ever encountered in descriptive form." *Charles Baudelaire: A Lyric Poet in the Era of High Capitalism*, trans. Harry Zohn (London: Verso, 1992), 121.
11. Baudelaire, *La Goût du néant* ("The Taste for Nothingness").

12. Thomas Isham, *A Christian Spiritual Psychology* (St Paul, MN: New Grail, 2006), 22.

13. Charles Baudelaire, *The Flowers of Evil* (Spleen IV, stanza 1), trans. James McGowan (Oxford: Oxford University Press, 1998), 149–50.

14. Baudelaire, by the way, was the French translator of Poe, who was a spiritual compatriot of sorts, and through Baudelaire Poe became better known and more popular in Europe than he was in America, where he was from.

15. Baudelaire, *Les Fleur du Mal* (Paris: Le livre de poche, 1972), 231.

16. Ibid., 233.

17. Baudelaire, *The Flowers of Evil*, trans. James McGowan (Oxford: Oxford World's Classics, 1998), 15.

18. Cf. Kenneth White, *Le Plateau de L'albatros: Introduction à la géopoetique* (Paris: Grasset, 1994).

19. *Romans* 1:20.

20. Wallace Fowlie, ed., "What Is Romanticism?" in *Charles Baudelaire: Flowers of Evil and Other Works* (New York, NY: Dover, 1992), 159.

21. Ibid.

22. Baudelaire, *L'Art romantique: Ouvres complètes* (Paris: Louis Conard, 1925), 52.

23. Walter Benjamin also falls into this error foreseen by Baudelaire. Benjamin quotes him as saying, in regard to Wagner (whom Baudelaire esteemed): "If in the choice of his subjects and his dramatic method Wagner approaches classical antiquity, his passionate power of expression makes him the most important representative of modernity at the present time." And Benjamin adds: "This sentence contains Baudelaire's theory of modern art in a nut-shell."[25] But Benjamin understands this in terms of an antiquarianism on Baudelaire's part. Benjamin can only imagine Baudelaire's sense of this correspondence, not as one of height but of historicity, and of trying to reconstitute that history in the way that Hölderlin, Hegel, Schelling, and later, Heidegger, imagined. But Baudelaire could see that Wagner was no more antiquarian than he was himself. They were trying to do something new, something with a future more than a past, and coming therefore from Baudelaire's sense of poetic mission and inspiration. Now naturally this dimension of height *resonates with* the past, because in the past the dimension of height was part of metaphysical thought, as in the Platonic tradition for example, but it is an error to imagine height reducible to historicity and therefore as a revivalism of antiquity; in short, Benjamin is historicist.

24. Paul Valéry, "Mallarmé," in *An Anthology*, Selected with an Introduction by James R. Lawler, (Bollingen Series XLV-A/Princeton NJ: Princeton University Press, 1977),169.

25. Adorno, *Aesthetic Theory*, 92. While using Adorno's concept here, I will not be following his argument exactly.

26. Ibid.

27. Of the Being of entities, Heidegger says "there lies *a priori* an enigma." Heidegger, *Being and Time* [1926], trans. J. Macquarrie and E. Robinson (New York, NY: Harper and Row, 1962), 23.

28. Paul Valéry, *Analects*, trans. Stuart Gilbert, with an introduction by W. H. Auden. *The Collected Works of Paul Valéry*, Vol. 14 (London: Routledge and Kegan Paul, 1970), 269.

29. For more on this point, see Italo Calvino, *Why Read the Classics?* (New York, NY: Vintage, 2001).

30. See Lou Andreas-Salomé, *Eros [Die Erotik*, 1910] (Paris: Éditions de minuit, 1984).

31. Valéry, *Analects*, 315. A footnote by Valéry adds: "In short the dimensions of a work should be determined by an analysis of the conditions needed for prolonging, heightening and reiterating the impression it conveys."

32. Valéry, *Analects*, 316. A footnote adds: "Music haunts the memory, cannot be defined or summarized."

33. Adorno, *Aesthetic Theory*, 161.

34. Baudelaire, *L'Art romantique*, 52.

35. Arthur Rimbaud, "Farewell," in *A Season in Hell*, trans. Louise Varèse (New York, NY: New Directions), 89.

36. Baudelaire, *L'Art romantique*, 66.

37. Ibid., 66–7.

38. While in *Aesthetic Theory* Adorno does not criticize the Baudelairean notion of the new, in *Minima Moralia*, composed during the war under the shadow of Nazism in Europe and first published in 1951, Adorno attacks Baudelaire and the concept of the new with the heavyweight intellectual muscle that simply floors all opposition—a style in which clearly Adorno is adept. Reading carefully, between the punches, Adorno criticizes a collective form of newness which he sees as a step on the path to dictatorship—whether by a political party or, today, by the commodity, both being possibilities—while in *Aesthetic Theory* he can tolerate the idea of newness where it lends itself to (and intends itself for) spiritualization. At least that is how I read it. It shows the weakness of Baudelaire's aesthetic (that it is so easily seconded), but that fact does not alter its truth. It simply means such an aesthetic, if it is to be grounded, needs able defenders: philosophers!

39. Baudelaire: "*car presque toute notre originalité vient de l'estampille que le temps imprime à nos sensations.*" *L'Art Romantique*, 69.

40. Ibid., 93.

41. Ibid., 103.

42. Put in Christian religious terms, Baudelaire is not afraid to consort with sinners, with the outcast woman, of whom the Samaritan woman who Jesus meets at the well is a prototype.

43. Adorno, *Aesthetic Theory*, 132.

Chapter 2: The Metaphysics of Nostalgia

1. Theodor W. Adorno, *Aesthetic Theory*, trans. Robert Hullot-Kentor (Minneapolis: University of Minnesota Press, 1997), 132.

2. www.maulpoix.net/US/indexa.html.

3. Buber, quoted by Maurice Friedman, in "Why Joseph Campbell's Psychologizing of Myth Precludes the Holocaust as Touchstone of Reality," *Journal of the American Academy of Religion* 66, no. 2 (1998): 394.

4. Quoted from Rabbi Itzchak Marmorstein, "Ha' Rav Kook: Master of Lights," *Tikkun* 25, no. 4 (July–August 2010): 27. For newcomers to the Rav, see Rabbi Hillel Rachmani, *Introduction to the Thought of Rav Kook* (public domain).

5. Wagner, "Beethoven," in *Actors and Singers* (Wagner's *Prose Works*, Vol. 5), trans. William Ashton Ellis (London: Kegan Paul, Trench, Trubner and Co., 1896), 61.
6. Christianity with *apostolic* roots that is not mere Christian*ism* (a mindset, a belief-based religion) such as psychologist James Hillman thought of Protestantism, for these are quite different things.
7. *Romans* 1:20.
8. Augustine, *Confessions*, Book 10. Chapter 26. Section 38 (various editions/public domain).
9. Jacques Lacan, *The Four Fundamental Concepts of Psychoanalysis. The Seminar of Jacques Lacan*, Vol. 11, ed. Jacques Alain-Miller, trans. Alan Sheridan (New York, NY: Norton, 1998), 127.
10. Ibid., 153.
11. Vladimir Jankélévitch, *L'irréversible et la nostalgie* (Paris: Flammarion, 1974), 360–1.
12. Ibid., 362.
13. *1 Peter* 1:4.
14. *English Hymnal* (London: Oxford University Press, 1906, 1933), No. 638.
15. We can learn more about the culture and literature of this nostalgia within Christendom in the writings of Helen Waddell: *The Wandering Scholars* (1927), *Latin Lyrics* (1929), and *The Desert Fathers* (1936), all in print today.
16. Yves Bonnefoy, *The Act and Place of Poetry*, ed. John T. Naughton (Chicago, IL: University of Chicago Press, 1989), 44. This aligns Baudelaire with a bardic tradition—as unlikely as that may seem—when we recall Baudelaire's dandyism and bohemianism. On the other hand, Bonnefoy is the most authoritative living reader of Baudelaire and we should not dismiss his comments lightly, but try to ascertain what he means, which, it seems, starts outside our preconceived ideas. After all, Ted Hughes, one of the greatest twentieth-century English poets, was in the bardic tradition, but if we look at his personal life, we may be disinclined to recognize the fact; so, therefore, with Baudelaire. Bonnefoy is assuming in his readers that they are not blinded to begin with by words such as "dandyism," "bohemian," "bardic", and neither should we be.
17. Ibid.
18. Ibid., 49.
19. Ibid.
20. Arthur Schopenhauer, *The World as Will and Representation* (2 Vols.), trans. E. F. J. Payne (New York, NY: Dover, 1969), Vol. 1, §.54, p. 275.
21. Ibid.
22. Valéry, *Analects*, trans. Stuart Gilbert, with an introduction by W. H. Auden. *The Collected Works of Paul Valéry*, Vol. 14 (London: Routledge and Kegan Paul, 1970), 288.
23. Nietzsche, *The Birth of Tragedy* (various editions/public domain), XVII.
24. Schopenhauer, *The World as Will and Representation*, Vol. I, §. 54, p. 275.
25. Nietzsche, "On Free Death," in *Thus Spoke Zarathustra*, trans. Walter Kaufmann (New York: Penguin, 1978), 72,
26. Ibid.

27. Ibid., 71.
28. Nietzsche, "Aphorism 125: The Madman," in *The Gay Science* (various editions/public domain).
29. Rainer Maria Rilke, "The Book of Poverty and Death," in *The Book of Hours*, trans. Stevie Krayer (Salzburg: Institut für Anglistik un Amerkanistik Universitat, 1995), 91.
30. Ibid., 90.
31. Rainer Maria Rilke, *The Notebook of Malte Laurids Brigge*, trans. John Linton (London: Hogarth Press, 1959), 9–10, 15–16.
32. Bonnefoy, *The Act and Place of Poetry*, 47.
33. The whole oeuvre of Michael Eigen eases us in this *other* direction, but see especially, *Contact With the Depths* (London: Karnac, 2011), *passim*.
34. Adorno, *Aesthetic Theory*, trans. Robert Hullot-Kentor (Minneapolis, MN: University of Minnesota Press, 1997), 39.
35. Ernst Bloch, *The Principle of Hope*, Vol. 3, trans. Neville Plaice (Cambridge MA: MIT, 1996), 1057ff.
36. Ibid., 1063.
37. Ibid., 51.
38. Baudelaire, *Journaux intimes* (Paris: Livres Généraux, 2010), X. Quotation given in Chapter 1 above.
39. Adorno, *Aesthetic Theory*, 40.
40. Ibid., 39; my italics.
41. Adorno goes so far as to say that "Schubert, who was later so widely exploited by the insistently happy, already felt compelled to ask if there were such a thing as happy music." Ibid, 40.
42. Ibid.
43. *1 Corinthians* 13:12.
44. Plotinus, *Enneads*, IX.10.
45. "*Vacabimus et videbimus, videbimus et amabimus, amabimus et laudabimus. Ecce quod erit in fine sine fine.*" Augustine, *De Civitate Dei*, XXII.30.
46. I am thinking here of Søren Kierkegaard, *Stages on Life's Way*, [1845] trans. Howard V. Hong, Edna H. Hong (Princeton NJ: Princeton University Press, 1988.
47. See my introductory discussion of *Faust* in Del Nevo, *The Work of Enchantment* (Brunswick NJ.; London: Transaction, 2011), ch.13.
48. Art is integral to Christianity from the start, from St. Luke who after Pentecost painted the first portraits of Mary the mother of Jesus, and also of Jesus, presumably from memory; the images have come down in iconographic tradition in the Eastern Churches (Leonid Ouspensky, *The Theology of the Icon* [Crestwood, NY: St Vladimir's Seminary Press, 1992], 60).

Early statues of Peter, Paul, and Jesus stood at Caesarea Philippi, where the woman with a hemorrhage, whom Jesus healed, had lived (cf. Mark 5:25–34). "This statue," says Eusebius, the historian, "was still there in my own time, so that I saw it with my own eyes when I resided in the city." (Eusebius, *The History of the Church*, trans. G. A. Williamson [Harmondsworth, UK: Penguin, 1965], Book 7, Chap. 18, p. 302.) A note there states that the statue is mentioned by three other writers, two of whom had seen it. Given the brotherliness of the new cult to Judaism, which was icono-clastic, and the prominence of Jews in the church still at that date, there is no reason for Eusebius to exaggerate in any case.

Luke's version of the Beatitude of Jesus is: "Blessed are those who mourn"—that is, artists—"for they shall laugh." That is, I take it, they shall have *the last laugh*. For the artwork will sublimate the mourning, and give something to rejoice over, that overcomes death.

Chapter 3: The Ladder of *Eros*

1. Paul Valéry, *Aesthetics*, trans. Ralph Manheim, ed. Jackson Matthews. *The Collected Works*, Vol. 13 (London: Routledge and Kegan Paul, 1964), 120.
2. Plato, *The Republic*, 617e.
3. Ibid., 618b.
4. William Wordsworth, Ode, Intimations of Immortality, *Wordsworth: Plain Texts of the Poets* (St. Lucia: University of Queensland, 1968), 84.
5. It may be conventional, but it is not neutral, if analysed one would find the whole notion of development goes back to Hegel's philosophy and Hege-lianism in a biological and psychological manifestation; in other words, the notion of development along biological and psychological lines is ideologi-cally governed and surreptitiously bears Hegelian philosophy with it as the presupposed ground of truth.
6. For an illuminating account of this perspective, see James Hillman, *The Soul's Code* (New York, NY: Random House, 1996).
7. A problem which, to some extent, we will see later, music actually avoids.
8. This world is not really *other*, but is the *hidden* side of this world, such as Rilke describes in his final Diuno Elegy, from which all his poetry issues.
9. I have not quoted it but I would refer my reader in thinking about the point I have made here to John Ruskin's lecture on "The Division of Arts," comprising Lecture 1 in *Aratra Pentelici*, toward the end, where he quotes from the second part of Goethe's *Faust* to express "what the whole science of aesthetics is, in the depth of it." The quote from Goethe is

> —the notable one that follows the song of the Lemures, when the angels enter to dispute with the fiends for the soul of Faust. They enter singing— "Pardon to sinners and life to the dust." Mephistopheles hears them first, and exclaims to his troop, "Discord I hear, and filthy jingling"—"*Mis–töne höre ich: garstiges Geklimper*." This, you see, is the extreme of bad taste in music. Presently the angelic host begin strewing roses, which discomfits the diabolic crowd altogether. Mephistopheles in vain calls to them—"What do you duck and shrink for—is that proper hellish behavior? Stand fast, and let them strew"—"*Was duckt und zuckt ihr; ist das Hellen–brauch? So haltet stand, und last sie streuen*." There you have also, the extreme, of bad taste in sight and smell. And in the whole passage is a brief embodiment for you of the ultimate fact that all aesthetics depend on the health of soul and body, and the proper exercise of both, not only through years, but genera-tions. Only by harmony of both collateral and successive lives can the great doctrine of the Muses be received which enables men "[Greek: *chairein orthôs*],"—"to have pleasure rightly"; and there is no other definition of the beautiful, nor of any subject of delight to the aesthetic faculty, than that it

is what one noble spirit has created, seen and felt by another of similar or equal nobility. So much as there is in you of ox, or of swine, perceives no beauty, and creates none: what is human in you, in exact proportion to the perfectness of its humanity, can create it, and receive."

This text is published in various Ruskin collections and is to be found on the internet and in *The Works of John Ruskin* on CD-ROM published by Cambridge University Press for the Ruskin Foundation in 1996.

10. If my soul is capable, if it has the capacity—this is one of the points Ruskin makes in the aforementioned reference to his lecture, "The Division of Arts," in *Aratra Pentelici*. See the previous note.

11. Laurence Binyon, *Music and Letters* 1, no. 1 (January 1920): 6.

12. Originally Valéry had entitled this poem "Psyche," until he learned his friend Pierre Louÿs—a better known writer—was working on a novel with that title. Valéry consequently retitled his poem to avoid a clash. Louÿs however abandoned his work. The reference to the Goethe novel is to *Die Wahlverwandtschaften* (1809).

13. Jacques Lacan, *The Four Fundamental Concepts of Psychoanalysis: Seminar XI*, trans. Alan Sheriden (New York, NY: Norton, 1998), 53; my italics.

14. Ibid.

15. Ibid. *Automaton* is an Aristotelian term from *Physics* book 2. In Lacan the automaton may be understood as the coincidence or collision of desire and language (or the pleasure principle and signifying networks). Žižek puts the general matter here more precisely as follows:

"Materialism means that the reality I see is never "whole" - not because a large part of it eludes me, but because it contains a stain, a blind spot, which signals my inclusion in it.

Nowhere is this structure clearer than in the case of Lacan's *objet petit a*, the object-cause of desire. The same object can all of a sudden be "transubstantiated" into the object of my desire: what is to you just an ordinary object, is for me the focus of my libidinal investment, and this shift is caused by some unfathomable x, a *je ne sais quoi* in the object which cannot ever be pinned down to any of its particular properties. *Objet a* is therefore close to the Kantian transcendental object, since it stands for the unknown x, the noumenal core of the object beyond appearances, for what is "in you more than yourself." *L'objet petit a* can thus be defined as a pure parallax object: it is not only that its contours change with the shift of the subject; it only exists - its presence can only be discerned - when the landscape is viewed from a certain perspective. More precisely, the object a is the very CAUSE of the parallax gap, that unfathomable X which forever eludes the symbolic grasp and thus causes the multiplicity of symbolic perspectives." Slavoj Žižek, *The Parallax View* (Cambridge MA: MIT Press, 2009) 17–18.

16. *Dasein* in Heidegger's sense.

17. Sigmund Freud, "Timely Reflections on War and Death," in *On Murder, Mourning and Melancholia,* trans. Shaun Whiteside (London: Penguin, 2005), 167–200; C. G. Jung, "Stages of Life" and "The Soul and Death," in *The Structure and Dynamics of the Psyche,* trans. R. F. C. Hull. *The Collected Works of C. G. Jung* (London: Routledge and Kegan Paul, 1960), 387–416.

18. Fyodor Dostoevsky, *The Brothers Karamazov*, trans. Constance Garnett (New York, NY: New American Library, 1957), 264. The quotation from *The Brothers Karamazov* is taken from the teaching of the fictional monastic elder, the saintly Father Zossima.
19. Schopenhauer, *The World as Will and Representation* (2 Vols.), trans. E. F. J. Payne (New York, NY: Dover, 1969), Vol. 1, 275.
20. Rainer Maria Rilke, *The Book of Hours*, trans. Stevie Krayer (Salzburg: Salzburg Institut für Anglistik un Amerikanistik Universität, 1995), 23.

Chapter 4: Shades of Melancholy

1. On depression, the best book is by Dorothy Rowe, *Depression: The Way Out of Your Prison*, 3rd ed. (London: Routledge, 2003).
2. *Grundstimmung* in the philosophy of Heidegger. His whole account of this in his early work make his work worth reading.
3. Martin Heidegger, *Being and Time*, trans. John Macquarrie, Edward Robinson (San Francisco, CA: HarperCollins, 1962), 173.
4. Ibid.
5. Ibid.
6. The passage from a letter of Letter, April 1819 reads as follows:

   Call the world if you Please "The vale of Soul-making." Then you will find out the use of the world . . . I say '*Soul-making*' Soul as distinguished from an Intelligence—There may be intelligences or sparks of the divinity in millions—but they are not Souls till they acquire identities, till each one is personally itself. . . . Do you not see how necessary a World of Pains and troubles is to school an Intelligence and make it a Soul? . . . Seriously I think it probable that this System of Soul-making—may have been the Parent of all the more palpable and personal Schemes of Redemption, among the Zoroastrians the Christians and the Hindoos.

   H. B. Forman, ed. *The Letters of John Keats* (London: Reeves & Turner, 1895), 326.

7. Quoting a line of Milton, 'To slumber here, as in the vales of heaven' [*Par. Lost*, Book I, I. 321]. Keats adds, " There is a cool pleasure in the very sound of *vale*." (. . .) "How much of the charm is in the word *valley*!" Keats cited in Lord Houghton, *The Life and Letters of John Keats* (London: Edward Moxon, 1867), 236–7.
8. Peter Holman, *Lachrimae* (Cambridge UK: Cambridge University Press, 1999), 50–60.
9. A *pavan* is a slow, stately, courtly dance. The *galliard*, the other main dance of the time, was a lively kicking and hopping dance. The third kind of dance, the *almand* (or *allemande*), was of German origin and a kind of line dance.
10. Ibid., 38.
11. Ibid., 49.
12. Ibid., 52.
13. Ibid., 4.
14. Ibid., 52

15. These details are taken from Karl Heller, *Antonio Vivaldi: The Red Priest of Venice* (Hong Kong: Amadeus, 1997).
16. Brian Newbould, *Schubert: The Music and the Man* (Berkeley, CA: University of California Press, 1997), 253.
17. Black refers here to Rudolf Otto's reference in his famous work, *Das Heilige* (1917)—in English: *The Idea of the Holy* (1923). Leo Black, *Franz Schubert: Music and Belief* (Woodbridge, Suffolk: Boydell, 2005), 146–7.

As he lay dying, Schubert wished to hear Beethoven's String Quartet no. 14, Op. 131, from this same year, 1826, and he is supposed to have said, "After this, what is there left for us to write?" Adorno writes in the essay, 'Beethoven's Late Style'(1937):

> The force of subjectivity in late works of art is the eruptive gesture with which it exits them. It breaks free of them—not to express itself but, rather, to discard expressionlessly the semblance of art. All it leaves behind are the ruins of the works, and it communicates—as if in code—only through the hollows it erupts from. Touched by death, the master's hand releases the heaps of material it had previously shaped; the tears and cracks in it, testimonies to the ultimate helplessness of the ego in the face of the existent, are its final work.

Theodor Adorno, *Night Music: Essays on Music 1928–1962*, trans. Wieland Hoban, ed. Rolf Teidmann (London: Seagull, 2009), 16.

18. Roger Scruton, *Understanding Music: Philosophy and Interpretation* (London: Continuum, 2009), 48.
19. Ibid.
20. Ibid. Chap. 5, esp. p. 50.
21. Ibid., 50.
22. Ibid., 49.
23. Ibid., 50.
24. Ibid., 50.
25. Theodor Adorno, *Night Music: Essays on Music 1928–1962*, trans. Wieland Hoban, ed. Rolf Teidmann (London: Seagull, 2009), 23.
26. Ibid.
27. Ibid.
28. I call something Hegelian in this book where the assumption is that thinking is all-encompassing (therefore reason, and ideas; where even *Geist*, spirit, is idea; where even the Absolute is idea, and so on). These ideas are not representative of anything else. The ideas represent themselves—hence "idealism"—and the self-referential system of thinking they relate to. This has been the dominating factor in Western philosophy, more so than the influence of Hegel. Marx tried to set Hegel to rights, but it was only ideas-led action, ideas-led change that Marxism espoused and in that regard Marx was as much under the sway of Hegel as a speculative idealist. Hegelianism is like a modern secular reiteration of medieval theology because of its totalising and self-referential, solipsistic quality. Kant had thought to break through this tendency, but Hegel in the very next generation reinstated it.
29. Ibid., 23–24.

30. Daniel Barenboim, *Everything Is Connected: The Power of Music* (London: Weidenfeld and Nicolson, 2008), 11.
31. Ibid., 12.
32. Scruton, *Understanding Music*, 51.

Chapter 5: Gardens of Delight

1. John Keats, On Melancholy, *The Poetical Works of John Keats* (Oxford: Oxford World's Classics, 1987), 207.
2. Jonathan Keates, *Purcell: A Biography* (London: Chatto and Windus, 1996), 234. Cf. Martin Adams, *Purcell: The Origins and Development of His Musical Style* (Cambridge: Cambridge University Press, 1995), 316.
3. Jonathan Keates, *Purcell: A Biography*, 234.
4. Donald Brook, *Five Great French Composers: Berlioz, César Franck, Saint-Saëns, Debussy, Ravel: Their Lives and Works* (London, Rockliff [1946] 1947; London: Books for Libraries Press, [1971]1977), 168.
5. Charles Hoffer, *Music Listening Today* (New York: Schirmer, 2008), 214.
6. Dedicated to his teacher, Gustav Fauré, and first performed in 1902.
7. Ravel (1875–1937) was born in the little town of Ciboure, in France, near Biarritz, on the Atlantic coast, right down near the border with Spain, at the foot of the Pyrénées. His mother was a Basque and his father a Swiss industrialist. Ravel grew up in Paris.
8. Ibid., 213.
9. Ibid., 213.
10. Scott Goddard, "Some Notes on Maurice Ravel's Ballet *Daphnis and Chloe*," *Music and Letters* 7, no. 3 (July 1926), 219.
11. Ibid., 219–20.
12. Lawrence Kramer, *Classical Music and Postmodern Knowledge* (Berkeley, CA: University of California, 1996), 201.
13. Ibid.
14. Ibid., 202.

Chapter 6: Listening across Time

1. Jürgen Lawrenz, *Art and the Platonic Matrix* (Newcastle upon Tyne: Cambridge Scholars Publishing, 2011), 102.
2. Ibid.
3. On Platonism in art, see Jürgen Lawrenz, *Art and the Platonic Matrix* (Newcastle, UK: Cambridge Scholars Publishing, 2011).
4. Plato, *The Republic*, 424b-c, in *The Collected Dialogues of Plato Including the Letters*, ed. Edith Hamilton and Huntington Cairns (New York, NY: Pantheon Books, 1961).
5. Plato, *The Republic*, 398d-399c.
6. Ibid., 242b.
7. Schopenhauer, "On the Indestructibility of Our Nature by Death," in *Selected Essays*, edited with an introduction by Ernest Belfort Bax (London: Bell and Sons, 1926), 244.
8. Schopenhauer, *The World as Will and Representation* (2 Vols.), trans. E. F. J. Payne (New York, NY: Dover, 1969), Vol. II, 164.
9. Ibid.

10. Schopenhauer, *The World as Will and Representation* (2 Vols.), trans. E. F. J. Payne (New York, NY: Dover, 1969), Vol. 1, 257.

11. Ibid., Section 52, pp. 262–3. This is an important point too readily overlooked by his commentators.

12. Ibid., 264.

13. Ibid.

14. Ibid., 263.

15. Ibid.

16. Ibid.

17. Michael Eigen, *Contacting the Depths* (London: Karnac, 2011), Chapter 3 entitled "I Don't Know" gives an account of what I am referring to here.

18. The name Hegel is almost a watchword for a muddled philosophy (and discursive twaddle, which goes with it) and inner disorientation (which goes along with misleading others). Except that Hegel's sense (taken from Judaism and Christianity) is right that there is a "Providence" with which human thought it bound up (of which the Christian notion is a pale deflection only).

19. On this subject, see Jacob Neusner, *Judaism's Theological Voice: The Melody of Talmud* (Chicago, IL: University of Chicago Press, 1995). See page 10 for the description of the Talmudic melody. On the point of *melos* in Judaism, which one would ordinarily think of as fundamentally textual religion, Rabbi Itzchak Marmorstein has found it natural to set Rav Kook's poetry to jazz.

20. *Luke* 2:14.

21. It has been a hallmark of the twentieth century to put the old wine in new skins, e.g. Rosenzweig's speech thinking (*Sprachdenken*), Buber's dialogical philosophy, and Levinas's ethics of infinity and the Other.

22. Schopenhauer, *The World as Will and Representation*, Vol. II, 162.

23. *The Wisdom of Lao Tse*, ed. Lin Yutang (New York, NY: Random House, The Modern Library, 1948), Section 18, p. 119.

24. Schopenhauer, *Selected Essays*, xv; emphasis added.

25. Wagner, Letter to August Röckel, January 25, 1854, in *Wagner on Music and Drama*, ed. A. Goldman and E. Sprinchorn (New York, NY: Da Capo Press, 1988), 290.

26. Jürgen Lawrenz, "Music and the Copernican Aesthetic Revolution of the 18th Century" (unpublished manuscript, courtesy of the author).

27. Quoted in Kurt Honolka, *Der Musik gehorsame Tochter* (Stuttgart: Cotta, 1962), 7.

28. Carl Dahlhaus, *The Idea of Absolute Music* (Chicago, IL: Chicago University Press, 1989), 8.

29. Paul Henry Lang, *Music in Western Civilization* (London: Dent, 1942), 11–12, 18–19.

30. Kant, *Anthropology from a Pragmatic Point of View*, trans. M. J. Gregory (The Hague: Martinus Nijhoff, 1974), 114.

31. I note, by the way, that Kant lifted this straight from Rousseau's pages.

32. Hegel, *Aesthetics*, trans. T. M. Knox (Oxford: Clarendon Press, 1975), 960.

33. This is all the more strange in that Kant *should* have been familiar with the music of Haydn and Mozart (but seems not to have been) and that Hegel in addition should have been fully cognizant of Beethoven, Hummel, Spohr, Clementi, and Boccherini (among others), who were all prominent in the

public eye. When translator Knox, however, permits himself the surmise that Hegel might have been thinking of Schubert in his discussion of instrumental music, he shows himself to be ignorant of music history, nor has this *faux pas* been picked up by writers who ought to know better (e.g. Peter Kivy, *Philosophies of Arts: An Essay in Differences* [Cambridge UK: Cambridge University Press, 1997], 21–2).

34.   "In the beginning was the word (*logos*) and the word (*logos*) was with God and the word (*logos*) was God." (John 1: 1). The prologue to John's gospel then goes on to say the word (*logos*) took flesh and became man (Jesus). In this way the Church (after the Nicean Council of 325) would define "true God" and "true man" according to the rational proscription of metaphysics. If however, one starts not with John 8: 1–11, with Jesus as the sand artist who sides with the disgraced woman rather than the religious authorities another kind of metaphysics comes into view.

35.   Charles Rosen, *The Classical Style* (New York, NY: Norton, 1997), 120.

36.   Lawrenz, "Music and the Copernican Aesthetic Revolution of the 18th Century", manuscript; cf. Rosen, *The Classical Style*, 194–5.

37.   Lawrenz, "Music and the Copernican Aesthetic Revolution of the 18th Century", manuscript.

38.   The seven sensibilities: that of ascetic or wilful as in Nietzsche; that of wisdom as in Schopenhauer; the intellectual and dynamic as in Hegel; the harmonious and sensual as in Wagner; the intellectual and technical as Kant or Husserl; the devotional as in Schleiermacher; the lyric and epic with Goethe.

39.   *John* 14:27.

40.   Obviously it is not *caritas* either; this is a bad translation of *agape*.

Chapter 7: Beethoven and Absolute Music

1.   Meister Eckhart, *Works*, Pfeiffer edition, trans. C de B. Evans (London: Watkins, 1924), 290.

2.   Ibid., 289.

3.   I imagine the greed body as a circle of colored desire, partly visible in people's body language and activity, which one could draw like a bubble around them. Some people's greed bodies would warrant drawing gigantic circles the size of a suburb. Our cities are crowded, but if we measure the crowding by the greed bodies rubbing stomachs with each other, we would be crushed in together with scarcely any room to move or breathe.

4.   I do not mean to say Beethoven's nine symphonies would comprise the *only* curriculum. One could take his piano sonatas as a curriculum, or even a set of symphonies by another composer, such as Tchaikovsky. But in my judgment, even if this is not the music of one's own sensibility, it is still the best "curriculum" I can think of. One absolutely crucial feature of any curriculum is that it should stand *outside* a person's personal taste and natural choice to begin with. And a curriculum at an entry level needs to cover both what is broad and what is central to the subject, here *melos*.

5.   Although this is a quotation taken out of context from one of his letters, it is not taken out of context unfairly, given the overall understanding of Beethoven and his music that is widely and historically held, as some recent

critics have tried to argue in their attack on any kind of value judgments in music.

6. Quoted in Marion M. Scott, *Beethoven* (London: Dent, 1947), 176.
7. Roman Rolland, *Beethoven the Creator*, trans. Ernest Newman (New York, NY: Garden City, 1917), 70.
8. Beethoven wrote: "My heart beats in entire concord with the lofty and grand art of Sebastian Bach, that patriarch of harmony (*dieses Urvaters der Harmonie.*)" to Hofmeister, 1801, cited by Roman Rolland, *Beethoven*, trans. B. Constance Hull (London: Kegan Paul, Trench, Trubner and Co., 1919), 105.
9. The issue that this is a discord is of only technical interest. The point is that the discord needs to be resolved. So what are we hearing? A question, establishing a mood of anticipation, expectancy.
10. Berlioz, *Beethoven's Nine Symphonies*, trans. Edwin Evans (London: William Reeves, 1958), 31.
11. Scott, *Beethoven*, 49.
12. Ibid., 51.
13. Berlioz, *Beethoven's Nine Symphonies*, 35.
14. Emil Ludwig, *Beethoven*, trans. G. S. McManus (New York: Putnam's and Sons, 1943), 61.
15. Ibid.
16. Ibid.
17. Berlioz, *Beethoven's Nine Symphonies*, 36.
18. Wagner, "A Happy Evening" [1841], in *In Paris and Dresden* (Wagner's *Prose Works*, Vol. 7), trans. William Ashton Ellis (London: Kegan Paul, Trench, Trubner and Co., 1898), 80. "R." was what Wagner's wife Cosima called him in her diary. We know Wagner was a great night dreamer, quite concrete ideas came to him in dreams, and he could conduct quite real conversations in the dream state.
19. Ibid., 77.
20. Ibid., 77.
21. Ibid., 78.
22. That legacy has not been "cashed in," so to speak. It is awaiting a New Dawn, a new, post-secularist culture, led by a new generation of musicians. From this point of view, which is *hardly that of any of the current musicology*, for which we do not apologize in the least, the rest of the nineteenth century can be seen as a frightened relapse to more staid forms of expression (Mendelssohn, Brahms, Dvorak) or else as an untamed mania for exaggeration, forgivable in its first flower (Liszt, Tchaikovsky), which became increasingly monstrous as European Christian culture and German culture unconsciously prepared to implode (Mahler and most twentieth-century "serious" music). The only composer who understood fully what Beethoven had unleashed with this symphony was Wagner, and now, again, we have to listen. We have another chance. We have to get it this time.
23. Rolland, *Beethoven the Creator*, 71.
24. Ibid.
25. For instance, make this comparison: in the Barenboim recording of the performance of the First Symphony, if you listen to the fourth movement, between 2 mins 50 secs and 3 mins 5 secs you have a good, traditional

example of violins playing an upward flourish several times in a row, and each time the flutes punctuate it with a change of harmony in order to get movement into a new key. Now, in Barenboim, Symphony no. 3, the "Eroica," compare the first movement, starting at 11 mins 5 secs, there is the same "trick"; observe the thrust and horsepower being marshaled. That is inventiveness.

26. Hector Berlioz, *Beethoven's Nine Symphonies*, 41; my italics.
27. Rolland, *Beethoven the Creator*, 79.
28. Ibid; my italics.
29. Wagner, "A Happy Evening," 79–80; my italics.
30. Rolland, *Beethoven the Creator*, 81–83; omitting Rolland's musical notation.
31. Ibid.
32. Wagner, "A Happy Evening," 80.
33. Berlioz, *Beethoven's Nine Symphonies*, 45.
34. Wagner, "Beethoven," in *Actors and Singers* (Wagner's *Prose Works*, Vol. 5), trans. William Ashton Ellis (London: Kegan Paul, Trench, Trubner and Co., 1896), 102. Adorno says of the dimension of Wagnerian harmonics that "the dimension of color is, properly speaking, his own discovery." Theodor Adorno, *In Search of Wagner*, trans. R. Livingstone (London: Verso, 1985), 71 (and throughout Chap. 5).
35. On the subject of music and color there is a curious page in a book by W. J. Turner, *Beethoven: The Search for Reality* (London: Ernest Benn, 1937), 250, where he attributes colors to composers. Wagner has purple and gold attributed to him; Beethoven, no color; and Mozart, shining silver. According to Turner the list is corroborated by "a very intelligent and musical woman." I do not know who that might have been.
36. Berlioz, *Beethoven's Nine Symphonies*, 46.
37. On one occasion he praised—in print!—Mendelssohn's "Scottish" Symphony for its "Scottish" sounds. The quotations in his essay reveal that he was reading the "Italian" Symphony. It happens in the best families, but you can imagine the laughter in the fraternity.
38. Apart from two or three "feminine" movements, none of Beethoven's symphonies strike a dominantly "feminine" note.
39. Berlioz, *Beethoven's Nine Symphonies*, 55.
40. Ibid., 61.
41. Ibid., 62.
42. George Grove, *Beethoven and his Nine Symphonies* (London: Novello & Co., 1896), 137.
43. Schopenhauer, *The World as Will and Representation* (2 Vols.), trans. E. F. J. Payne (New York, NY: Dover, 1969), Vol. 1, 186.
44. Scott, *Beethoven*, 170.
45. Berlioz, *Beethoven's Nine Symphonies*, 118.
46. Rolland, *Beethoven the Creator*, 375.
47. Wagner, *Religion and Art* (Wagner's *Prose Works*, Vol. 6), trans. William Ashton Ellis (London: Kegan Paul, Trench, Trubner and Co., 1897), 224.
48. Ibid.
49. Berlioz, *Beethoven's Nine Symphonies*, 97.
50. Ibid., 95–6.

51.   Edward Carpenter, *Angel's Wings* (London: Swann Sonnenschein & Co., 1898), 187–197.
52.   Ibid., 187.
53.   Ibid., 187–190.
54.   Ibid., 191.
55.   Ibid., 192.
56.   Ibid., 192–3.
57.   Ibid., 197.
58.   Ibid., 197.
59.   Ibid., 197–8.
60.   Ibid., 198–199.
61.   Ibid., 195.
62.   Wagner, *Beethoven*, [1870] trans. William Ashton Ellis, *Prose Works*, Volume IX, 27.
63.   W. J. Turner, *Beethoven* (London: Ernest Benn: 1927), 327.

Chapter 8: Wagner and World Music

1.   Daniel Barenboim, *Everything Is Connected: The Power of Music* (Weidenfeld and Nicolson, 2008), 182.
2.   Michael Eigen, *Contact With the Depths* (London: Karnac, 2011), 119.
3.   Alain Badiou, *Five Lessons on Wagner* (London: Verso, 2010), 83.
4.   David P. Goldman, writes, "we have lost the capacity to hear it the way Baudelaire and Mahler did. And our inability to hear Wagner's music constitutes a lacuna in our understanding of the spiritual condition of the West." 'Why We Cannot Hear Wagner's Music,' *First Things* (December, 2010), http://www.firstthings.com/article/2010/11/why-we-cant-hear-wagnerrsquos-music
5.   This, incidentally, he was quite capable of performing himself. In the *Mastersingers*, he produced a fugued "stretta" which deliberately alludes to Bach, and in which four different melodies are heard simultaneously.
6.   See Chapter 11, where I discuss this sonata briefly.
7.   Cited by Matthew Rampley, in *Nietzsche, Aesthetics and Modernity* (Cambridge: Cambridge University Press, 2000), 120.
8.   Today we would not feel the Tristan chord as people (especially musicians) might have felt in the nineteenth century, because we do not *expect* resolution as they did—at least, not so readily; we still expect it one way or another, but we are more accustomed to *bear delay*. Now the eponymous Tristan chord is symbolic: of an era of transition, which it inaugurates. The end of the old era of expectation of resolution—of Hegelianism, with its certainty of the future and Absolute Spirit—is gone and what gradually takes its place is an era of irresolution, of delay, that can only be resolved on a human basis by love, and by the liberation through love of both of the sexes. First, the emancipation of women (a subject forever on Wagner's heart), but as Wagner realized, this was dependent upon the emancipation of men from themselves, so that they are able to release women, so that women can, as Goethe put it, eternally lead them on to greater feats of love and to love triumphant, the only resolution. This is the vision of a new age, which is

partly reliant on the Christian symbology, but not wholly subscribed to it as a faith or mythology (theology) any longer; the church is as much in need of redemption as the world as far as Wagner's art is concerned.

9. By the way, an interesting sidelight on this is that Verdi, of all people, imitated this exactly in his *La Traviata*, where it depicts the love torments of the heroine and her "love death." Contrary to many opinions of those who like Verdi and hate Wagner, Verdi was well aware of Wagner; and although his handling of the orchestra was primitive by comparison, Verdi was never above purloining a good musical idea when it suited him. Late in life, after he gained independence from the impositions of Italian and French theaters, he revised *Don Carlos* and *Simon Boccanegra*, and composed *Otello*; and in each of these the influence of Wagner's orchestra increases. His last work, *Falstaff*, employs Beethoven's orchestra and style. All this is very interesting, coming from an utterly tradition-bound opera composer; the moment he was "free" to do his own thing, he upset all the canons of "good" Italian opera.

10. Theodor Adorno, *In Search of Wagner*, trans. R. Livingstone (London: Verso, 1985), 72. However we should note that Adorno says this only in order to make nasty, personal criticisms against Wagner and taste in music. Retrospectively, these criticisms rather rebound on Adorno, the fan of Schoenberg and "agenda" art music.

11. Wagner, *Opera and Drama* (Wagner's *Prose Works*, Vol. 2), trans. William Ashton Ellis (London: Kegan Paul, Trench, Trubner and Co., 1900), 18.

12. Alain Badiou, *Five Lessons on Wagner*, trans. Susan Spitzer (London: Verso, 2010), 89.

13. He saw *Tannhäuser* performed in Paris in 1861; his essay was then subsequently published in 1869 in *L'Art Romantique: Ouvres Complètes* (Paris: Louis Conard, 1925), from which I have already quoted several times in Chapter 1.

14. Baudelaire, "Richard Wagner et *Tannhäuser* à Paris," in *L'Art romantique*, 207; my translation, Baudelaire's italics.

15. Ibid., 208.

16. Ibid., 206.

17. Ibid., 208.

18. Ibid., 208.

19. Ibid., 203.

20. Robert L. Jacobs, *Wagner* (London: Dent, 1947), 137.

21. Baudelaire, "Richard Wagner et *Tannhäuser* à Paris," 203.

22. Ibid., 208.

23. Ibid., 213–4.

24. Ibid., 214.

25. Ibid.

26. Ibid.

27. Ibid., 217.

28. Ibid., 230; my italics.

29. Ibid., 229.

30. Ibid., 222.

31. Ibid., 232.

32. Ibid., 222–3; my italics.

33. Wagner, *Religion and Art* (Wagner's *Prose Works*, Vol. 6), trans. William Ashton Ellis (London: Kegan Paul, Trench, Trubner and Co., 1897), 217.
34. Wagner, quoted by Ernest Newman, *Wagner Nights* [1949] (London: Picador, 1977), 137–8.
35. Wagner, "Beethoven," in *Actors and Singers* (Wagner's *Prose Works*, Vol. 5), trans. William Ashton Ellis (London: Kegan Paul, Trench, Trubner and Co., 1896), 68.
36. Ibid., 74.
37. Newman, *Wagner Nights*, 116.
38. Ibid., 115.
39. Wagner's comments on the folk and art in *The Art-Work of the Future* (1849) gain credence in this context. He writes: "The redemption of thought and science and their transmutation into artwork would be impossible could life itself be made dependent upon scientific speculation. Could conscious autocratic thought completely govern life, could it usurp the vital impulse and divert it to some other purpose than the great necessity of absolute life-needs: then were life itself dethroned, and swallowed up in science. And truly science, in her overweening arrogance, has dreamed of such a triumph; as witness our tight-reined state and modern art, the sexless, barren children of this dream." (in *The Art-Work of the Future* (Wagner's *Prose Works*, Vol. 1), trans. William Ashton Ellis (London: Kegan Paul, Trench, Trubner and Co., 1892), 73–4.
40. *Wagner on Music and Drama*, ed. A. Goldman and E. Sprinchorn (New York, NY: Da Capo Press, 1988), 270.
41. Derryck Cooke, *An Introduction to Der Ring des Nibelungen*, 2-disc audio CD (Decca, 2005). The *Ring* cycle is made of four music dramas: *Das Rheingold* (composed 1853–54), *Die Walküre* (1854–56), *Siegfried* (1856–69), and *Götterdämmerung—The Twilight of the Gods* (1869–74). Wagner composed *Die Meistersinger von Nürnberg* during 1862–67 and his final work, *Parsifal*, 1877–82.
42. *Wagner on Music and Drama*, 270.
43. Jacobs, *Wagner*, 72.
44. Jean Jacques Nattiez, *The Battle of Chronos and Orpheus* (New York, NY: Oxford, 2004), 182.
45. Ibid., 179.
46. Wagner laid aside the work on the music drama *Siegfried*, which he began in 1856, to devote himself to *Tristan and Isolde*, composed 1857–59, staged in 1865, and *The Mastersingers*, composed 1862–67 and staged in 1868.
47. Thomas Mann, "Richard Wagner and The *Ring*," in *Essays of Three Decades*, trans. H. T. Lowe-Porter (London: Secker & Warburg,1947), 360–1.
48. Paul Valéry, *Analects*, trans. Stuart Gilbert, with an introduction by W. H. Auden. *The Collected Works of Paul Valéry*, Vol. 14 (London: Routledge and Kegan Paul, 1970), 272.
49. Mark Litchfield West, *The Orphic Poems* (Oxford: Clarendon Press, 1983), 146; Eli Rozik, *The roots of theatre: rethinking ritual and other theories of origin* (Iowa City: University of Iowa Press, 2002) Chapter 4: The Shamanistic Source.
50. I am thinking also, as I write this, of the essay by Georg Lukács, "The Tragedy of Modern Art," in *Essays on Thomas Mann* (London: Merlin,

1979), 47–97. The main character of Leverkühn is a modern musician. Lukács writes:

> Behind Leverkühn's music, therefore, lurks the deepest despair, the despair of a real artist for the social function of art, and not only art but bourgeois society itself in our time. He may attempt to break free from his position (although all such attempts will be purely in terms of his art). But he will only exacerbate these inner contradictions and hasten on the destruction of his art, whose premise is its divorce from life. Such attempts must lead objectively to the death of art. (p. 70)

The tragedy of art so finely described in that essay shows Thomas Mann speaking ahead of his time, much the same way as I am saying Wagner was. The tragedy Mann is writing about with his main character of Leverkühn is a tragedy of Western culture (that Nietzsche famously defined in terms of the "death of God"). Mann diagnoses this devastation with which music is caught up, through its being confined to the study, Lukács rightly says. Mann also realizes the greatness of Wagner (so he would agree with the view I am putting forward): that Wagner's music is the absolute opposite of art confined to the tiny, enclosed space of the study. It is world art and points forward to much greater works along the same principle, but without their being mere repetitions of it either.

51. Western religion symbolizes and institutes this vision as the Promised Land. This is the place of our building, dwelling, thinking in peace. Bayreuth is a symbol etched into the earth to this end by Wagner, although it may have become a mere festival hall in a country town and look for all intents and purposes like little more than that. Wagner chose this place from sensitivity to its propitious nature, the way those looking to build a Buddhist monastery will examine the energy of a place, the *deus loci* in our tradition, the *feng shui* in Eastern tradition. Wagner was conscious of these traditions.

Chapter 9: The Work of Mourning

1. Peter Banki, "The Forgiveness to Come: Dreams and Aporias" (PhD thesis, Department of Germanic Languages and Literatures, New York University, 2009).
2. Vladimir Jankélévitch, "Le Pardon," in *Philosophie Morale* (Paris: Flammarion, 1998); *Forgiveness* trans. Andrew Kelley, (Chicago, IL: University of Chicago Press, 2005).
3. Banki, 161.
4. The story is taken, analysed by Banki, as it appears in Jacques Derrida, "To Forgive the Unforgivable and the Imprescriptible," in *Questioning God*, ed. John Caputo, Mark Dooley, and Michael J. Scanlon (Bloomington, IN: Indiana University Press, 2001), 21–51.
5. Banki, 187.
6. Ibid., 188–9.
7. *Lamentations* 1:4.
8. Juan F. Riano, *Notes on Early Spanish Music* (London: Bernard Quaritch, 1887), 3.
9. See http://www.ecmrecords.com/Background/New_Series/1700/Bgr_1765 .php.

10. Berthold Litzmann, ed., *Letters of Clara Schumann and Johannes Brahms, 1853–1896* (New York, NY: Hyperion, 1979), 16.
11. *Matthew* 27:46.
12. Of Picou's longstanding research and publication in this area, see "The Day the Water Died: Cultural Impacts of the Exxon Valdez Oil Spill," in J. S. Picou, and D. A. and M. J. Cohen, eds., *The Exxon Valdez Oil Spill: Readings on a Modern Social Problem* (New Delhi: IA Press, 2008), 167–92.
13. Joseph Stevenson, *All Music Guide to Classical Music: The Definitive Guide to Classical Music* (Montclair, NJ: Backbeat, 2005), 843.
14. *Revelation* 10:1–2, 5–7, King James Version of the Bible.
15. *Psalm* 29 (30):6.
16. *Psalm* 129 (130):6.
17. Alexander Poznansky, *Tchaikovsky: The Quest for the Inner Man* (New York, NY: Schirmer Books, 1991). See review by David Brown in his *Tchaikovsky: The Man and His Music* (New York, NY: Pegasus, 2007), 16f.
18. Timothy L. Jackson, *Tchaikovsky: Symphony No. 6 (Pathétique)* (Cambridge UK: Cambridge University Press, 1999), 83f.
19. Edwin Evans, *Tchaikovsky* (London: Dent, 1948), 121.
20. Sainte-Beuve was a famous and powerful critic in Proust's day. Proust argued against his approach to art through the artist's biography. Proust argued that in art, the artist—the composer, in this instance—in solitude, *suppresses* all that which belongs as much to others as to ourselves, "and with which, even when alone, we judge things without being ourselves," and laying all this aside, we come face to face with the *art* in ourselves, the aspect of genius, which we cannot share in conversation or in any other way, *except as art*, and we then "seek to hear and to render the true sound of our hearts." Marcel Proust, "The Method of Sainte-Beuve," in *Against Sainte-Beuve and Other Essays*, trans. J. Sturrock (London: Penguin, 1988), 14–15.
21. Schopenhauer, *The World as Will and Representation*, Vol. 1, Section 52, 260.

Chapter 10: When Time Stands Still

1. Bassi Guen, "Oblivious to the Music," www.aish.com.
2. Schopenhauer, *The World as Will and Representation*, Vol. 1, 393. See my discussion of Goethe's *Faust* in Matthew Del Nevo, *The Work of Enchantment* (New Brunswick, NJ: Transaction, 2011), Chaps. 12 and 13.
3. Roger Nichols, *The Life of Debussy* (Cambridge UK: Cambridge University Press, 1998), 131.
4. Elie Robert Schmidt, *The Piano Works of Claude Debussy* (New York, NY: Dover, 2010), 146.
5. Glenda D. Goss, *Jean Sibelius: A Guide to Research* (London and New York: Garland, 1998), 212.
6. Ibid.
7. Cited in Andrew Barnett, *Sibelius* (New Haven, CT: Yale University Press, 2007), 323.
8. Burnett James, *The Music of Jean Sibelius* (Rutherford, NJ: Fairleigh Dickinson University, 1983), 87.
9. James Arnold Hepokoski, *Sibelius: Symphony No. 5* (Cambridge UK: Cambridge University, 1993), 1.

10. James, *The Music of Jean Sibelius*, 67.
11. Ibid.

Chapter 11: Beauty and Sadness

1. Cf. Lao Tzu, *Tao Te Ching*, 28.
2. Lacan misses this as well. Winnicott has the best sense of purity and innocence in psychology. See Will W. Adams, "Love, Open Awareness and Authenticity: A Conversation with William Blake and D. W. Winnicott," *Journal of Humanistic Psychology* 45, no. 1 (2006): 9–35.
3. James Hillman's development of Jungian analytical psychology into archetypal psychology picks up this difference. See, for instance, Joanne Stroud and Gail Thomas, eds., *Images of the Untouched* (Dallas, TX: Spring Publications, 1982).
4. Vladimir Jankélévitch, *Le pure et l'impur* (Paris: Flammarion, 1960), 273.
5. S. Kierkegaard, *Fear and Trembling/Repetition*, (*Kierkegaard's Writings*, VI) trans. Howard V. Hong and Edna H. Hong (Princeton NJ: Princeton University Press, 1983), 125–176; Jaques Lacan, *The Four Fundamental Concepts of Psychoanalysis*, 17ff.
6. Jankélévitch, *Le pure et l'impur*, 275.
7. Ibid., 276.
8. Ibid., 276.
9. St. Francis de Sales, *Treatise on the Love of God*, 1. 12.
10. Jankélévitch, *Le pure et l'impur*, 301.
11. Plato, *Symposium*, 203d.
12. Ibid., 204b.
13. Jankélévitch, *Le pure et l'impur*, 301–2.
14. Ibid.
15. Ibid., 204d.
16. Ibid., 206b.
17. Ibid., 205c.
18. Ibid., 206d.
19. Ibid., 206e.
20. Nietzsche, *Thus Spoke Zarathustra*, Prologue, 5.
21. Jankélévitch, *Le pure et l'impur*, 165. Jankélévitch gives a section to this whole problem.
22. See http://www.ravkooktorah.org/HAYEI-SARAH-72.htm.
23. See the following: Kathleen Raine, *Defending Ancient Springs* (New York, NY: Lindisfarne Press/Inner Traditions, 1985); *William Blake*, 2nd ed. (London: Thames and Hudson, 1985); *W. B. Yeats and the Learning of the Imagination* (London: Golgonooza Press, 1999). Yeats is the world poet who best exemplifies this tradition, which is "inner" or soulful in a strong sense. This soulfulness is the keynote of all the greatest poetry written in English, and perhaps what English poetry has over French and German.
24. This he does in his multivolume novel, *À la recherché les temps perdu* (literally, "In Search of Lost Time," or, more poetically, "In Remembrance of Things Past").
25. Jean-Jacques Rousseau, *Émile*, trans. Barbara Foxley (London: Dent Everyman, 1974), 356.

26. Robert Schauffler, *Franz Schubert, The Ariel of Music* (New York, NY: Putnam and Sons, 1949), 252.

27. Brian Newbould, *Schubert: The Music and the Man* (Berkeley, CA: University of California Press, 1999), 362.

28. Ibid.

29. Julian Rushton, *Mozart* (Oxford: Oxford University Press, 2006), 89.

30. Marcel Proust, "Camille Saint-Saëns, Pianist," in *Against Sainte-Beuve, and Other Essays* (London: Penguin Classics, 1988), 132.

31. The French *charme* comes from the Latin *carmina*, which means "song." Like the English word, charm, *charme* has connotations of a kind of power which is lovely, bewitching, enchanting. I take the term from Vladimir Jankélévitch.

32. *Charme* has a more subtle and magical quality in French. Let us keep this in mind. *Charme* is the *shine* of innocence, its glory more than its aura. Then the perfect symbol is a girl. We have this in Rilke.

33. Vladimir Jankélévitch, *Music and the Ineffable* [1983], trans. Carolyn Abbate (Princeton, NJ: Princeton University Press, 2003), 7.

34. Augustine, *Confessions*, 10. 7. 11. [John K. Ryan translation]

35. Vladimir Jankélévitch, *L'irréversible et la nostalgie*, 373.

36. Ibid.

37. Ibid., 373–4.

38. Paul Verlaine, *Fêtes Galantes* [1869] (Paris: Gallimard, 1973), 97.

39. Cited by Arnold I. Davidson in "The *Charme* of Jankélévitch" in the introduction to Jankélévitch, *Music and the Ineffable*, x.

40. "*L'âme encore stupide, et comme/Interdite au seuil de la chair.*"

41. "*Je l'ai, cette essence du Ciel/À des fins plus douces que miel.*"

42. Rilke, The Tenth Elegy, *Duino Elegies* in *The Selected Poetry of Rainer Maria Rilke*, trans. Stephen Mitchell (New York: Vintage, 1989), 211.

43. *Matthew* 26:69–75 (New Revised Standard Version of the Bible).

44. This is Emmanuel Levinas, cited in *Otherwise than Being*, trans. Alphonso Lingis (The Hague, and Boston, MA: Martinus Nijhoff, 1981), 110. Levinas was a philosopher whose 1962 essay "Transcendence and Height" encouraged my own account of height as it pertains to inner sensibility and sensitivity, cf. Chapter 2 of Emmanuel Levinas, *Basic Philosophical Writings*, ed. A. T. Peperzak and others (Bloomington, IN: Indiana University Press, 1996). Levinas's account of *eros*, combined with his account of height, filtered into my image of a Ladder of *Eros*, cf. the relevant sections (which cannot in any case be read out of context) in Emmanuel Levinas, *Totality and Infinity* [1961], trans. Alphonso Lingis (Pittsburgh, PA: Duquesne University Press, 1992).

45. Emmanuel Levinas, *Otherwise Than Being or Beyond Essence*, [1974] trans. Alphonso Lingis (Dordrecht, The Netherlands: Kluwer, 1981), 3. Chapter 1 of this book is relevant to my discussion of transcendence and disinterest.

46. See Jürgen Lawrenz, *Art and the Platonic Matrix* (Newcastle, UK: Cambridge Scholars Publishing, 2011), where there are numerous references in the index (p. 287) to where he works this out.

47. See my account of this in Matthew Del Nevo, *The Work of Enchantment* (New Brunswick, NJ: Transaction, 2011), Chap. 4.

48. Ries quoted in: Joachim Kaiser, *Beethovens 32 Klaviersonaten und ihre Interpreten* (Frankfurt/M: Fischer Verlag, 1979), 502f. (transl. supplied by Jurgen Lawrenz).

49. Ibid.

50. This is the adagio movement of the Deutsche Grammophon recording I am referring to.

51. It is the philosopher Emmanuel Levinas who breaks up this French word: dis-inter-esse-ment. This way we can see its Latin components and understand it better. *Esse* means existence or Being (in Heidegger's sense of the Being which is in every entity, because *it is*, but which is not itself an entity). *Inter* means, as in English, between, as in "inter-change"; it refers to the *nexus* quality of existence or Being, how ultimately it is whole—but this whole, this One, is *not a totality*. *Dis* refers to a break or caesura, as in "disengagement," or at least to a distance toward, or presence "other than," this *esse*.

52. Augustine, 'On the Magnitude of the Soul' in *The Immortality of the Soul; The Magnitude of the Soul; On Music; The Advantage of Believing; On Faith in Things Unseen* (*The Fathers of the Church*, Volume 4), (Washington DC: Catholic University of America Press, 2002), 136ff.

Chapter 12: Blue in Green

1. Theodor Adorno, *In Search of Wagner*, trans. R. Livingstone (London: Verso, 1985), 71.

2. John Gillock, *Performing Messiaen's Organ Music* (Indianapolis: Indiana University Press, 2009).

3. Miles Davis, with Quincy Troupe, *Autobiography* (London: Picador, 2012), 232.

4. Ibid.

5. Ibid, 401.

6. Ibid.

7. John Coltrane became a name synonymous with avant-garde jazz in the 1960s, for instance, the forty-minute piece, *Ascension* (1965), a collective improvisation.

8. Baudelaire, Intimate Journals, trans. Christopher Isherwood http://centre-truths.co.uk/fahdtu/INTIMATE%20JOURNALS.htm

Chapter 13: Attunement

1. Alain Badiou, *Five Lessons on Wagner*, trans. Susan Spitzer (London: Verso, 2010), 83.

2. Ibid.; italics in original.

3. Adorno, *Philosophie der neuen Musik* (Frankfurt am Main: Europäische Verlagsanstalt, 1958).

4. Hans Heinz Stuckenschmidt, *Schoenberg: His Life, World and Work*, trans. E. T. Roberts and H. Searle (London: Calder, 1977), 468, 491.

5. Plato, *Apology* 31c-d, 40a.

6. Plato, *Symposium* 202d-e.

7. Jürgen Lawrenz, *Art and the Platonic Matrix*, 86, 87 and 101. I am aware of raising a major point here. Productive power of the imagination is studied

beautifully and sensitively in the poetic works of the philosopher of science Gaston Bachelard e.g., *L'eau et les rêves : essai sur l'imagination de la matière* (José Corti, Paris, 1942); *L'air et les songes : essai sur l'imagination du mouvement* (José Corti, Paris, 1943); *La terre et les rêveries de la volonté: essai sur l'imagination des forces* (José Corti, Paris, 1948); *La terre et les rêveries du repos : essai sur les images de l'intimité* (José Corti, Paris, 1948); *La Poétique de l'Espace (P.U.F., Paris, 1957);La Poétique de la Réverie* (P.U.F., Paris, 1961); *La Flamme d'une Chandelle* (P.U.F., Paris, 1961). English translations of this whole series of works are available through The Dallas Institute of Humanities and Culture (Dallas, U.S.A.) http://www.dallasinstitute.org/books_thebachelardtranslations.html

8. Jean Baudrillard, *Simulacra and Simulation*, trans. Sheila Faria Glaser (Ann Arbor MI: University of Michigan Press, 1994), 6.
9. Samuel Beckett, *Collected Shorter Prose 1945–1980* (London: John Calder, 1984), 145–147.
10. Valéry, *Aesthetics*, trans. Ralph Manheim, ed. Jackson Matthews. *The Collected Works*, Vol. 13 (London: Routledge and Kegan Paul, 1964), 225.
11. Ibid., 230.
12. Ibid., 229–30.
13. Rainer Maria Rilke, poem of August 1914 in *Werke in drei Bänden, Zweiter Band, Gedichter und Übertragungen* (Frankfurt am Main: Insel Verlag, 1966), 93 [translation Stephanie Dowrick in *In the Company of Rilke* (Crows Nest NSW Australia: Allen & Unwin, 2009), 92.
14. *Exodus* 31:6.
15. *Makkos* 10b.
16. Adorno, *Minima Moralia: Reflections on a Damaged Life*, trans. E. F. N. Jephcott (London: Verso, 2005), 247.

Index

A

Adderly, "Canonball", 237
Adorno, Theodor, 9, 14, 17, 33, 76, 77, 78, 85, 111, 159, 227, 231, 246, 250
   Aesthetic Theory, 9
   Dialectic of Enlightenment, 111
   Minima Moralia, 111
   new music and, 859
   Philosophy of New Music, 250
   poor judgment, 250
   spiritualization and, 9
Aesthetics, 31
   "Copernican turn" in, 116ff.
   ethics and, 31ff.
Albinéz, Isaac, 241
   Iberia, 241
Anda, Geza, 218
Aphrodite, 45, 46
Aquinas, Saint Thomas, 112
   Summa Theologica, 112
Arisotle, 48, 220
Art
   aesthetic experience and, 10f., 21, 39, 44f., 50, 51, 74ff., 97, 126, 127, 128, 155, 160f., 218, 224f., 249ff., 257
   aura, 10, 238ff.
   bad art, 21, 128
   commodification, 35, 44, 52, 78, 126, 243
   correspondence, 12, 17ff., 25ff., 36ff., 45, 53, 76, 224, 251, 255, 256
   critical acclaim, 9
   indomitability, 11
   irreducibility, 10
   Jesus and, 37
   longevity, 10
   memorability, 11
   modernity, 12

noir, 35
   productiveness, 11
   radical, 35
   redemption, 163ff.
   religion and, 170ff., 210
   science and, 152
   synchronicity, 12
   translatability, 10
   truth, xii, xiii, 1, 7, 13, 14, 25, 30, 32, 33, 34, 36, 37, 43, 61, 76, 77, 166, 207f.
Aspiration, 53
Athos, Mt., 107
Attunement, see soul under Music
Augustine of Hippo, Saint, 7, 22, 23, 24, 219, 228–9
   Confessions, 23, 219

B

Bach, Johannes Sebastian, 93, 94, 99, 102, 128, 134, 153, 155
   Chaconne, 183–4
   Well Tempered Clavier, 99
Bacon, Francis, 13
Badiou, Alain, 153, 245
Banki, Peter, 175, 177, 178
Barenboim, Daniel, 53, 78, 151, 227
   West-Eastern Divan Orchestra, 151
Barfield, Owen, 14
Baroque, 86, 120, 121
Bartoli, Cecilia, 120
Basho, 195
Baudelaire, Charles, 1ff., 25ff., 36, 43, 72, 221, 225, 243, 244
   Les Fleurs du mal, 1, 2, 5, 6, 12, 21, 25, 30, 32, 3, 83, 135, 161ff.
   aesthetic, 1–15, 17, 18, 21, 31, 72, 75, 119, 218, 243, 245, 246, 251, 255, 265

authority and, 1
beauty and, 4ff., 35
Correspondances, 7
double passion, 25
Fusées, 244
spleen and, 5
volupté, 13, 82
Beauty, 3ff., 22, 28, 205ff. 218
death and, 36, 81, 190
ethics and, 33f.
feminine and, 37
free, 3, 45, 224f.
ground-moods and, 256
harmony and, 160ff.
ineffability and, 226
innocence and, 56, 69, 93, 206ff.
love of, 28
melancholy and, 30
melody and, 164
modishness, 35
perfection and, 228, 252
sadness and, 205–228
shyness of, 46
soul and, 45ff., 228–9
strength and, 92
time and, 197
truth, goodness and, 122
Beckett, Samuel, 178, 253
Beethoven, Ludwig, 20, 71, 101, 102, 125–149, 152, 153, 155
1st Symphony, 129
2nd Symphony, 130
3rd Symphony "Eroica", 131
4th Symphony, 138
5th Symphony, 20, 139, 202–204
6th Symphony, "Pastoral", 141
7th Symphony, 142
8th Symphony, 144
9th Symphony "Choral", 145ff.
"Hammerklavier" Sonata, 156
"Heiliger Dankgesang", 202
Bell, Joshua, 196
Benjamin, Walter, 254
Illuminations, 254
Berg, Alban, 111
Bergson, Henri, 97, 194, 207, 234
Bible, 19
Big ideology, x
Black, Leo, 71
Blake, William, 207, 214, 215
Songs of Innocence and Experience, 214, 215

Bloch, Ernst, 33
Blue, 66, 231ff.
Boehme, Jacob, 5
Bonnefoy, Yves, 25ff.
Bosch, Hieronymus, 3
Brahms, Johannes, 33, 89, 120, 156, 184, 217, 275
Bridgeman, Duncan, 255
Bruno, Giordano, 4
Buber, Martin, 18, 47, 273

C
Carpenter Edward, 145
Cassian, Saint John, 107
Catto, Jamie, 255
I Giant Leap, 255
Cavafy, C. P., 219
Cherry, Don, 239
Chopin, Frédéric,179, 219
Christensen, Jon, 240
Christianity, 210, 256
Catholic, 7, 196
Church fathers, 24
Council of Trent, 117, 223
mythologism, 22, 110
Codona, 339
Codona Trilogy, 239
Coltrane, John, 237, 240
Consumerism, x, xi, xii, 29, 66, 87, 102, 140
Connoisseurship, 51
Conrad, Joseph, 113
Heart of Darkness, 113
Corbin, Henry, 108
Crumb, Arthur, 247
Black Angel, 247, 248, 249
Culture,
Americanism, 176
collapse of sensibility, 3, 102
commodification, 189
Communism, 190
conceptualization of, 194
industry and, 32
prostitution of, xiii
symbols of, 31ff.
taste and, 253

D
Dalai Lama, 20
Dance, 171
Dark enchantment, 4
Das, Krishna, 229

Davis, Miles, 232ff., 240
  Aura, 238
  Birth of Cool, 236
  green, see color under Music
  Kind of Blue, 236
  "Saeta", 233–237
  Sketches of Spain, 232
Death, 26ff., 83, 105ff., 114, 180
Debussy, Claude, 83, 89, 197f., 22
  La Cathédral engloutie, 197
  Nocturnes, 89
  Suite Bergamasque, 220
Decadence, 83
Delight, see ground-moods under Listening
Delphic Oracle, 40
Desire, xii, 18, 22, 23, 27, 35, 46–56, 68, 98, 125, 137, 165, 168, 177, 183, 208, 211, 222, 258, 269
Diaghilev, Sergei, 32
Dickens, Charles, 10, 213
Dionysius, St. (the Aeropagite), 126
Discernment (*diakrisis*), 8
Disenchantment, 31
  science and, 31
Dis-inter-esse-ment, 198, 225f., 298
Dostoyevsky, Fyodor, 10, 40, 213
  The Idiot, 213
Dowland, John, 63f.
  Lachrymae, 63, 67
Durchfürung, 128, 133, 136

E
Eastwood, Clint, 237
Eckhart, Meister, 104, 125
ECM recording label, 184, 238, 239
Eicher, Manfred, 238
Eigen, Michael, 152, 267, 273, 277
  Contact With the Depths, 32
Einstein, Albert, 23
Eliot, T. S., 225
Enchantment, 197, 219
  and self-presence, 194ff.
Eriugena, John Scotus, 125
Eros, 39–57, 97, 132, 138, 163, 183, 189, 193, 208ff., 224, 252
  innocence and, 209
  Levinas and, 283
  Lou Andreas-Salomé and, 265
Ethics, 26, 321–37, 98, 102, 185, 211, 257, 273
  and aesthetics, 31ff

Evans, Edwin, 192
Evans, Gil, 232, 237
Exaltation, see ground-moods under listening
  and rapture, 154ff.
Existential phenomenology, 104

F
Fauré, Gabriel, 220
  Masques et Bergamasques, 220
Faustian age, 2
Fashion, 8, 13, 45, 46, 226
  commodification and, 49, 102
Femininity, 14, 36, 37, 46, 290
Francis de Sales, Saint, 34, 207
Fresu, Pablo, 243
Freud, Sigmund, 18, 23, 56, 68, 82, 103, 111, 172, 179, 206, 180

G
Gabareck, Jon, 240
Genius, 225, 352–3
Geo-mourning, 186ff.
Gillock, Jon, 232
  Performing Messiaen's Organ Music, 232
Girard, René, 98
Gluck, Christoph, 117
God, 19, 22, 23, 24, 26, 27, 29, 39, 60, 67, 105, 106, 107, 110, 111, 125, 128, 180, 183, 184, 185, 188, 196, 202, 210, 214, 215, 219, 222, 229, 257, 274, 280
  death of, 29
  glory of, 36
Goddard, Scott, 92
Goethe, Johann Wolfgang, 37, 39, 46, 72, 139, 194, 197, cited, 259, 268, 269, 274, 277, 281
  Elective Affinities, 46
  Faust, 37, 46, 197
  Wilhelm Meister, 46
Goldman, David, P., 277
Goss, Glenda, 198
Gray, Cecil, 199
Grief, 183
Ground-mood, see under Listening
Grünwald, Matthias, 3
Guy, Constantin, 6

H
Handel, 101, 134
Han Shan, 195

happiness, 7, 8, 29, 35, 55, 59, 62, 68, 69, 103, 149, 160, 209, 210, 222
Haydn, 130, 131, 134, 137, 142, 144, 145, 155, 190, 219, 120, 121, 126, 129
Harmonium mundi, 98, 152
Heidegger, Martin, 9, 25, 61, 18, 103, 104, 123
  Being and Time, 104 cf. 205
Hegel, G. W. F., 26, 101, 104, 105, 112, 118, 119, 152, 165, 234
Hegelianism, 31, 77, 78, 91, 92, 103, 104, 105, 112, 140, 225
Height, see under Music ladder and, see under L
Herzog, Werner, 113, 152
  Fitzcarraldo, 113
Hewitt, Angela, 93
Hilliard Ensemble, 183
  Morimur, 183f.
Hitler, Adolf, 98, 225
Hockney, David, 128
Hoffer, Charles, 89
  Music Listening Today, 89, 92
Holloway, Robin, 73
Holocaust, 175ff., 189
Homer, 18, 156
Horkheimer, Max, 111
Husserl, Edmund, 104, 225

I
Incarnation, 41, 42
Ineffable, 76. 164, 205, 218ff., 224ff.
Immortality, 105ff.
Inner ceiling, 78
Inner ecology, 7
Innocence, 206
  experience and, 206ff.
Inspiration, 53, 153ff.
Intuition (*nous*), 8, 148, 56
  Schopenhauer and, 107
  Wagner and, 159

J
Jacob's ladder, 47
Jankélévitch, Vladimir, 23, 178ff., 191, 207ff., 220ff.
  charme, 198, 218, 219ff., 283
  Le Je-ne-sais-quoi et le presque-rien, 220
Jarrett, Keith, 238
Jaspers, Karl, 103

Jesus, 37, 123, 180, 184, 185
Jonathan Sacks, Chief Rabbi, 20
John the Evangelist, Saint, 21
  Gospel of John, 37
John Climacus, Saint, 47
John of Damascus, Saint, 112
  De Fide Orthodoxa, 112
Joy, 68, 69, 127, 131, 146, 147, 149, 165, 180, 181, 189, 205, 214, 215
  enjoyment, 258
Joyce, James, 18, 250
  Finnegan's Wake, 250
  Ulysses, 250
Jung, Carl, 56, 111, 172, 212, 269

K
Kant, Immanuel, 3ff., 20, 23, 26, 27, 33, 34, 46, 47, 68, 72, 82, 83, 104, 105, 152, 193, 194, 224, 252, 257, 269, 273
  Critique of Judgment, 3, 225
  Critique of Pure Reason, 116, 193, 117, 118, 119, 225
  dependent beauty, 3
  free beauty, 3, 4, 45, 224
  Haydn and, 273
Keats, John, 36, 60
  Ode on Melancholy, 36, 59, 62, 81, 82f.
King, Martin Luther, 20
Kinski, Klaus, 113
Kook, Rabbi Abraham Isaac, 19, 20, 265, 273, 282
Kramer, Lawrence, 93
  Classical Music and Postmodern Knowledge, 93
Kristeva, Julia, xi
Kundera, Milan, 207
Küng, Hans, 20

L
Lacan, Jacques, 9, 22, 23, 49, 68, 98, 207, 269, 282
  delta, 23
  jouissance, 22, 83
  objet a, 9, 269
  tuché, 48
Ladder of listening, 47ff., 53, 127, 131, 165, 209, 224
Ladder of *Eros*, 39–57, 97, 132, 163, 193, 209, 218, 224, 297
Ladder of *Melos*, 131, 132, 139, 149
Ladder of Soul, 228f.

Lao Tzu, 113
Lassus, Orlando de, 222f.
  Lagrime, 222
Lawrenz, Jürgen, 97, 98, 115ff., 225
  Art and the Platonic Matrix, 98, 225, 284
Leone, Sergio, 237
Lévinas, Emmanuel, 20, 224, 225, 273, 283, 284
Li Po, 72
Listening, philosophy of, ix, x, 17ff., 97 123, 128f.
  accomplishment, 53
  aesthetic differentiation, 51
  audibility, 50
  color, 231ff.,
  ground-moods, 5, 12, 25, 48, 61, 62, 63, 69, 82, 175, 256
    blue, 231ff.
    delight, 81–95.
    exaltation, 125ff., 151ff., 165
    green, 231ff.
    melancholy, 59–79.
    mourning, 175–192
    rapture, 154ff.
    sadness, 205ff.
    timelessness, 193–204
    white, 159, 160, 197, 198, 233, 238
  height in, see under Music
  individual taste, 50
  initiation, 50
  metaphysics of nostalgia, 17–37
  practical proficiency and, 52
  symbolism, 49
  time, 193–204
  tuché, 48
  understanding, 52
Liszt, Franz, 90, 91, 160, 161, 252
  Lohengrin and Tannhaüser, 161
Locke, John, 23
Longing, 14, 17ff., 45ff., 189, 97–123, 128f.
  sites and symbols of, 31ff.
Loss, 36
Loveliness, 72
Luck, 40
Ludwig, Emil, 131
Luther, Martin, 223

M
Mahler, Gustav, 133, 227, 235
Mallarmé, Stéphane, 27

Mandela, Nelson, 34
Manet, Édouard, 32, 225
  Dejeuner sur l'herbe, 32
Mann, Thomas, 103, 169
Marx, Karl, 6, 103
Marxism, 103
Maulpoix, Jean-Michel, 18, 40
Melancholy, see ground-moods under Listening
Mendelssohn, Felix, 139
Messiaen, Olivier, 188f., 231
  Quartet for the End of Time, 188
Michelangelo, Buonarroti, 13, 137, 227
Miller, Henry, xiii
Modernity, 12, 23, 264
Mompou, Frederico, 220
Monet, Claude, 35, 36, 117, 217f.
Morales, Cristobel de, 181f.
Morricone, Enio, 237
Morrison, Rabbi Chanan, 212
Morrison, Van, 25, 220
  Astral Weeks, 25
Mourning, see ground-moods under Listening
Mozart, Wolfgang Amadeus, 94, 130, 132, 137, 142, 153, 217f., 218–222, 227, 228
Music
  absolute, 108, 125–149, 245
  charme and, see Jankélévitch under J
  color and, 159, 231ff.
  conceptual, 85
  contrapuntal, 94
  emotion and, 74ff.
  harmony and, 120
  height and, 8, 12, 83, 125f., 127, 132, 221, 224 (See also ladder under L)
  impressionistic, 89ff.
  initiation and, 165
  melody and, 112, 121, 138
  melos as, 109, 118f., 133, 135, 173, 224, 228, 229, 233, 243, 246, 248, 256, 273, 274
    dead *melos*, 122, 232
    experience and, 209
    free *melos*, 122, 126, 126, 139, 153, 166, 243
    genius and, 127
    imagination and, 128
    ladder of, see ladder under L

logos and, 110, 114, 117, 208, 239
new age of, 109, 110, 111, 112, 113, 172, 173
nostalgia and, 220
techno and, 240
voice and, 148
modes, 99, 101, 121, 138, 203
new age and, 144, 179
new age music, 240
philosophy of, 108ff., 218ff.
physiognomy of, 155
redemption and, 163ff.
soul and, x, xi, xiii, 2, 6, 8, 9, 11, 15, 20, 23, 25, 28, 31, 33, 36, 41, 42, 43, 44, 45, 46, 47, 51, 52, 53, 56, 59, 60, 61, 62, 63, 65, 67, 68, 69, 70, 72, 74, 75, 81, 82, 83, 87, 91, 93, 97, 103, 105, 114, 122, 125, 127, 134, 137, 140, 141, 142, 158, 160, 162, 164, 165, 167, 175, 180, 181, 193, 202, 205, 245, 233, 235, 244, 253, 254
aspiration of, 228ff.
attunement of, 8, 245–259
color and, 159, 231ff., 240
definition of, 256
experience and, 211
flourishing of, 236
indestructibility of, 105–108
ineffable nature of, 224
innocence and, 212, 215
instruments and, 251
purity and, 206ff.
soul of the world, 122, 180, 182, 255, 258
soul to soul, 44m, 251, 253f.
soullessness, xi, xii, 55, 84, 132, 196, 231, 235, 239, 241, 247, 249, 250, 253, 254
stillness and, 196
time and, 97ff., 128, 193ff.
understanding, 75
Valéry, Paul and, 170, 253f.
Valley way of, 206
spirit of, 155ff.
techno, 240
technology, 250ff.
the Real, 253ff.
truth and, 122, 131ff., 145ff.
Musical sense, xii
Myth of Er, 43
Mythologism, see under Christianity

N
Nature, ix
Nazis, 151, 188
Newbould, Brian, 217
    Schubert: the Music and the Man, 217
New consciousness, 114f., 179
Newton, Isaac, 23
Nietzsche, Friedrich, 25, 28, 30, 31, 34, 39, 114, 140, 156, 172, 210, 214, 245
    death of God, 29
    Dionysius, 28
    The Gay Science, 111,
    Thus Spoke Zarathustra, 28, 29, 210, 213
Nijinsky, Vaslav, 32
Nostalgia, metaphysics of, 17–37, 175ff., 246

O
Ockeghem, Guillaume, 117
    Ecce ancilla Domini, 117
Orphic mysteries, 172
Oxford, 198

P
Paracelsus, 5
Paris, 5–6
Pärt, Arvo, 238
Paul, Saint, 7, 21, 36, 83
Perfection, 226
Picasso, Pablo, 227
Picou, Steven, 186f.
Pinto, David, 67
Plainchant, 180
Plato, 17, 21, 23, 41, 43, 97ff., 194, 208
    Republic, 41, 100f.
Platonism, 17ff., 27ff., 45,
    and Christianity, 27
Playlist, x, 63, 87, 197, 217, 221, 223
Plotinus, 21, 36
    Enneads, 21
Poe, Edgar Allan, 6
Poetic temperament, 5
Poppen, Christopher, 183
Powell, Anthony, 97
Pozansky, Alexander, 192
Prana, 105
Proust, Marcel, 27, 215, 226
    In Remembrance of Things Past, 226
    Swann's Way, 215
Psyche, 45, 46
Puccini, Giacomo, 170

Purcell, Henry, 84ff.
    The Fairy Queen, 84ff.
Purity, 25, 46, 65, 207ff.
    death and, 25
    innocence and, 209
    in Wagner, 164ff.

R
Ravel, Maurice, 90, 91, 92
    Daphnis and Choe, 91, 92
Rebirth, 41
Recordings, 53f.
Reed, Lou, 240
Reification, 31, 34
Religion,
    art and, 170ff.
    melody in, 112
    mourning and, 183f.
    two types of, 107
Rimbaud, Arthur, 12
Rilke, Rainer Maria, 2, 29, 31, 195, 225
    Book of Hours, 29
    Duino Elegies, 30
    Notebooks of Malte Laurids Brigge,
        30
    Sonnets to Orpheus, 30
    the dark interval, 56
Roerich, Nicholas, 32
Rolland, Roman, 127, 133, 135, 136, 137
Romanticism, 7, 59, 126
Rosary, 184
Rosen, Charles, 194
Rousseau, Jean-Jacques, 115, 213, 215,
    216
    Émile, 215
Rushton, Julian, 217
    Mozart, 217

S
Sacramentality, 7
Sadness, 205, 211ff.
Salomé, Lou Andreas, 2, 14, 26, 206
Sand drawing, 37, 73
Scarlatti, Domenico, 120
Schauffler, Robert, 217
    Franz Schubert, The Ariel of Music,
        217
Schiele, Egon, 13
Schneerson, Rabbi Menachem Mendel,
    34
Schoenberg, Arnold, 85, 154, 240, 247, 249
    Pelleas and Melisande, 154

Schopenhauer, Arthur, 103ff., 119, 121ff.,
    135, 140, 152, 153, 193, 195
    World as Will and Representation,
        103, 105, 193
    metaphysics of, 106f.
    philosophy of music, 108
Schubert, Franz, 71ff., 130, 152, 153,
    201f., 216f.
    8th Symphony, 201f.
Schumann, Clara, 184
Schumann, Robert, 138, 184
Scriabin, Alexander, 154
    Poem of Ecstasy, 154, 247
Scruton, Roger, 52, 77
    Aesthetics of Music, 52
    Understanding Music, 52, 73, 74
Sensibility, x
    see soul under Music
    see ground-moods and height under
        Listening
    the seven sensibilities, 274
Shakespeare, William, 86m, 137, 194
Shostakovitch, Dmitri, 145, 189, 190,
    192
    A Midsummer Night's Dream, 86
Sibelius, Jean, 197ff.
    Tapiola,198
    4th Symphony, 200f.
Simplicity, 65
Soul, see under Music
Spengler, Oswald, 123
Spinoza, Baruch, 18, 23
Stanford, Charles Villiers, xi
Stevenson, Robert, 181
    Spanish Cathedral Music, 181
Stiegler, Bernard, 255
Stravinsky, Igor, 32, 225
    Le Sacré du Printemps, 32
Swedenborg, Emanuel, 5
Szabó, István, 21
    Taking Sides, 21

T
Tammaro, Feruccio, 194
Tao, 113
Tchaikovsky, Pyotr Ilyich, 191f.
Telemann, Georg Philipp, 120
Tennyson, Alfred, 143
    *Ode on the Death of the Duke of
        Wellington*, 143
Thoene, Professor Helga, 183
Three ages, 109ff. 123

Tolstoy, Lev, 91, 156
War and Peace, 91, 103
Towner, Ralph, 239ff.
Blue Sun, 240
Chiaroscuro, 243
Diary, 239
Old Friends, New Friends, 242
Solstice, 240
Transgression, 2
Translation, 79
Transubstantiation, 194
Truth in art, xiii, 43, 76–77, 122
as aesthetic, 1–15
beauty, 3ff., 7f.
correspondence, 7–15
Tshuvah, 19
Tu Fu, 72
Turner, J. M. W., 4
Turner, W. J., 127, 148

U
Ubiquity, 253ff.
Uniqueness, 41

V
Valéry, Paul, x, 9, 11, 28, 39, 41, 46, 81, 170, 193, 205, 221f. 222, 253ff.
Le Jeune Parque, 41
Dance and the Soul, 81
Charmes, 221
Vasconcelos, Nana, 239
Vedanta, 106, 193
Verdi, Guiseppi, 161, 170
Aida, 161
La Traviata, 161, 216
Verlaine, Paul, 1, 220
Virgil, 23
Aeneid, 23
Vivaldi, Antonio, 68ff., 70, 120
Venice, 71
Volupté, 12–13, 82, 160

W
Wagner, Richard, 20, 28, 39, 40, 43, 103, 114, 115, 125, 132, 136, 137, 138, 143, 148, 151–173, 198, 231, 233, 245
Artwork of the Future, 115
Bayreuth, 173
Color, 159
Flying Dutchman, 158, 159
Götterdamerung, 155, 169
Leitmotif, 164
Lohengrin, 159, 160, 165, 166, 167, 197
Mastersingers, 171, 277, 279
New age, 114, 152, 163, 173
Parsifal, 171, 279
Rheingold, 155, 169
Rienzi, 157, 233
Ring Cycle, 168ff., 279
Siegfried, 157, 169, 184. 251, 279
Tannhäuser, 151, 160–167, 197
Tristan and Isolde, 39, 154, 156, 158, 167, 171, 172, 199, 247, 259, 277, 279
Walcott, Collin, 239
War, 176
just war, 177
technology, 176ff.
Webber, Andrew Lloyd, 225
Weber, Eberhard, 240
Weber, Max, 31
Wheeler, Kenny, 242
White, Kenneth, 255
Wordsworth, William, ix, 42
Intimations of Immortality, 42, 43, 207
World religions, age of, 20

Y
Yoga, 102, 171
Young, Lester, 237